What's Missing?

This Large Print Book carries the Seal of Approval of N.A.V.H.

What's Missing?

*Inspiration for Women Seeking
Faith and Joy in Their Lives*

Rena Pederson

Walker Large Print • Waterville, Maine

Published in 2004 by arrangement with DHS Literary Agency.

The text of this Large Print edition is unabridged.
Other aspects of the book may vary from the original edition.

Set in 16 pt. Plantin by Elena Picard.

Printed in the United States on permanent paper.

Library of Congress Cataloging-in-Publication Data

Pederson, Rena.
    What's missing? : inspiration for women seeking faith
and joy in their lives / Rena Pederson.
       p. cm.
    Includes bibliographical references (p. 581).
    ISBN 1-59415-024-9 (lg. print : sc : alk. paper)
    1. Women — Religious life. 2. Spiritual life. I. Title.
BL625.7.P45 2004
   204′.4′082—dc22   2003066561

What's Missing?

As the Founder/CEO of NAVH, the only national health agency solely devoted to those who, although not totally blind, have an eye disease which could lead to serious visual impairment, I am pleased to recognize Thorndike Press★ as one of the leading publishers in the large print field.

Founded in 1954 in San Francisco to prepare large print textbooks for partially seeing children, NAVH became the pioneer and standard setting agency in the preparation of large type.

Today, those publishers who meet our standards carry the prestigious "Seal of Approval" indicating high quality large print. We are delighted that Thorndike Press is one of the publishers whose titles meet these standards. We are also pleased to recognize the significant contribution Thorndike Press is making in this important and growing field.

Lorraine H. Marchi, L.H.D.
Founder/CEO
NAVH

★ Thorndike Press encompasses the following imprints: Thorndike, Wheeler, Walker and Large Print Press.

Contents

Acknowledgments

My heartfelt thanks to —

All the women who trusted me with their stories and shared their faith.

First Lady Laura Bush for sharing her mother, Jenna Welch.

The members of my women's Bible study for providing prayers and proofreading.

My bosses, Bob Mong, Jim Moroney, and Robert Decherd, for their generous support.

My agent, David Hale Smith, and editors, Jennifer Repo and Michelle Howry, for their encouragement.

Ann Carruth for thinking of the title.

Libby Norwood for innumerable suggestions.

Bill Blackburn for golden quotes.

The patient, efficient researchers in the *Dallas Morning News* reference department.

My dedicated secretary, Carol Portele, who remembers everything I forget.

White House Press Secretary Noelia Rodriguez for making interviews happen.

Addie Beth Denton for connecting me with Wickham Boyle and Ground Zero.

Ruth Bell for connecting me with Anne Graham Lotz.

Lillian Calles Barger and the Damaris Project for their intellectual questioning.

Becky Sykes of the Dallas Women's Foundation for providing invaluable statistics.

Elaine Agather of Chase Bank for sharing Justice Sandra Day O'Connor at the National Cowgirl Museum.

Yvonne Pendlelton and Anne Crews of Mary Kay Cosmetics for connecting me to Sherril Steinman.

All those who read chapters and provided feedback — Jan Hart Black, Anne Blakeney, Debra Decker, Diana Holbert, Deedie Leahy, Bob Moos, Libby Norwood, Jeanine Sandifer, Ann Sentilles, Lee Smith, and Nancy Solana.

Lauren Murray for sorting out the Bibliography.

The Rev. Mark Craig in Dallas for his inspiration.

My sons, Gregory Gish and Grant Gish, who make the world a happier place.

Introduction

"The spirit is an area of growth most of us set aside, half hoping the day will come when some soul-stretching peak experience will lift us out of our ordinary consciousness for a glimpse of the sacred and eternal. But we have to prepare our consciousness for taking such a path. We need to change the way we measure time and to relax our insistence on control."
— AUTHOR GAIL SHEEHY

Come on in. I'm glad you're here. Since September 11, many Americans have felt the need to get their spiritual house in order. This is a book to help you come home to faith. This is a book for women who may need reassurance in the midst of life's uncertainties that there really is "someone watching over you." This is a refresher course for women who feel worn down by it all and who are in need of hope. This is a book for women who feel incomplete or unconnected in a world too busy to notice.

This is a book for women who yearn to know, at the end of the day, that their life means something. This is a book for women who've made mistakes — big ones and a million little ones — and want to repair their faith. This is a book for women who want to learn from the faiths of others, finding wisdom in the three great monotheistic faiths: Judaism, Islam, and Christianity. This is a book for women who want real-life examples of how to go forward and grow.

Perhaps you have had some of those feelings yourself. You try to be good and do good, but you still don't feel settled or soothed inside. Something's missing in your life, but what? You may have kept up a church life year after year, but the old embers of faith don't make you feel warmhearted through the week — or comforted in the dark of night. You may feel unfulfilled even with a home and family. You may have tried several careers and still feel discontent.

Have you ever had the feeling that your life is like a pantomime act? You've got the motions down, but when trouble comes, you feel an ache. "Why me?" you think. Perhaps you've struggled with raising your kids and now struggle to care for your parents. Life doesn't seem fair. If this story were on TV, you'd change channels.

What's missing?

A good bet would be the faith factor. Sometimes even the most well-intentioned woman may have the words right but not the music. How do you find that fullness of heart that comes from knowing your place in God's universe? How do you find meaning? Purpose? Balance?

What you may be seeking is that "sweet zone," where what you yearn for in life is in sync with what God would have you do. Where the way you live is in harmony with what you believe. Where you can rest assured that what you are doing makes sense. Where you can wake up in the morning excited at the prospect of learning more. Where you look forward to discovering the people who have been brought into your path for a reason. It's like *syzygy,* the astronomical term for moments when the sun and moon and earth are in alignment, perfectly yoked. To get to that sense of order, you have to open yourself to a closer relationship with God, whatever your religious background might be. It makes great sense: The antidote for what ails you is more faith, not less. When you are searching for the right direction, you need a compass.

Look closely at the women who keep their equilibrium despite the hurly-burly around them. You will find they have a spiritual foundation that gives them strength. Look at the women who navigate life's storms and sail on. You will find their faith has guided them. It is often said these women are "centered." That means they have learned to organize their life around their faith — not the other way around.

Over the years, I have noticed that most people do not put their church affiliation or activities on their bios, separating their professional selves from their private selves. However, when I was researching a book called *What's Next?* about women changing direction at mid-life, I discovered that the majority of women credited their faith — whatever their denomination — as a major factor in helping them grow. Women like Anna Quindlen, Elizabeth Dole, Linda Ellerbee, Alma Powell, Susan Molinari, Beverly Sills, and Jane Goodall found comfort and steel in their faith. My impression later was confirmed by author Carol Gallagher, who found something similar when she interviewed hundreds of the top female executives around the country for her book, *Room at the Top.* She said some 80 percent of the women at the top reported their faith was an essential part of their life.

Although that's higher than the 60 percent of Americans who say their faith is important to them, when you think about it, it is rather logical. When you are walking on a high wire, as women do while they balance the many demands on them, you need a gyroscope. As you get older, you discover you need that guidance more, not less. When you are young, you think you're invulnerable, bullet-proof. You may assume you can handle whatever life throws at you, so faith is not at the top of your to-do list. However, after you've spent some time in the rodeo barrel, as everyone does, you begin to appreciate the wisdom of faith. Hard knocks — disappointments, divorce, deaths of loved ones, frightening illness — come to everyone. Faith gives you the sense of purpose and hope to move on.

The good news is that it is never too late to embrace faith. You may be turning to faith for the first time or renewing beliefs that have been put on hold while you raced after other goals. Or fell into a ditch or two. It doesn't matter how you come to faith. It's just good that you do.

On September 11, many Americans

looked at their TV screen and came face-to-face with their own mortality. Stunned by the tragedies of that day, they had to ask themselves the blunt question, *What would I want to be caught dead doing?* Or *What would I want to be caught dead having done with my life?* There was a rush to prayer and church after September 11, and the hearts of many may never be the same. But the question after more time has gone by should be: *How do we keep the spirit of that moment in our lives?* How do we keep growing spiritually, so this is not just another trend, a fashionable faith that fades in a year? What can we learn from the faiths of others that enriches our own understanding? Let us open our ears so we can hear each other. May we focus more on how we are the same and less on how we are different.

And who am I to chronicle this? No, I am not a theologian — just a journalist trying to report what I see happening around us, a storyteller sharing the stories of women of our time, a believer seeing what's happening through the eyes of faith. My faith has provided a safe harbor for me since I was a young girl. It has helped me survive life with an alcoholic mother and a divorce from someone who is now my best friend. Faith has helped me deal with single parenting and the constant pressure of newspaper work. I used to tell my friends that I was made out of rubber, so you can't keep me down long. But the truth is that I am simply blessed to believe.

For me, Christianity is decisive and true. But that's all the more reason to love all the people I met in these pages. I don't endorse the views of all the women profiled here, and I don't expect you to. But I respect all of them and I learned something from each one. These women represent a spectrum of views. Having the privilege of talking with them stretched me to define my faith. I hope I am a more mature Christian because of it. I'll try to be your guide in the chapters ahead, adding context where I can.

Exciting things are happening in the world of faith, as you will see. Thousands of women have graduated from theology schools since the 1970s, so there are now many women in positions of influence, if not authority, in many faiths. The views of women like Rabbi Janet Marder, Sister Joan Chittister, and Islamic teacher Ingrid Mattson are adding richness to interpretations of the Torah, the Bible and the Qu'ran. Women like Beth Moore of Houston

19

and Anne Graham Lotz of Raleigh are emerging as master teachers of scripture and drawing huge crowds of women hungry for scriptural wisdom. Freed from cultural constraints that limited the participation of women in the previous generations, baby boomer women like Judy Collins, Representative Nancy Pelosi, and Senator Kay Bailey Hutchison are embracing the need to heal the world.

From here on, it may help you to see how other women have incorporated their faith into their lives, particularly since September 11. Quite frankly, I think we can use more real-life role models of faith in our muddled world, because the believers who often get the ink and airtime are extremists. Most women in the mall and the office cubicle are looking for more thoughtful examples, people who try to do right without being self-righteous. In the pages ahead, women ranging from First Lady Laura Bush to tennis player Zina Garrison will tell you how their faith is a factor in their lives. To

> "Let nothing disturb you
> Let nothing affright you
> All things are passing;
> God never changes.
> Patient endurance attains
> all things,
> God alone suffices."
>
> — ST. TERESA OF AVILA

be honest, some were a little apprehensive about talking about their faith — it's a very personal thing, after all. They didn't want to seem "holier than thou." Most of them would rather walk with faith in their own fallible-but-sincere way than talk over-much about it; they've grown a bit leery of sanctimonious people who merely wear the jewelry of faith. They know they aren't perfect, but they also know that God loves them anyway. And they are the better for it. I hope you will find something in their stories to help you in your own journey. Just as we teach with our lives, there is much we can learn from the lives of others. So look ahead, my friend, and see what you can find.

ONE

Listening

"If God speaks to us at all other than through such official channels as the Bible and the church, then I think that he speaks to us largely through what happens to us . . . (so) listen to your life. See it for the fathomless mystery that it is. In the boredom and pain of it, no less than in the excitement and gladness: touch, taste, smell your way to the holy and hidden heart of it, because in the last analysis all moments are key moments and life itself is grace."

— FREDERICK BUECHNER

I can't really remember a time when I didn't believe in God. When I was growing up in West Texas, I always pictured myself riding along with God in one of those little sidecars attached to a motorcycle, barreling ahead full-throttle into life. God was a large and reassuring presence at my side. I could never see exactly what was on the road ahead, but I felt connected. I still feel that way. Only now,

I realize that where he was bringing me was here.

Sure, my attention wandered. I've rushed along from mistake to mistake, probably just like you. There were times I would despair that life wasn't fair, that I wasn't strong enough, that God wasn't listening to my cries — the whole pitiful human being thing. It was then that I would realize I needed to get closer, get quieter, get back in.

Those separations were almost like a lover's quarrel with God. It was not that I didn't believe; I didn't understand what God was doing or what I should do next. Then I would have to struggle back somehow, find my way back into the perimeter with him and into that feeling of close communion. It has taken me a while, but as I get older, I am learning to open myself even more to faith, to surrender, to make myself vulnerable to others, to stretch, to be truer, and then, darn, to try again.

One thing I have learned for sure, is that if you yearn for more faith, if you want answers, you must begin by *listening*. It sounds too simple, but it's true. You must be still and listen. To the clock ticking. To the rustle of leaves. To the beat of your heart. And in the quietest of moments, to the voice of God. It is not just a coincidence that when God gives the most important instructions, he begins by saying, "Hear this."

Yet listening is one of the hardest things to do in our wound-up world, isn't it? How often have you had time to stop and listen to life around you as if it were a chambered conch shell at your ear? The busier you are, the greater the need to tune out the rush and tune in the subtle tones of life. Remember when your teacher said, "Put on your listening ears"? Learning to listen for faith lessons is like learning to listen with your "third ear" to what is between the words. We swap details of the day with friends and spouses, but do we really listen carefully for indirect messages about their hopes and fears? Parents chide and prod their children but don't pay attention to what their children are trying to telegraph about their feelings. We worry so incessantly about our

> "I always begin my prayer in silence, for it is in the silence of the heart that God speaks. God is the friend of silence — we need to listen to God because it's not what we say but what He says to us and through us that matters."
>
> — MOTHER TERESA

24

own fortunes that we cannot hear the voices of the poor and the needy in the world around us. We pray to God, asking for favors and miracles, then walk away without listening.

To be fully human is to take enough time to think about who we are and what we are to do with our lives. The rabbis teach, "Each of us should have two pockets. In one should be the message, 'I am dust and ashes.' And in the other we should have written, 'For me the universe was made.' " It's up to us to figure out how those two messages form a whole. You have to stop hurrying through life to do so.

When was the last time you watched the rain falling a . . . drop . . . at . . . a . . . time . . . and reflected soberly about your life? Visitors to a one-hundred-year-old Methodist church in tiny Basalt, Colorado, are greeted with a pamphlet containing this message: "It rained today. And I thought about my life. And how many years it's been since I laughed the way I laughed when I was eight years old. About how the choices we make in life add up to define how we live, how our children will live, and what our lives will ultimately mean to others. I'm forty-two years old. And it rained today. That's why I came."

That's the spirit. You don't want to miss the miracle in the noise, so you must learn to listen carefully for the whisper of God.

For singer Judy Collins, that learning process was painful. At sixty-three, she is a survivor of four decades in the music business. She's recorded thirty-seven albums, and her signature songs have become themes for several decades. She helped make "Where Have All the Flowers Gone?" one of the antiwar anthems of the 1960s, and she made Leonard Cohen's haunting "Suzanne" a coffeehouse staple. Few have sung better about love and loss. Her 1970s recordings of Joni Mitchell's "Both Sides Now" and Stephen Sondheim's "Send in the Clowns," are still selling strong. Bill and Hillary Clinton named their daughter Chelsea after their favorite Collins song, "Chelsea Morning."

> "Listen to me, O coastlands, and hearken, you peoples from afar."
>
> — ISAIAH 49:1

But it is the hymn "Amazing Grace" that has become the theme song of her life.

Today, Judy Collins is an artist in residence at the Cathedral of St. John the Divine in New York City, the largest cathedral in the world. If you attend the services, every now and then you just might find a striking woman with incredible crystal blue eyes helping with the liturgy. When she read the scriptures at an Easter service I attended in 2001, there was great feeling to her words. That great feeling was earned, paid for at a dear price. Over the years, Judy Collins has survived polio, divorce, alcoholism, lost loves, depression, and the suicide of her only son, Clark. Her faith has helped her recover from those blows and find real joy in new ways.

Tracing her story is like reliving the cultural ups and downs in our society since the 1950s. Born in Seattle, Judy grew up in Colorado, where her father, Chuck Collins, was a bandleader and radio talk show figure. Her father had lost his sight at an early age, but he had learned to cope so well that most people did not realize he was blind. He was beloved and feared, a charmer with a drinking problem. When he was on the wagon, he was all smiles and songs. When he wasn't, he was a bully and womanizer. His young daughter sang harmony with him while he shaved; he encouraged her to study music. Judy dutifully began studying piano at the age of five and proved to have considerable talent. Music, she said later, gave her shelter from the pain of thinking her father's problems were her fault. Music was a way to please the man who was so supportive, and music was a refuge from the man who also was so scary. At the tender age of thirteen, Judy made her debut with the Denver symphony. But by the time Judy was in high school, it was not Mozart, but folk music that she was drawn to. She rebelled from the tight discipline of a concert pianist and gravitated toward the coffeehouse scene, where she could sing heartfelt songs like "The Gypsy Rover." She was intrigued by the down-to-earth quality of songs by Woody Guthrie and Pete Seeger and taught herself to play the guitar.

When she was eighteen, she married Peter Taylor, a handsome college student who shared her reading tastes — Camus, T. S. Eliot, Sartre, Graham Greene. For a while, she worked in a state park and did filing at the University of Boulder. Then they had a baby. Judy was nineteen. To help make ends meet, Peter suggested she try making money singing. When she was hired at Michael's Pub, Peter quit his job delivering newspapers and stayed home with the baby. But the bright lights that beckoned and nights on the road meant the end of Judy's marriage. She was drawn into a larger, livelier world, where she was becoming a new kind of music icon.

As the 1960s grew more rebellious, Judy's ethereal voice was a perfect fit for the songs about making love, not war. She became a shining star at peace demonstrations. She was at the center of a cultural-political shift with the likes of Joan Baez, Bob Dylan, Arlo Guthrie, and Peter Paul and Mary. She shared stages and good times with many rock 'n' roll stars who didn't survive those heady times. Janis Joplin once said in an interview that of the two of them, Judy Collins would be the one to make it. By the time Janis died of an overdose, Judy was "doing whatever I thought I needed to get me through the night." Living on the edge was fashionable, even required, she wrote later, for the interesting lives they were leading. As she wrote, "I have often thought that Janis knew we were the same and were both burning out, she at the greater speed and with a bomb, not an inferno. I was lucky and lived, I was touched on the

"God of wilderness, God of wildness, lead me to the quiet places of my soul. In stillness, in openness, may I find my strength."

— JAN RICHARDSON, Sacred Journeys

shoulder, I was pulled from the wreck before it blew."

While her career was soaring, her personal life crashed. She lost custody of her son, Clark, to her former husband. She would later admit, "I cried until I couldn't speak. I drank until I couldn't walk or speak." Drinking took away her regrets, her inhibitions, her shyness. She thought the liquor high was a spiritual high to go with the holy feeling of the music she sang. In her memoir, *Trust Your Heart*, she writes, "People ask if I miss the sixties. I do not. I was filled with misery and pain for many of those years. I went places and did things in a daze." At one point, Judy got so drunk that she fell in a pool at a wedding with a plaster cast up to her hip.

In 1978, Judy realized she had to get sober to save herself and sought treatment. She began getting back in touch with her faith. As a girl, some of her happiest moments were singing in the Methodist choir, and she loved the Christmas music best of all. Now she returned to God with prayers for help. And just as she was seeking assistance, she met the man who remains the love of her life, designer Louis Nelson.

Judy found healing in meditation and prayer. She found comfort in Gregorian chants. She learned from reading Pope John Paul II that we begin with the impression that prayer is our initiative, "but it's always God's initiative with us." She learned from Emmet Fox, a metaphysical writer of the 1930s, that practicing prayer is the only thing that changes character, that you must stop thinking about your difficulties and think of God instead, that to get rid of something negative, you must substitute something positive. She learned from Antoine de Saint Xupery, the French writer, and Elena Poniatowska, the Mexican writer, that everything truly essential is "invisible." Like love. And health. And faith.

She was somewhat embarrassed to admit her spiritual search in her artsy circles. "To see auras, to wear flowers, to light incense was all right; to admit to a spiritual search might be viewed as a weakness. To go to church, fine, but to be caught praying, meditating? Very suspect," she wrote in *Singing Lessons.*

Yet she began singing the hymn "Amazing Grace," which she had recorded in 1971, more often because she thought people needed the message that God can save even the most wretched of people. The story of the hymn's creation in 1779 was as inspiring as the music. The composer, John Newton, had led a successful life as trader, sailing from Liverpool to Africa and on to Antigua. His lucrative cargo was human beings. But on one trip, a fierce storm struck. His ship seemed lost. He prayed that if only salvation would come to "a wretch like me" he would leave the slave trade and work toward its abolition.

That moment became a turning point in Newton's life. He became an ardent opponent of slavery and a Methodist minister. But his greatest legacy was turning his story into a hymn, which still brings comfort hundreds of years later. The words are powerful:

"Amazing grace! (How sweet the sound!)
That sav'd a wretch like me!
I once was lost, but now am found;
Was blind, but now I see."

Judy Collins would need that same grace and more to deal with the toughest challenge of her life in 1992. Her son, Clark, who had struggled with his

"Grandfather, Great Father, let matters go well with me, for I am going into the forest."

— BAMBUTI PYGMY PRAYER

own drinking problem, committed suicide at the age of thirty-three by pumping carbon monoxide into his car. He left behind a wife and young daughter. At his funeral, his mother stood by his casket and sang "Amazing Grace" a cappella. How did she get through that moment? It was difficult, she says, but she felt she had to do it for him.

The depth of her grief forced Judy to quit working for a time, but she held on to God to get through the dark times. She poured out her pain into prayers in her journals. Music helped her heal — both the music she made and the music to which she listened. "Listening is important for artists, listening to music and to yourself," she says now.

Through it all, Louis Nelson stayed by her side. They were married in 1996 in the cathedral of St. John the Divine. They are

> "If I cannot listen to all of life, then any part that I do hear will only be partial or distorted. If I am listening only in chapel, if I am listening only to my peers, if I am listening only to my profession, if I am listening only to my routine, then I have cut out the poor, the children, the needy, the holy where it is calling me to be present."
>
> — JOAN CHITTISTER, Living in the Breath of the Spirit

on the church board and attend services there when they are in town.

To see Judy Collins perform today is to see how joy can survive. When she strides on stage in a lilac pants suit and pinkish boots, she certainly doesn't look like the grandmother she is.

Today, Judy says she has restored herself physically and emotionally and energetically, but it takes continuing effort. "I've gone through many, many things. I tell you something, if it doesn't kill you, you do get stronger," she told the *New York Times* in 1995. "I think I have gone through the single most difficult thing that a person can survive. I think suicide recovery is both the bottom of the barrel and the height of emotional stretching, psychic stretching. I don't think there's anything more horrible or more revealing."

Talking about her son's suicide helps her recover from the blow, she told me, adding, "You're not supposed to forget it." But as deeply as you go into grief, she explained, you also can reach new heights in spiritual contact. "Suicide is always a blow," she said. "There was a piece in the Sunday *Times* magazine this week about a young man who killed himself, and the person writing it was basically discussing whether it was preplanned, asking *Could I have stopped it? Was it depression? Was it treatable?* You know there is a link between depression and alcoholism. Those who kill themselves sometimes have been drinking and using. But there is so much to learn and so much we never know."

She said she probably will be talking the rest of her life about the importance of mental health treatment because "It is so important when people have issues of depression and conflict that they seek help. People think nothing of going to see the doctor when they need to check out their blood pressure. It shouldn't be any different when you need to seek help about emotional struggles with mood swings and body chemistry. It should be absolutely acceptable. And it should be included in health coverage."

When families of suicide victims call, she said she is happy to help, to listen to them. "Part of the recovery process is figuring out that there are other people who have done this and what kinds of help they got and thinking maybe I could survive, too." She tells the families to "take it one day at a time, connect with others, and not stop talking about it, not bury the suicide as a secret, go see someone if you need to, talk to a friend, talk to someone who has been there, walk, keep up exercise. Don't stop your work, don't retire from the field, so to speak. You have to get on with life, go to work, go to church, pray.

"The solution to so many problems is a spiritual solution," she emphasized, adding dryly, "I can say that, having overcome a *lot* of things."

Music has been a spiritual connection for her, Judy said, a kind of side door to church. And it pleases her that her music has been a conduit for others.

"I really think music serves as a kind of spiritual healing force," she said. "Certainly after September 11, I have seen it in the way people in the audience respond to the music. They want to hear something with meaning, something with depth. They don't want to be mindlessly engaged in things that are not going to capture their minds and their hearts."

And in the weeks after the attacks, as a gesture of caring for the families of victims, she offered to perform one song for free at many of the funerals for the victims. Usually the song the families chose was "Amazing Grace."

Rejuvenated at mid-life, Judy has poured herself into a host of activities:

ೲ She has formed her own record label, one of the few women to do so.

ೲ She has written a steamy novel about the music business for fun and is working on another.

ೲ Always a social activist, she has campaigned against land mines and championed assistance for children in the war zones of Bosnia for UNICEF.

ೲ A lifelong feminist, she has performed at many benefits for women, and as a staunch Democrat, she was a frequent guest at the Clinton White House.

ೲ She is trying to be of help to families of suicide victims and is writing another book called *Sanity and Grace* about dealing with suicide.

ೲ She is trying to write a song in memory of Mychal Judge, the fire department chaplain who died during the attacks on the World Trade Center, because he was "so devoted to humanity."

Her greatest hope now, she says, "is to fill out whatever the plan is for me. To have the courage and the strength to do the work in front of me. So often you have to remember not to focus just on the big challenges but the little things that add up to a life as well . . . like remembering to be patient with my husband, be forgiving with this other one, or be understanding with a woman struggling with something, watching my language. I pray to improve. I pray to be of service. I hope I will forgive as I am forgiven. I am a believer in miracles when you think about it, living through a lot of things is a miracle. And if you come to a point like I have where you have your health and your career, when you try to do some good and have some fun, that is a small miracle right there, isn't it?"

> "One of the best ways to demonstrate God's love is to listen to people."
>
> — BRUCE LARSEN

Yes, it is. And when you can come to see your life as a small miracle, that revelation is like finding something that was hidden in plain sight, right there in front of you the whole time you were looking. Carol Van Aken Oppel took the long route to answer God's call, but when she arrived, she was better prepared. Carol's journey from homemaker to a pastoral chaplain in Austin shows how listening to others can become your vocation.

Back when Carol was growing up in Tallahassee, Florida, church was a formative part of her life. She had gone to youth camp for seven summers and then worked as a counselor. "I would say I was a fairly typical teenager growing up in the 1950s in a small southern town where everyone went to the same high school." She was pretty enough and smart and close to her friends, but she often felt frustrated by the mold she felt she and other girls were put in during those times and the peer pressure to follow the crowd. "It didn't cut it with me. I was more serious, independent-minded. I didn't want to go along with the crowd if it wasn't fully me."

She felt a different tug, a tug to translate her youthful faith into some kind of service to others. A pivotal moment came when she was sixteen years old and had arisen early for the eucharist service at summer church camp. The camp chapel was in an old Army barrack and the altar faced over the Gulf of Mexico, she recalls, as if she could still see it clearly: "It was one of those early mornings. The sun was coming up over the Gulf. I remember the priest stood there as the sun was coming up behind him and held up a coquina shell with the markings of a sunrise on it. He said, 'This is a unique shell. There has never been anything like it, and there will never be anything like it again. You are the same way, and God loves you just the way you are.' I remember looking up at him and his body was washed in brilliant white, almost too strong to look at, and I knew then my life would forever be tied to the church. But I did not know how."

As she looked back, at the age of sixty, Carol could see that moment as the call to ministry she searched the rest of her life to fulfill. After college, she married a college classmate, Richard Oppel, who became a reporter with the Associated Press and moved steadily up in the profession as a newspaper editor. His career would take them all over the United States. There were some nine moves in all, she recalled with an easy laugh. "Let me see if I can get it straight: Tallahassee, Tampa, Miami, Tallahassee, Miami, Detroit, Tallahassee, Charlotte, Washington, then Austin. We were nomads, but I became good at it. I've learned a lot from all the places we've lived and feel very accomplished that our family life moved right along with us from place to place. I have very good friends in every place we lived."

And wherever they moved, Carol would find an Episcopal church to be part of their life. She wrote articles for church publications and started a small seasonal tabloid for her church in Charlotte. "It was a fabulous little newspaper, if I do say so myself," she says.

By the mid-1990s, she began to feel a yearning to live out the calling she felt in other ways. She began volunteering as a pastoral caregiver in her parish. She found that work very satisfying, but felt she would need to go to seminary to be taken more seriously than a volunteer.

They were moving soon to Austin, so Carol faced an opportunity and a crossroads.

"And he told them many things in parables, saying, 'Listen!'"

— MATTHEW 13:3

Should she make a bigger leap of faith and apply at the Episcopal Theological Seminary of the Southwest? Her son and daughter had gone off to college and had careers of their own. Should she go back to school herself in her 50s? She sought advice from her rector, Jim Holmes. He asked her pointedly, "What is it that you have to do?" She replied, "What I need to do and would regret not doing at the end of my life if I had not done it."

She found herself telling him that she wanted to say to teenagers — and others, but to teenagers especially — "that they are beloved children of God and made in his image. That they are okay and affirmed and pleasing in his sight just as they are." And Rev. Holmes said softly, "Then you better go do that."

Studying sometimes full-time and part-time, she earned a degree that would allow her to pursue pastoral ministry with proper credentials. She did her chaplaincy internship at St. David's Hospital, sharing the concerns of patients who were critically ill and in intensive care, and at a correctional facility for female inmates. She offered pastoral visits to women jailed for offenses ranging from drug use to murder. While there, she learned, "There was not a whole lot of difference between me and them. Only they had a lot of bad breaks. Most of them were victims themselves."

It was an adjustment in thinking from the rest of her life, she acknowledges. She was by then the wife of a successful newspaper editor with a comfortable home. She looks the picture of quiet, good taste, tall, striking, slender, and silver-haired. But every day she would go to work and be locked in cells with women who had violent pasts. "I would drive home in my Lexus to my house in Westlake Hills and try to make some sense of the lives I'd shared that day. I learned to trust the guards who told me if I would stay in their view they would protect me. I learned that this was the kind of work I wanted to do the moment I looked into the face of a crying woman whose life was in shreds and be able to say to her, 'I hear you. I hear your pain. I hear you, friend. I am here to tell you that you are beloved and good and we all screw up, but God loves you anyway.' "

One special moment of connection, Carol remembers, was with an African American woman in her mid-forties. "She taught me so much about faith and endurance. She was getting ready to get out of jail. She told me that her children had forsaken her and sold her house and car when she was in jail, so she had nothing left on the outside, but she had a spirit about her. She was in for bad checks — nothing terribly bad. I had asked her what she would do on her first day out and she said, 'I am going to go home to Louisiana, and I'm going to plant me a mess of greens and when the dew is on the grass in the morning, I am going to walk out in my bare feet and feel the mud between my toes.' I'll never forget that. I've always wondered what happened to her."

After graduation from seminary, Carol went to work with Life Works, an agency that provides housing, parental counseling, and credit counseling to families in need. "I learned buckets from that," she says. The agency had not had a chaplain before, so she created the position and discovered what she provided best was a ministry of presence. She learned how to develop a rapport with young people who were young enough to be her grandchildren. They came from the streets, multiple foster homes, and the police department. Some came for help on their own out of horrible circumstances. Some were young mothers with babies. Carol not only had to get them to trust her, but the staff as well. Some were suspicious of her as a Christian, thinking she would come with a Bible and "hit them over the head with it," especially those who worked with domestic abuse shelters and had encountered fundamentalists who insisted the battered women just needed to buck up and obey their husbands. "I had to develop a trust with them that I was there in an ecumenical role, to represent the possibility of something better happening to those kids."

One of the staffers, who saw her struggling to establish a connection with the teenagers early on, suggested, "Why don't you go in the kitchen and make cookies with them?" Nobody had taught her at seminary to use kitchen theology. But it worked.

"I started out with the most recalcitrant kid I could find," she recalls. "He had nose rings and a black doom-and-gloom T-shirt. I told him, 'Let's go in the kitchen and stir up a batch of chocolate-chip cookies.' And the most amazing thing happened. He told me, 'My father raped me, then he made me go to church. I hate God, and I don't want to talk to you anymore.' So I said, 'Well, then, you better get back to baking the cookies.' Then as we kept baking cookies, and eating a few, more stories would come out along with the cookies, and we began to develop a rapport."

It was not the kind of work where she could say, "This is my theology." More likely, she would find herself calming a fearful, pregnant girl who was almost a child herself by sitting with her at a picnic table and talking about what mothers do when the baby is up at three a.m. "That was just grace that day," Carol said as she recalled that scene. "It's hard to measure in this kind of work, but when something clicks, it feels good."

Carol's work until recently has been as chaplain at El Buen Samaritano, an Episcopal mission, where she worked with Hispanic, African American, and Anglo families in need. Most came for food, clothing, and medical services. And she was there to listen if they wanted to talk about whatever was going on in their lives. She now works as pastoral care coordinator for her parish, where she spends time one-on-one with parishoners struggling to survive grief after a death or divorce.

As human beings, we all need someone to validate our concerns by simply hearing them. Carol Oppel offers a caring presence as chaplain, just as you would offer an understanding heart for a friend who calls at two a.m. "You are listening. You're fully there for them, available to them without talking about yourself and saying *I've been there, I've done that.* I'm not there to talk about me. I am there to hear them. It is a very humbling opportunity. These are good people. They are trying to make it day to day, and they need a lot of help. At Buen Samaritano, I could also be there for the staff when they were worn thin and frustrated from having to tell people there are no more food baskets. I was grateful to be able to do the kind of work that reflects the church into the world and the world back to the church."

Looking back, she can now see "how one thing led to another." Her favorite subject in school was Spanish, so she went to Mexico twice when she was in college to study in Monterrey. It was not a usual choice for coeds in the 1960s, but one that now helps Carol connect with Hispanics at El Buen Samaritano. Likewise, raising her own children, being a homeroom mother, and being a Brownie leader decades ago now make it easier for her to talk to at-risk youth. Being a chaplain for low-income families was not something she ever would have envisioned in those days. While some are called to serve by a dramatic event, she was drawn forward in a step-by-step process.

> "The Lord came and stood there, and called as he had before, 'Samuel! Samuel!' Samuel answered, 'Speak; your servant is listening.'"
>
> — 1 SAMUEL 3:10

For other women who may feel a similar tug to serve in some way, she urges them to listen to their own inner voices as a guide. "Follow your yearning. Follow the restlessness. God is the restlessness. God is the yearning. God is in the inklings and the intuitive knowledge that there is something more. Follow it. Even if you don't know where you are going, follow it. One of my favorite quotes is from Vaclav Havel, who said, 'Hope is not knowing where you're going. Hope is knowing that you are headed in the right direction and that when you get there, it will be the right place.' You must follow what feels right and ask yourself along the way, just as Jim Holmes asked me, 'What is it that you *have* to do? What is it you *must* do?' If you open yourself to grace, in time, you hear yourself answering."

TAKE HOME:

Listening to God must have been just as difficult thousands of years ago, too, because the three great monotheistic faiths — Judaism, Christianity, and Islam — pointedly remind followers to remember who they should be trying to please with their lives. In fact, one of the most beautiful prayers in any faith is the "Sh'ma," which translates in Hebrew to "listen." Even the name is like a whisper:

Shhhhhhh. The most important line of the Sh'ma is the very beginning, "Hear, O'Israel," it says for emphasis, there is only one God and he wants you to know that love is the way of acting in the world. The Sh'ma goes on to remind that human actions make a difference in the world. The Sh'ma declaration of faith is one of the first things learned by Jewish children. For the rest of their life, the prayer will be said upon awakening and at the end of the day. It is often the last words that the faithful utter as they die.

You can find the Sh'ma in Deuteronomy 6:4–10, where Moses called on the people of Israel to listen to the message about how to awaken the love and compassion in their beings: "Hear, O'Israel: The Lord is our God, the Lord alone. You shall love the Lord your God with all your heart, and with all your soul and with all your might. Keep these words that I am commanding you today in your heart. Recite them to your children and talk about them when you are at home and when you are away, when you lie down and when you rise. Bind them as a sign on your hand, fix them as an emblem on your forehead, and write them on the doorposts of your house and on your gates."

Many Jews to this day place a mezuzzah, a small decorative box, by their doors. They often touch it on their way into their homes or as they leave. Inside are the words of the Sh'ma, a reminder to "hear" God as we go about our lives.

Not coincidentally, when Jesus of Nazareth was asked by a teacher of religion which is the first commandment of all, Jesus answered him, "The one that says, 'Hear, O Israel! The Lord our God is the one and only God. And you must love him with all your heart and soul and mind and strength.' The second is: 'You must love others as much as yourself.' No other commandments are greater than these." (Mark 12:34)

"Listen carefully my child, to my instructions, and attend to them with the ear of your heart. This is advice from one who loves you; welcome it and faithfully put it into practice. The labor of obedience will bring you back to God from whom you had drifted through the sloth of disobedience."

— THE RULE OF BENEDICT

That wording also is echoed in one of the most memorized passages in the Qu'ran: "Allah! There is no God but He, the Living, who needs no other, but Whom all others need." (Qu'ran 2:25)

We are in a century saturated with information but sorely lacking in reflection. As a way of learning to listen more carefully, imagine for an entire day that you have ears but no mouth. That means you cannot talk, only listen. Spend the day paying special attention to what others are saying. As is often the case, whenever you accentuate one sense, it heightens your perceptions. We can "see" others better when we listen carefully to them. In the same manner, try listening to music with your eyes closed instead of watching television when you come home in the evening. When you shut out the world for a while, you can experience it more clearly. Consider having a quiet weekend, when you don't speak a word. Fill your soul, so you will have more energy when you return to the world. It's not practical for most of us to spend our days in total quiet, but we can learn to savor time to think. The first step to take when you need to shut out the noise of the world is to quiet yourself.

"The first duty of love is to listen."

– PAUL TILLICH

Do you have a listening heart? Or are you part of the noise of the world?

TWO

Praying

"Prayer draws down the great God into the little heart."
— SAINT MECHTILD OF MAGDEBURG

When I was a little girl, I would sometimes have an earache, like most children. My mother would come and lie down on my bed with me and gently blow her warm breath in my ear. She would pat my back and say quiet things until I went to sleep. In one way or another, God does the same kind of thing for us if we tell him where we are hurting.

Many women turn to faith because of a devastating moment — divorce, death of a loved one, illness, hardship. For many others, the steady accumulation of disappointments may have lead to deep despondence. Either way, prayer is the gate for finding your way back to God.

Seven out of ten Americans reported praying more in the weeks after the terrorist attacks on September 11, 2001. The threat of mortality literally brought them to their knees. They had to check their moorings: *Hello up there,* they asked, *are you still there?*

And so it has been for ages. When the ground shakes under our feet, we reach for the sky. But how do you pray for help if you've gotten out of the habit? Or never got the hang of it? You can start by understanding a few basic things:

ᔛ You learn to pray by praying. It's like learning to dance the box step. At first you are terribly self-conscious. After a while, you don't need to look at your feet, you just lean in and go.

ᔛ There's a simple five-point formula that you can check off using your upheld hand. Touch your thumb first to begin with praise for God, the almighty, the merciful, because that's the most important thing of all. Next, touch your index finger to give thanks for your blessings, which are more than you realize, and for your problems, which are fewer and smaller than you think. Third, count your tall middle finger, to remind yourself to ask forgiveness, for yourself, then to forgive others. Fourth, your ring finger reminds you to make your prayer requests for others. Fifth and last, the smallness of your little finger shows your prayer requests for yourself shouldn't always be at the front of the line.

∾ Don't expect to get everything on your list like a catalog order. Sometimes the answer is "Wait." Or sometimes it's "No, I've got something better up my sleeve." Remember, even Jesus did not get everything he prayed for.

∾ Pray out loud. It becomes more real, more bold, more empowering.

∾ Yes, he is listening. Eminent psychologist Carl Jung had these words carved over the front door of his house in Zurich: "Bidden or not bidden God is present."

"What is the use of prayer if at the very moment of prayer we have so little confidence in God that we are busy planning our own kind of answer to our prayer?"

— THOMAS MERTON

∾ As Brother Lawrence pointed out, prayer really is like a conversation with God, not a monologue. Just as when you are talking with a friend, it is not wise to dominate the conversation.

ᑫ If you can't think of anything to say, it is helpful just to place yourself in God's presence, just hanging out with The Beloved. It is a way to get close to him.

ᑫ Remember, prayer is not just for emergencies, like the emergency cord on the bus. You should also pray when your heart is full of joy and your house full of abundance. It should be your first resort, not your last.

ᑫ In centering prayer, your mind is kept on the prayer focus by the repetition of a key word over and over until you drive distracting thoughts to the corner. Think of something like "hope," "grace," or "shalom."

ᑫ If your worries keep distracting you, try laying those matters at God's feet like a tangle of yarn that you can't unravel. Leave it to God, and let go.

ᑫ If you fall asleep before you finish your prayers, don't feel guilty. Perhaps God wants you to know you are tired. His answer may be to get some rest so you can start over fresh in the morning.

ᑫ Prayer can be physical. Some find it effective to raise their arms to the sky as they pray, palms up as if to receive. Some kneel to show submission. If your prayer life seems stagnant, perhaps you need to get out of your physical comfort zone.

☙ Prayer can be enriched by your senses. Light a candle to sanctify the moment. Say, "Let me come into the presence of God." Listen to music, chants, or bells. Add something to look at — a cross, an icon, elegant script from the Qu'ran, a Menorah, or a prayer cloth. Some like to anoint the moment with oil or burn incense.

☙ Look at photos of your family as you pray. Ask God's blessings for them. Ask forgiveness for any misunderstandings. Ask God to hold them in his hand and grant them peace. Likewise, if there is someone that you have negative feelings about, place something in your prayer area that reminds you of that person. Look at it and ask God to lift away any hard feelings; pray for forgiveness in the matter; pray for God's blessings for that person.

☙ Pray always, anywhere. Even when you can't feel it or believe, pray. As Lady Julian of Norwich advised back in the twelfth century, "Pray inwardly, even though you do not enjoy it. It does good though you feel nothing, even though you think you are doing nothing."

❧ Don't stop. PUSH — Pray Until Something Happens. And then keep praying.

I had to chuckle when I heard Peggy Noonan admit on C-Span one afternoon that when she applied for a job as a White House speechwriter, she wanted the job so much she said a novena, the recitation of prayers for nine consecutive days, even though she was not as seriously religious at that time in her life. The day after she finished, she got the call from the White House. "But I don't usually tell that much," she admitted. "It's a little too woo-woo."

> "I pray on the subway going home, in the train filled with commuters — just sit there with my eyes closed, breathing in and out. I let each person I've encountered that day float into my heart, where I embrace them and then let them go."
>
> — ALISON LUTERMAN,
> *This Thing About Goodness*

Woo-woo or not, it is a reminder that even when we thought we were too cool to need faith in younger years, it was waiting for us. Today, Peggy Noonan can say she is a much happier person because she has re-embraced faith at mid-life. "Faith and love of God have made me much happier," she says.

Her faith has informed her writing as well as her life, making her a unique figure in American politics. When she got that job as a speechwriter for Ronald Reagan, and later George H. W. Bush, she was an anomaly: a brainy, attractive, conservative, Catholic woman in a field where just about everyone else was a middle-aged man.

When the *Challenger* space shuttle crashed in 1986 and the country was in shock, it was young Ms. Noonan who suggested President Reagan quote from a 1940s poem called "High Flight" when he addressed the nation. The words had popped into her head as she wrote the speech. She wrote that the *Challenger* astronauts had "slipped the surly bonds of earth to touch the face of God." It was the phrase that Americans remembered long after their tears had dried.

Whether she has realized it or not, Peggy Noonan's ability over the years to insert religion into political discourse has added immeasurably to the ability of others in the media to do so without blushing or feeling unsophisticated. Her writing about her own faith journey in her books as well as her application of spiritual values to her political analysis for the *Wall Street Journal* has broadened the acceptable range of intellectual commentary to include religion in a refreshing way. For example, she was able to pick up a telling anecdote in a 2001 interview with newly elected President George W. Bush that many others might have dismissed. As she told in her book *When Character Was King*, when President Bush first met with Russian president Vladimir Putin, the Russian leader told him that he had taken to wearing a cross his mother had given him. One day he inadvertently left the cross in a house he was visiting, and the house burned down shortly thereafter. Putin wanted to find the cross, but the task seemed impossible. Just then, a worker walked over to Putin and showed the leader something he had found in the ashes. The cross was in his open palm.

President Putin told Mr. Bush, "It was as if something meant for me to have the cross." President Bush interpreted that to mean the Russian was saying, "There was a higher power." It was the beginning of

Mr. Bush's sense that he and the Russian leader could establish a personal connection. Peggy Noonan understood where the president was coming from.

Though she had tried to distance herself from her faith for a time as a young adult, Peggy never got too far from it. Like many baby boomers, she didn't think she really needed her Catholic religion. It was old hat, she thought; something for "immigranty" grandparents. The more modern World War II generation was more relaxed about religion, and their children, the boomers, just didn't consider it cool. As she told in her book, *Life, Liberty and the Pursuit of Happiness*, her faith was like a nice handbag that she carried but rarely opened. The Me Generation's plan was to have years of exploring the thrills and edges of the world, "a real full wallow," then become religious in your 70s, "about ten minutes to death." But by the time she was in her forties, she sensed that something was missing. Peggy came to see that success boiled down to "getting invited to things I don't want to go to but liked saying I went to."

In 1992, she called a friend who was a

> "To wish to pray is a prayer in itself."
>
> – GEORGES BERNANOS

former priest to ask for advice about praying. She had moved beyond a mild engagement with Christianity to a kind of hunger — she wanted to grow from being a person who approves of faith to someone who lives it. Her friend told her to "read, think, pray, and get a regular spiritual counselor." So she did. She began reading Thomas Merton, histories of the early church, and essays by theologians. She joined a Bible study group with her friends and discovered she hadn't really known what was in the Bible. So "Acts" was about how the disciples went into the world after Jesus died and started the church? Ohhh. "Acts of the Apostles." Right.

She started trying to pray more, even though she really didn't think she knew how. She knew the "Hail Mary" and "Our Father," but she wanted to move from recitation to engagement. Then she met a priest at a PBS taping and asked him to help her learn to pray. He counseled her to read the scriptures, have a regular prayer time, study the lives of the saints, and observe the sacraments, Mass, confession, and communion.

> "To pray is to change. Prayer is the central avenue God uses to transform us."
>
> — RICHARD J. FOSTER

He wrote her, "St. Francis de Sales advised: Only two kinds of people need frequent communion — the not-so-good, that they might become better; and the good, that they might stay that way. If you haven't already, look for a church with good liturgy and good preaching — and God will take it from there . . ."

Her instinct was to seek expert advice, just as you would with any problem, and it was a good one. If you aren't quite sure how to pray yourself, Rabbi Zalman Schachter suggests that you sit with a "prayerful person" and pray together. It will help you catch on.

When we talked, I asked Peggy if, at fifty-one, she believed you need your faith more as you get older. She laughed, "Oh, honey, I'm smack in the middle of life even if I live a long life, and you do need it more. You always need God, and always need more God than you think. Maybe as you get older, you are simply more aware of it. I don't know that I need more God than when I was fourteen, because when I was fourteen,

> "If a dead person were allowed to return to this world and pray, you can be sure that he would pray with all his might."
>
> — RABBI NACHMAN OF BRATSLO

I knew I needed him. I was thinking the other day when I was making notes for a *Wall Street Journal* piece, that America makes you ambitious and life makes you religious. After a certain amount of time, you realize ambition isn't enough. Meaning and God are the only happiness. Everything else is just commentary."

It was her faith that gave Peggy a maturing perspective about the emotions of September 11. Walking the streets near her Manhattan home, she could smile when she saw someone had written in new concrete, "Smile. Today is what you have." It had a Psalmlike wisdom to it. While other columnists wrote of retaliation and revenge, she mused that it is easier to fight than to pray, but we should pray anyway. She remembered the story about Mother Teresa and the Catholic writer Henri Nouwen, who was a priest. He had gone to the nun once and poured out all his problems — he wasn't appreciated, he was misunderstood, higher-ups weren't helping him in his good work. Mother Teresa replied simply, "You wouldn't be having all these problems if you prayed more." At first Nouwen was resentful, Peggy recalled, because he had expected encouragement, sympathy, and solidarity. Instead, he got a blunt statement that he knew, in his heart, was true. So he went home and prayed. And sure enough, his problems became more manageable.

"Prayer is the hardest thing," Peggy concluded. "And no one congratulates you for doing it because no one knows you are doing it, and if things turn out well, they likely won't thank God in any case. But I have a feeling that the hardest thing is what we all better be doing now, and that it's not only the best answer but the only one."

> "Dear Jesus, as a hen covers her chicks with her wings to keep them safe, do you this night protect us with your golden wings."
>
> — PRAYER FROM INDIA

And it's true. Prayer is our lifeline in time of need. Prayer helped Cheryl Polhill Watts start over after her husband died of a heart attack while he was playing basketball with their sons in the driveway of their home. A registered nurse, she tried to administer CPR. It was too late. She had to begin a new life alone.

She was a thirty-seven-year-old African American single mother with three sons. Steven was only four years old. Justin and Willis were in their early teens and hoped someday to go to college. First, Cheryl had to help her youngest son understand that his father was not coming back. He worried at the funeral that his daddy wouldn't be able to breathe in the ground. She told him "Daddy's making rainbows in the sky."

She wrote a children's book just for him called *Loving One Another*. Justin drew illustrations of black and white children playing together, praying, helping other children in wheelchairs, and holding hands with Jesus Christ. The text reads:

"If people don't love other people, they do not truly love God.

Loving other people is one of the best ways to show that you love God.

Some people hurt other people because they want things they don't have, and they don't have things they want because they don't know God to ask him for them . . .

People are always saying how they love God, but if they are not loving and kind to other people, they don't really know God. God is love. When we love God he lives within us . . . he makes us strong. He wants us to be humble. He does not make anyone better than the other person . . . He loves each of us the same. When we make other people feel bad, we are fighting

against God's law of 'loving one another.'"
(1 John 3:11)

Cheryl continued working for a health agency, but her heart was not in the work any longer. She went to her office with her résumé in her briefcase every day. As she looked for a way to change her life, she realized she found comfort in baking tea cakes — large fluffy sugar cookies like her aunt and grandmother used to make back in Pearson, Georgia. When she was young, she had watched with fascination as her aunt Dora baked and told her, "If you'll be good, I'll make you tea cakes. Just sit on the sofa and wait."

Now, when Cheryl baked her own tea cakes, her sons and friends would eat them as fast as she could get them out of the oven. The thought occurred to her that she might be able to sell them to others. She was a fan of cooking shows on The Food Channel and liked to bake. But improvising in her kitchen from memory was one thing; selling to strangers was another. Could she come up with the right recipe to make the tea cakes a commercial success? She prayed she would figure out a recipe that would appeal to other people. She tried variation after variation until she got the taste and consistency she wanted and remembered. The result was something like a cross between a cookie and a biscuit. Cheryl's tea cakes are soft and slightly chewy. The ingredients are basic — flour, sugar, butter, vanilla, and a little salt. Cheryl jazzed hers up with nutmeg, cinnamon, and a sprinkling of cinnamon-sugar.

Then she headed out in her family car to look for places that might sell the tea cakes. Stopping for gas at a nearby service station, she prayed that the station manager would try her tea cakes and agree to sell them over-the-counter. She went in and offered him a sample, suggesting, "Why don't you just try it and see if it works? You could put them right there next to the cash register." It just took one bite for him to say "Yes."

Within a few years, she was on her way to a full-fledged baking business, "Tea Cakes by Cheryl." Her tea cakes were on sale in forty area service stations, restaurants, and convenience stores in the Dallas area. By the time she was forty-two, she was baking ten dozen cookies at a time, thanks to a used Cookie

"Prayer is happy company with God,"

– CLEMENT OF ALEXANDRIA

King machine she bought from a restaurant supply company. Her older sons helped her design the packaging on their personal computers. "At first they thought I was crazy to leave nursing for baking," she says. Now they call her from college with suggestions on how to "grow" the business.

She believes that it is not just the taste that compels people to buy her sweet treats, it is the memories they represent from a time when "afternoon calls" from friends meant that women had to be prepared for guests. Many customers tell her that the tea cakes are "just like the ones I had when I was growing up." Explains Cheryl, "I sell memories of love and family."

> "One single grateful thought raised to heaven is the most perfect prayer."
>
> – GOTTHOLD LESSING

When I first met Cheryl, it was difficult to imagine her hauling her cookies into service stations and making a deal. She is soft-spoken and modest and wears a small gold cross around her neck. With her hair pulled back and her wire-rimmed glasses, she looks rather like an accountant. But as you get to know her, you notice how carefully she watches everything, how composed she remains, how steady her center is. Speaking with an unassuming naturalness over lunch at a neighborhood Chinese food restaurant, she credited her faith with helping her launch herself in a new direction. "I always pray. I don't do anything without praying about it," she confided. "I don't guess I've ever told anyone how much I pray, but I do believe in the power of prayer."

Usually, she prays three times a day, she said: in the morning with her daily devotional reading, at noon when she's baking, and in the evening as she goes to bed. At home she has a corner where she can kneel on a pillow to pray, and when she's baking, she takes a time-out to sit in a favorite "prayer rocker" and pray. She keeps a prayer journal so she can go back and see where her prayers were answered and write underneath, "Thank you, God, for answering this prayer."

What does she typically pray for? "Oh, since September 11, I've prayed for the president and Laura Bush," she said. "I pray for the prosperity of my business and all the locations I sell to. And of course, I pray for my family." Her sons don't like it when she "preaches" to them, she admitted with a smile, so she makes sure they see that she reads the Bible and when one of them sits in her rocker, she tells them, "You are in the prayer rocker, so you are going to have to pray."

Her own role model is her mother, who prayed over her children and would call to pray with Cheryl while she was at college in Georgia. "My family used to say 'There's nothing like a praying mother' and it's true," she said. "Mothering is holy work."

Prayer, she said, also can be a very subtle witnessing tool. When a friend or customer expresses concern about a problem, she gently suggests, "I will pray for you. Do you mind if I pray for you? I'll put you on my prayer list." Since September 11, she noted, people have been especially receptive. "I think a lot of people want to be closer to God, but they just don't know how."

In a way, she said, her tea cake business has become a kind of ministry for her. She sometimes gives tea cakes to the homeless and encourages them to share the cakes with a friend. When people ask how she started her baking company, she tells them that she prayed for the recipe

"Prayer should be the key in the morning and the lock at night."

— OWEN FELLTHAM

70

and the customers and that God answered her prayer.

As she looks for ways to expand her business, she said she is praying for guidance and praying that "God will give me favor with the people I meet."

> "Is prayer your steering wheel or your spare tire?"
>
> – CORRIE TEN BOOM

She is keeping her nursing license up to date so she can go back to health care if necessary. But she doesn't think she'll need to: "I feel this is what I am supposed to do — because I have been happy ever since."

In the final analysis, it's hard to do better than the Lord's Prayer. Start with it as a warm-up for your other thoughts, or use it as a perfect closing. You can be assured that God will give you something important to pray about every day of your life. It's up to you to do so.

TAKE HOME:

There is much to learn from prayer practices through the ages.

∽ Methodist founder John Wesley was

such a strong believer in prayer, he scheduled five minutes out of every hour for prayer. It refreshed him. It helped him keep his focus. It reminded him whom he was working for.

∾ Taking their cue from the Psalm reference "Seven times a day have I praised you," the Benedictine monks schedule seven prayer times during the day: Lauds, Prime, Terce, Sext, None, Vespers, and Compline. Benedict, the founder of the order, scheduled prayer times to coincide with the changing of the Roman Imperial guard. While the secular world sought order by force, he sought order by prayer.

∾ The Arabic word for prayer in Islam is *salat*, which means "red-hot connection" — a hot-link so to speak. In Islam, believers are supposed to pray five times a day. These memorized prayers are before sunrise, just after noontime, late afternoon, just after sunset, and at night. As onerous as that may sound, Muslims will tell you that you become used to it as it becomes woven into your life, which is the whole point. The practice takes Muslims out of the temporal world for the humbling reminder that "Allahu Akbar" — God is greater.

∾ Observant Jews also pray several times a day, as do Hindus, Buddhists, and others. A believer should pray three times a day, according to Judaism, because the soul should be fed as often as the body. The three prayers honor the three founders of the Jewish religion, honoring Abraham in the morning, Isaac in the afternoon, and Jacob at night. The goal of regular prayers during the day is to hallow daily life. In Jewish tradition, stepping into the holy space of prayer is like stepping into the ocean of people praying everywhere, a sort of a world wide web of faith.

∾ Even God prays. According to the Talmud, God's prayer is this: "May it be My will that My mercy overcome my anger, and My loving qualities overcome My strict traits; that I treat My children with a quality of mercy and that I always deal with them beyond the letter of the law."

∾ Many Christians take Jesus at his word to his disciples that he would hear what they asked in his name. Early Christians chanted "Kyrie Eleison," which means "Lord, have mercy." Today, many rely on the repetition of what has become known as the Jesus Prayer: "Lord Jesus Christ, son of God, have mercy on me." The shortest Jesus prayer is simply to say the name Jesus with the verb that matches your present need, such as "Jesus comforts," or "Jesus rescues," or "Jesus heals."

Whatever the denomination, it has been shown that prayer can heal. More than 191 studies have been done on the relationship between healing and prayer. Though the methodology sometimes has been ragged, prayer always made a positive difference in varying degrees. In one recent study at Duke University Medical Center, one thousand heart patients were studied. Half were prayed for; half were not. The result: The prayed for patients had 11 percent fewer heart attacks, strokes, and complications. In another study by Dr. Elisabeth Targ in San Francisco, twenty critically ill AIDS patients were studied. All ten patients who were prayed for lived, while four of the others died.

Keeping a prayer journal is a good way to see how your prayers are answered. It also is a revealing way to see what kinds of supplications you make over time, to see what you're preoccupied with. Just as you might look at your checkbook register to see where your money goes, it is worth checking to see where your prayers go and what that says.

Are there conditions to getting answers? Yes and no. The stern fine print in the Old Testament tells us disobedience, unconcern, and injustice may prevent God from answering prayer because those supplicants may not have a genuine relationship with God. The New Testament reassures that if we seek the Lord, knock, and ask in Jesus' name, our prayers will be heard, particularly if two or more join in prayer. But the idea is that prayer should have some ramifications for our lives. As Henry Ward Beecher observed, "It is not well to pray cream and live skim milk." Sincere prayer should lead to a closer relationship with God, which then grows to include harmony with others.

> "Prayer is the rope that pulls God and man together. But it doesn't pull God down to us; it pulls us up to him."
>
> – WILLIAM FRANKLIN (BILLY) GRAHAM

When my sons were very young and away at camp, I would pray for them and ask God to wrap them in a light golden blanket of protection, so that they would feel comforted and protected as they slept, rather than homesick or alone. Even later, when they were in their twenties and off in new places, I would pray that a sunny envelope of God's love would be with them, surrounding them with a warm golden feeling of well-being. If you know someone who is sick or in trouble, it's a comforting way to pray for them. At the least, it always made me feel better just thinking of my sons with love wrapped around them.

THREE

Blessing

"May the road rise to meet you. May the wind be always at your back. May the sun shine warm upon your face. And rains fall soft upon your fields. And until we meet again, May God hold you in the hollow of his hand."

— IRISH BLESSING

If our lives seem depressingly mundane and monotonous, it may be because we have evolved away from the practices that hallowed the everyday business of life. Too much of our day has been emptied of the divine.

In the past, rituals and blessings gave meaning to the tasks at hand. There were blessings of the fleets as fishermen set out with their nets. Crops were blessed as they were planted and harvested. Houses were blessed as they were built. The changes of the seasons were blessed. What we need to do is reclaim the traditions of blessing what we do and those we love.

Blessings are different from prayers. Prayers primarily are petitions and communications addressed to God. Blessings are verbal expressions of God's love to others in hopes that their lives will be fruitful, abundant, and godly. All blessings flow from God, of course, but they may be offered by others in his name. In the Old Testament, blessings were pronounced on children or subordinates by the heads of households or others in authority. The idea was to endow them with the faith that leads to prosperity, longevity, and wisdom.

Today, we can use blessings to put God back into the details of our daily living, not just the holidays. If you take special care to sanctify the mundane, you begin to understand that whatever your problems may be, you are indeed blessed.

Cooking dinner after a long, tiring day? Ask God to bless each member of your family with health as you prepare the meal. You have food. You are together.

Working in your yard? Look at your green space as a blessing, a chance to make your corner of the world beautiful, worthy of the original gardener. You are alive and able.

Painting the house? Let every stroke be full of gratitude that you have a home, shelter from the cold and the storm. Ask protection for all within.

Sure, it may sound like Pollyanna, but give it a try. It works. Even when you are paying bills or filing records, your attitude changes if you ask that your efforts be blessed, file by file, bill by bill, and that those blessings be passed along the chain to everyone whose hands the paper passes through. It's a way of reminding ourselves that every task is valuable. It's a way of reminding us that even on our worst days, our blessings exceed our burdens. Whatever the task at hand, whether cooking or computering or mopping, we should invest the act with a sense of God's loving presence. If we put more divinity into the minutes of our lives, it will add up to a life well spent, no matter what our particular vocation.

A telling example comes from Brother Lawrence, a seventeenth-century Carmelite monk who saw God at work in the every day. Brother Lawrence spent forty years working at his assignment in a French monastery kitchen, chopping vegetables and cleaning. When he died at the age of eighty, he left no writings, but his spiritual wisdom was captured by a visiting member of the cardinal's staff, M. de Beaufort, who recorded their conversations. Kneeling at his scullery work, Brother Lawrence explained to Beaufort, was his gift to God. His oratory was in his heart as he served God in the kitchen, rather than in the chapel. As he put it, "The time of business does not with me differ from the time of prayer, and in the noise and clatter of my kitchen, while several persons are at the same time calling for different things, I possess God in as great tranquility as if I were upon my knees at the Blessed sacrament." It is telling that the humble monk's words live on today, while the words of those who were in more elevated stations around him do not. He knew well that the monotony of repetitious tasks can free our minds to think on God.

As Teresa of Avila said, "Christ moves among the pots and the pans." Life is humdrum — just one darn thing after another — if you do not color the everyday events with reverence. If you look at each task as a gift, then you will begin to see God where you did not see him before. As Sister Joan Chittister says, "God does not come on hoofbeats of mercury through streets of gold. God is in the dregs of our lives. That's why it takes humility to find God where God is not expected to be."

She points out that Benedict, founder of the Benedictine order, used to remind his colleagues that humble work was as sacred as prayer. He would bless the kitchen servers in the middle of the chapel service. With that simple gesture, she says, life begins to look different. Suddenly, it is not made up of "higher" and "lower" activities, but the sense is communicated that all of us play a role in making the world work. Each plays a part.

Indeed, after September 11, we became acutely aware that policemen, firemen, and flight attendants might be more important in our lives than the people who get paid millions of dollars to play baseball or make movies or run corporations. For once, the "heroes" on the news after September 11 were workaday people who had risen to the occasion and deserved the applause. It reminded me that at one time in Japanese society, it was tradition to bow politely to even the street sweepers in the train station. That courtesy signaled that we all are valuable. Without

"Lord through this day,
In work and play,
Please bless each thing I do.
May I be honest, loving, kind,
Obedient unto you."

— FROM *THE INFANT TEACHER'S PRAYER BOOK*

the garbage collectors and the plumbers and the painters and the waitresses and the carpenters and technicians, we could not move forward in this biosphere called life. So when you see a worker from now on, maybe you should bow to them mentally in your mind and heart. Or pray blessings for them.

The Jewish faith excels at making all occasions, large and small, an opportunity to embrace God. In the Talmud, eating or drinking without first making a blessing over the meal is compared to robbing God of his poetry. Tradition teaches that each Jew should say at least one hundred blessings a day. True, when you repeat memorized blessings, human nature is to slip into automatic pilot and forget the inner meaning of the words. Yet there is something comforting even in going through the motions; and like buying insurance, you're better with it than without. The goal should be to make saying blessings a sincere habit, not just a habit. Your words and acts should flow with intentionality.

Jewish families are supposed to say several blessings ("berachah") before the Sabbath meal — for the children, the wine, the washing of hands, and the bread. Before eating bread, for example, the Jewish blessing is "Blessed are you, Eternal One our God, universal presence, who brings forth bread from the earth." It is customary for a father to bless the children, but women can do so as well. The parents place their hands on the heads of the children or wrap their arms around all of them. Part of the ancient blessing is "The Eternal One blesses you and protects you. The Eternal One shines God's Presence upon you and is gracious to you. The Eternal One lifts up God's Presence to you and grants you Peace."

Rachel Naomi Remen recalls in her memoir, *My Grandfather's Blessings*, how her grandfather would call her to him for a blessing, saying, "Come, Neshume-le — beloved little soul." He would rest his hands lightly on the top of her head and thank God for her and for making him her grandpa. He would mention her struggles during the week and tell God something about her that was true. If she had told the truth about making a mistake, he would praise her honesty. If she had learned to sleep without her night-light, he would praise her bravery. "Then he would give me his blessing and ask the long-ago women I knew from his many stories — Sarah, Rachel, Rebekah, and Leah — to watch over me," she recalled. "These few moments were the only time in my week when I felt completely safe and at rest."

Couldn't we all use that sense of security, even as adults?

You can find similar blessings for children in some Protestant churches. In the Unity church, for example, children are regularly blessed at the Sunday service with these words: "We love you. We bless you. We appreciate you just the way you are." After one service, one of the youngsters ran up to her father and hugged him, saying, "I love you. I bless you. I appreciate you just the way you are."

Traditionally, a Jewish father also may bless his wife at the Sabbath meal time by reading from Proverbs 31:10–31, the famous "Proverbs Woman" passage, which extols, "What a rare find is a capable wife! Her worth is far beyond that of rubies. Her husband puts his confidence in her and lacks no good thing." According to Dr. Karen J. Prager, a professor at Southwestern Medical Center in Dallas, feminist Jews are reviving traditions honoring women that have fallen into disuse. They also are creating new blessings for life-

"God is in me or else is not at all."

— WALLACE STEVENS

cycle events, such as the good news of a pregnancy, which can be determined much earlier these days thanks to home pregnancy tests. The modern rituals are married to the ancient by using wording from patriarchal covenants, such as God's promise to Abraham and Sarah in Genesis that their descendants would be "as numerous as the stars in the sky and as plentiful as the sand." That continuity is reassuring. The old becomes new again and meets our deepest human needs, to know God and be known, to love and be loved.

A woman sitting by me on an airline flight once taught me a new way of thinking about blessings. Meeting her brought home to me that you never know when you get up in the morning who will be brought into your path that day that you can learn from — or can teach. The secret is to leave yourself open to the possibility. And listen. The woman I met on the plane was a kindergarten teacher named Irene Molina. I was struck first by her big smile and hearty laugh. This was the kind of person who offers everyone around a piece of gum when she pulls a packet out of her purse. There was a naturalness to her that was very appealing. She felt perfectly comfortable closing her eyes for a moment's grace before she began eating her airline sandwich and bag of chips. She mentioned as we talked that her late husband had been a teacher as well. Something about the name sounded familiar, so I asked, isn't there a school in Dallas named after your husband? "Yes, Moises Molina was my husband," she acknowledged, beaming. "Did you know him?" No, but I remembered his story, because it was so unique.

A new high school was named after Moises Molina in 1998 because the school band director had been such an inspiration to so many students. He was something of a legend for helping needy students. If students needed lunch money, he gave them his. If they had problems at home, they could bunk a night at the Molina's. If they needed a part-time job to help make ends meet, Mr. Molina would help them find bookings for their music groups. It came as a shock when he died suddenly of a rare liver ailment at the age of forty-six. The school district took the unusual step of naming a school after him, making him the first band director and one of the few Hispanics to receive such an honor. His name and story had stuck in my mind. And this exuberant woman with the shoulder-length, chocolate brown hair was his wife. I was to learn that her story was just as interesting as his.

She had grown up as Irene Saldovar, the child of migrant agricultural workers. She worked in the fields from an early age, picking cotton when she was a little girl and traveling with her family wherever there were crops to work. She picked watermelons, onions, and tomatoes ("Your hands get all red"). She harvested sugar beets in Colorado and pecans in Texas. She was a precocious student who threw herself into her schoolwork and made friends easily with her puppy dog openness. Her father died when she was nine, so she worked to stay in school. The Girl Scouts gave her a scholarship to continue her education at Texas Christian University in Fort Worth. Her dream was to become a teacher and help other young people.

She was twenty when she met twenty-five-year-old Moises Molina and they discovered their birthdays were the same week. "I always told him, 'You were the best birthday present I ever got,'" she says. He was home on leave from an assignment to Germany with the U.S. Army. After he went back to Germany, they corresponded so regularly that the postman would recognize his letters and hand them to her first. The next time Moises came home, it was to ask Irene to marry him. She said yes, putting aside her teaching plans to join him in Germany. Soon she was making friends from Nuremberg to Berlin. She would boldly announce to generals and Germans as she traveled with him to Army band performances, "Hi! I'm Irene Saldovar from Fort Worth, Texas." They made a good team. He performed; she applauded. He generously gave away whatever he had; she tried to make ends meet. Moises was one of those rare talents, a man who could play the saxophone, the clarinet, and the mariachi guitaron. He had a gift for teaching others to play, so when they returned from duty overseas, he went on to become a band teacher while she worked as a teacher's assistant.

Irene wanted children of her own but had great difficulty starting a family. She miscarried with twins and then had a series of miscarriages, possibly from working with so many pesticides throughout her young life, she thought. Finally, she gave up and said to God, "I'm not going to worry about it anymore, God. I'm going to put it in your hands." Two months later,

Irene was pregnant with her first child. She then gave birth to two more.

As their family grew, she applied lessons she had learned by observing others. She had noticed that when her sister's husband left for work, everyone in the house would kiss him good-bye and wrap around him before he left in his truck. And when he would return, they would rush to him as if they had not seen him in a long time. She recalled, "I would say to myself when visiting them, 'I love this. I am going to do this.' Because you could feel the love."

She also had observed when visiting her friend Delores' home as a child that Delores' father would bless her when she left for school. Because Irene was with her, he would bless her, too. "When we'd leave, he would bless us and when we would eat, he would bless us. I thought, *I like this. I'm going to use this.* And I did. I would bless my children and their friends when they left for school. Pretty soon the kids would come up to me when they were in our house and remind me, 'Mrs. Molina, don't forget to bless me, too!' When they were older, sometimes my

"O Lord who fed the multitudes with five barley loaves, bless what we are about to eat."

— ARABIC GRACE FROM EGYPT

kids would come back and honk and call me out and say, 'Mom, you forgot to bless me.' It makes them feel good."

Irene would need her well-trained faith when her husband was diagnosed with a rare liver disease called hemochromatosis. He was ill for more than a year and needed a liver transplant, she said, but their insurance company was reluctant to pay. The hospital said it would cost at least $150,000. They were trying to raise the money when suddenly his condition worsened. Moises was bleeding internally when she called 911 to get him to the hospital. He lapsed into a coma as his family, students, teachers, and administrators gathered at the intensive care unit. Some of the students were still in their mariachi outfits, having come from an after-school engagement that he had arranged for them. A minister arrived to pray with them.

"Everybody was crying and looked real sad, so I told them, 'You know, Mo and I were almost going to have our twenty-fifth wedding anniversary. Instead of saying the last rites, I would like to repeat our wedding vows while we can.' So we did. We got married again right there in the hospital room and everyone we loved was there with us until his heartbeat stopped. I didn't want to leave. I just sat there a little numb. But at the same time, I felt this odd joy of knowing that I had so many happy years with him. Most people don't even get one year like that."

Later, Irene discovered that one of the last things Moises had done before he collapsed was to take several students to lunch. She found the charge to his credit card when the bills came in after he died.

The months ahead would prove a challenge as she struggled to bring up their children on her salary as an elementary school teacher. Then, adding tragedy to tragedy, their house burned down the year after Moises's death. Irene's first thought as she realized that flames were engulfing the house was to rush in and find her photos of Moises. They were in two storage containers because she had gathered them for a school ceremony in his honor. She ran into the house to search for the containers even though the flames singed her hair. She found the photos, but did not have time to get her letters from him, which were in a plastic bag in her dresser. She stood outside and prayed for the safety of the firemen and prayed that she would find the letters. After the flames were extinguished, she walked through what was left of the house with her children. She found the letters in the water that covered the floor. The dresser was gone, but the letters were intact and dry in the plastic bag.

Eight years after Moises's death, she admitted, life was still something of a struggle since her children are college age. But she expressed confidence that they would get by. "One day after Mo had died and the house burned down, one of the other teachers came up to me and said, 'Mrs. Molina, I can't believe you. Your husband died and your house has burned down. And you are still smiling.' But I told her, 'The worst that could have happened to me has already happened.' I can be a little stinker, too, but God doesn't let me get away with it long. I always come back to blessings that we have. I am

"Go with each of us to rest; if any awake, temper to them the dark hours of watching; and when the day returns, return to us, our sun and comforter, and call us up with morning faces and with morning hearts, eager to labor, eager to be happy, if happiness should be our portion, and if the day be marked for sorrow, strong to endure it."

— ROBERT LOUIS STEVENSON, written the night before he died, 1894 thankful that God saved our lives."

Irene's positive attitude stuck in my memory after the flight. I did an Internet search to look up the newspaper stories about Moises. In the news story about the christening of the new school in Moises Molina's honor, a teacher who had known him for nineteen years said, "Although he was teaching band, what he taught me was the very little generosity in my life. He was known to give students his lunch and lunch money and even expensive shoes to students going on job interviews. I don't know how many coats and shoes Mr. Molina gave away, but he taught me generosity."

I regret that I never met Moises Molina, but I am glad I got to sit next to his widow on that flight. I still smile at the image of children crowding around her asking to be blessed before they leave for school, entreating like baby birds, "Bless me, bless me." Irene's story shows how we can demonstrate love and faith at the same time. In our post-modern, too-cool-to-be-religious culture, the idea of saying blessings might sound unsophisticated, but remember that the everyday words "Good-bye" are a truncation of "God bless ye." The way to make blessings a part of your life is to try to say at least one every day. Experience has shown it just takes twenty-one days of repeating something for it to become a habit.

In most families today, people are together and yet apart, rushing in and out on different tracks. Adding blessings could be the way to reconnect your family that you have been looking for. And isn't that what people are longing for? To be connected, to have a sense of place? One of the Biblical names of God is "Makom," which is translated as "place." Perhaps what that means is that you are truly "in place" when you are in sync with God. Rabbi Jeffrey Dekro reminds, "In the place where your thoughts are, there you are." And one of the best ways to strengthen that sense of being "with" God all the day long is to remember to say your blessings.

TAKE HOME:

If you are still hesitant about how to go about it, there are many other helpful models in Jewish tradition. Before drinking grape juice or wine, it is said: "Blessed are you, Eternal One our God, Universal presence, who creates the fruit of the vine." A blessing for nourishment, the "Birkat," also can be said after a meal as well as before. A side benefit of joining for thanks at the end of a meal is that it encourages families to finish the meal together, instead of just getting up to leave one at a time as people finish gulping down their food. Marcia Falk, in her modern versions of blessing, offers this after-meal blessing: "Let us acknowledge the source of life, source of all nourishment. May we protect the bountiful earth that it may continue to sustain us, and let us seek sustenance for all who dwell in the world." That's the spirit.

Blessings are such an integral part of Jewish tradition that there are prayers for lighting candles, for studying the Torah, for putting on a prayer shawl, and for getting good news and bad news. Rabbi Nancy Flam explains that the ancient rabbis knew of the human tendency to drift through life in spiritual dullness, so they invented a series of blessings that would help us stay spiritually awake. There are blessings in gratitude for opening our eyes and for standing on the firm earth. There's even a blessing to say after using the toilet, in gratitude for the body's proper functioning. There's also a blessing for seeing exceptionally beautiful people, trees, or scenery — "Blessed are You, Eternal One our God, Who has such as this in the Universe." And there's a blessing for seeing a person or thing that is disturbing — "Blessed are You, Eternal One our God, Universal Presence, Who creates variety among living things." One of the sweetest Hebrew blessings is for children: "Be who you are — and may you be blessed in all that you are." There are lessons in each blessing — making a ritual out of washing the hands before a meal, for example, brings to mind the holiness of the body.

The Old Testament concept of blessing had conditions. The abundant life would be found in the Lord if people lived his way. God made a covenant to bless Abraham and his descendents if he was obedient. Moses passed along the Commandments of the Lord with the explanation that people would be blessed if they obeyed but cursed if they disobeyed and followed other gods. The New Testament concept emphasizes that we are to be a blessing to others no matter how they treat us.

Blessings, quite simply, are a way of looking at life. Today, you can find that attitude in the folkways of other cultures. A friend from Mexico, for example, once told me that when someone spills a glass of water, it is said, "An angel passed by." That's smart psychology — you don't get as irked about the spill if you believe something celestial just happened. Likewise, when a baby would cry loudly, the tradition was to say, "God is saying, 'Here I am.' " Again, that's good psychology and faith — the wailing child is not seen as a negative, but a gift from God. Just imagine how calming it might be during the hectic Christmas holidays if you blessed all your gifts as you wrapped them, imbuing each with good wishes and gratitude.

As part of a national prayer effort in recent years, many church women around the country agreed to think blessings for each house they passed in their neighborhoods as they went for walks. Each family was blessed and prayed for as the women walked by. Extra effort was made to speak warmly to people down the block and down the street. Again, it was a simple matter of making a practice of looking at the world in a different way.

"God regards not the greatness of the work, but the love with which it is performed."

— BROTHER LAWRENCE

What effect do you think it would have on your marriage to ask God every day to bless your marriage and to greet your spouse with thanks in your heart? Have you ever asked God to bless even your failures, your disappointments, and your doubts?

What comfort would it bring to bless your new house as you move in? A second marriage? A youngster going off to college? Could a ritual of thanks make such changes seem less unsettling? At the end of the day, what are your blessings? Who has blessed you? And who have you blessed?

FOUR

Learning

"*Ancoro imparo* — I am still learning."
— MICHELANGELO,
AT THE AGE OF EIGHTY-SEVEN

Just as the truly educated never graduate, the truly faithful never quit studying for the final exam. Whether you are called to study the Bible, the Qu'ran or the Torah, you can apply Martin Luther's advice that you should study as you would gather apples: "First, I shake the whole tree that the ripest might fall. Then I shake each limb, and when I have shaken each limb, I shake each branch and every twig. Then I look under every leaf." He was right about the need to dig deep. You cannot really know what you believe until you have made a practice of studying your religion.

This was brought home to me when I volunteered to teach Sunday School. It was the only way of getting my fourth-grade son to attend. For a while, my scheme worked. I knew enough about the Good

Book to get through the stories like Joseph and his coat of many colors. It helped that much of the lesson plan for that age group was cutting up construction paper and placing flannel figures on a board. Then one Sunday, while I was telling the Moses story, putting the flannel baby behind the flannel bullrushes, I discovered how much I didn't know. After I explained that Moses was saved from the Pharoah because his mother and sister Miriam hid him in a basket of reeds in the river, one of the little girls piped up: "What was her name?" Who? "The mother, Moses' *mother.*" I hurriedly flipped through the lesson plan. No mention of the mother's name. "It doesn't say," I replied. "What? Where does this story come from?" the girl asked. "The Bible," I answered, adding "Book of Exodus." Score one for the teacher. "Maybe her name is in there," the girl suggested. "Good idea," I agreed. We looked. It wasn't there. The little girl was shocked: "*What?* What kind of book is this if it doesn't even have the name of the mother in it? *She's* the most important person in the story. If it hadn't been for *her,* Moses would have *died.* Who wrote this book?" I gulped. "Moses." "*What?* He didn't put his *own* mother's name in?" I frantically signaled to the other teacher to get her guitar for a quick rendition of "Michael Row the Boat Ashore." It was my last semester as a Sunday School teacher. I realized I didn't know enough to teach fourth-graders.

I've been trying to catch up since then. That quest to learn has made my faith more real, more exciting, more fun, and more reassuring. I later learned that most reputable scholars do not believe Moses actually wrote his own story. And I found out his mother's name: Jochebed. Scripture merely notes that she was an Israelite woman. But as a fourth-grader could tell you, she is one of the most important people in the Bible. Jochebed defied a pharoah to save the life of the man who would lead his people out of Egypt and give them ten rules from God that shaped not only the faith, but the jurisprudence of much of the world.

As I struggled over the years to squeeze in more study between working and parenting, I was amazed to find things in the Bible I would swear weren't there before. Was it that I had not studied — or that it was not taught? I learned that Moses' sister Miriam later suffered with leprosy. And that when Isaac's wife, Rachel, died in childbirth, she was buried by the side of the road. I learned that a prostitute named Rahab helped Joshua conquer Jericho. She hid his spies from the king because she believed in the God of Israel. What I had not fully appreciated before was that she subsequently left prostitution, got married, and became the mother of Boaz . . . who married Ruth . . . whose descendants included a carpenter named Jesus.

The realization began dawning on me that many of the gutsiest figures in the Bible were women. Sarah left her home in Ur of the Caldes, the Paris or Rome of the day, to trek with Abraham across vast arid lands to parts unknown, forsaking the old gods of their families for a new God, who said he was the Only God, which *really* was something new under the sun. Their journey was a radical leap of faith on many levels. And when the angels announced that Sarah would have a child at the brittle age of ninety, she laughed, becoming one of the few people in scripture to demonstrate an earthy sense of humor.

After I looked at the Bible in a new way, the stories registered more clearly about the women in the Bible who were judges (Deborah) and queens (Esther) and pushy moms (Rebekah). There were lots of bad girls. Jezebel was so bad, she ended up being eaten by dogs like trash in the street.

On closer inspection, the Bible proved a darker tapestry, a family history of strivers, whiners, cheaters, charmers, and schemers — but full of wisdom and life lessons nevertheless. The weak-kneed and weak-willed often rose to the occasion. I realized that in comparison to the obstacles faced by women in Biblical times — a world of harsh desert living, constant warfare, and toting water from the well — women of today have little reason not to be stronger in their beliefs. Especially when you consider the models of faith in the New Testament:

∾ Who was the first to bless the baby Messiah? A woman. Elizabeth, the mother of John the Baptist. When the pregnant Mary came to visit Elizabeth, Elizabeth recognized the holiness of the moment and proclaimed God's blessing on Mary and the fruit of her womb.

∾ Were there important women prophets? Yes, Anna, the prophetess, who prayed in the temple without leaving until she was in her 80s, predicted that a child liberator was coming.

ॐ Were women originally accepted as leaders, teachers, and deacons in the early church? You bet. Lydia, a businesswoman who sold prized purple dye, was one of the earliest leaders in the church of Philippi. Phoebe traveled hundreds of miles to deliver an epistle for Paul and was described as a deacon in the church at Cenchreae. Priscilla ("Prisca"), who hosted the church in her home in Corinth, was thanked by Paul for risking her neck for him. Three others are commended by Paul in Romans: Tryphaena, Tryphosas, and Persis. And two more, Euodia and Syntyche, are named for sharing the Apostle Paul's struggles in the cause of the gospel. Paul cautioned them to try to agree more, so we can assume the women were, well, vocal.

ॐ And the first evangelist? You could say it was the Samaritan woman at the well. (When people gather at a well in the Bible, you know something important is about to happen.) When Jesus told the Samaritan woman he was the expected Messiah, she went straight to the town and brought back people to hear him preach.

ॐ Who loyally stood by Jesus at the

cross? A brave handful of women. Mary of Magdala, Mary the mother of James and Joseph and the mother of the sons of Zebedee.

ᔋ And who was first at the tomb to proclaim that Jesus had been raised from the dead? Mary of Magdala and the other Mary. In fact, at a time when women were rarely named in public documents, Mary of Magdala, a wealthy and devoted believer, is mentioned in Scripture fourteen times. Indeed, at a time when women did not have the standing to serve as witnesses in court, God gave women the honor of being first to witness the empty tomb. The women brought the good news back to the disciples.

So yes, there is much to learn in the Bible that is faith-affirming for women. They were serious players, not merely bystanders or baby-sitters. It has taken a while, but now, two thousand years later, there are growing numbers of female religious scholars who are putting the roles of women in a fresh perspective. More than half the students in many theology schools are women. In the recent edition of *Women's Bible Commentary* alone, some forty-seven women who are Ph.D.s or professors in theology schools are cited as contributors. Most of those female scholars weren't at their desks two decades ago. They are making Bible study a different experience. And think tanks like the Dameris Project in Dallas are springing up to host serious intellectual discussions and write papers about women and faith.

"Eve Was Framed."

— BUMPER STICKER ON A NEW FORD PICKUP TRUCK, 2002

A good place to begin revisiting the roots of faith is, naturally, at the beginning. It's important to look at how male and female roles were first treated in the three monotheistic faiths, because those early interpretations — or misinterpretations — still shape the roles of women today. In the Hebrew Bible, which is known to Christians as the Old Testament, the first man and woman were called "Adam" and "Chavah." In Hebrew, *Adamah* means "from earth," which referred to his past, his origin from clay, and *Chavah* means "mother of all living things," a reference to her future role. It is written in Genesis that Eve was created to keep Adam from being lonely, but in recent years, there has been more debate whether she was to be a helpmate *for* him, indicating a subordinate status, or *opposite* him, indicating more of a partnership. More rabbis teach today that Eve was intended to balance Adam's hunter-gatherer qualities with a totally different nature that complemented his. The Talmud also adds that when "building" the woman from the rib, God built in "profound understanding," endowing women with more insight and intuition than men.

Rabbis also use the symbolism of Adam and Eve to underscore another idea: If all humans are descended from the same two parents, then no person can insist that he or she is of better blood. This principle is mentioned numerous times in the Hebrew Bible, laying the foundation for the equality of people in faith.

It's especially intriguing to compare the Hebrew version of the creation story with the Islamic version. In the Qu'ran, the Arabic *Adam* means "black" and *Hawwa* means "brown." Because the first humans were believed to have been dark-skinned, this makes sense, although it may be jarring to those accustomed to Renaissance art renditions. The Qu'ran also does not share the belief that Eve was created because Adam was lonely, but says they were made *for each other's welfare*. The rather charming way of describing the relationship is that they are to be like "garments" for each other, protecting each other. And the Qu'ran does not lay all the blame on Eve for spoiling the garden party. According to the Qu'ran, the blame starts with the devil, whose name is "Shaytan," which means "the separator," an apt name for someone who tries to separate humans from the Creator. Shaytan tempts both Adam and Eve by promising them eternal life and never-ending power. Both are blamed equally for taking the bait. The Qu'ran says, "They both sinned." As a result, Islam also does not share the Judeo-Christian teaching that women must endure the pain of childbirth as a punishment for tempting Adam. In Islam, labor pains are looked on as noble suffering that women endure for the sake of children, which entitles them to have some of their sins forgiven.

Nevertheless, Muhammad incorporated some patriarchal themes into the Qu'ran, writing: "Men have authority over women because God has made the one superior to the other and because they spend their wealth to maintain them. So good women are obedient, guarding the unseen parts as God has guarded them." (Qu'ran 4:34)

And even though in early Judaism some women became judges and prophets, the cultural norm was for women to primarily serve as wives and mothers. Women were not allowed to lead services or teach from the Torah. Jewish men are still taught in some congregations today to offer the daily prayer, "Blessed art Thou O Lord our God, King of the Universe, who has not made me a woman."

The heart of the debate is whether male church leaders have been right to sublimate females in the name of faith over the centuries. Did God originally intend for the playing field to be more level? Fresh light on the subject is being added by women scholars who now have the prominence and platforms to speak out.

For Naomi Harris Rosenblatt, excavating clues in the Hebrew Bible about the human condition has been a lifelong process. She has been passionately studying the Hebrew Bible since she was a six-year-old in Haifa, Israel. "My teachers and parents believed you could not be a civilized, cultured, decent human being without a thorough knowledge of the Bible, so we studied it from our first years of school until we finished. Whether you were religious or not was your private business," she says, "but we were engrained with the moral, ethical, and spiritual ideas in the Bible."

She has combined her lifelong Bible study with a career as a psychotherapist, which has given her a unique perspective. Her vocation has been listening to the problems of people. Her avocation has been teaching the Biblical prescriptions for a good life. For more than fifteen years, she taught a unique Bible class on Capitol Hill for U.S. senators, where some of the most powerful figures in the country stopped the political clock for an hour to learn about ancient wisdoms. The participants have included senators from both sides of the aisle and many sides of religion — Jews, Catholics, Mormons, Episcopalians, and Baptists. Naomi also ran a Bible class for women around her dining room table for more than twenty-five years — the same group of women, every Friday morning. There was healing, there was laughing, and there was sharing of life's triumphs and tribulations. Some of the women have moved on to other cities and have started similar discussion groups, all of them revolving around the Biblical text.

Both the senators and the women turned

to Bible study to answer basic questions about humanity. Why are we here? How are we supposed to live? What are the conflicts between our careers and our personal lives? What on earth does it mean to live in the same culture as Anna Nicole Smith and *Sex and the City*?

"There is a tremendous hunger," Naomi says. "There is a fear in our society that there is no buffer zone between our beliefs and the popular culture of today. People are looking for an anchor, a compass. Often people start thinking about spiritual values when they start bringing up children or grandchildren . . . without an anchor of some sort, they feel like a cork on the ocean at the mercy of every breeze that comes along. We then look to our past and our religion to find out what's solid and what's transcendent. How do we prevail over the tragedy that flows into everyday life?"

Part of the material she used in her Washington classes was gathered into a book about Genesis called *Wrestling with Angels: What Genesis Teaches Us About Our Spiritual Identity, Sexuality and Personal Relationships*. As a result, she was featured on the Bill Moyers program *Genesis* on PBS in 1996. She recently has been writing a book about Adam and Eve to be called *After the Apple*.

"The most sobering information that Adam and Eve glean from the tree of knowledge is their mortality," she says. "We are not gods. Our tenure on earth is limited by the life span of our bodies. The lesson of this story of banishment from a garden of eternal life is clear: Our goal is not to escape death, but rather to embrace life and savor its challenges and gifts. Mortality is NOT God's punishment for eating of the tree of knowledge . . . Death is what endows life with meaning and a measure of urgency. With the awareness of death comes an understanding of just how finite and precious each day of our life is."

She describes that learning process as a continuum, a constant challenge to comprehend what life is all about. That quest never ends, she mused, even for senators. Or Bible teachers.

Her personal journey has been illuminated by her girlhood in Israel. If you have seen Naomi in one of her television appearances, you might remember her as the lady with the charming and unusual accent, a consequence of the fact her parents immigrated from Scotland and Canada to what was then a British mandate called

Palestine in the 1920s. Her father was a respected art critic and her mother a nonpracticing lawyer. Young Naomi grew up in a world of ideas and political conflict.

"Two themes run throughout my growing up and invariably inform my faith and point of view about life. Loss and grief were a part of my life because I grew up during the Second World War. The Holocaust was like a Greek chorus in the back of my mind because immigrants were flowing into Israel with numbers that had been tattooed on their arms in Nazi concentration camps. At a very young age, I was aware that there was pain in life. But the other theme, which runs parallel to the first, was of faith, redemption, overcoming, prevailing, and transcending. I got the sense that we can survive terrible things, that there is always a chance for a new beginning in life. The two themes were interwoven, just like in the Bible, loss and overcoming."

It was a heady time, growing up in Haifa, a bustling port on the Mediterranean, not far from the Lebanon border. Political intrigue or rumors of war were always in the air, but still oranges were grown and music was played and young people were passionate about life. When Naomi was just fifteen, she met her future husband, Peter Rosenblatt. He was about the same age and a summer visitor from the United States. He asked her to marry him that first summer, but she was too young. So he asked again the next summer. And the next. She did her duty for her young country by serving in the Navy for a year, then they married. That meant at age nineteen, she left her home in Israel to travel across the ocean to a new country and a new husband. They ultimately settled in Washington, D.C., where they raised three children. He served in the government and practiced law; she became a therapist, specializing in individual and marital counseling.

Learning more about faith remained important to Naomi, part of her intellectual drive and spiritual hunger. At the urging of friends, she began teaching Bible studies, first in her home, then in a community center as well as the Capitol. In her interpretations of Bible women, she focuses on the positive, emphasizing that you don't need to tear down men in order to give the women their due. Take Eve, for example. "Yes, there was disobedience," Naomi says, "but I don't see her as the culprit. I see her as a trailblazing pioneer who has to deal with the greatest setup of all time. God set it up, but you know, he is a teacher with a capital 'T.' You can't teach people about the consequences of their actions without *showing* them and walking them through the choices they can take."

Naomi's study has convinced her that men and women are intended to be different because they are broken down into two sexes, two halves from the first human being (Adam). The bottom line is that they are equal and unique, complementing each other. Every generation has to re-learn the balance between those roles, she observed, and those are very much in tension today. "For one thing, the male is physically stronger, so he always has to be socialized as to how to deal with it. We see physical strength being abused today when it comes to rape and domestic

"When Eve was brought unto Adam, he became filled with the Holy Spirit, and gave her the most sanctified, the most glorious of appellations. He called her Eva, that is to say, the Mother of All. He did not style her wife, but simply mother — mother of all living creatures. In this consists the glory and the most precious ornament of women."

— MARTIN LUTHER

violence. The male must be taught through the values of our society that physical abuse and rape are absolutely non-negotiable, unacceptable," she emphasized.

"As for women, as makers of life, we are the ones who create the next generation, and it is our responsibility to set priorities around that most important of roles. We can't really have it all. We must set priorities whether we choose to be primarily a stay-at-home mom or primarily a career mom. That's hard for Americans because they are brought up believing that we can choose anything we want, achieve it all, and have it all. What does it mean to have it all? It doesn't mean a whole box of chocolates; it means choosing a few of the chocolates out of many and then deciding you are going to be at peace with the choice you have made."

Her own faith, Naomi said, has helped her deal with whatever adversities have come her way. "From when I was very little, my mother's mantra to me was, 'Naomi, develop your inner resources. That can never be taken from you.' I used to hear that over and over again. And when I was in the midst of the difficulties we all encounter, I returned to the Bible. I've never stopped. For me, it was sheer nourishment. I could always identify with the conflicts or issues the Biblical characters were wrestling with. We are still studying the stories of people who lived three thousand years ago. We read about women dealing with infertility, sibling rivalry, sexuality, social injustice, and death. All those themes resonate with me and my women friends today."

Naomi emphasizes that the story of Genesis is more than a nice tale about long ago people. It shows us how we are to order our lives. "We are to put moral order and compassion into our lives, just as God put order and love into the world when it was all darkness. Otherwise, our lives are chaotic. And religion gives you an organized system of values with which to do that," she says.

Though her teaching is based in Scripture, it is open-minded and defies pigeonholing. Though she has feminist leanings, Naomi dismisses the criticism that the Bible is sexist. It's not fair to judge their ancient lives by our contemporary standards, she says. She sees the Biblical women as proactive, risk-takers, and courageous. They had no birth control, high infant mortality, and none of the options women have today. Yes, she says Adam erred by denying his personal responsibility and pointing the finger of blame at his wife, but she sees that as a common human weakness, not necessarily a male trait.

She also is highly skeptical of the modern, excessive emphasis on self-realization, worrying in one interview that "We have turned the concept of choice into an idol and the pursuit of happiness into a religion." Instead, she says Genesis teaches us that the three steps to having a meaningful life are spiritual identity, accountability, and purpose.

She also worries about the decline of the multigenerational family, which cuts people off from their cultural, moral, and spiritual roots. She sees the negative results every day as a psychotherapist. Because modern life provides little human warmth and a sense of belonging, she finds that 90 percent of what she does in her therapy practice is help her patients combat the anonymity they experience because of the breakup of old patterns of bonding in families and the community. She says, "Every day I meet people adrift in the world without an inner compass — filled with self-doubt, empty of any sense of purpose." Although many of them are successful professionally and may be wealthy, she said, they are distanced from their families with no real ties to their communities. "Often their job descriptions have become their only anchors for their identity."

After the September 11 attacks, Naomi said many of her clients in therapy were unsettled and anxious, so she suggested they read from the Book of Psalms aloud. Usually, she is careful not to bring up religion in her professional work, although over time her clients know where she stands just as she knows where they stand. But in the weeks after September 11, Naomi sensed that something was needed to help many of them calm the waters. She advised them to read some of the Psalms aloud twice. "The first time we don't really absorb it. The second time, we go a little slower, absorbing the meaning and mood. It then brings us into a calmer place. We tap into the Psalmist belief that faith transcends the immediate crisis and that God is indeed our Shepherd. As my rabbi suggested, when we are studying the Bible, God is talking to us. When we read the Psalms, we are talking to God. Some of the Psalms talk about anger, feelings of rage, or even hatred. And we feel all these things. The Bible acknowledges the tapestry of the human condition. Just pouring it out provides us with a sense of validation and understanding. In return, we feel healed and strengthened. It takes time, though. You can't be running to catch a cab and trying to read a Psalm at the same time."

Naomi said she feels terribly fortunate to be able to interact through the Biblical prism in her classes with other human beings about timeless issues, "perhaps because I am so in harmony with the Biblical philosophy on life and faith. But I do believe that anybody who has been fortunate to have any body of knowledge — biology, theology — should share it in some way with others, making sure that the next generation benefits — a way of planting seeds. If you teach a woman, you inevitably are teaching her daughter or son."

She often closes her letters and messages to her children with the advice, "Go forth and fear not." Those are the two powerful and interdependent calls that resound through the Book of Genesis, she said.

"Go forth" is our destiny to venture into life and discover our personal destiny. "Do not wait for life to come to you, to rescue you. Go forth and find a mate, build a family, repair your community."

"Fear not" tells us not to fear struggle,

not to fear the doubt that besieges all faith, not to fear the pain that comes with relationships, not to fear the unknown around the corner. Bless life and seize the day. She says, "We must always remind ourselves that we are created in God's image, so we are each valued, and that what we do with our life matters. Faith is not a blind insurance policy, but it will help us overcome panic, cynicism, depression, and alienation. It is a rope we can hold on to in the midst of a stormy sea."

TAKE HOME:

There are Creation stories in many other cultures that mirror the Genesis story. The earliest of the *Upanishad* metaphysical treatises about the ancient Hindu religion, which are thought to date somewhere about the ninth century B.C., contain this story: "In the beginning, there was only the Great Self in the form of a Person. Reflecting, it found nothing but itself. Then its first word was, 'This am I!' To throw off the burden of loneliness, the 'Person' caused itself to split into two, from which a man and a woman were born."

A Bassari legend from Togo in Africa has

a tradition in which a man and a woman, having been created by the god Ununbotte, eat of forbidden fruit and are then confronted by Ununbotte. "Who told you that you could eat that fruit?" the god asks. "Snake did," they reply.

From the Pima tribe of Southern Arizona comes "a song sung by the Creator at the beginning of the world": "In the beginning there was only darkness everywhere — darkness gathered thick in places, crowding together and then separating, crowding and separating until at last out of one of the places where the darkness had crowded there came forth a man. This man wandered through the darkness until he began to think; then he knew himself and that he was a man; he knew he was there for some purpose." The Creator then sings, calling himself the maker of the world. He creates the world and then the stars to light the darkness.

For believers, it should be reassuring that other traditions echo the Biblical Creation story. That such explanations sprang up in independent cultures calls to mind Carl Jung's idea of a collective unconscious. For women, it should be reassuring that they generally are not stigmatized in such stories.

In the Jewish tradition, women play a special role in bringing light into the world. The women of the house light the Sabbath candles. This usually is no later than eighteen minutes before sundown on Friday. While most Jews use just two candles, others may light a seven-branched menorah, or oil lamps, or one candle for each person in the family. Because Judaism contains a set of practices and guidelines, it is often called a Way of Life. These practices, which are ways an individual can connect to God, are called mitzvot in the plural and mitzvah in the singular. The most famous mitzvot are the Ten Commandments, including remembering to keep the Sabbath holy. The beginning of Sabbath is signaled by the lighting of candles. First the candles are lighted, then you cover your eyes and say a blessing: "Blessed are You, Eternal One our God, Ruling Presence of the Universe, Who makes us holy with mitzvot and gives us the mitzvah of kindling the Sabbath lights." Then uncover your eyes and imagine that you are seeing light for the first time. The symbolism of light is very much at the heart of Judaism. Dawn and dusk are times of prayer because of the mystical changes of light. Candles at the beginning and end of a holy time set off and distinguish the sacred from the profane. Even the form of the menorah is taken from the shape of a burning or lighted tree. This is related to the ancient image of God as a cosmic tree of life. Lighting candles in the dark is a way we can signal back to the God above who gave us light.

> "So God created man in his own image; in the image of God he created him; male and female he created them. And God blessed them, and God said to them, 'Be fruitful and multiply, and fill the earth and subdue it, and have dominion over the fish of the sea and over the birds of the air and over every living thing that moves upon the earth.'"
>
> — GENESIS 2:27–28

Some women feel alienated from institutional religion because they do not feel included in the stories that are taught. Has it been difficult for you to identify with Biblical figures? Perhaps you will find it helpful to seek out some of the newer commentaries and Bible studies that include the female perspective. It might help you to grow in your faith to simply sit and read the Bible. You might want to memorize some scriptures you can retrieve quickly when you need them. Or you might want to join a Bible study group, where you can learn with others. The end goal should not just be to have useful information, but an encounter with the divine.

FIVE

Understanding

"If we cannot end our differences, at
least we can make the world safe for diversity."
— JOHN FITZGERALD KENNEDY

Funny how Karen Armstrong's life brought
her to the United States just as the battle for
God went global. When terrorist attacks hit
on September 11, the British historian was
at Harvard University for the fall, working
on a new book about the Axial Age. That's
the era (800–200 B.C.) when many of the
great religions of the world came into
being — Confucionism and Taoism, monotheism (Judaism, Christianity, and Islam),
Greek rationalism, and Hinduism. Despite
their differences, they share common
threads, which she found fascinating. She
relished the chance to delve into the research
at Harvard.

But suddenly, the book project had to be
put on hold. After September 11, everyone
in the country wanted to talk to Karen

about Islam and the reverberations that were rocking the world. So she put aside her books. She appeared on TV. She spoke to the lofty Council on Foreign Relations in New York. She tutored members of Congress at a special retreat in Mexico City. And everywhere she spoke, she was greeted by hundreds of people who stayed afterward and peppered her with questions:

Is Islam really a violent religion?

The dark side of Islamic history contains about as many massacres as the dark side of Christianity, she would reply. The Qu'ran does justify defensive war, but it does not sanctify unprovoked warfare.

Does the Qu'ran require submission of women?

The Prophet Muhammad actually broke with the harsh treatment of woman that prevailed in seventh-century Arabia by giving them considerable respect and freedom, Karen explained for the thousandth time. And the scriptures in the Qu'ran gave women rights to divorce and inheritance long before Christian Europe did. Yes, there certainly are those who subjugate women in many parts of the world, but they are following the dictates of patriarchal cultures more than the Prophet Muhammad.

Is a clash of the civilizations inevitable between the Judeo-Christian countries and Islamic countries?

This is a dangerous moment, Karen acknowledges. It is crucial that we convince those millions of Muslims who abhor the September 11 atrocities but have been alienated from the United States, that Americans are indeed religious themselves, that they care about the poor, and that they care about a just world.

By November, when I heard her speak at St. Bart's Episcopal Church in Manhattan, Karen was beginning to feel drained. She was under constant pressure to explain the complexities of faith in sound bites. But she graciously stayed long after her talk to answer more questions from the huddle of listeners who were gathered around her with worried expressions. Even though she was feeling wrung out afterward, she agreed to an interview, because she sensed there was an urgent need to understand the world of Islam and what on earth was going on. As fate would have it, she was uniquely suited to the task.

One way or another, studying religion has been Karen's life. She has written twelve books, including *Through the Narrow Gate*, the story of her seven years as a Catholic nun. Perhaps her best-known book is *The History of God*, an overview of monotheism. Her most recent is *The Battle for God*, a look at the fundamentalist extremes that have erupted in the Muslim, Christian, and Jewish faiths. *The Battle for God* was hitting the best-seller lists just as the terrorists attacked the World Trade Center and Pentagon. Readers immediately began clamoring for her pocket-size history *Islam*, which soon was outselling mystery novels.

"I never intended to be a writer," she mused in our interview, giving a shorthand version of her life. "It just happened by accident. I wanted to be an academic. There was a shortage of jobs and I failed my Ph.D. in a rather spectacular way. Then there was a series of career accidents, and I found myself in religious broadcasting. I didn't even study religious *history;* I studied religious *literature*. But I'm rather glad it didn't come out that way."

> "Wisdom begins with sacrifice of immediate pleasures for long-range purposes."
>
> – LOUIS FINKELSTEIN

Karen Armstrong's journey began in Birmingham, England, when she decided at the age of seventeen to enter a Roman

Catholic convent. "I wanted to find God so that he would fill my life, and that meant giving my life back to him," she later wrote. "I wanted him with a desire that was frightening in its urgency. And I knew that looking for God had to be a full-time job; no half measures would do." As Sister Martha, she threw herself into the sweeping, scrubbing, and praying. This was before the liberalizing decrees of Vatican II, so everything the young novitiate did was strictly regulated, from the layers of cotton garments to the hours of sewing and solitude. She was once required to treadle a sewing machine that didn't have a needle for a month. Recognizing that she was a so-so seamstress but an absolutely brilliant student, the sisters sent her to Oxford University to continue her education. Once there, her studies pulled her steadily toward literature and away from convent life. The tug-of-war between her intellectual and spiritual yearnings eventually exhausted her. She decided not to take her final vows. The scene in her memoir of her final confrontation with her superiors is cinematic. She fainted to the floor from the strain. After seven years of submission, Sister Martha became Karen Armstrong again. She walked out the door to a very complicated world. She taught at a girl's school for several years until fate took her to BBC-TV for work on religious documentaries. The next step was writing comparative histories on religion, which eventually led her to the United States for what was supposed to be a leisurely fall semester of research on the Axial Age.

"I've been dreading something like September 11," she told the St. Bart's audience in New York. She said she has had the increasingly unsettling hunch that something was going wrong as she studied fundamentalist movements in recent years, "We in the West simply do not understand the Muslim world, which encompasses 1.2 billion people. The stereotypical thinking about Islam is appalling. I felt we were heading for some kind of catastrophe." The West has made the mistake, she contends, of making Muslims "the example of everything we think we are not."

An even worse mistake, Karen said in our interview, would be equating the twisted religious views of Osama bin Laden with true Islam. "There are passages in the Qu'ran that sound ferocious when quoted out of context," she said. "But there are always verses succeeding those very passages with injunctions of peace and forgiveness." She pointed out that in the Qu'ran, "as soon as an enemy asks to make peace, Muslims are told to stop at once and agree to any terms, no matter how humiliating, so peace can be restored."

She takes considerable pains not to seem an apologist for the terrorist attacks. She emphasizes that there is nothing that would justify the horrific wickedness of September 11, but it is possible to analyze the contributing factors: The modernization process in the Muslim world in the twentieth century was more brutal and abrupt than the gradual evolution in the West, she said, and many countries are still struggling with how to enter the postmodern world. In Turkey, for example, madrassas (religious) schools were closed by the government and women were compelled to wear Western dress. In Iran, the Shah's soldiers ripped the veils off women. In Pakistan, mullahs were tortured to death. In Egypt, members of the Muslim Brotherhood were jailed, many without evidence. Then there was the use of Saudi territory to launch the Desert Storm war against Saddam Hussein in Iraq. And there is continued friction between Israel and Palestine over disputed territories. All this fueled fundamentalist reaction and anti–United States resentment. Yet the West was generally oblivious to the clues.

Now, however, the West is desperately trying to understand the Middle East. "We've got a long way to go; we can't pat ourselves on the back. But something has moved," Karen said. She said she has sensed a spiritual swell in the United States over the past few years, which seems to have been accelerated by September 11. Indeed, a survey released by the Pew Research Center after the attacks in December 2001 tended to corroborate her observations. Some 78 percent said they believe religious influence in American life is growing — up from 37 percent eight months before and the highest mark in four decades. Unfortunately, attacks against Muslims in the United States have gone up, a sign that more bridge-building is needed.

> "God is everywhere and in everything and we are all His children."
>
> — MOTHER TERESA

"Our planet has shrunk since September 11," Karen said. "We are one world. We can't afford to demonize one-fifth of the human race. I suppose I am most concerned that America doesn't spoil itself in hatred and a lust for revenge, because that ultimately doesn't help. Over the weekend, I was reading work by Simeon Weil, talking about how we are infected by evil just as we are by good. We can infect other people with goodness, so when we are good to people, they become better and the cause of evil is harmed. The trick after September 11 is to contain evil and not project it onto someone else. We have a long, hard struggle ahead.

"The United States has now joined the community of suffering," she said. "The United States is sharing the kind of pain and fear and terror that most people in the world have always felt, so you are sharing the experience of the people of the Middle East, Ireland, Rwanda, and Yugoslavia. That can work two ways. It can make you furious, and it can make you want to go back to the way it was before, safe and secure. But things can never go back to the way they were before. We've moved on now. We can see the security we thought we had was an illusion. We thought a great ocean would protect you and there would never be terrorism on American soil, but now it is not the case, so you can't go back to normal.

"But it can deepen your spiritual life, which begins with the experience of suffering. That is very clear in Buddhism; you cannot begin the spiritual life until you experience suffering on some profound level. What keeps us from God is a sense of self-sufficiency and pride that we can manage without God. That's why suffering is important, because it can make us more compassionate. It is easy to deny the suffering of others if you have never experienced it. Now we can use the pain and anguish of this time to reach out in sympathy to others who are suffering in less-fortunate parts of the world. If we could do that, it would make America a much better, holy place."

In the meantime, Karen said, there are beginning to be signs of change in the Muslim world. Women are reclaiming the traditions, making the menfolk look again at the earliest traditions of the faith, and demanding some form of equality. "More women are getting ordained in Judaism and Islam and Christianity," she said. "There is a Muslim feminist sense growing whereby women are making their men re-examine the teaching of the Qu'ran itself, which was kind to women originally."

To be sure, she said, there are appalling situations in the Islamic world, where women are cruelly subjugated, such as the

Taliban's mistreatment of women in Afghanistan. But she pointed out, there are horrible situations in the Western world as well, where women are subjected to domestic violence, rape, and prostitution. "We talk very piously about the dignity of women, but we do exploit women's bodies in the West and we do waste a lot of time worrying about our appearance, our makeup, our clothes. I remember when I wore the veil there was something very freeing about not having to think about what I was wearing every day. What the Muslim women are saying is that there is more than one way of expressing your femininity, and there is nothing sacred about Western dress."

Karen tends to choose unostentatious attire herself. She was dressed in a simple but stylish black pants-suit with a white blouse. At fifty-seven, she is attractive in the way her British compatriot Judi Dench is, with grayish, pixie-cut hair. She speaks with authority in a brisk cadence that was once clocked by an observer at 130 words per minute.

Karen doesn't elaborate on her own faith, other than to say she is a "freelance monotheist," not tied to a particular denomination at this point. Initially, she said, after her convent experience, she was very opposed to religion. But her study of faiths has brought her back to a new, more complex and rich sense of the divine. She explained in a 1993 interview, "I have a far more positive view by studying other traditions than my own. By studying Judaism, by studying Islam, by studying the Greek and Russian Eastern Orthodox tradition . . . I found what my own tradition was trying to do at its best. Comparative religion does that for you. It doesn't make you convert to another religion necessarily, but it makes you see your own differently." She now feels closest to God, she said, when she studies. She had missed that study, in the aftermath of September 11, she said, much as someone else might miss her prayer time.

Dealing with sensitive religious issues in public is definitely not an easy path. After her frank memoir about convent life came out, she was tagged the "runaway nun." A few Catholics in England were angry enough to send her excrement in the mail. Some Jewish critics thought her

"Tolerance implies a respect for another person, not because he is wrong or even because he is right, but because he is human."

— JOHN COGLEY

history of Jerusalem was pro-Arab. Christian critics have claimed she slights Christianity. "It is a tough role," she says, "But if everybody is blaming you, then you must be getting it right." Agree or disagree, it can be seen that Karen brings rare gifts to the subject of religion. She is a good storyteller and has a knack for making the most abstruse religious concepts accessible.

About her current role as interlocutor between the Muslim and American worlds, she says, "If a better understanding of the Islamic world comes out of this horror, that is something that has been gained. This problem is not going to stop if we manage to get rid of bin Laden. We will only sow dragon's teeth and more people will rise up to avenge him. The best antidote is mutual understanding, and we in the West might have to learn to see ourselves as others see us."

One example of how Muslims see us, she pointed out in an article in *Gentleman's Quarterly*, is the nickname "the great Satan." That sobriquet usually shocks Western Christians who see Satan as a figure of absolute evil and resent being demonized. But there are other interpretations of that taunt that might be even more telling about how Westerners are perceived, Karen explains. She says that in Shiism, the "Shaitan" is a pathetic creature, incapable of appreciating true spirituality. In one folk legend, he complains to God that humans are acquiring gifts that he wants. Shaitan would like to have a Scripture and beautifully illuminated manuscripts. God tells him to get himself a few tattoos. Next, Shaitan wants a mosque, so God tells him to go to the bazaar. Then Shaitan wants prophets of his own, and God gives him fortune-tellers instead. The surprise is that the shallow Shaitan is content with the inferior gifts. He is hopelessly trivial and superficial, unable to see that there are deeper dimensions to life. So when many Iranians mocked the United States as "the great Shaitan," they might have meant the great trivializer and wastrel. To them, Karen says, the bars, casinos, and secular shops of the Americanized zone in Tehran typify the materialistic Shaitan. What's more, the word *Shaitan* also can mean "tempter." Karen says that many Iranians also thought the United States had tempted the Shah away from the true values of Islam to a life of unspiritual secularism. In a way, those interpretations are more painful than simply demonizing the United States as a devil

139

figure. Misusing our power is one thing. Being incurably crass and sleazy is another. Yet that side of American culture has come to dominate our image in many parts of the world. As one well-educated Afghanistan woman put it when reporters asked her if she wanted to have the same freedoms as women in the United States, she said, "Yes, but not your bikinis."

Karen Armstrong also is striking a nerve with her warning in *The Battle for God*, that the fundamentalist stirrings around the world appear to be a troubling rejection of the excesses of the post-modern world, with its materialistic frenzy and impersonal, technological trappings. As the world changes faster and faster around them, she says, people are feeling disoriented and lost. They aren't sure where society is going and are troubled by the changes in their everyday lives. As old myths, national traditions, and family values that gave meaning to their lives crumble, post-modern people experience a loss of identity and community. Often they feel helpless, hopeless, and purposeless. Karen contends that such anxiety is drawing people in many cultures — not

> "Where is God? Wherever you let God in."
>
> — HASIDIC SAYING

just Islam, but Judaism and Christianity as well — to the more fundamental branches of faith that promise certainty and rules in an ambiguous, uncaring world.

Karen sees fundamentalism in its many forms as a response to the spiritual deficit in the post-modern world and says people are looking for a sense of belonging and purpose. That in itself wouldn't be a problem, but difficulties are created when fundamentalists who feel threatened try to crush or silence those with a different view. What can be done about the downside of the fundamentalist revolts? The antidote might be a broader spiritual revival that emphasizes tolerance as well as compassion. The best medicine for flawed faith is true faith.

> "A man came to the Prophet Muhammad (peace be upon him) and requested to join a military expedition. The prophet asked him, 'Are your parents alive?' The man replied, 'Yes.' The Prophet then said, 'Then do your jihad by serving and caring for them.'"
>
> — IMAN KUKHARI'S *BOOK OF MORALS AND MANNERS*, HADITH 20

She reminds audiences that the word *jihad* does not refer only to a "holy war," as most Americans think, but also to the internal struggle or "effort" that everyone faces with self in a broken world. Indeed, the Prophet Muhammad once said on returning from battle, "We are returning from the lesser jihad (the battle) to the greater jihad (the more difficult battle of re-forming our hearts, our attitudes, our own societies)." Karen sums up, "In our present crisis, we have begun the lesser jihad in Afghanistan, but we must make sure we conduct a greater jihad and scrutinize our own conduct and our own policies, in the interest of peace."

If the jihad — inner struggle — means being better tomorrow than yesterday, we could start by seeking a better understanding of those around us. Not to change our beliefs, but to illuminate them. As Karen says, learning more about other faiths doesn't dilute your own beliefs; to the contrary, it can affirm your faith by helping you understand more about spirituality overall. That is, you don't have to be Buddhist to meditate. You don't have to be Jewish to appreciate the value of traditions. You don't have to be Catholic to respect the brave contributions of saints. You don't have to be a Muslim to see the wisdom in praying throughout the day. But we do need to learn to live together as religious pilgrims. In many ways, the globe's future depends on it.

Like many Americans, I did not know a lot about Islam before September 11. I had to make it my business to learn more quickly. How had we been so oblivious to the festering resentments in the world around us? As the news magazines plaintively asked on their covers, "Why do they hate us?" And what can caring people do about it?

> "When a man has made peace with himself, he will be able to make peace in the whole world."
>
> — MARTIN BUBER

I began gaining new understanding just a few weeks after September 11, when I had a chance to sit down with two young Muslim women during a business trip to Washington, D.C. I asked them to give me a mini-tutorial on how they see the world. I had just seen the CNN documentary *Beneath the Veil* about cruel conditions for Muslim women in Afghanistan, where women were being shot by the Taliban for adultery and were barred from schools and jobs. The first thing on my mind was what the young Muslim women thought about the harsh treatment of Muslim women in other places.

"That's politics, not religion," insisted Farkhunda Ali, a twenty-one-year-old employee at the Muslim Council. She said the

Muslim faith as intended by the Prophet Muhammad wouldn't countenance the mistreatment of women that had occurred in Afghanistan. Muslim women have had rights since the beginning of Islam, she maintained, pointing out that the Prophet's first wife was an accomplished woman and his respected confidante. Indeed, history shows that the Prophet not only sought and respected the views of women, he often performed household chores himself. He also ended brutal practices of the time, such as female infanticide, and changed laws so women could own land and retain their money.

Farkhunda contended that Muslim women can not only work, they can keep all the money they earn, whereas Muslim men are instructed to use their income to support the family. And in open societies like the United States, Muslim women can choose when to cover their heads and who to marry, although often it is done in consultation with their parents. Farkhunda chose to cover her head with a white scarf when she was nineteen, she said, but it was because her faith had become more important to her and she wanted to reflect that. She had experienced the death of several close family members, which drove her to seek comfort in her religion. As a girl, she had taken her faith for granted, assuming "things would turn out right." After she got serious about her faith, she said, "I realized whatever I had achieved was not because of me, but because of an external force. I began studying more about Islam because I wanted to get back in touch with my faith. It made me grow. I am probably a more patient person because of that, and I am still learning," she said.

Jihene Ben Moussa, also twenty-one, recently graduated from American University. She teaches religion classes for girls in the Washington, D.C. area. Like Farkhunda, Jihene became a more devout Muslim after she moved to the United States with her family from Tunisia. She does not cover her head, but she does keep her arms and legs covered. Still, she manages to do so with a sophisticated flair, wearing a fashionable denim top and long, black skirt. With her long, straight hair, she looks just like any other attractive coed. But she finds the American culture too "liberal," and has moved closer to her faith the longer she has lived in the United States. As she put it, "You see thirteen-year-olds here and they look like they are twenty-five."

"It's the American women who are repressed," Farkhunda agreed. "You are exploited by your culture, by the advertising. Look at the ads with half-dressed women in them. You don't know whether they are advertising cars or batteries or women most of the time."

That makes women look cheap, the two agreed. Both said they would prefer to dress conservatively and keep their self-respect. As college students, both helped create Muslim student centers where they would go to pray. They carried their prayer rugs in their backpacks with their books so they could keep up the requirements of praying five times a day. They said it is helpful to withdraw from the chaos of everyday life to find a quiet moment with God. And it is healthy to prostrate yourself for a few minutes, straightening your back and breathing deep. "It's like yoga," said Jihene. "You get more blood to your head." Likewise, they said there were common-sense benefits to Muslim dietary restrictions, such as avoiding alcohol.

They believe their Muslim faith will help them keep a sense of community that has dwindled in the American culture. "One of my primary goals when I marry will be to let my children know who they are and to have a strong home life," Farkhunda said. "In Islam, every person has a role, the moms and the dads. When the roles are not filled, it is not good. Someone has to sacrifice for the others. In American culture, we have lost the sense of community and what's good for society. We focus on the self too much."

As we talked through the afternoon, I came to respect that the young women had given serious thought to their values, probably more than I had at the same age. No, I would not want to switch places or faiths with them. But I enjoyed hearing their perspective. For the record, both said they shared the sorrow of Americans about the September 11 attacks and made it clear their religious beliefs would not condone such crimes against others. And yes, they might have glossed over the repressive tendencies within some Muslim countries, but considering the time and place, I thought they were fairly candid. And they raised some valid complaints about the way women are treated in Western culture. It's hard to win that culture argument when Britney Spears's belly button is a leading export.

So yes, our wide-open culture can degrade women just as the covered-up culture in some Muslim countries can restrict them. We shouldn't have needed a war to tell us our slips were showing. We could have just looked around — perhaps at the signs in front of the warehouse-looking buildings that promise "Live Girls." A *Texas Monthly* story about drunken spring break guys reports the fraternity chant, "Roses are red, orchids are black, I like my date flat on her back." A crowd gathers on the beach as a young blonde chugs beer until she passes out. Doesn't this fuel the image of women as disposable commodities? Did we lose something back there a couple turns after Woodstock? You get the nagging feeling that in the absence of commonsense standards, a sexual revolution can turn into degradation instead of liberation. We have not sorted out the unintended consequences of birth control and no-fault divorce. Women deserved to be more than baby machines, but somehow we lost the pride that women were vessels of life. Women deserved a way out of punishing marriages, but too often they found they were the ones cast aside. What was good for

> "The most perfect in faith, amongst believers, is he who is best in manner and kindest to his wife."
>
> — PROPHET MUHAMMAD

148

the gander did not turn out to be good for the goose or the goslings in fractured families. Perhaps in this century we can learn something from other faiths about how to balance freedom and modesty. Perhaps we can do a better job of showing our young people that the answer to the ambiguity of the world is personal responsibility.

September 11 was not the first attack that disrupted Rula Bibi's life. Back in 1990, she was visiting friends and family in the United States when Saddam Hussein invaded Kuwait. She had been having a fine time until the surprise take-over of her country. Suddenly, she was stranded in New York. She and her two-year-old son couldn't get back to their home in Kuwait City. It was not long before her tourist visa and money were running out. She was worried sick about her family. She was worried that she was overstaying her welcome with relatives. ("The house was getting a little crowded.") The more time passed, the more isolated she felt. "I was just lost in space. I didn't know who to turn to or even how to plan my day."

She went to Norman, Oklahoma, to a friend's house. After many tense weeks, her parents managed to send some money to her through the son of a family friend, who advised her to get a student visa. She could stay in the United States and go to college, since it was uncertain how long it would be before she could go back to Kuwait. Rula ended up at Midwestern State University in Wichita Falls, studying to get another degree in medical technology. And she ended up marrying the helpful fellow who came to her assistance. But she never got to go back to Kuwait. After the war was over, her family left Kuwait. Her father was a businessman with a Master's degree from the University of Chicago, and her mother was a teacher. But now they were displaced, too. Her parents had to relocate to Jordan. "Even though I was born and lived all my life in Kuwait, I was looked upon as being foreign there, too, and not accepted. I always grew up feeling insecure. My dad was never secure in his job because, as a non-Kuwaiti, he could lose his residency if he lost his job. If he lost his job, that meant we all had to go, and we were aware of it all the time. So I always grew up feeling insecure, an outsider."

"For thirty years I went in search of God, and when I opened my eyes at the end of this time, I discovered that it was really He who sought me."

— BAYAZID BUSTAMI, d. 874

When she was younger, Rula grew up in the Muslim faith, and as a teenager, she was quite religious. She married after college and when she had to get a divorce several years later, it was a dramatic disappointment that shook everything in her life. "I came away with the disillusioned feeling that everything was relative, that what was right for me might not necessarily be right for someone else, that there was not an absolute right and wrong that you could count on. Therefore, I could not explain religion anymore. If God was there, he wasn't going to leave those people dying from hunger and poverty and concentrate on me."

When she had been religious, she wore the hijab head covering. After her divorce she removed it and later gave up praying and fasting as well. She became more involved in contemporary life, more open to the socialization and secularization she had shied away from before. "I didn't become bad," she says, "just more liberal." It took her three years after her divorce to begin healing her hurt feelings, she said, but eventually she saw the good side of it and felt relief of not having to stay with her husband. She even called him up and thanked him that they had divorced. "It turned out to be liberating. It exposed me to new things. It made me stronger. You know, what doesn't kill you makes you stronger. I figured, if I can take this, I can take anything."

After she remarried, she became a U.S. citizen along with her husband Hussam ("Sam"). She began to feel more settled, she said, and pointed out that their daughter and son consider the United States "home" because it is all they have ever known. "I feel that way, too," she says, but there is still a little emptiness inside because I am isolated from the land where I grew up and the land of my parents. Where is home? What is home to me?"

She still felt a subliminal sense of being adrift. Then she came across a book that changed her life. It was by a Syrian engineer who had written a modern adaptation of the Qu'ran. "It brought me back. It fulfilled my religion as I thought it would be or should be. Your religion should be flexible for your time." She started praying and fasting again, but with a new understanding that "religion is mostly morality and behavior, and that praying and fasting is part of it, but not the main part, which is conduct and behavior and conscience. Your religion really is a private relationship between you and God, and you are not to impose it on others, who must find their own relationship."

One of the benefits of her journey to the United States, though it certainly had its hard spots, was that she gained a better understanding about other faiths and other people. She has many American friends and says she's gratified that her job at Baylor Hospital brings her in contact with other people "because many Muslim wives are stay-at-home moms and don't get to know others in the community as well."

On September 11, Rula was busily working in one of the labs at the hospital where she is a medical technologist, helping with a DNA research project. She emerged from the lab to discover her colleagues standing in shock listening to the radio. "I don't know how to describe it," she says, "I just put myself on the plane with the others. It just made my heart and stomach hurt. It was a weird feeling because I was very sad and heartbroken about what happened, but it felt like we were the victims and we were also the accused. We were caught in the middle. Those people's identity was tied to my identity, but their behavior is not connected to me. They are Muslim and Arab.

I am Arab and Muslim. But I am certainly against what they did. I remember looking my husband in the eye and saying, Where can we go from here? What can we do? There is not a good place on earth for us." Once again, she felt isolated and homeless.

She remembers that when she was studying at Midwestern, the Oklahoma City bombing occurred. Her history professor took her aside and said, "If I were you, I would keep a low profile and not tell anybody that I was an Arab and Muslim." She remembers, "This was before they found Timothy McVeigh. I was so relieved when it was not one of us because of the guilt by association."

Then, when September 11 happened, there was speculation in her office that "the Palestinians" did it. "There's no way," she told them. "The Palestinians don't have the capability to do such a thing — they are busy fighting for their liberation back home." Thinking about what a horrible situation it was, her stomach started to hurt and she put her hands on her stomach. When she mentioned to someone near her that her stomach hurt, the coworker said, "It better be." She didn't say anything, knowing that emotions were high. She stuck to her own corner and worked. If people who knew her could think she would be associated with the terrorists, she worried, what would the average person on the street think?

Then a friend e-mailed her and invited her to help with an interfaith group that was being formed to bring together Christian women and Muslim women for mutual understanding. A female Lutheran minister put out the word in the various faith communities, and sure enough, a diverse group of women showed up at Perkins Theology School at Southern Methodist University. There was a seventy-year-old woman who came because she was worried about the world; a lawyer raised as a Catholic who now had Buddhist leanings; several protestant ministers; women from Iraq and Palestine; and a filmmaker who wanted to help raise money for women in Afghanistan. The participants all shared their personal faith stories. One week the Muslim women prepared an astounding feast of Middle Eastern dishes and explained the concept of fasting and Ramadan. One week there was dancing. One week there was "show-and-tell" with books and photos about Muslim countries. And always there was group prayer. By the time six months were up, the group had dwindled to a core group of about two dozen who were getting more candid and comfortable by the week. No one quite knew how to proceed from then on, but it was clear that those who had attended regularly had learned something. Some wanted to expand the group to include Jewish women. Others wondered if men in their life could be encouraged to follow the example.

"It has opened many avenues in my mind," Rula admitted. "I am a firm believer that if something is mysterious to you, you deal with it as if it were an object, not a human, but when you get to know each other on a personal level, that you are a mom, just like them, you go through the same things others go through, then it becomes all the more important to me to have you heard. The way you worship your God may be different, not bad, just different. In a way it is so tasty and beautiful. When we have a society like ours where there are so many ethnicities and backgrounds, you can use it as strength rather than a weakness. Unfortunately, it becomes messed up and people think if you are different from me, you are the bad guy."

Rula was one of five Muslim women who

agreed to help organize the meetings; she proved a highly personal and efficient facilitator, which surprised and pleased her. She got more involved with a peace coalition, although with two young children, there wasn't much time left after soccer and music and Girl Scouts. Rula said she gets up very early so she can begin work at 6:30 a.m. and get off in time to be with her son Nauman and daughter Deena. "But I have come to realize that my being a Palestinian has affected me a lot more than I understood. The reason I was so insecure all my life was that I was so emotionally attached to that cause as part of my identity, but without a way to express it. I would love to be a bridge to make people understand what is going on, help them realize why this is happening, and help them see what kind of peace would be achievable. We need a just and lasting peace. I hope I can be an example that all Arabs are not terrorists. I hope I can help people understand Islam. People ask me questions all the time. They really think our God is different from their God. The word *Allah* is just the Arabic translation of 'God.' Even Arab *Christians* use the word *Allah* for God. It's like the Spanish word *Dios* for God. It's not a different God." She repeated a verse by heart from the Qu'ran. It was the same verse she had read at the first interfaith meeting, standing up before the group of strangers, nervously holding a little scrap of notepaper on which she had written down the words in case she forgot them: "Oh mankind, we created you from a man and a woman . . . and made you into peoples and tribes, so that you may come to know one another. Truly, the most honored of you in God's sight is the greatest of you in piety. God is All-knowing, All-Aware." As she read the words to the hushed group of women sitting on parlor sofas and chairs, her brown eyes filled with big tears. Five months later, she was dancing with them as a friend, swaying in a circle to a traditional Palestinian dance, roaring with joyous laughter as they tried to count and dip with the music. In just a few months, the differences in faith had been bridged by respect.

"There is no compulsion in religion. Truth stands out clearly from falsehood; whoever rejects evil and believes in God has grasped the strongest rope that never breaks. And God is all-hearing and all-knowing."

– QU'RAN 2:256

TAKE HOME:

The Islam theme of following the "straight path" in life is summed up in the opening surah (chapter) of the Qu'ran: "Guide us in the straight path, the path of those on whom Thou has poured forth thy grace." How do you walk in the straight path of life? Islam provides a set of rules that were given to the Prophet Muhammad by the angel Gabriel. The Five Pillars of the faith are:

Shahadah — The Declaration of Faith is a simple formula pronounced by the faithful: "There is none worthy of worship except God, and Muhammad is the messenger of God."

Salah — The name for the obligatory prayers that are performed five times a day. The ritual prayers include verses from the Qu'ran and are said in Arabic. Personal supplications can be offered at any time in one's own language.

Zakah — Almsgiving to the needy is based on the principle that everything belongs to God and that wealth is, therefore, held by human beings only in trust. The word *Zakah* means "purification" and "growth." Muslims believe that setting aside a portion for those in need purifies our possessions and like the pruning of plants — this cutting back encourages new growth. Annually 2½ percent of one's possessions — the Poor Due — are supposed to be distributed to the poor.

Sawm — Fasting is required every year in the month of Ramadan, when all Muslims fast from dawn until sundown. They are to abstain from food, drink, and sexual relations with their spouses. By cutting oneself from worldly comforts, each person is more inclined to focus on his or her purpose in life, the presence of God, and the deprivations of others.

Hajj — Pilgrimage to Mecca is an obligation only for those who are physically and financially able. For the rite, pilgrims wear simple garments that strip away distinctions of class and culture, so that all stand equal before God.

For those who have come to think of the Muslim faith as predominantly violent because of the al Qaeda crusade against the West, religious historian Huston Smith points out that Allah's compassion and mercy are cited 192 times in the Qu'ran as opposed to seventeen references to his wrath and vengeance. And for those who are still trying to learn more about Islam:

- *Qu'ran* means "recitation."

- *Allah* means "The God."

- *Islam* means "peace and surrender to God."

- Muhammad's first convert was his wife, Khadija.

- Arabic and Hebrew are both Semitic languages, and the words for *peace* are similar — *Salaam* in Arabic and *Shalom* in Hebrew.

- Today, a fifth of the world's population is Muslim. Only one-third of Muslims are Arabs.

- Muslims say the first half of the Shahadah often, not just in ritual prayers. "La ilaha ill Allah," "There is no God but God."

- The Qu'ran permits a Muslim man to

have up to four wives, but according to historian Huston Smith, more careful readings of its regulations point toward monogamy. The injunctions in the Qu'ran regarding the veiling and seclusion of women are actually minimal: "Tell your wives and your daughters and the women of the believers to draw their cloaks closely round them when they go abroad." (Qu'ran 33:59)

"The Prophet Muhammad said, 'Spread peace abroad and you will remain safe.'"

— IMAN BUKHARI'S *BOOK OF MORALS AND MANNERS*, HADITH 982

∾ Muslims believe in angels, who are made of light energy and can materialize in any form. They have no gender and exist to serve Allah. The bad spirits in the world are known as Jinn.

∾ Islam stresses racial equality, dating back to Abraham's willingness to marry Hagar, who was black.

∾ Muslims are directed by the Qu'ran to respect the faiths of other "people of the book."

∾ No images of God or people are allowed in holy places, to avoid drawing attention away from the words of teaching to the image.

૭ Islam teaches that people are basically good, rather than tainted by original sin, but the religion does include the concept of "forgetting," a recognition that human beings tend to forget their divine origin and may choose to sin.

Do you feel secure enough in your own faith to study the beliefs of others? Do you generally find the beliefs of other religions threatening or interesting? Do you think your faith would be enriched by reading more about another religion or joining an interfaith study group?

SIX

Challenging

"Dare to do things worthy of imprisonment if you mean to be of consequence."
— JUVENAL, C. 55–C.130

Let's face it. Most of us get off light when it comes to faith. We think finding the time to bring a spaghetti casserole for the potluck dinner is a testament. We give the money for the altar flowers and the summer camp and hope somebody upstairs takes note. But the truth is, we don't often put our faith on the line. We don't enter the arena with the lions or even the courtroom with the judges. Yet with all the injustice and poverty and inequality that remains in the world, the pesky, nagging question begs, why aren't we more outraged and engaged? If the status quo is not just or merciful or forgiving or loving, shouldn't we be challenging those conditions?

Every so often in life you get a chance to meet someone who does put her faith on the line, and with stunning clarity you realize you've only been going through the motions — like one of the earnest drill-team girls on the fifty-yard line, smiling and dutiful and in step but, well, marking time. I knew the minute I saw Joan Chittister coming across the hotel lobby that I was about to encounter something rare and life-changing. Joan Chittister barrels across a room with an intensity for life that you can feel. Sitting down to a quick breakfast before a speech, she looked up from her menu to exchange warm greetings with people passing by her table. I asked if she knew them. "Oh, no, but they look like wonderful people," she said.

With her graying hair and pale blue suit, she looked, at sixty-six, like a matronly teacher. It just goes to show that courage comes in unexpected guises. Sister Joan, a Benedictine nun for fifty years, risked her life's work for the sake of more openness in the church. She refused orders from the Vatican in the summer of 2001 not to speak at a worldwide conference in Dublin. She had been invited to speak about the controversial issue of ordination of women. Authorities in Rome opposed the speech, saying it would "create scandal" if the nun spoke her mind. The Vatican warned that "just penalties" would follow if the order were disregarded. The suspense and pressure mounted as the date of the conference neared. All but one of the 128 nuns who worked with Sister Joan at Mount St. Benedict convent in Pennsylvania co-signed a letter of support. Additional support came from twenty-two monasteries for Benedictine women across North America. Knowing that she might be expelled from her order and that many of her colleagues might be punished as well, Sister Joan went to Dublin nevertheless. She modestly made light of her jeopardy, saying, "We're not going to let a little letter from Rome get us down." She delivered an address that was bold and brilliantly written. It was a challenge to the church to do the right thing.

Then something wonderful happened. Nothing. The Vatican backed down. A spokesman said Sister Joan would not be punished. This was certainly a surprise, since Pope John Paul II declared in 1994 that the church has no authority to ordain women. The Vatican had decreed there would be no further discussion about whether women could serve as priests. Total silence was ordered on the matter, which became an issue in itself. Many of the sisters supporting Sister Joan felt open discussion of church issues should not be forbidden. They contended that raising questions was well within the traditions of the early desert monastics, who lived on the margin of society in the fourth century precisely so they could be a questioning presence to both church and society.

Sister Joan explained in later interviews that she was not trying to be defiant by speaking in Ireland, but she genuinely felt, as a matter of conscience, that it would not be good for the church if she did not go. "If people cannot find a depth of ongoing reflection in the church," she said, "they will go somewhere else to get the guidance."

She has been ostracized by some Catholics for challenging the system. Just a month before the Dublin showdown, five U.S. dioceses boycotted her appearance at the national Catholic Educational Association in Milwaukee. Some critics have accused Sister Joan of spreading heretical ideas. She responds that she is merely raising the intellectual, moral, and doctrinal issue of how the church can continue to say that "half of the human race is less holy." It took four hundred years of debate to end church support for slavery, she notes. While the hierarchy stonewalls the issue of ordaining women, she points out, the supply of priests is shrinking even as the number of Catholics is increasing.

And she's right — today, two-thirds of the American parishes have only one priest for thousands of members. To get around the shortage — and avoid using women — authorities have begun using more retired priests and male deacons. And the size of parishes has been stretched, so that in some areas, one priest serves as many as six thousand parishioners.

Though Sister Joan continues to argue passionately that women could help fill those shortages as priests, she insists she would never become one herself. "Absolutely not," she said emphatically. "I know exactly who I am, and it's not a priest. But I have met women who I really believe have a call for priesthood. I do not. I love being a sister. If there weren't a priest left on the earth and they said, 'Joan, would you like

> "It takes some extra examination to find the numerous women who worked side by side with Paul and the other 'well-knowns.' Possibly we are slow to notice their names because our own culture has trained us to see women more in strictly family roles than in ministry roles."
>
> — WINNIE CHRISTENSEN, American Bible teacher

to be ordained?' it would be an agonizing moment."

She added that she did not expect to see women as priests in her lifetime, but that it might be possible someday for female deacons to preach and minister, but not celebrate Mass. "That would be a sensible opening step," she says. "And church history is filled with examples of women deaconesses from the time of the Apostle Paul, who worked with women like Prisca and Phoebe, to well into the Middle Ages."

Though the Vatican is not behind Sister Joan, the polls are. Numerous polls show some American Catholics approve of women's ordination by more than a two-thirds majority. But because of the Vatican gag order, the issue cannot be officially debated.

In the meantime, Sister Joan is doing what she does best: writing and speaking about faith. She has written more than twenty books and recently traveled to Ireland to finish writing on *Scarred by Struggle, Transformed by Hope: The Nine Gifts of Struggle*. She has a website (eriebenedictines.org) and distributes videotapes, audiotapes, and newsletters through Benetvision, a nonprofit operated by her monastery. The monastery also runs a job-training program, soup kitchen, children's feeding and sports programs, a neighborhood art center, low-income housing for seniors and the disabled, an environmental educational center, and a summer camp.

Sister Joan does not shy away from challenging the status quo. When she was serving as abbess in the 1970s, a local business leader called to complain that as a Catholic he was embarrassed that some of the "lunatic fringe" nuns were holding prayer vigils against the arms race and war. She thanked him for accusing the nuns of being Christian.

Likewise, once a local newspaper sent a novice reporter to interview her who began by saying, "I don't know anything about religion, could you tell me what to ask?" She walked the cub reporter through the interview, then called his editor and asked him if heart surgeon Dr. Michael DeBakey were in town, would he send someone to interview him who didn't know anything about science or medicine? Absolutely not, said the editor. "Then don't ever do it in religion again," she told him, "It is not only insulting, it took my time away from people who needed it. And you indicated the incompetence of the newspaper itself."

The incident got her ire up, she explains, because she feels strongly that it is inappropriate to trivialize religion, which "Frankly, is at the base of all our lives, our beliefs, our very Constitution. We can't permit that."

She also once challenged a policeman who called to tell her some of her nuns had been arrested for refusing to leave their prayer vigil in the U.S. Capitol. According to the *Los Angeles Times*, Sister Joan asked the policeman why it was a crime to recite the Lord's Prayer on government property but not to build nuclear weapons? When he said he was just following orders, she asked him, *"Why?"*

Sister Joan sees it as the proper role for the faithful to ask "Why?" That's the way believers — and the church — grow. However, she says she was drawn rather inadvertently into the role of activist because of her writing. She doesn't like traveling to speak, she explains, and probably would have been more content to be teaching school or writing.

"I did know at the age of fourteen that I was a writer. I love it. I would write whether anybody read it or not. But I never expected to be one. I gave it up to enter the order, because in those days women didn't write in large part, but nuns, *never* wrote. How many books do you know that were written by nuns? Being a sister was the most important thing for me in life, and I just took it for granted that I would have to give up writing," she recalled. "I had agonized. It was the one thing that stood between me and entering the order." She chose God over writing. And yet she has ended up writing eloquent books about faith. "It just came back," she said with an amused twinkle in her eyes. "God is so *clever*."

> "No one can make you feel inferior without your consent."
>
> – FIRST LADY ELEANOR ROOSEVELT

She also gave up high school to enter the convent. But the dropout was encouraged by the sisters to go back to school. She earned her doctorate and now teaches complex theological issues at universities. She was barely sixteen when she entered the order and came down with polio six weeks later. It was four years before she could walk again. Still, Sister Joan managed to finish her high school courses and receive her bachelor's degree by the age of twenty-three. She caught up fast and has not slowed down since.

Sister Joan went on to become a tireless

champion of the poor, perhaps a consequence of her background as well as her faith. Her father died when she was three. She and her twenty-one-year-old mother had to move in with her grandmother. Her mother did sewing for people to bring in what little money they had during the depression and later married a welder named Dutch Chittister, who adopted Joan and gave her his name.

True discipleship, she says, always, always, always takes the side of the poor despite the power of the rich: "Not because the poor are more virtuous than the rich, but because the God of love wills for them what the rich ignore for them." Sister Joan teaches that true discipleship takes umbrage at systems that are more bent on keeping "those kinds of people" — improper people, that is — out than they are in welcoming all people in.

In one of her speeches, Sister Joan reminded the Catholic audience that if the world's population were reduced proportionately to a village of one hundred persons, seventy would be nonwhite, seventy would be non-Christian, seventy would be illiterate, and fifty would be malnourished. More than half of the resources of the village would be held by just six villagers —

and they would all be white male Americans. She bluntly told them that it would be bogus faith to be content with private pieties and go about business as usual in what is *not* a business-as-usual world. The church must reach out, she says, explaining, "Church is not the place where people go; church is the place where we must go to the people."

That also applies close to home, Sister Joan warns. "We had better be percolating — it's not a white Anglo-Saxon world anymore. When we say we are a pluralistic country now, we don't mean Methodist and Catholic. The Muslim population is now larger than the Jewish population. They are starting their own schools and social centers, just as we did years ago. We have to have some understanding." She agrees that September 11 was a clarifying moment. "We cannot refuse as a nation to look at the underlying anger in the rest of the world, especially

174

the Arab world. I'm not saying they are right. I'm saying they are *there*. We have to look at the causes."

She suggests that healing may have to start in the United States with more ecumenical understanding and respect. "We have to go the next step ourselves. You and I have to work to realize where these faiths converge. If we don't come to a sense of the one great God who is everyone's God and recognize that God has worked differently in every culture . . . we will be back at the level of tribal history where we are pitting one God against another. That sets up a me-against-the-infidel mentality. As much theirs as ours, as much ours as theirs."

In our attitude toward other faiths, she suggests, we should remember that Jesus did not "beat anybody into the Way." He was open to the Samaritan woman, the Caananite woman, and the Roman soldier, she reminds. "They were all models of the Other, who Jesus accepted, cured, and allowed to be exactly as they were. He doesn't say to the Roman soldier, 'I'll cure your daughter if you become *Jewish*.' He takes people where they are, he allows their own lives to lead them to the Way. In my opinion, of course, Jesus is our way to

God. At the same time, if God didn't think that people could discover goodness in any other way, how do we account for the fact that two-thirds of the world would be just left by God to be lost? God's plan is a plan for this world."

Sister Joan likes to challenge audiences to live in the world the way Christ lived his — touching lepers, raising donkeys from ditches on Sabbath days, questioning the unquestionable — and — consorting with women! Women, she points out, are most of the poor, most of the refugees, most of the uneducated, most of the beaten, and most of the rejected of the world. The pauperization of women, she says, flies in the face of the Jesus, who repeatedly showed respect and concern for women — healing the woman with the chronic bleeding problem and refusing to allow his apostles to silence the Samaritan women on whose account, Scripture tells us, "thousands believed that day."

> "Well-behaved women rarely make history."
>
> – LAUREL THATCHER ULRICH

Indeed, Sister Joan said the ministry of Jesus shows us that the invisibility of women in the church threatens the very nature of the church itself. "Religion that preaches the equality of women but does nothing to demonstrate it within its own structures, that proclaims an ontology of equality but insists on an ecclesiology of superiority, is out of sync with its best self and dangerously close to repeating the theological errors that underlay centuries of church-sanctioned slavery."

"Surely God did not make one sex simply for the sake of waiting on the other. Surely God did not give women minds in order to taunt them by not allowing them to use them — an argument which is now losing ground in the secular community, but which is alive and well in the Synods and Seminaries of the Church," Sister Joan tells audiences.

She believes the origins of the suppression of women can be traced back to a Greek philosophy that was based on male supremacy as well as to unscientific biology that for centuries saw women as passive incubators of male sperm (hence the belief that she's carrying *his* baby, not *their* baby, as if the womb were less important than the sperm carrier). The result of those influences was a church that taught that women were inferior by nature ("the weaker sex") and deficient of soul (the seducers of civilization). Sister Joan contends that the church learned from the pagan philosopher Aristotle what it then taught as doctrine in Christianity for centuries — that all life is graded from the lowest to the highest — from inert matter to males. She regrets that the church interpreted Genesis to demonstrate the inequality of the sexes rather than the universal equality of humanity that being "bone of my bone, flesh of my flesh" surely implies.

Her complaint can be corroborated in examinations of church history. According to *Sacred Origins of Profound Things*, a wave of misogyny swept through the church in the second, third, and fourth centuries. Whereas Jesus did not criticize women as being more sinful than men, church leaders in later centuries did so with a vengeance, and unfortunately, that characterization has colored cultural perceptions of women ever since. St. Ambrose, bishop of Milan, said chastity was higher than marriage and only by remaining a virgin could a woman redeem the sin her parents had committed in conceiving her. St. Jerome said that sex was so polluting that married couples should abstain from cohabitation three nights before receiving communion. Tertullian, church leader of Carthage, branded women as "a temple over a sewer" and the "devil's doorway." St. Augustine warned of passion and portrayed women as temptresses.

In contrast, Hebrew authorities of the same era had a much healthier view of sex and women. Rabbi Eleazar wrote in the third century, "Any Jew who has no wife is not a man." Indeed, the Talmud proclaims that "Were it not for the sexual instinct, no man would build a house, marry a wife, or beget children." Sex was not evil, but necessary. Women were seen as vessels of life.

Yet as the Christian Church evolved, the role women played in Jesus' ministry and the early growth of the church was overlooked and overruled. Some women today still might not feel comfortable with Sister Joan's argument that women can be a conduit to God as priests, because our culture has said otherwise for lo these many years. But our culture has been wrong about many other things. Remember, as recently as the 1950s, students were taught there was only one galaxy. By the time the children of those students went to high school, we learned that there are a million galaxies! That gives us a more awesome picture of the nature of God. As Sister Joan points out, when you read the Psalms, you see almost a stick drawing of God, because the map of their world at that time was a dome over the earth and the earth was a ball that sat on lakes somewhere. As we learn more, we have to integrate reality into what we believe. And the good news is that because what you thought before was smaller or more limiting, our new understanding paints God more to size. God gets bigger and bigger, not smaller and smaller.

She points out there have been considerable changes in the Catholic church in the last forty years:

ᕲ Both women and men can now sing in Catholic choirs, a task once reserved for only men and small boys.

ᕲ Women can read the Scriptures out loud inside the sanctuary, and women can touch the vessels of the altar, a privilege once reserved for altar boys but not their moms. There are even some altar girls and women homilists.

ᕲ The Churching Ceremony, wherein a woman was readmitted to the church after childbirth in a process similar to the Jewish purification ceremony, has been dropped. (Dropping with it, the feeling of ostracism and banishment that came with giving birth, something that women must do to keep the species alive.)

❧ Catholic bishops have written, but unfortunately not published, a document that declares that sexism is a sin and that wife-beating is immoral.

❧ In dioceses where women have been part of the parish process, the cases of priests accused of assaulting youngsters have been resolved more openly and fairly, with more compassion to the victims.

Yet if you look around and listen, you realize that women are still considered "less than" by the church, even though Scripture says both male and female were made in God's image. Asking that women be treated fairly is not a radical departure, but a return to the essence of faith. Sister Joan

"Perhaps it is no wonder that the women were first at the Cradle and last at the Cross. They had never known a man like this Man — there never has been such another. A prophet and teacher who never nagged at them, never flattered or coaxed or patronized; who rebuked without querulousness and praised without condescension; who took their questions and arguments seriously; who never mapped out their sphere for them."

— DOROTHY LEIGH SAYERS,
British novelist

challenges audiences: Are women full human beings or not? Did Moses come down from the mountain and say women were unequal to man? Of course not. Did Jesus relegate women to second-class status in the Sermon on the Mount? To the contrary, he included women in key parts of his ministry and defended Mary's efforts to learn from him while Martha fussed over the household chores. If we no longer cling to Biblical Scriptures telling slaves to obey their masters, why do we still cling to the few verses from the same disciples that women must defer to men in church matters? How would anyone be harmed if women today were treated as respectfully by the church as Jesus treated the women around him?

Sister Joan smiles a Cheshire-cat smile as she challenges women, "Quit waiting for someone else to give you the right to make a difference. A right is not what someone else gives you. A right is what no one can take away."

Unfortunately, sisters like Joan Chittister are waning. In an exceptionally poignant centerpiece called "Women of God" in *Atlantic Monthly* in January 2002, author Mary Gordon surveyed the state of nuns today, finding that their numbers are declining. "Nuns are an endangered species," she wrote. "With a median age in the country of sixty-nine, and little new blood coming in, their numbers have dwindled markedly." From a high of 180,000 nuns in 1965, the number has fallen to 80,000. But spiritually, Gordon found, the sisters still have something that the secular world can envy: a higher calling. Our imaginations have been fed by the sugary images of the smiling, flying nun or the Julie Andrews singing nun. But most of us have also had at least a passing acquaintance with a Sister Mary Agnes who seemed to have a sense of purpose or serenity that was memorable. Author Gordon wrote, "Since Freud, we all believe that sex makes one if not happy then whole. But look at these women's lives. How can we understand that even without sex, they are happy, and whole, and free? Freer than many of my friends." As she tried to put the nuns' stories into words, she found herself crying. The tears perhaps were for the end of something, if the cloistered life dwindles. And perhaps the tears are for the lost parts of our lives as we settle for a lesser calling, a partial understanding, and less-courageous paths.

Not that all is rosy in the cloistered life.

There are other nuns besides Joan Chittister who are daring to ask questions and sometimes paying dearly for it. Sister Jeannine Gramick, a member of the School Sisters of Notre Dame, was ordered along with a priest to stop a ministry to gays and lesbians as well as support groups for their parents. She was ordered to be silent. She ended up having to leave her order and was accepted by the more open Sisters of Loretto. She has raised questions that the authorities have yet to answer. If, as many church leaders have estimated, as many as 30 to 50 percent of priests are homosexual, why has the church stifled debate on the subject? Regardless of how you might feel about homosexuality — and it is certainly a highly charged and sensitive issue — the issues Sister Jeannine has dared to raise are not so much about sex as about authenticity in church practices as well as about compassion. The discomfiting reminder from Sister Jeannine is that Jesus did not draw boundaries to exclude people from his love and forgiveness.

"People ought not to consider so much what they are to do as what they are; let them but be good and their ways and deeds will shine brightly."

— MEISTER ECKHART

Other women of faith continue to bring up difficult issues that those in authority wish they wouldn't. In Mexico, Elena Poniatowska has found creative ways to speak for the poor and the powerless. "Elenita" is one of Mexico's most popular novelists. As a pioneering newspaper columnist, she also became the first woman to win the Mexican National Award for Journalism.

When we met before one of her speeches, Elena said teasingly, "I am usually second choice to Carlos Fuentes." It was an impish reference to Mexico's more celebrated novelist. But Elena has proved second to none when it comes to capturing Mexico in words.

In 1968, she wrote courageously about the massacre of 250 students who were killed by government soldiers when they marched in protest of the Olympic Games. Most other journalists, under government pressure, kept quiet. But Elena doggedly found eyewitnesses and reported that the students had been gunned down like the row of mechanical targets in a shooting gallery.

Often the words she writes are really theirs, the people of Mexico. Elena has pioneered the technique of testimonial literature, taking what real people say as a way of dramatizing their stories. In the 1960s, she immortalized a scrappy working-class survivor named Josephina Borquez from the slums of Mexico City. Elena overheard Borquez talking and asked to hear more of the stories about life in revolutionary Mexico. Meeting once a week for months, she took notes that became a "novel" narrated in first person by a woman named "Jesusa." So illiterate she could not read a "Help Wanted" sign, Josephina/Jesusa survived a forced marriage at fourteen, rejection, robbery, and poverty. Foul-mouthed and irrepressible, Josephina/Jesusa survives by working as a maid, nanny, hog butcher, boxmaker, whorehouse manager, and janitor in a print shop.

By allowing the woman to speak for herself, Elena showed the humanity of the working poor, something that often gets overlooked in politics. Her lifework has been getting Mexico's literate class to read about the illiterate underclass. She has written more than forty books of journalism and fiction, almost always contrasting the lives of the have-nots with the haves. The irony is that she is one of the privileged elites of Mexico, yet she has proved one of the most talented and bravest observers of her era. Her full name is Helene Elizabeth Amelie Paula Dolores Poniatowska, known to her many readers and friends by the diminutive "Elenita," because she is, even in stylish pink heels, around four-foot-ten.

She is the daughter of a French-Polish nobleman Jean Poniatowska and a member of one of Mexico's privileged families, Paula Amor Iturbe, Princess Poniatowska. Young Elena was born in Paris and spent the first nine years of her life in France. She was sent to boarding school at the elite Eden Hall in Pennsylvania along with the daughters of ruling families of other Latin countries. She remembers those years fondly and can name several of the nuns who impressed her with their character and teaching. "It was a very religious school. What I learned really was a Christian doctrine. We spent lots of hours in the chapel and lots of hours in the hockey game. We even played against Grace Kelly when she was at Ravenhill. And we won."

Did that Christian upbringing give her the strength she would use to question the government in later years? "Maybe," she says, noting that she still attends Mass now and then and that her mother was very religious. "Or that could also be from my

Polish background. Poles are very courageous. They went to war on horseback against the German tanks."

If they ever do a movie of Elena Poniatowska's life, it ought to be called, *The Countess Was a Muckraker.* After she dared to document the 1968 massacre, the government sent goons to stake out her house and photograph her. She posed for their cameras and smiled prettily, saying coyly that she only thought she had become "popular." Because the photographers had been waiting all night without food to catch a photo of her, she invited them to come in and have breakfast.

While other women writers were relegated to the "Sociales" section of the newspapers, Elena insisted on writing serious stories — profiles of the rich and famous as well as the poor in the dust. A collection of her profiles, which fill fourteen books titled *Todo Mexico,* is being released in Spanish two volumes at a time. The interviews include Americans such as Susan Sontag and

> "The ability to find joy in the world of sorrow and hope at the edge of despair is woman's witness to courage and her gift of new life to all."
>
> — MIRIAM THERESE WINTER, medical mission sister

Barry Goldwater as well as cultural icons like cinematographer Luis Bunuel, who went to jail with Elena to visit prisoners. To duplicate her in U.S. terms, you would have to mix up Joyce Carol Oates, Lesley Stahl, Barbara Walters, and Ellen Goodman. Now nearing seventy, the petite *escritora* shows no signs of slowing or piping down. She is busy at work on another novel. Asked where she gets her ideas, she said, "From the jail, from the streets."

It was important perhaps that Elena was born in France rather than Mexico, she muses, because otherwise "I would have accepted everything in Mexico — the poverty, the misery, the violence." There were interesting people in the safety of her family's circle, she said, but she could guess what they were going to say. The people in the street were always a surprise. "What I have tried to do, since I was not born in Mexico, was try to document my country so others would know it. So much was unknown about Mexico in the 1940s when I arrived. It was like a map that did not have the rivers and landmarks clearly drawn. For me, it was very important and I wanted to do this. It was a way of discovering my country and myself."

During the 1985 earthquake, Elena went out on the streets not only to chronicle the damage, but to help. The countess was put to work helping fumigate the bodies in the morgue. Most had died in poorly constructed buildings built by corrupt contractors. One was an eight-year-old boy. "It's not fair," Elena said. "Tragedy always hits the poorest, most deprived, most screwed-over people."

Elena Poniatowska has been awarded many prizes that she did not seek or accept. She has been courted by presidents and ministers, but she stays as far away as possible from them saying, "If the government starts inviting you, it's a very bad sign." So she carries out the struggle her way, listening to the poor, who usually can't get a countess or a president to listen.

> "Do one thing every day that scares you."
>
> — ELEANOR ROOSEVELT

TAKE HOME:

The church has a long history of stubborn individuals who have dared to challenge the status quo — and they have not always won.

ॐ St. Hildegard of Bingen has been rediscovered as a feminist icon in recent years. Born in 1098 in Germany, she was the tenth child in her family and given to the church at the age of five — perhaps because the tenth child was often tithed to the church in the Middle Ages. When she was in her forties, she emerged as an exceptionally gifted prioress — she composed music, wrote poetry, painted, and compiled herbal remedies. She corresponded with the leading intellectuals and rulers of the day in many countries and was considered their peer. But late in life, she ran afoul of church authorities after she gave permission for a young man, who had been excommunicated, to be buried in the monastery cemetery. She was ordered to have the body exhumed. She refused. She insisted that before he died, the young man had been reconciled with the church and received the sacraments. The Bishop of Mainz punished her by forbidding her from receiving or celebrating communion. She protested bitterly. Eventually, she won her battle with the Bishop and the ban was lifted, but she died a few months later.

ॐ Or consider Anne Hutchison, the Puritan prophet in Massachusetts. She was a skilled midwife and used herbs for healing. She began inviting women into her home for prayer and religious conversation, sometimes offering her own commentary. She contended that God speaks to us from within. She constantly challenged the standard Puritan interpretation of the story of Adam and Eve. Women were regularly blamed as the source of sin, which was used to justify the strict patriarchal social structure. By challenging that orthodoxy, Anne was branded a "Jezebel," a heretic, and an instrument of the devil. Still, she would not be shushed. When critics cited the Scriptures about the need for women to keep silent in church, she shot back a verse from Titus saying the "elder women should instruct the younger." She was castigated by one minister, "You have stepped out of your place, you have rather been a husband than a wife, a preacher than a hearer, and a magistrate than a subject." She was held in prison during the bitterly cold winter, then banished with her children. They were all massacred as they tried to make their way to Rhode Island.

℘ Soujourner Truth is the memorable name of the unique prophet and preacher

ও Soujourner Truth is the memorable name of the unique prophet and preacher who began life as a slave in New York in 1797. She was the ninth child, but she was never to know her brothers and sisters because they were sold to different masters. Her parents named her Isabella, but she dropped that "slave name" when she took up her calling to preach at the age of forty-six. She was bought and sold several times and bore on her back the scars of the beatings she endured. She poured out her sufferings to God and later would tell audiences that she spoke to God and he spoke to her. She felt called to be a soujourner for truth about the evils of racism and sexism and even traveled to the White House to encourage Abraham Lincoln to keep up the struggle against slavery.

Although some abolitionists were reluctant to tie slavery to the suffrage issue, Soujourner Truth insisted that if black men got their rights, women must as well, or else they would still be slaves to men. She continued to campaign for equal rights until she died in her eighties. In one of her most famous speeches, she argued, "That man over there says that women need to be helped into carriages, and lifted over ditches, and to have the best place everywhere. Nobody ever helped me into carriages, or over mud puddles, or gave me any best place — and aren't *I* a woman?"

᷈ Women of the church have historically led the way in caring for the poorest and most ignored of this world. Many today may know the name Drexel from the Wall Street financial firm of Drexel Burnham Lambert. What they might not know is that a member of the Drexel family became the first American saint canonized in the third Christian millennium (2000). Katherine Drexel was the foundress of the Sisters of Blessed Sacrament for the Indians and Colored People in 1891. She was the daughter of a wealthy Philadelphia banker whose firm later became a financial powerhouse. She not only devoted her life to the poor, but she also poured her fortune (worth some $80 million today) into charitable projects. After visiting Indian reservations in the Dakotas, she felt a special call to do missionary work among Native and African Americans.

In 1984, Katherine established the first Native American school in Santa Fe, New

Mexico. She went on to create eleven more schools on reservations as well as nearly one hundred for African Americans in rural areas and a teachers college for African Americans that became Xavier University in New Orleans. Even though she was housebound after a severe heart attack, she continued to fight for civil rights causes. When informed by her sisters how they were jeered at as "nigger sisters" when walking the streets of New Orleans and Harlem in the 1950s, Katherine replied, "Did you pray for them?"

For many people today, the "saints" may seem so perfect and idealized that they do not bear resemblance to our modern lives. But look carefully. These women prayed. They listened to God. They performed good works. They spoke up about their beliefs. They stood on principle and did not bend to prejudices of the day.

> "If God had wanted us to think with our wombs, why did he give us a brain?"
>
> — CLARE BOOTH LUCE

Saints have gone before us, yes, but there are saints around us still. The Hebrew adjectives for saintly mean "kind, merciful, benevolent; zealous in the pursuit of good and doing good." In the Old Testament, the Hebrew word for "godly" is *hasid,* meaning "grace." It also is translated as "saints," indicating that those who were recipients of God's grace showed the impact of grace in their lives as a result. The Greek references to saints, *hagios,* in the New Testament means "believers," not necessarily those of exceptional holiness or to those who died. They are described as "those who believed."

Often we are intimidated about speaking up about our beliefs. If you anonymously could tell your church leaders about something that really needs changing, what would you say?

SEVEN

Grieving

"Brief is this existence, like a brief visit in a strange house."

— ALBERT EINSTEIN

After the tragedies of September 11, many Americans got a glimpse of their own mortality. And many got serious about faith. Bible sales soared 28 percent. Seven out of ten Americans reported praying more in the weeks after the terrorist attacks. The attacks were a collective shock to the entire country, much like the *Sputnik* space shot of 1957. *Sputnik* was a telegram to the United States that we weren't as smart as we thought, so we tried to recalibrate our education system and space program. September 11 was a telegram to the United States that we weren't as safe as we thought. We would have to recalibrate our defenses — and ourselves. We would have to get right with God.

It reminded me of a scene from the movie *Apocalypse Now* in which U.S. soldiers are slogging through the jungle in

Vietnam, nervous as cats. They are looking over their shoulders out of fear. One of their own might accidentally shoot them. An ambush might be ahead. Then suddenly, a tiger leaps out from the side and catches them totally by surprise. It's that tiger we don't expect in life that usually stops us in our tracks, not the things we worry about every day. We buy flood insurance and are surprised by the tornado; we take our vitamins and are surprised by breast cancer. Tigers rise up. And we are stunned how much is beyond our control.

On September 11, our country lost a great deal of innocence as well as a great many lives. We don't like to think in our modern society that death may be crouching at the door. Now we know it is. Our perpetually youth-oriented society has had to come to terms with death. Mortality is not a subject we normally like to talk about. The Navajo don't speak the names of the dead out of respect, but we don't because it makes us uncomfortable. We don't wear mourning clothes like people did in other times and places. Widowers and widows rarely wait the polite year before dating, or even marrying. We are so wrapped up in the here and now that death would be an inconvenient interruption. Death? Now? But I'm booked solid this week.

Since September 11, more people have realized that death doesn't care about your puny little plans. One of the victims in the World Trade Center attack called home to his wife as his office filled with smoke and flames. He told her he had bought airline tickets to Europe to surprise her for her fortieth birthday. She should cancel those, he suggested. And then he was gone. Another sent a message to a friend on his Blackberry that read simply: "I'm scared." It is said that Alzheimer's patients often are startled when they look in the mirror and see their reflection because they don't recognize themselves; they think they have seen a ghost. We looked at the profiles of the September 11 victims and were startled because we did recognize ourselves. What death whispers in our ear at such moments is "live" because he is coming. God whispers in the other ear for us to live right — and right now — because we must come to him.

Some of the impermanence of life began dawning on many people in the 1990s with the sudden deaths of cultural icons like Princess Diana and John F. Kennedy Jr. If the rich and beautiful could disappear in a heartbeat, so could we. As Franz Kafka bluntly said, the meaning of life is that it stops. Brevity really is the soul of life. It's a discomforting thought to realize that our brief life is indeed like a bird that flies in one window of the cabin, flutters across the room, and flies out the other window, gone.

So when the tiger interrupts, as it did on September 11, we wonder what it is all about and where God is. And though it might seem at such times that God has turned his phone off, he speaks to us though others and by what happens to us. I heard him in the phone calls the victims of the hijackings made to their loved ones, when the only message that mattered was "I love you." I saw him go into the rubble with the firemen who worked for days on end. I heard him in First Lady Laura Bush's calm voice as she encouraged parents to hug their children a little more. We were reminded September 11 that faith in God changes our manner of living and of dying.

We are still learning from the September 11 tragedies, about what the world thinks of our culture, about what is worth fighting for, about fear we've never felt before, about beliefs we had been too busy to practice. We have indulged ourselves for a very long time and have been indulged. Now we are learning again what it means to take care of each other, what we stand for, what we are made of. It is an awakening and perhaps, an exhilarating opportunity. Who are we, and what do we believe in? Who are *you,* and what do you believe in? How will you face your maker?

Perhaps human beings have always carried on as if there is no tomorrow, but I suspect that delusion has been exaggerated by the peace and prosperity since World War II. Older cultures were much more conscious about the specter of death. Tribal custom in Africa was to wear masks to scare away death. Wooden war canoes were protected by carvings of people who had died before. The Romans pictured death as an old ferryman named Charon, who rowed the dead across the River Styx into subterranean darkness. Death with his scythe was a familiar spectre in Medieval art; when he knocked at the door, he brought the plague. Black bunting was used to mark houses of grief in the Victorian age, and mourners wore black armbands for long periods as a symbol of their loss. Not so today. Americans tend to keep death and all its ramifications out of sight and out of mind. Perhaps that's why it comes as such a shock.

When death occurs, the loved ones left behind often feel that they have lost their bearings. They are numbed by grief. At such times, when you are going through the motions of life and feel detached from reality, rituals can walk you through the process. The rituals of faith give you something to hold on to. Increasingly, traditions from long ago are being reintroduced to help believers deal with the cycles of life. For example, at the Chalice of Repose Project in Denver, volunteers provide soothing, uplifting music therapy for the dying, a tradition learned from the ancient monasteries. It is telling that they describe the process as "midwifing," or "midwifery." They are assisting in the birth of the individual to the next world — a consoling image for mourners to keep in mind.

> "May God's love wrap and enfold you, embrace you, and guide you, and bring you comfort."
>
> – JULIAN OF NORWICH

When Hind Jarrah's mother died in a tragic accident, she was devastated. Her mother was only forty-nine. A gas heater in a bathroom had malfunctioned in their home in Beirut. Her mother was overwhelmed by the fumes. "It was the biggest shock of my life," Hind recalls. "She was my greatest friend — more a friend than a mother." She had to tell herself, "This is God's will, and we are not to object to his will." True to Muslim custom, her mother was buried immediately. She died in the morning and was buried by afternoon prayer. She was wrapped in a shroud after her body was bathed and covered completely. Hind insisted on being able to go in to kiss her farewell and say a funeral prayer, "God is great, forgive the dead." Then she and her family stayed at their home, numb with shock. "Both life and death are God's order, God's decision," she knew. "You deal with death as a part of life. It is obvious that you are going to miss your loved one, but you don't yell or scream because it is God's will. The hurt is inside." For the next week, family members gathered at her home, bringing food and condolences.

In the Muslim faith, forty days after burial, the whole family goes to visit the grave of the departed to ask forgiveness and mercy for them. Then every year, on the anniversary of the death of the loved one, the family gives to the poor and the needy in the loved one's name. Muslims include the dead in their daily prayers, asking God for mercy for themselves and the deceased. And at the end of Ramadan fasting, mourners often go to the cemetery to visit loved ones, to honor them and pray for them.

Those prescribed rituals helped Hind's family make the passage back to "normal" living. Though she still missed her mother, she came to see death as one of the tests in life we all have to deal with. "We can't truly believe unless we are tested and put our beliefs into action," she says. "Then, when our own day of judgment arrives, we will see a record of our actions because God has kept track even though we our-selves have forgotten. That fact keeps you focused."

To see Hind in the grocery store or mall, you would not assume she is a devout Muslim. Hind (whose name rhymes with bend) does not cover her head except for when she prays, and she often wears pant-suits and looks like what she is: a suburban soccer mom. Yet she says, "I have always been a religious person. I come from a family who is very religious. My dad taught me that your faith is sort of your companion in life; your faith is what makes things understandable for you and makes things tolerable for you."

Hind's family was Palestinian but had moved to Lebanon in 1948. Her father was a civil engineer who worked on projects through the Middle East. He was a patient teacher and told her stories related to the Qu'ran to explain things in life to her. She proved a good student at the American University in Beirut, where she graduated with a pharmacy degree. She worked for a year and then married a medical student. The young couple moved to Dallas in the mid-1970s, where Hind earned her doctorate in pharmacology from Southwestern Medical School. Along the way, she had three daughters and decided to be a stay-at-home mom so she could have the kind of relationship with them that she had with her mother.

For many years, Hind was homesick for her homeland. She wanted her daughters to learn Arabic and learn about Islamic culture, so she helped start the Arabic Heritage Society. She gradually became more involved in community activities that helped explain the Muslim faith to others — she helped make presentations in the schools and organized an exhibit about the Arab world for a city festival. "I never felt Islam was different," she says, "so I tried to address the preconceptions that people had. But I must admit that the first time we tried to set up a booth for the International Festival at City Hall, I was scared to death. I was scared people would yell at us, shout 'Go home!' But they did not. People asked questions, and we tried to explain that the message of Islam is the same, but God sent different messengers to speak in the language or way that people would understand."

Then September 11 happened, and Hind experienced grieving on a different scale. "It was an earthquake," she says. "It has been one of the hardest things in my life. When it first happened, my mind stopped working. I found myself sitting in front of the TV, trying to understand what was going on. It took a while to realize a lot of the sadness, the shock. What helped me was the Qu'ran. I was sitting sideways and could see a chapter that caught my eye. It said, 'Did you think I would leave you to say that you believe without testing you?' The Qu'ran says that the prophet himself and his companions were tested. There was an earthquake with everything shaking, and the prophet pleaded with God for his support. That reminded me that September 11 was another test. But for weeks after September 11, I would walk into the house, whispering. It was very strange." Hind did not leave the house unless it was absolutely necessary. If she went to a restaurant with friends, they were careful not to speak Arabic because they could see other diners looking at them warily. "You felt the uneasiness," she remembers.

It was hard for her to deal with the anger she sensed around her toward Muslims, and she ached to explain that the actions of the terrorists "were not the kind of faith in Islam I grew up with." Later she said, "To see how people misrepresent or stereotype Islam makes me very sad. But I also see God's design for the world in this. Through this difficult time, there is more interaction. People of different faiths here are dealing with each other and learning from each other." Indeed, Hind played a constructive role in that interfaith process by helping form a discussion group of Muslim and Christian women who met once a month to talk through the emotion of the moment and learn more about each other.

Hind explained to the group that many of the rituals in Islam are to make believers more conscious of God's presence — such as the fasting at Ramadan and the five prayers a day. "You are supposed to reflect your faith in everything you do, the way you talk to people, the way you conduct yourself, the way you address people, the way you interact with elders or little ones."

Though her mother is gone, Hind prays for her daily and honors her at Ramadan. The rituals give her something to hold on to. And since September 11, her religion has assumed a new role in her life. She had planned to go back to work after her daughters graduated from college, but that will have to wait. She now feels that she has a duty to reach out to others and explain her faith.

Like Hind Jarrah, Jan Fuller Carrothers learned early that loss is part of life. Her parents were missionaries in the Middle East, and she grew up surrounded by war. During the 1967 war between Israel and Egypt and its aftermath, her family lived in Jordan. Her family went into hiding during some of the tensest times. They were in Jordan when the civil war broke out between the king's army and Palestinian guerrillas. In the 1970s, they lived in Beirut, where civil war erupted. Death was a neighbor, but they lived in a house of faith. Growing up, one of Jan's best friends was a Palestinian Muslim who lived across the street. Her parents, who were Southern Baptists, taught and modeled toleration toward the faiths of others. Yes, they wanted to help others come to Christ and a Christian point of view, but they did their missionary work in a respectful way, without putting different beliefs down. So Jan thought tolerance for others should be the norm.

Even though she was a very blonde American, Jan grew up feeling like an Arab. She spoke English, Arabic, and French, but felt more Arab than anything else. She left Lebanon at eighteen to attend college in the United States, graduating from Hollins College in Virginia in 1970. Her heart was still in the Middle East, so she returned to Lebanon to teach in a Lutheran orphanage. "It was a very valuable experience, but I knew in two weeks that it was not my calling," she says now. She married a handsome Arab businessman named Said Ziyadi and began setting up a home of her own. Then, suddenly, Said was killed in a blast while going to work. "He was in the wrong place at the wrong time," she says softly. "What a big waste." He was twenty-seven. She had just turned twenty-one. After that, she recalls, "I grew up really fast. My sense of life is that I have lived a lot in a very short time. But I wasn't sure how to live through that kind of loss. Of course, no one does at the time. When you are living through grief, you have one foot in this world and one foot in a different world. You are kind of living in limbo. And yet you are hooked into the eternal in ways that other people aren't. You know you are distracted and don't hear what other people say to you. You feel as if you are in your own time zone. It later became clear as I lived through more experiences that I was going to have to learn more about grief in order to help others, because I kept being called on to be with other people who were grieving because of what I had been through."

She applied to several seminaries because she wanted to learn why the world was the way it was. Why does God allow evil in the world? Why does God allow the faithful to suffer? What is that all about? She left Lebanon again at the age of twenty-three to study at the divinity school at Yale University. Once again, she was in a multi-cultural world, but this time she was surrounded by Episcopalians, Catholics, Jews, and Methodists. "Yale was great experience, academically and existentially.

You must think about who you are, what you believe, and where you need to be. I had to process what I had been through. I didn't realize it when I came back to the United States, but I was suffering from post-traumatic stress. It taught me that you cannot tell by looking at people what they have been through. So many people have abusive families or have been through the death of someone close. We carry those burdens silently and try to fit in. You have to ask. I have used that in the way I do ministry."

Jan wrote her dissertation at Yale on grieving and attributes the fact that she is in the ministry to her first husband's death. "Somehow that turned me around or that opened me up. It just changed me. I needed to know some things that I had never asked before. It might be that in order to live with a loss like that, it needs to be redeemed in some way. This might be my way of finding some redemption for those empty spaces. But it was a transformative moment for me. I became somebody I had never been before. It empowered me to search of the existential questions of life and try to name them. I still struggle with it, but I have found a way to put those feelings to good use."

When she graduated from divinity school, Jan was hired to be the Baptist chaplain at the university. For five years, she taught and ministered to students there. But she was ordained at a time when "it was not cool for women to be ordained," so her options were limited. She was beginning to realize that her calling was not for a parish ministry, but a campus ministry. She had returned to her alma mater in Virginia several times to preach; when they offered her the job as acting chaplain, she accepted. She's been there since then.

"I love to work with students who want to learn. They are so refreshingly honest. What I love about the chaplaincy at the college is that I have spent the rest of my life proving it is possible to be faithful and be smart, especially as a girl. So many come to college having already decided that they can't possibly have a religious life because they think it is so narrow and so limited and doesn't honor the mind. They think those things can't mix. They come in feeling alienated from their personal religion. I have noticed increasingly in the last couple years, maybe the last ten years, that they will say, 'I am a Presbyterian,' but then not even have the slightest clue how to spell it. They have no idea what their religious traditions mean. That's when I really began to appreciate and love this work, because I can help them discover what their faith really means."

Until recently, Jan admitted, it was not cool to express an interest in faith on many campuses. "There has been more interest in the last couple years in things that are spiritual, but before that, you could still put down Christians on campuses and get away with it. What I am trying to do is heal that intellectual animosity toward religion. Religion is a format for spirituality, but sometimes the form can get in the way. The students might say they generally believe in God, but they might not be able to answer the questions, What kind of God do you believe in? Do you believe in a God who orders tragedy to happen so you will become somebody else? A God who causes you to be hurt so you will face reality? Or do you believe in a God who mourns with the mourning? A God who cries with people? It's very important to think what kind of attributes your God has, so you can accept that he is there for you, not against you."

It is important, she thinks, that she lives on campus at Hollins with her husband

and their son, Samuel. Her husband previously was a minister, but now builds handcrafted furniture from a workshop in their home. Students walking by their house can see her playing with her son, walking her dog, or riding her bike. "That's important to me, that they see that religion doesn't make you separate, but makes you more able to enter the world." She often eats lunch with the students and attends the sports events. "I try to be in places so they can see I live a satisfying life and that I am not afraid of the challenges. It is important that my life is an open book."

Students have seen her struggle with a severe illness that has left her with chronic vision problems and neurological pain. She had surgery in the late 1990s to remove a brain mass that was putting pressure on her nerves. She still has to live with pain and the possible loss of more eyesight. At times, struggling with the neuroma was "a scary time," she says. "I thought, *Well, I guess I'm going to die now.* I know that's what my family was thinking! But I found I wasn't really panicky. I was really, really sick, but I somehow felt I was never alone. It was a real experience of God's presence, and I had the assurance that I didn't know what the outcome would be, but I knew it would be okay. I knew I was not alone and I wasn't being punished, but being loved the whole time. God's love was more tangible to me in those days than it has been at any time. I don't know how to analyze that, but possibly I was just open to it. When we are busy and efficient, we might not be as open because we think we've got it all together."

Jan's friends speak with admiration of her great courage and say she has modeled skills for overcoming that her students will need in their own lives. She acknowledges that more of today's college students come from broken homes and bring with them emotional problems related to a culture that revolves around money and appearances. She said increasing numbers of students struggle with such things as substance abuse, eating disorders, the scars of emotional and sexual abuse, and depression. "Many students have to choose every holiday which family to go to, because so many of their parents are divorced and re-married. There might be strength that

> "Even in our sleep, pain that cannot forget falls drop by drop upon the heart, and in our own despair, against our will, comes wisdom through the awful grace of God."
>
> — AESCHYLUS
> (525 B.C.–456 B.C.)

comes from that, but it is a really hard thing, too." Students of this generation, she says, "also show more signs of depression because they are not being given good answers to the questions, What does life mean? What does it mean to live and die? The lack of meaning can be very troubling. What do you do in this world? You want to make something of yourself, and you try to contribute something, but sometimes it is hard to contribute. There's a sense that the system is fixed and what they do doesn't make a difference. They want to know, What kind of difference could I make in this world?"

Jan has spent a lot of time since September 11 helping the students deal with the anxieties that the fear of terrorism has stirred up. That took some adjusting herself, because the event raked up many feelings from her past about living with violence, which "is distorting to the heart and soul." She added, "Much of the world lives like that. I don't want us to be like that."

She often recommends students read from Psalms as a way of dealing with concerns. And she coaches them on how to pray. "Archbishop Anthony Blooms tells a wonderful story about a woman he met when he had been appointed to a rest home. A woman who had lived there many years told him that she had asked the same question of every priest and had gotten highfalutin answers that were not helpful. She told him he was so new to the job that he might just have a helpful answer. 'I need help with my prayer life,' she said. 'I keep saying the Jesus prayer over and over, but I feel like nobody's listening and I am just saying it.' The bishop said, 'I want you to go to your room, clean up your room, and place your rocking chair in front of the icon of Jesus. Get out your knitting and sit and look at Jesus and knit for fifteen minutes. Then come back and tell me what happened.' She was skeptical, but she went and did it. She came back and said to him, 'It was the best thing. First, I got to understand for fifteen minutes that I didn't have to be doing anything. And second, as I knitted, I felt a presence with me.' The woman realized that when she stopped talking, she could hear that somebody is with her. That's a fabulous story that has really shaped me."

We need prayer to get through life, Jan suggests, because there are some things, like grief, "that we never get over and need to keep working on." She says that the landmark work on the stages of grief by Elisabeth Kübler-Ross has often been misinterpreted by our culture: "Her description of the stages of grief is that you come to a point where you are reintegrated with the world. But that has been misinterpreted to mean that you have resolved it, you get over it. We have all these people running around pretending that they have resolved everything because that's what they think they are supposed to have done. But it is not resolution, but transformation that occurs. You can partner with it or block it in some way. We have the ability to shape the ways in which we are being transformed by grief. These are very holy moments because we are being transformed.

"But we live in a culture that doesn't want to hear about suffering or pain. We say you can have seven days off from work under our insurance plan and then we want you to come back and not bother us about it anymore. We want you to get over it. We need to understand what goes on in those moments. It is not clinical, but spiritual. It is not the medical community's job, but the spiritual community's job. We all need a pastoral leader at such times to say something about the meaning of that moment when we are most disoriented and then reoriented."

Jan agrees that other cultures have more rituals to help guide mourners through grief. "In Lebanon, a widow wears black at least one year. Then they have a memorial service and she changes her clothes. In the Jewish tradition, where you sit shiva for seven days, they cover the mirrors and you sit on low stools because you feel low. People bring you food and you don't go out of the house. Then you go out of the house, around the block, then you go back to work. But every time you go to the synagogue, you say the prayer of the mourner, the Kaddish, for a whole year, so you can't forget that you are a mourner and other people can't forget who you are. The Kaddish is a beautiful prayer, there is no word about death, but 'Blessed are you, king of the universe,' which is a statement of faith in God's power. That statement of faith is very helpful at a time when you might not have any."

Too often, she says, we tell people they should buck up when instead we should allow them time to fill the empty space they feel. "I don't mean mope around twenty years," she cautions. "I remarried after nine years. I thought that was an awful long time. But it took me five to get back on my feet and figure out who I was again. And nearly another five to find anybody worth being with! I don't know what the proper amount of time is, but I do know you should not deny your feelings."

Even after September 11, she said, she had to reassure students that it was okay to be upset. "You cannot imagine how many students would come into my office and say, 'I don't know what's wrong with me. I just burst into tears at the weirdest times. What is it?' That's what happens when you have lost something. It is hard enough to explain when somebody close to us has died, but when it becomes a national loss and we all have an amorphous piece of it, that's even harder to articulate. We had a national grief reaction, which is normal. We can take those feelings to God. We need to say what we are feeling. But then you need to shut up and listen for as long as you spoke."

"One of the most transforming ways of prayer I've discovered in the last ten or twenty years is the prayer of silence. The lack of silence in our lives is very unhealthy in almost every way. Prayer is one of the things that can save us — not only in the divine access, but in the need to be still.

We have to realize we are not gods and we are tired. As long as you stay busy, you don't have to face things. If you can stay still, weep, feel who you are, and face your disappointment, the way you are, the honesty is healing."

I was struck when I interviewed women for my first book, *What's Next?*, that everyone had survived stiff blows by the time they got to mid-life: divorce, death, illness, betrayal, and disappointment. Many were changed at the root by such experiences and emerged wiser and stronger because they were drawn back to deep resources, drawn closer to faith. Nobody gets through life without some laundry marks on her. In time, you learn to wear that survival with quiet pride.

> "In time, I hope and believe the anguish with you will be covered over. That is the only way to express it. It is like new skin covering a wound. That doesn't mean that one forgets the people who have gone away."
>
> — EDITH SITWELL

Like most leaders of a congregation, Rabbi Stacy Offner is called on often to help people in St. Paul, Minnesota, through the grieving process. She points out that the grieving process is itself healing. It should not be short-circuited with false bravado in an attempt to get on with the business of life. She cautions that the stages of grieving are not necessarily linear, where you go one, two, three and then you are home free. The process of grieving is more of a spiral. You might find yourself heading back to painful feelings you felt before. One way to deal with the reality of death, she advises, is to prepare yourself for that eventuality and express your love while you can for the people close to you. She often counsels members of her synagogue to prepare an "ethical will," no matter what their age. It's a thoughtful way of helping others deal with your passing when the time comes. As September 11 reminded us all, even the young can be taken in an eyeblink on a beautiful blue sky morning. Just as many of the victims in the World Trade Center used their last minutes to tell someone they loved them, those with more time to plan the message in an "ethical will" will feel a certain peace of mind in knowing that it will be delivered.

What exactly is an "ethical will"? Stacy counsels that in addition to a legal will for their possessions, people should give thought to an ethical will that passes on the lessons of their life to their family. It is an ancient Jewish tradition that faded out of use and is being revived by rabbis like Stacy. "It makes so much sense," she says. "When you think about the legacy you pass on to your children, the monetary legacy is one thing, but it is just one thing." She's right. It is a commentary on the pervasiveness of money in our thinking that our last instructions to our loved ones are how much dough we are leaving behind. In addition to a legal will, some people now have "living wills" to specify that they do not want extraordinary medical measures taken to prolong their lives. Adding an ethical will makes good sense as well.

Stacy's Shir Tikvah congregation in St. Paul offers classes on how to create such wills. She says it is a wonderful exercise, not only for those who receive the will, but for those who write it. Those who have a phobia about writing should just consider it a heartfelt letter. You simply write down in a tender way what you have learned, what you believe in, and what blessings you wish for those you love.

The concept of ethical wills dates back to Biblical times. In Genesis, you might recall, Jacob summoned his family to his deathbed and talked to each son about the family heritage as they gathered around his bed. But you shouldn't wait until you are on your deathbed to start thinking about your testament of life, because, quite frankly, your head and heart might not be working well then. It's better to spend a few minutes now jotting down a brief summary of your life and expressing your blessings to the rest of your family.

What would you say if you left a statement of life for your family? You might want to specify how you would like people in your family to treat each other after you are gone. Or you might want to specify what accomplishments you feel good about or what mistakes you made that you would hope your survivors will avoid. You might want to ask forgiveness for any wrongs.

My friend Libby Norwood takes a trip every year with her parents and her grown children, a tradition her parents started as a way of getting the whole family together after they have dispersed to different cities. Her parents always pay for the trip, having explained, "We're going to leave you memories rather than money." And isn't that a wise idea, to give of yourself, your time, your conversation, and your understanding, rather than your cash?

It all comes back to what counts most. Stacy has written a Torah study about the concept of counting. Back in the time of Moses, counting was considered a privilege belonging to God, a divine act. That's because God counts what's important. We count to quantify what we have or don't have — our money, our attendance, our votes, the things we collect. But as Stacy points out, we cannot count love, we cannot count faith, we cannot count patience, and we cannot count belief. But God can. Perhaps that's why we use the word *count* to show what's important or worthwhile. We say "Let's make this one count" when what we really mean is "Let's make it matter." We say, "I'm counting on you" when we mean we are depending on someone because it is crucial. When you examine the word, you see that counting is not about numbers or money, but about significance and dependability as well, Stacy says.

Using that context, she asks, how would the story of our lives be different if instead of counting our money, we made our money count? If instead of counting the days until our next vacation, we made each day count? And if we asked ourselves, *Can I be counted upon? By God and those around me?*

Writing an ethical will helps us see how

our lives are part of a continuum. Rabbi Abraham Joshua Heschel believes that a devout life cultivates surrender to divine will, so that by life's end, death becomes its ultimate, seamless expression. Perhaps that's why they call it going home. For many years, one of the auto dealers in Dallas advertised that it treated its customers with the best service because they were considered customers for life. The brackets that held on the license plates for the dealership's cars read, "Customer for Life." Not to be outdone, another auto dealership put on its license plates holders, "Customer Beyond Death." Perhaps that's the theological message in a nutshell. God isn't finished with us when we die. We are customers beyond death. And the service is truly the best.

"The day of death is when two worlds meet with a kiss: this world going out, the future world coming in."

— JERUSALEM TALUD, YEBAMOT

One of the women I interviewed for *What's Next?*, a physically fit widow who had hiked her way across Europe in her seventies, was planning to celebrate her eightieth birthday by going around the world in eighty days. So I asked her if she was planning on living to be one hundred?

Oh, no, she said with some firmness, "Life's a party, but even a good party has to end sometime." Exactly.

TAKE HOME:

There are other lessons about dealing with death in the Jewish tradition. In the Jewish view, death is a matter of going from one room to another. The world to come, "olam ha ba," is compared in the Talmud to the eve of the Sabbath, that is, the world is the eve, or the vestibule, and the next is the palace. One of the oldest Hebrew traditions is that during Biblical times, when it was time for someone to die, she sneezed — and her soul departed through her nose, the place where God breathed in the breath of life, "nephesh," when God created Adam and Eve. Perhaps that's why we say "God bless you" or "gesundheit" (good health), because the breath is a holy gift.

At the moment of death or at the funeral, it is tradition for the immediate relatives to tear their garment or a black ribbon to signify grief. This "k'riah" is not only a symbol of the heart that is torn, it is also a cathartic act to help release pent-up anguish. According to Rabbi Benjamin Blech, k'riah also may have the more profound meaning that the body is merely the garment of the soul. Death rends the garment, but the inner soul remains intact.

Like the Muslims, the Jews carefully prepare the body for death with washing. The plain white shroud is distinctive in that it has no pockets: a reminder you can't take it with you. Special prayers ("taharah") are said to purify the soul for the next, purer world. The dead are never left alone before the body is buried. Friends and loved ones stay to pray over the deceased twenty-four hours a day.

Sitting Shiva, meaning "seven days," is the time when people visit with the grieving family and share meaningful stories about the deceased to keep the positive aspects of the person's life in mind. At the end of seven days, the mourners walk around the block, symbolizing that they now must rejoin the world and not live in the past.

But because it takes time to heal, remembrances of the dead do continue. The next thirty days of mourning are called the "sheloshim,"

"You don't get to choose how you will die. Or when. You can only decide how you are going to live. Now."

— FOLKSINGER JOAN BAEZ

228

and mourners are restricted from some activities. For the next year, mourners are not expected to resume their normal lifestyles completely. For eleven months after the death of a loved one, the "kaddish" is recited by mourners: "My mother (or father) tried to live as a Jew who brings glory to God. My parent is no longer alive, and so I will take her (his) place. By reciting the kaddish, I show my determination to live 'Jewishly' and sanctify God's name in my life as my parent did. In this way, I keep the memory of my loved one alive, since if it were not for her (him), I would not have been able to come into the world to make this declaration. Because I am committed to the values of my ancestor, my parent still lives in the most powerful way of all."

Approximately a year after the death, a stone is placed at the gravesite and the ceremony is called "the unveiling." This might follow the act of Jacob when Rebekah died by the side of the road. He "set a pillar upon her grave." Interestingly enough, the Hebrew word for funeral is *levayah*, which means "to accompany." The rituals of death allow us to escort our loved ones to God, like an honor guard, we do them honor by saluting their life, their departure from the room, and their arrival into the next.

EIGHT

Overcoming

"You think I'll crumble? You think I'd lay down and die? Oh no, not I! I will survive!"

— GLORIA GAYNOR SINGING "I WILL SURVIVE"

If you open yourself to it, there are people all around who may have a message for you about faith. Later you realize you had an appointment with them, you just didn't realize it. Several years ago, I flew to Chicago to appear on the *Oprah Winfrey Show* to talk about *What's Next?* I was a nervous wreck as the limo pulled up in front of the Omni Hotel in Chicago to take me to the TV studio. I had not slept all night, worrying about what to say and how to say it. My anxiety was mounting by the minute as two women got into the limo. One of them was carrying a satin pants outfit on a hanger. *Oh-oh,* I thought. *Maybe the attire for the* Oprah *show was dressier than I thought.* I had on a plain black pants-suit. So I leaned over and asked the woman with the satin outfit, "Are you by any chance going to the *Oprah Winfrey Show?*"

She nodded her head, "Yes. Are you?"

"Um-hum," I said.

"What are you on the show for?" she asked.

"Oh, I wrote a book about women," I answered. "How about you?"

"I used to be a hooker," she said, very matter-of-factly.

I was at a total loss what to say next.

Then it dawned on me: This was the hooker I had heard about from a friend who had attended a Drucker Foundation meeting earlier in the year. My friend Lyda Hill had called to tell me about a woman who had gotten a standing ovation for her inspiring work helping prostitutes in San Francisco. Lyda said there was not a dry eye in the ballroom as they showed the video of her encouraging the women to leave the street life and start a new life. "You ought to write an article about her. She's *incredible,*" Lyda suggested. "Her name is Norma Hotaling." Several months later, her name was still on a piece of paper on my desk, buried in a pile of things to do. So I leaned over and asked the woman in the limo, "What's your *name?*"

She said, "Norma Hotaling."

Bingo. This unassuming-looking woman with short sandy hair was the founder of the SAGE Foundation, rescuer of hundreds of "women of the night." Norma received an "Angel Award" from Oprah Winfrey that morning along with $100,000 for her foundation. And yes, they showed the video. Onscreen Norma explained, "I see these women and really know who they could be — that's what drives me to do what I do." Then she pointed to a corner where she used to sell herself for sex, explaining, "This is where I got beaten up. . . ."

It's an amazing story. Thirteen years before, Norma was homeless, a heroin addict, who had been arrested more than thirty-five times. She slipped into cars with strange men in the Mission and Tenderloin districts of San Francisco, hiding butcher knives in her purse to protect herself. She slept in subway stations and doorways. Then one bleary day, she realized as she woke up in the detox unit in jail that she must change to save her life. She finally found help with city social services but thought getting that help was much too hard for most people to manage. Someone needed to provide a more user-friendly way to help women off the streets. She decided she should do it. She would help other women follow her lead, because without help, most of them would die or be broken by beatings, AIDS, hepatitis C, venereal diseases, or drugs. So Norma went back to school at San Francisco State and earned a degree in health education. She graduated magna cum laude.

In a fitting twist of fate, Norma was encouraged to counsel prostitutes by one of the policemen who used to arrest her, Lieutenant Joe Dutto, who heads the San Francisco Police vice squad. He had read letters to the editor that Norma had written to local newspapers opposing the legalization of prostitution. He recruited her to mentor the prostitutes who wanted to get off the street and to counsel the men who were arrested for soliciting them. She also began testifying at trials as an expert witness. Dutto tells reporters that Norma, with her raw talk and real wounds, is perfect to explain to juries what kind of control pimps have over prostitutes. "She's a lot more effective than a cop," he says.

In the video, one of the prostitutes Norma helped said, "If not for Norma, I'd be dead." Another young girl said that Norma "let me know I have some worth . . . that I could be more than *naked* . . ."

And, yes, when the video was over, there wasn't a dry eye in the TV audience. Including mine. It's not often that you meet a miracle in a satin suit, but Norma Hotaling surely is one.

ᖆ Consider Angel Cassidy, twenty-two. Angel had been a hooker since she was fourteen. As a child, she had been abused by her parents' friends. She ended up homeless, on drugs, and selling sex in an environment that was becoming increasingly violent. She was raped, beaten, and burned. At her lowest point, she weighed only eighty pounds. She shot heroin "to try not to feel how lonely, worthless, and unlovable I felt." Norma convinced Angel to stop in 1993. Norma told her, "You deserve more." Norma didn't judge; she offered a safe way out. Angel is now a drug counselor.

ᖆ Consider Tracey, a heroin addict who was the wreckage of a human being in an HBO documentary on *Black Tar Heroin: The Dark End of the Street*. When it was aired, filmmaker Steven Okazaki told the San Francisco press that he was worried that the ending was too bleak, the situation too hopeless. The documentary ends with a shot of Tracey, who had lapsed back on heroin just eight hours after getting out of jail. But Norma Hotaling found Tracey. She found her in the "kick tank," vomiting and twitching from withdrawal. Again, Norma didn't judge. She pointed out that she was living proof that people like her can get clean. Tracey now is a violence prevention counselor. Since she's been clean, four of her friends on the street have died from overdoses or AIDS.

୬ Consider Vanessa, eighteen. She told Norma, "My pimp knocked me out with a baseball bat. I woke up and he was sewing my head up. He wouldn't even take me to the hospital. How could I get away? He'd kill me first. Besides, he was all I knew. I had been with him since I was twelve." SAGE provided a safe place for Vanessa so she could get away from her pimp.

Their stories sounded familiar to me, because over the years as a newspaper reporter, I've had the opportunity to interview hookers and "exotic" dancers for various features. Back in the 1970s, I wrote what life was really like for the topless dancers in white vinyl go-go boots (not glamorous). I interviewed high-priced hookers who made thousands a night in the plush hotels downtown but were filled with anger about the hypocrisy of "polite" society that winked at men spending their family money and time on randy debauchery yet scorned the women they used. Many of the hookers were school dropouts who rented their bodies because they didn't think they had any other skills. Many had been sexually abused when they were young or had been sexually exploited when they were temptable teenagers, naive and ripe for the picking. Some came to the big city from rural areas to be "models" and ended up prostituting themselves. Others trusted older boyfriends to take care of them but were taken for a ride.

Most of the women I have interviewed in prison have had a similar profile: little education, early abuse or pregnancy, and a slide into drugs and petty crime. The thought has often nagged me that our system failed these people at multiple times in their young lives when they could have been salvaged. If only someone had reported the child abuse, if only a teacher or relative had noticed the signs of struggle.

Granted, their prostitutes' view of their problems often is self-serving. They have made bad life decisions. But based on what women in prison have told me, they rarely — if ever — received counseling or remediation at any stage of their downward slide. Once such girls get the stigma of being prostitutes, they become untouchables to the rest of society and live in an odd sort of limbo. They are visible to those looking for sex, invisible to the rest of the world passing by.

So I wasn't surprised to learn that Norma Hotaling's life fit the same general pattern: fondled, then abused at a very young age, a rebellious teen, a self-destructive woman. The surprise was how she found the will and the way to change. She was in drug rehab about twenty-five times. She estimates she was raped twenty or thirty times. Once she woke up in Palo Alto wrapped in cellophane. Her rehabilitation is a powerful example of will and grace.

When we finally got around to our interview, Norma had just gotten back from Japan, where she was a speaker at the Second World Congress Against the Commercial Exploitation of Children in Yokohama. While there, Norma presented recommendations for cracking down on child prostitution on behalf of the United States, Canada, and Mexico. She also now works with the State Department and the Justice Department to save children from a life of prostitution. The streetwalker who once sold sex for drugs has addressed the United Nations and has spoken at Harvard and in Paris. Norma Hotaling has overcome her past rather than let it overcome her.

> "I'm not what I have been, I'm not what I am going to be, but thank God, I'm not what I was."
>
> — GOSPEL SONG

The way Norma modestly describes it, she "runs a job-training program for prostitutes." It's a shoestring operation. Just Norma and two others, who, yes, are also hookers turned reformers. So far, SAGE has helped hundreds of prostitutes get off the street in San Francisco. But Norma has done much more than that. She has led the charge to change laws in California, so that fines from "Johns," the customers of prostitutes, can be used to rehabilitate the hookers, creating a model for other states. Fledgling efforts to work with prostitutes around the country now look to the SAGE Foundation for inspiration. And Norma is educating people in California to think differently about the whole concept of prostitution. She's a regular letter writer to the *San Francisco Chronicle* and a frequent guest on radio talk shows. She's bright, she's outspoken, and she's passionately driven to do more.

In fact, at fifty, she now realizes that saving lives is her calling. "I really believe there is a spiritual path for all of us," she says. "If we are just open to that, no matter what our lives have been about, they have been having a purpose. I believe this is my purpose. I believe that all the things that have happened to me have been part of my purpose. On one hand, I have to acknowledge it has been hard. I have sat and cried deeply about the lasting impact of everything that happened to me. But I feel just as strongly on the other hand, that this was a life I chose for a reason. And that I am guided very clearly to this point."

> "You are amazing grace. You are a precious jewel. You — special, miraculous, unrepeatable, fragile, fearful, tender, lost, sparkling, ruby-emerald jewel rainbow splendor person."
>
> — JOAN BAEZ

Norma is an overcomer, and so are the women who make it through her program. To listen to a group session at SAGE is to hear voices of new strength.

★ ★ ★

Alexis: "I didn't have a person in my life to say 'Go to school,' to say 'What are you going to do when you don't look pretty no more?' I didn't have anybody to say that. Now I have women in my life that say, 'No, it's not okay to do that. You need to make your life okay.' I had so much shame around what I did. My dad was a pimp, and that meant he was out all night and would sleep all day. So I had to be loud to get attention. I'd be loud and wake him up. It was usually negative attention. And I saw that the lady who was bringing home the money, she was getting his attention. And still she was getting hit on, he was hitting her. And so I always thought, if you were getting love, then you were supposed to get hit. And yelled at. When I was younger, I was raised by my grandparents. But I felt, since my real parents weren't there, that I wasn't lovable. Abandoned. I did all those things to get all this attention, and it was usually negative, acting out in negative ways, so I would get a negative response. [We need to] teach parents — and to teach people period — to be encouraging. I'd like to hear someone say, 'I like that' instead of 'Why'd you do that?' "

Norma: "We need the men in the world

more involved in the girls' lives. We need men to value girls. I think we also need programs in schools so girls know how not to be recruited by pimps, how not to be recruited by drug dealers, and how not to be recruited by gangs. The tactics are the same. They pick vulnerable girls. And if parents were more involved in girls' lives, there would be a lot less vulnerable girls to be preyed upon.

"All of my work is meant to say: 'You may encounter many defeats but you must not be defeated.' In fact, the encountering may be the very experience which creates the vitality and the power to endure."

– MAYA ANGELOU

"Systematic change has got to happen so that women and girls are not just there as objects or commodities. When they talk about legalizing prostitution, they very often compare us to alcohol. They say, 'Oh, look at prohibition. Alcohol was illegal and look at it now.' The problem with that is that alcohol gets abused and then it gets urinated out somewhere. And what happens to the woman when she gets abused? The legalization thing says to me, well they'll just put a band around her neck or something and say '99 percent pure' because she's had her vagina checked — and then you'll market her and you'll traffic her and then that makes it okay. It really oversimplifies a very complex issue, and it totally objectifies women. If women get abused, what is there then? Where are the services for her, what does she need? We've never had services for prostitutes. We've only put them in jail. And like you were saying, when I got out of jail, all I thought was that I was a criminal and a bad person. Nobody in forty years ever asked me about my life."

Laurie: "When I was on the streets on Christmas Eve, the look that chilled my blood was the look from a woman. A woman in a Jaguar, on her way to, you know, her family's big dinner. It wasn't necessarily that the men would look at you as if you were so disgusting, but other women. Women who had never had that experience would look down on you. That was the look that would make me cringe."

Norma: "And how many in here need to get their GED? [Show of hands — about half of the twenty participants raise their hands.] This is after seventeen or twenty-four years of prostitution, and the rapes, the beatings, the kidnappings, the being left for dead — and then at forty-five or so, needing to get your GED. And your first job ever. And learning how to live with people, how to pay rent, how to build a social support system, how to have healthy relationships. It's going to take a long time. . . . I was incested throughout my whole childhood. And then when I started developing behavioral problems, they said *I* was the problem. But I don't have any shame about that. Who should have shame are the ones who are incesting our children. . . . Who are the ones who are making the laws? People who, at the very least, don't care about women and girls."

Ben: "In my work, part of what I do is working with men who have really deeply numbed themselves. You know, do what you've got to do to protect yourself from pain. All the control stuff that's going on — and yeah, it's mostly getting acted out through men, for several thousand years, I wouldn't argue with that. And yet, the thing that's going to change it, if anything will change it, is people opening their hearts. So what I wanted to say is that most men I've seen who are real addicted to that male domination control thing — and it's not only control of women, it's control of other men, too — when even men like that go really deep into their healing, they don't need ter-rified women, they need strong women. That's real. I've seen that's true over here. That's really a big service to the whole human race, not only to your sisters, to be doing these things you're doing."

Susan: "That's a beautiful statement that 'They don't need terrified women, they need strong women.' For all these years, women have been co-ing [co-dependent] this stuff, putting up with this stuff. And we really have to start putting our feet down. And that's when this will change. And that's what I mean, by the women driving by in their Jag-uars. These are the women who need to start getting it together, doing some work with us, and finding out that we're people, that we're women just like them. These are the women who could really change it for us, because they're already in there, they've already achieved, they had a somewhat decent up-bringing, or they struggled through somehow, they made it. If we could just get some of these types of women to come with us and help us with this thing. That's some-thing we need. Women high up in the big buildings. These are the women we need to educate. To let them know that we're WOMEN."

Meerin: "When I first got here, I thought I would never have a job. And I have a job today. I think there are many forms of prostitution. I think that some of these women who are in the Jaguar married that man for that money — and not for who that man really was."

Unidentified: "And people who can't read need help. People who don't even know they can do it until they get people pushing them, helping them. I was one of those people. And I read something the other day. I'm at a third-grade level. Every day now I got a book in my hand."

Meerin: "What was said before about the different kinds of prostitution — when I stopped prostituting for money, I prostituted in other ways. I think that recognizing behavior patterns around what is internalized in women as children and continues . . . maybe you get married, maybe you work the streets. There's this service orientation of women. And what we get back from that, there's something we have to clear up in our brains, because we are made to be nurturers and we are made to be strong. And we need to recognize that will only come from loving ourselves and other women . . . when I did that, and then I loved the blessed mother and I loved all the saints and I loved the nuns I used to hate and I brought that back to myself . . . I didn't receive my GED until I was thirty-seven. And I'm in graduate school. And I have a degree in acupuncture. And I will probably go to law school. And I'm fifty-one."

Laurie: "So hopefully when the media looks at us they will show that we are survivors, not just see prostitutes. They'll also be able to see that we are the survivors of this destruction."

Norma: "I think that it's amazing that the world hasn't even figured out how to deal with us, except to put us in jail. Around this room, we're doing this from a girlfriend-to-girlfriend kind of healing, and I think that's very powerful. What's really helped me is to learn to love others. It's why I'm here. It's my air. Just look at these incredible women — who's luckier on this planet than me, sitting in this circle?"

When she testified to the United Nations in 2000, Norma pointed out that 90 percent of the SAGE clients had experienced sexual abuse. Some 82 percent had been assaulted, and 84 percent had been homeless. Because the abuse and prostitution often begin at an early age, Norma now is trying to focus more on prevention and early intervention. "Even though most of the girls we deal with have already been sexually assaulted or have sexual abuse in their backgrounds," she explained, "getting to them early will help them not go into drugs as heavily as we did, and they won't be cycled through the adult criminal justice system.

"If I am not for myself, who will be for me? And if I am only for myself, what am I? And if not now — when?"

— HILLEL

"When a girl is exploited, she has the symptoms of low self-confidence, depression, post-traumatic stress disorder, then she goes to school and she can't study, she is disorganized in her thoughts, angry, and maybe acting out, disheveled, yet she often gets treated as if *she's* a *problem*, rather than given a chance to recover. She becomes the target for people who target vulnerable children. Lots of times, it starts with a date rape or boys who target girls who are emotionally needy, who don't have confidence or self-esteem. We are working in the schools with boys and girls," she said. "I really feel the boys need re-education or better education on lots of issues, including gender equality."

But after more than a dozen years working on the issue of prostitution, Norma sees progress in a few areas. A state law she helped promote requires that men arrested for trying to buy sex from prostitutes not only have to pay a fine that helps pay for the hookers' remediation, but they also have to attend a class for "Johns" about responsible sex. She also has influenced international efforts to crack down on child prostitution around the world. Dealing with international prostitution of women is difficult because of entrenched macho attitudes in many countries, she said, but dealing with sexual exploitation of children is more approachable because most countries do consider that taboo. In Thailand, for example, life sentences are now being ordered for men caught buying sex from children who have been forced into prostitution. "This is really the direction we need to move in," Norma says.

There also is a need to put curriculum in place that teaches mutual respect between boys and girls, she said, "because the boys don't know how to deal with women who are equal. Even in domestic violence, we really are not going to be successful until we have women and men saying, 'I am not protecting you anymore, I'm teaching my sons that it is not okay to be a trick, it is not good for them, not a wink-and-nod gentleman's agreement.' It hurts everyone. I think everyone needs to start talking about what it means to have a relationship where you really have intimacy and meaning and depth and equality."

Toward that end, Norma now has men as well as women on her SAGE board. "The men now work so hard for our organization as well as the women, and that's the way it should be. Those men who are Johns have sons, and those men have daughters. Their involvement in prostitution is taking them away from their families and making liars out of them. You can't really be a good role model for your son or you can't really have a good relationship with your seventeen-year-old daughter when you are picking up seventeen-year-olds on the street. It is impossible. We are not paying enough attention to our sons and daughters in our communities," she says. She tells the men in the "John" education classes, "If you have all this extra time to cruise the street, then you need to get involved with your community. If you sit in the chair and complain about the drug addicts and the homeless, look what you're doing. You are one of the people who thinks you're good and yet you're doing really bad things."

A lot of people who hear Norma speak tell her, "I'm just one person, what can I do?" And she shoots right back, "Well, I'm just one person, look what I've done! Get off your asses. You have a responsibility. If you're taking up space in this world, then you're either part of the problem or you are part of the solution. There are no compromises in that."

Those she doesn't offend become devoted volunteers, helping find clothing for the girls and women who often are brought in with only the clothes on their backs, and not much of that. The foundation is in constant need of new sweatshirts and socks and underwear and jeans and tennis shoes. She's also trying to do more fund-raising to replicate the SAGE model in other cities, such as Washington, D.C.

"It is incredibly hard work," she admits, "But I believe that I have been spared for a reason. This is my calling. It is such a phenomenal opportunity that I just feel really blessed to have this opportunity to make such a difference in my lifetime."

Although she does not belong to any

particular denomination, the evidence of Norma's own spiritual generosity is all around her. SAGE helps transport women to church and encourages the different spiritual celebrations at the foundation. Sometimes the women want to sing hymns together, which helps them through their recovery. That's not Norma's thing, as she says, but she is understanding, saying "There is a spiritual path for us all. . . . I believe we are all connected, that there is a higher being."

She often tells people who want to work with SAGE, "We are all connected — all of us. If you feel like learning to be with somebody with a totally open heart and unconditional love, this is a place for you to work. But if you feel you have to judge and confront and challenge and look down on others, then I'm sure you can find somewhere else to work. This isn't it. But if you really think that you benefit in this lifetime by opening your heart more and more, this is the perfect place to work."

When she is asked how she handles the emotional strain of dealing with subjects that are taboo, secret, dark, and violent, she says, it is more energizing than depressing. "We do the work that other people can't do. And because we do it, we

> "Difficulty, my brethren, is the nurse of greatness. A harsh nurse, who roughly rocks her foster children into strength and athletic proportion."
>
> — WILLIAM CULLEN BRYANT

help create a world that is safer and healthier. We used to be the tossaways in many places, where people would say, 'Who cares if they die? We don't care what her name is. Put Jane Doe on her pine box. She is nobody. We're glad she's gone.' But it is a good thing we're here."

Norma says she is not a church member because her mother and grandmother weren't. But she probably also did not feel particularly welcome in church circles as a woman with a "history." Leanne Riley, who also slid into prostitution, has had a different experience. She was embraced by a church that is befriending women in the sex trade. She says her dad was an alcoholic and moved her family around all the time. She was raised in church and had an early grasp of faith, but fell into a self-destructive pattern. She was a single mom by the age of twenty. She had to work four jobs to keep her apartment and vehicle, but ended up in the Family Gateway shelter with a four-month-old baby. Desperate for money, she went to work as an exotic dancer in an "adult" club. She was making $1,000 a week and thought that was the greatest thing in the world. But before she knew it, eleven years later she was an alcoholic, addicted to drugs, and a prostitute.

"You lose little pieces of your morality night by night," she recalls now. "Because you see other women doing things, you slide into it, too, as time goes on, because you become desensitized." The customers were of all ages and professions. Some were in their early twenties and into the sleazy thrill of lap-dancing and boozy sex. Some of the older ones just wanted somebody to talk to, Leanne says, so they would pay her by the hour to talk to her. Just by listening, she says, she made them "feel special and cared about." Yet most nights she sold herself for grinding sex. It was so painful doing what she was doing, she says, she began using drugs to "medicate the pain from all I was doing there." She anesthetized herself with speed and cocaine, which was easy to get at any of the clubs. She knew "this is not the way I want to live," but she did not know a way out. She started going back to church without telling anyone what she did for a living. "I had no self-esteem," she recalls. "I did not feel worthy to go into the doors. I just knew if they knew what I had done, they would not have anything to do with me."

One Sunday morning, she was feeling low as she returned to her car in the parking lot, thinking she would not go back because it was too painful. Then a woman she had glimpsed a few times at the church spoke to her in the parking lot. She told Leanne that she had felt drawn to speak to her. "I don't know who you are, but God has placed you in my heart," she said. Leanne blurted out that she was a dancer and a prostitute. "I figured I would never hear from her again. But she just said, 'I still love you.'" It taught Leanne that "even if you can't do anything else, you can be alert to people who are hurting."

She began attending the church and became one of the first participants in "Amy's Friends," an outreach program started by a former topless dancer named Amy to help other dancers. Now called "New Friends," the women-to-women program has been shepherded by the Preston Road Church of Christ in Dallas. New Friends provides a wide range of assistance to women who want to leave sexually oriented businesses. Women who agree to do their part can receive living expenses, medical assistance, counseling, and job training during a transition period.

Leanne earned her GED, went to work for an auto parts dealer, and got custody of her three children back. She's now thirty and working with New Friends full-time, counseling other "protégés." She is also taking classes at El Centro Community College — and making straight As. Carolyn Pool, the executive director at New Friends, says, Leanne gets an A at work, as well.

Since the faith-based program was started in 1998, it has helped more than sixty women and girls. A big part of that success is due to the spiritual direction that the program encourages. The protégés attend a Wednesday night spiritual group, where they are encouraged to read the Gospel books of the New Testament. "It's not heavy-handed," Mrs. Pool says. "They just say here's how Jesus lived and here's the way he treated people — and that's pretty good." Leanne nodded her head in agreement: "It's the way anyone would want to be treated."

Few churches have similar outreach ministries. Sexuality is still a sensitive area in most churches. Ministers like Mark Craig, who pastors the Highland Park United Methodist Church in one of the most affluent areas of Dallas, bluntly tells his congregation that most of his time is spent dealing with problems in families created by the "three As" — adultery, alcoholism, and absenteeism. You can see a lot of squirming in the pews when he names the problems. Yet Americans still seem inhibited about talking about the sexual urges that are among the most powerful drivers of human behavior. We still are reluctant to face the untouchables in our society, the hookers with the Fu Manchu nails and platform shoes, the teen runaways with the tattoos, the prison parolees without high school degrees.

Not everyone has the harsh circumstances that Norma Hotaling and Leanne Riley faced, but everyone has hurdles to overcome. Their stories invite us to ask ourselves how we would react if a former prostitute joined our Sunday School class. Would we be judgmental or loving? When you

> "Some steps must be taken defiantly, against the grain. There is no growth without a bursting, without pain; primitive peoples in their wisdom place pain at the center of initiation."
>
> — NOVELIST JOHN UPDIKE

come right down to it, we are all misfits until proven otherwise. Redemption comes in many sizes.

One of the best things women can do is take the word *failure* out of their vocabulary. Do that for yourself and for your friends. Since women today live as much as twenty to thirty years longer than women a century ago, there are many more experiences to try, more careers to begin, more relationships, more difficulties, more false starts, more lessons learned. If you make them teaching moments, they can be valuable experiences, not failures.

Actress Jane Fonda, now in her sixties, had the added difficulty of having her learning played out in the tabloids. As it turned out, the easy part was the acting. The tough part was unscripted. Many American women thought they knew Jane Fonda from her movies, where they saw her evolve on the big screen: from her ingénue role as a wide-eyed cheerleader in *Tall Story* with Tony Perkins . . . to the honeymooner in *Barefoot in the Park* . . . to the interstellar sex kitten *Barbarella* . . . to the chastened daughter in *On Golden Pond* . . . to one of the girls in *9 to 5* . . . and a maturing woman in *Stanley and Iris*.

Her off-screen roles have been talked

about as much as her cinematic turns. Her father was the emotionally distant Henry Fonda and her mother, Frances Brokaw, cut her own throat when Jane was twelve. When Jane was in Lee Strasburg's acting class in New York with Marilyn Monroe, Jane was too shy to ask a question. She sought intimacy in a series of marriages — first French director Roger Vadim, then activist Tom Hayden, then cable millionaire Ted Turner. She wanted to make a serious contribution by visiting Vietnam to protest the war but was vilified instead for being unpatriotic. She sought physical perfection with rigorous exercise tapes that became a national craze, but eventually she was too burnt-out to exercise again.

Does she have regrets? Sure. Mostly that she posed for photos with the Vietcong with an antiaircraft gun. She has publicly apologized to the American people for that misjudgment.

Has she found what she has been looking for? Yes. As Jane told Oprah Winfrey in an interview in *O* magazine, she grew up in a nonreligious environment, but wanted as a child to go to church on Christmas Eve. For many years, she felt guided somehow. Then she heard Bill Moyers say, "Coincidence is God's way of remaining anonymous." She realized that she had been feeling a spiritual tug. She began praying, and felt the presence of God. She started attending church, often at a predominantly black church in Atlanta. And she took on the mission of improving the lives of inner-city girls by leading the Georgia Campaign for Adolescent Pregnancy Prevention. Jane often has helped with fund-raisers for GCAPP, contributing her own wildflower photos for auctions, and has successfully lobbied the state to pay for a home for unwed mothers.

Jane sees her evolution as a process of finding her authentic voice. That's why she has donated $12.5 million for a gender center at Harvard to help find out why cultural sex roles distort learning for girls and boys. The idea is to find out why more boys end up on Ritalin and why middle-school girls stop speaking up in class after they go through puberty. That's the kind of research pioneered by Carol Gilligan in her hallmark book *In a Different Voice*, which established the notion that girls start out eager at the age of nine and lose self-confidence by age thirteen, as they hear messages to be docile and look for a man. At the same time, boys are taught that repressing their emotions is manly and strong.

"I don't think women suffer any more than men do," Jane told one reporter. "In some ways I think men suffer more. The damage done to boys and men as a result of these gender strictures is very profound."

Tennis player Zina Garrison had to overcome the sexism in sports as well as the racism in the world to find her voice. She grew up a shy, insecure girl in an all-black neighborhood in Houston. She willed her way to the top of the mostly white tennis world. It wasn't easy. But she believed God would help her during the lonely and tough moments.

Garrison began as a postman's daughter. She went on to win the Olympic gold medal in doubles with Pam Shriver in 1988 and became one of the top-ranked players in the world. How did she do it? You get a clue when you call and get her recorded message of "God bless you" and a list of numbers where she might be reached if you are lucky. She used to include a scripture verse until so many people called to listen, it jammed her machine. She has been very public in giving

"If you give in to intimidation, you'll go on being intimidated."

— AUN SAN SUI KYI

God the credit for giving her a victorious drive: "It didn't matter to me that tennis was not the game of choice among people in my neighborhood, and I didn't care how many barriers were put in my way. With the Lord's help, I knew I'd find a way to overcome them all."

Her foundation came from her grandmother, who took her to church at Jones Memorial United Methodist Church in Houston. "I learned very early about having a relationship with God," she says. But it was not until her divorce that she understood how God was there for her no matter what. The crowds may have been cheering for her on the court, but she got more comfort from praying alone. "Lots of times people say to me, was your divorce the worst thing that ever happened? And I say it was the best thing that ever happened. It was when I truly understood my relationship with God. All the things I have gone through, good and bad, having faith and knowing that there was something better on the other side, was what got me through." Faith has helped her conquer a fear of flying and deal with bulimia. She had always been self-conscious about having a "basketball butt" that didn't look like the trim white players. But she was to learn that eating disorders are about control as much as appearances; food intake was one of the few things she felt she could control. "It's still a learning experience day to day," she says. "but I know he is always there."

Her first coach was a former cotton picker who taught her how to hit a strong backhand. He encouraged her to read *The Autobiography of Malcolm X*. She also benefited from legendary athletes like Althea Gibson and Arthur Ashe, the first black players to win Grand Slam titles. It was thirty years after Althea broke the tennis color barrier in the 1950s that Zina came along and broke barriers of her own. Now the next generation of stars, Venus and Serena Williams, say they were motivated by watching Zina on television.

Today Zina spends most of her time trying to pass along her blessings by mentoring other young players. Her outreach started when she literally tripped over a homeless person in San Francisco and was moved to collect blankets for people living on the streets. That led her to begin collecting tennis shoes for the needy when she was back in Houston, and eventually to create a foundation to contribute money to the homeless shelter in Houston.

Once she got the feel for philanthropy, she started the Zina Garrison All-Star Tennis Program for inner-city youngsters. Thanks to her fund-raising and coaching, hundreds of low-income children have gotten a boost in self-esteem and a game for life.

"I've always felt that in some way I was meant to minister to a large number of people," she said. "I've been very fortunate. Being a role model is an honor. The burden comes when people only see the image and don't want to allow you to be the person you really are. You have to be the same person on the court and off the court. That's when you get into trouble, when they are two different people."

She had just gotten back to Houston from coaching the U.S. Fed Cup team in Florida when we talked late one weeknight. Her team had lost. She said she was tired and needed time to sink into the comfort of her own home, but she wasn't going to dwell on the loss. At thirty-nine, she's learned that being a winner means you have to understand losing is part of the game. And move on.

Tennis colleague Billy Jean King, who has coached Olympic teams with Zina, says she admires her unshakeable faith. "She continues to move forward," Billy

Jean once wrote, "eager to confront new challenges and determined to grow as a human being. I'm convinced that her best years are yet to come."

If you have something to overcome, keep in mind some advice from Gene Roddenberry, the creator of *Star Trek*. He said, "You go the direction you look." I think he was talking about outer space, but it is true about inner space as well. The secret of overcoming is not to look back or look down. Look up and look forward. That's the direction you will go.

TAKE HOME:

God often uses unusual people to do some of his best work. The Catholic Worker movement — which is grounded in the belief of the God-given dignity of every human person — was cofounded in 1933 by Dorothy Day, a bohemian journalist who had a child out of wedlock. Her cofounder was Peter Maurin, an itinerant French scholar and illegal immigrant. Today, more than 175 Catholic Worker communities remain. They are committed to nonviolence, voluntary poverty, prayer, and hospitality for the homeless, exiled, hungry, and forsaken. Their movement — which provided the template for many nonprofit organizations to follow — drew its inspiration from the teachings of Jesus, especially the Sermon on the Mount and the social encyclicals of the modern popes, to bring about a "new society within the shell of the old, a society in which it will be easier to be good."

Dorothy was the epitome of a New York Leftist. She wrote for Socialist publications like *The Call* and *The Masses*, which was closed by the U.S. Attorney General during the Red Scare after World War I. She was jailed for picketing President Woodrow Wilson's White House for the women's vote. She participated in a hunger strike at Occoquah Prison. Her friends were socialists, anarchists, Communists, and labor organizers who despaired about the inequities of wealth in pre-depression days. Her life in those days was pushing the status quo intellectually and personally — by her own description, her lifestyle was dissolute, wasted, and full of sensuality. Yet she had been haunted by God during this time. She had gone to church as a young girl and sang in the choir. She felt the tug to return and began attending Mass while she was living with a biologist who she deeply loved. He vehemently opposed religion. Her budding faith strained their relationship. She became pregnant. He opposed children as well as marriage, and the relationship was torn apart. Dorothy transcended that experience by having the baby girl baptized into the Roman Catholic Church, where she proceeded to spend the rest of her life helping others.

Over the years, hundreds of thousands were fed in the "no questions asked" soup kitchens Dorothy helped establish in New York and around the country. Her favorite saint was Therese of Liseux, a Carmelite nun who taught that the "little way" — endowing humble daily acts with love — was the path to holiness. Dorothy wrote prodigiously and founded the *Catholic Worker* newspaper, which grew to a circulation of 100,000 and became a forum for asking persistent questions such as:

"Why are there so many poor and abandoned?"

"What is honest work?"

"What is due workers and the unemployed?"

"What is the relationship between political, social, and economic democracy — and between these and the common good?"

"Just where are we, where do we want to be and how can we get there?"

"What of means and end?"

"What does it mean to follow Jesus Christ today?"

Those questions are still meaningful today. Though she was at times considered a radical, the spiritual journey of Dorothy Day is illuminating. Her classic autobiography, *The Long Loneliness*, is still being read as a beautifully written testimonial to the power of faith. Her words spring off the page with feeling:

> *"Let us pray that we do not hear our Lord call out to us, 'Woe unto you rich!' 'Woe unto you who judge!'"*

> *"One of the saddest and sorriest things about poverty is the envy, hatred, venom, and despair suffered by the poor. It is part of their suffering."*

> *"There is that which is of God in every man, as the Quakers say. We believe that we are all members or potential members of the mystical body of Christ, members of one another as St. Paul said. We are all one body in Christ. St. Peter himself said that St. Paul was hard to understand, but the I.W.W. [Industrial Workers of the World] understood this particular doctrine*

when they said, 'an injury to one is an injury to all,' with beautiful simplicity."

Dorothy Day was a lifelong pacifist who opposed wars from the Spanish Civil War to the Vietnam War. She opposed racism and supported the Rev. Martin Luther King Jr. She met with Mother Teresa and protested migrant labor conditions with Cesar Chavez — at seventy-six she was arrested and jailed for ten days for supporting the striking farm workers in California. She was controversial most of her long life. She was shot at and investigated by the FBI. Somehow she integrated her radical social positions with conservative piety. When she died on November 29, 1980, it was reported that so many people attended her funeral in New York, that many had to stand on the

> "We have all probably noted those sudden moments of quiet — those strange and almost miraculous moments in the life of a big city when there is a cessation of traffic noises — just an instant when there is only the sound of footsteps which serves to emphasize a sudden peace. During those seconds it is possible to notice the sunlight, to notice our fellow humans, to take breath."
>
> — DOROTHY DAY

sidewalk outside the Nativity Church.

Her cause for canonization was introduced in 2000 by Cardinal John J. O'Connor, who considered her (among other things) a model for women who have had or considered an abortion. Dorothy once had an abortion, regretted it deeply, and subsequently had a daughter Tamar Teresa, who was baptized and brought up in the church.

NINE

Giving

"This is what you shall do: Love the earth and sun and the animals, despise riches, give alms to everyone that asks, stand up for the stupid and crazy, devote your income and labor to others, hate tyrants, argue not concerning God . . ."

— WALT WHITMAN

God calls us to give as long as we live. There is no magic age at which we put aside our soul work and stop giving. So long as there are needs to be met, believers are called to help however they can. That process doesn't end at fifty or sixty. Or even eighty. During the first half of our lives, we usually seek the good life. In the second half, we try to make our lives good for something. We give back. That's because as you mature, you begin to understand the meaning of your story. And you feel the urge to pass on what you have learned or earned to the next generation. Our lives gain more of the very meaning we have been seeking as we pass along those blessings to others, full circle.

The journey of Marty Evans, from the U.S. Navy to the Girl Scouts to the American Red Cross, shows what can happen to enrich your own life when you start giving back. We first met at the Women's Philanthropy Institute, where we appeared on a panel discussion. Marty spoke last. And stole the show. No one could compete with her riveting description of how two airplane flights — in the same day — changed her life. She explained that in 1994 she was flying from Andrews Air Force Base to Pensacola, Florida, at the controls of a seven-passenger military plane. "All of a sudden, all hell broke loose in the cabin," she recalls. "There were loud sirens going off. My oxygen mask did not descend." Someone handed her an oxygen pack like the firefighters wear. It wouldn't open. The plane was dropping thousands of feet. She pried open the oxygen pack with a screwdriver and struggled to stabilize the plane.

"When you are falling out of the air, it is one of the most frightening sensations. It feels like an elevator out of control. I was getting a little woozy because we'd lost the oxygen in the compartment. The adrenaline starts flowing when you realize you are going down; the heart starts racing. The sensation of time is intense. In less than a minute and a half, the plane had gone from an altitude of 41,000 feet to 10,000 feet. Even though I was woozy, you can think about a million things during the short period of actual time. I immediately thought of my husband and were we on good terms? We were, but how good? And I thought, *If this is it, how am I going to be remembered?* I guess I'm egocentric, but those were the two predominant thoughts I had. My husband and I are very particular about not parting with any venom. If we have any disagreement, we will take the time to figure it out even if it means missing a plane. So I felt pretty good there, but then there was still the other question: Have I done enough with my life? Again, I was pretty satisfied with what I had achieved, but I knew it wasn't my real potential. I was a two-star admiral in the Navy, but why wasn't I head of the Navy? Did I do all I was supposed to have done? That was the theme of my thinking while I was trying to get the plane down safely. You do the accounting of your life. Was it good enough? Was my life ready to be tallied up? Was there more to give?"

Somehow, Marty piloted the twin-engine plane to safety. It was a small utility jet that the Navy Marine Corps use to ferry senior people from place to place. Every seat was full with her closest staff members. When they landed, she was still hyperventilating. She was informed that another plane was being made ready, so they could go on to Pensacola. "Oh sure," she said, trying to be calm and appear confident. But after they took off again, the cabin began filling with smoke. She thought, "Oh no, this is unbelievable!" The rest of the crew was surprised as well. A broken seal in the air-conditioning system was allowing jet exhaust to flow into the cabin. She did a 180-degree turn and made another emergency landing at Andrews Air Force Base. After two heart-pounding emergency landings in one day, she thought, *I don't think I want to go to Pensacola anymore*. When she got to the parking lot, she was so drained, she says, "I didn't have enough muscle tension to hold on to the steering wheel. So I just sat there a few minutes while I tried to regain my strength." She made it back to her office at the Pentagon and continued working.

That's the kind of determination that helped Marty Evans rise to the upper ranks of the U.S. Navy, only the second woman to become a rear admiral. It's also the kind of dedication that caused her to leave to help others. She retired from the Navy after twenty-nine years to become National Executive Officer of the Girl Scouts of the USA in 1998. After she took the helm of Scouting, the organization grew steadily. Adult volunteers increased to an all-time high — nearly one million. Membership grew to 2.8 million girls. But 50,000 girls were on waiting lists, so she criss-crossed the country, week after week, calling for more leaders and more scholarships. Her new mission in life was to make the benefits of Scouting available to all girls — poor inner-city girls as well as comfortable suburban girls, girls whose mothers are in prison as well as girls whose mothers are in corporate offices.

How did she go from Pentagon insider to National Den Mother? She hadn't thought of leaving the Navy after her jet plunge; she still had six more years of potential service. But she continued mulling her life's work. When a search firm contacted her, she was intrigued by the idea of leading the Scout organization. She was well aware of the problems facing young women today because she had spent much of her career increasing opportunities for women in the military. She had served as head of the Navy's worldwide recruiting and as chief of staff for the U.S. Naval Academy in Annapolis. She knew that teenaged pregnancy and the high drop-out rate in schools were seriously affecting the ability of the military to recruit qualified women. "I saw how many were derailed. I knew I wanted to do something."

The tradition of service ran in her family. Her dad was a career chief petty officer. When she graduated from Occidental College in Los Angeles, she had a Phi Beta Kappa key and two graduate school acceptances. She was weighing which graduate program to choose when she decided on the spur of the moment, to join the Navy. Joining the Navy meant she could go to graduate school with G.I. Bill assistance. Thanks to that military support, she completed her graduate studies at the prestigious Fletcher School of Law and Diplomacy at Tufts University. And she was able to travel the world with her Navy assignments to San Diego, San Francisco, London, and Tokyo. Along the way, she met and married her husband, Jerry Evans, a Navy pilot. It was a challenging, full life, but when the Scouting offer came, it felt right to Marty. She had been a Girl Scout herself from the second to ninth grades.

She knew that girls learned more in Scouting than how to make "The Ask" for cookies. They learned survival skills for life. So she left the Navy and went to work teaching girls self-confidence.

"I can see now it was a brilliant match," she told me four years later. The job answered her yearning to make a difference because it offered so much potential for profound change. "When you see the things that affect these girls in such a negative way from such an early age, you start thinking about what to do to intervene. We now are taking Scouting to juvenile detention centers. We have Scouting for girls whose mothers are in prisons. Even in the suburbs where girls have relative advantages, there are still serious issues they are struggling with. We can change the course of history if we can get it right."

"The greatest good you can do for others is not just to share your riches but to reveal to them their own."

— BENJAMIN DISRAELI

By 2002, there were twenty-seven Scouting programs in prisons, and Marty Evans was seeking grants to expand. She explained, "The vast majority of female prisoners used drugs immediately before they were incarcerated. We have the wonderful opportunity to intervene and stop the generational cycle. The women who participate have programs on parenting and self-esteem. The girls go to the prison twice a month and do work on their badges with their mothers. The mothers have to stay infraction-free to stay in the program, so there is an incentive to be a model prisoner."

Finding adult volunteers to lead troops is the number one limitation for Scouting, Marty said. To fill the gap, councils are seeking nontraditional volunteers, such as women who do not have children of their own or young women who have just graduated from college. Girl Scouts is now partnering with other organizations — such as the Junior League and sororities — to find helpers. To make the task easier, she said, volunteers are not asked to commit for a troop meeting every week, but instead might be asked to help on a Saturday for a special program or to serve as a mentor. Likewise, she was seeking a broader base for funding. The Thin Mints and Samoa cookies don't cover all the costs of handbooks, uniforms, and camp equipment, so she's knocking on the doors of foundations as well as individuals who might remember the needs of girls in their wills and bequests.

Most of the changes she implemented were well received — like trading in the un-cool green uniforms for something more updated in a softer gray-green. Still, Marty Evans often had her hands full handling controversies that predated her — questions persisted about the decision in 1996 to make belief in God optional in the Girl Scout promise. ("On my honor, I will try: To serve God and my country to help people at all times and to live by the Girl Scout Law.") Marty explained that God was not dropped from the pledge, as some contended. She said the organization still believes that there is a spiritual basis to life, but had to recognize that "there is a diversity of spiritual views, from Shinto to Buddhism to Protestant, Catholic, Jewish, and so on" in its membership. So a footnote was added to the promise advising that a girl, in concert with her parents, could decide on the expression of God that she would personally make. Because that flexibility was added and because girls were encouraged to work out their personal beliefs with their parents, the Girl Scouts avoided the same kind of controversy and court suits that have plagued the Boy Scouts, who have kept the pledge to God obligatory.

The Girl Scouts also have avoided controversy over the issue of homosexuality by having very strict, specific standards of behavior that prohibit overt displays of sexual behavior, whether heterosexual or homosexual. "We treat it as a behavior issue, not a sexuality issue," Marty explains. "If a girl has a question about sexuality, it is not generally the role of the leader to deal with those issues. She should talk to her parents."

So Scouting has been trying to keep its core values while evolving to meet post-modern needs in a new century. There is now a "Domestic Violence Awareness" badge as well as badges for stress management and a "Decisions for Life" badge relating to teen pregnancy. The girls learn how demanding caring for a child can be by carrying around a raw egg for a week. (They can't part with the egg or allow it to be broken.)

Back in 1912, the first Scouts learned how to tie a burglar up with eight inches of rope. Today, girls can earn "Ms. Fix-It" badges for learning how to fix a leak, rewire an appliance, or re-caulk a window. They can earn a "Car Care" badge by checking fluids and filling tires to proper pressure. There's even a "Ms. President" badge to teach about women leaders and community matters.

As the public service ads proclaim, it's not your mother's Scouting. But then it's not your mother's world. As the Senior Scout resource book advises about eating disorders, "One fifth of the girls have used diet pills. More than one in six have forced themselves to vomit, and half have skipped a meal in order to lose weight."

While critics have complained the Girl Scouts have become too "politically correct," the truth is the Scouts are having to deal with problems that schools and dysfunctional families are not.

෬ **Sexual abuse:** At least one in five girls and one in seven boys have been sexually abused by the age of eighteen, according to the most reliable studies of abuse in the United States.

෬ **Drug use:** Today's fifteen-year-olds are fifteen times more likely to use illegal drugs as their mothers were. Marijuana is the most popular illegal drug. According to the Centers for Disease Control, the number of teens who say they have tried cocaine has gone up from 5.9 percent in 1991 to 9.4 percent a decade later.

Date violence: Statistics from the National Coalition Against Domestic Violence show 25 percent of America's teenage girls have been or are in a violent relationship. That's one in four girls, compared with one in seven a few years ago.

Teenaged pregnancy: The rate of pregnancies has declined slightly, but the numbers and ages are still of concern. Some 900,000 teenaged girls become pregnant each year. For those in junior high, the father is usually 6.5 years older than the mother. When the mother is twelve years old or younger, the average age of the father is twenty-two. Most of those fathers abandon the "used" girls when they become pregnant. Figures compiled by the Centers for Disease Control in 2001 also showed that 46 percent of teens had tried sex.

Smoking: Some 30 percent of high school seniors smoke, an increase from the 26 percent in 1992.

Obesity: About 13 percent of children and adolescents are overweight or obese, according to the Centers for Disease Control, more than double the number two decades ago. Experts blame TV, computer games, lack of safe playgrounds, as well as more reliance on junk food for meals.

ॐ **Teen drinking:** At least a quarter of the teenagers who become pregnant were under the influence of drugs and alcohol. Binge drinking is on the rise among teens. According to the National Center on Addiction and Drug Abuse, 42 percent of the ninth-grade girls admitted drinking regularly, and 31 percent of the sophomores admitted binge drinking, drinking five drinks in a row.

"So many girls are affected by violence in families," Marty says. "Wherever there is spousal abuse, there is fallout for the children. And then there is drug abuse or alcoholic abuse on the part of the parents. Sometimes these girls are affected by two or three of those factors. If you can reach those kinds of behaviors, it is really astounding. You can choose not to do anything about those problems, or you can do something."

Her "do the right thing" ethic compelled her to do something. She grew up in the Baptist Church but has affiliated with the Presbyterian Church as an adult. She regularly attended the Marble Collegiate

Church, the church where Norman Vincent Peale used to preach, when she lived in Manhattan.

"When you face ethical dilemmas, where do you get the strength to navigate through some of those? Your faith," she says. "It's very important when you face family challenges. I grew up in an alcoholic home, so having a church and a strong youth group was very important to me. As an adult, I feel very gifted. Often I'm incredulous at the experiences and the opportunities I've had. Why me? I don't deserve it. I think having the opportunity to be centered in a guided process is really important. My mother always talked about not getting a swelled head and remembering to take time to reflect on what's important — relationships, trying to do the right thing, trying to model the right values. Fortunately, the Girl Scout Promise and Law are very consistent with the Judeo-Christian teachings I grew up with, so there's no cognitive dissonance."

Even though she traded in her military uniform for tailored suits, Marty still has the erect posture and perfect-polish look you would expect from a rear admiral. She has a bearing that invites respect. People approach her with awe. At fifty-four, she is trim, poised, and fit. When she's home, she's usually up at 5:30 a.m. to go for a power walk. To stay in shape and relax, she has taken up golf and Rollerblading with her husband. But she spends most of her time in airports and airplanes, working on her laptop, clipping news stories from newspapers.

Her travel schedule as head of the Girl Scouts was rigorous — one day she was at the White House with seventy-five girls as President Bush asked the Scouts to help raise donations for the children of Afghanistan. Another day she was in the California wine country honoring two high school seniors who were "gems of girls." She said later, "When I see what they're doing, the kinds of causes these sixteen-, seventeen-, and eighteen-year-olds are working on in the community, it's easy to have hope. Almost every week I get to go out to an event like that. There are some amazing things happening out there that make you believe that these women will grow up and be successful."

Marty is a strong believer in giving to future generations. "When I was growing up, people were kind to me — teachers, especially. We can never directly repay to people what they've done to help make us what we are. The only way we can repay is to pass it on. When my father was a young sailor in 1955, we had a family emergency. A woman officer helped him get through it and arranged his transportation home from a foreign country. Years later, I was able to write a speech for that officer. Those are favors you just sort of pass along. It's kind of exciting when you think about it. It's the chain of life."

With that philosophy, it was not a surprise that the American Red Cross recruited Marty to take over its top job in August 2002. The organization had been rocked with controversy about its administration of money raised for the victims of the September 11 attacks. The Red Cross had planned to use some of the donated money for other relief efforts, but was hammered by criticism. Bernadine Healy, the president at the time, was forced out by the charity's board in a dispute over policy. The board searched for five months for a successor who could right the troubled organization — and chose Marty Evans. If they wanted impeccable credentials, the board got it. If they wanted a disciplined manager, they got it. And if they wanted a serving heart, they got it. Marty in turn, got a heckuva challenge.

Reached on her last day of work at the Girl Scouts, she said she didn't look for the Red Cross; they looked for her, but it seemed a fitting segue. "I realized how many times my life had been touched by the Red Cross," she said. As a five-year-old, she had taken swimming lessons from the Red Cross, then as a college student she had worked as a lifeguard. When her family received word that her father had died, the news was delivered by the Red Cross. Later, when she was commanding officer of the Treasure Island Naval Station in San Francisco, she directed the Navy's response to the 1989 earthquake in the Bay Area, working alongside Red Cross staff and volunteers.

"The Red Cross has been there for my family, and I have every confidence they will be there when most needed," she said. As for the September 11 controversy, she said every organization has its ebbs and flows, but the fallout was a "Good reminder to everybody in the not-for-profit sector that we have to focus on credibility issues. What are the values of our organization, and do we daily live the values? How do people know? How do we manifest it?" She wouldn't be going to the Red Cross, she added, if she did not have a high level of confidence that the organization was already addressing the problems from September 11.

There are other daunting problems facing the agency — preserving the quality of blood supplies, addressing waves of need from floods and fires and earthquakes. But for those who had any doubts the agency could rebound, hiring Marty Evans ought to send a reassuring signal.

When asked why she would take on the challenge, which would mean more travel and more controversy, she said, "The answer is, quite simply, service."

Women have a long history of philanthropy to be proud of — Girl Scouting was started ninety years ago by Juliette Gordon Low, a Savannah socialite. She sold

"And as we pray, give us such an awareness of your mercies, that with truly thankful hearts we may show forth your praise, not only with our lips but in our lives, by giving up ourselves to your service."

– BOOK OF COMMON PRAYER

her pearls to keep the movement going. Sophie Smith gave the $400,000 that started Smith College. Jane Stanford sold off her jewelry to finish the construction of the first building at Stanford University. Women in Dallas banded together in 1985 to start the Women's Foundation because so few resources were going to help women.

Their examples raise the question, Do women have a special obligation to support programs benefiting other women and girls? Have women learned to take care of other women as well as guys do?

When the founders of *Ms.* magazine were trying to get funding in the mid-1970s, no lending institution would help them. They finally got a grant from the John K. Whitney Foundation — under the funding category of "powerlessness."

Around the country, less than 6 percent of philanthropic giving is specified for programs that benefit women and girls, including all the giving for women's colleges.

Yet the needs for women and girls are great and sometimes unique:

∾ Women comprise two-thirds of all poor people in the United States over eighteen.

∾ Seven out of ten low-income Medicare beneficiaries are women.

∾ More than 75 percent of working women earn less than $25,000 a year.

✺ Girls constitute 76 percent of all children murdered by abductors.

✺ One in four women will be battered during her lifetime. Family violence is the leading cause of injury to women age fifteen to forty-four.

✺ Nearly three-fourths of the elderly poor are women.

✺ More than 12 million women have no health insurance.

There are many ways to give — like they say in church, by offering your prayers, your gifts, your time, or your service. But believers are cautioned in 2 Samuel 24:24, "I will not sacrifice to the lord my God offerings which cost me nothing." We each have to ask ourselves what our faith really "costs" us. How does that relate to theologian Dietrich Bonhoeffer's warnings about "cheap grace" — a conversion that costs you nothing? Women are such great givers, giving care to their families, listening hearts to their friends, time to many causes. Faith asks us to give deeper still. And perhaps, in ways we never thought of before.

The prophet Isaiah answers people who ask why God does not heed their prayers and fasts. He reminds them of the "fast" that God desires of them. "It is to share your bread with the hungry and to take the wretched poor into your home; when you see the naked to clothe him, and not to ignore your own kin . . . If you banish the yoke from your midst, the menacing hand, and evil speech, and you offer your compassion to the hungry and satisfy the famished creature — then shall your light shine in darkness, and your gloom shall be like noonday."

— ISAIAH 58:7–10

After twenty-nine years in the investment field, Angela "Angie" Allen decided there must be more to life than making money. She founded a nonprofit enterprise in Atlanta to raise awareness in the business world about the value of contributing to the common good. She calls it "Full Circle Living," and at fifty-one, she is a prime example of someone who has found a way to merge her talents and her calling.

"We need to counter what Madison Avenue is telling us — 'you need to spend' — and what Wall Street is telling us — 'you need to accumulate' — with another voice telling us — 'you need to give.' We need to change the lens that we have been looking through. We need to change the way we measure ourselves and other people. We need to change the way we measure a successful life," Angie says. If that happens, she believes that more people will turn their talents to helping others.

To the outside world, she says, her previous life was a success. To her, it did not seem so. She started at the entry level in the investment business after college. That meant she spent long hours proving she was smart. Her career flourished, but her marriage to another up-and-comer did not. After fifteen years, they divorced. She now refers to those early years as "the gap," before she realized the need to compose a life based on the spiritual values she learned as a young girl in Catholic schools, rather than business goals. "I realize that I have lived my entire adult life in some kind of automatic pilot mode," she says. "I have devoted the vast majority of my time and effort to my career."

She had been CEO of GLOBALT, Inc., an investment firm that managed $2 billion in client assets. Today, her husband, Sam, runs the company while she convinces other business leaders to do good, not just do well. Her goal is to put more business brainpower into improving the environment and bridging the divide between the haves and the have-nots of the world. She says, "I think there are a lot of people that are just waiting to get involved in something bigger than themselves."

When she talks about "Full Circle," she means the logical progression of humans who move from infancy to adolescence to early adulthood to the wisdom of middle adulthood. "If we are developing in a healthy, mature way, our faith changes in stages as well. If we keep expanding — who we include, who we embrace, who we reach out to, and what we understand — then the ultimate would be a universalizing faith. Our circle would widen so everyone on earth would count as being our neighbor."

But "Full Circle" also describes how she came back around to the faith of her girlhood. Both of her parents were Italian immigrants, and her father was a strong authoritarian figure. Though her father only went to church at Easter, Angie dutifully attended Catholic schools. Her image of God was that of a very powerful, stern, old, male father. "The hierarchy of the Catholic Church was such that males maintained their superiority — from the

Pope down to the parish priest — over all females, including the nuns who taught us. I was supposed to accept this without questioning, and I think I did until the eighth grade, when I tied in the vote to elect our class president. The principal decreed that 'the boy' had to be the president — and that was that."

She kept trying to please others, attending Mass, making A's in school. But when she went away to college at seventeen to a very large public university, for all intents and purposes, she also left her girlhood faith as she experienced her first real personal freedom in college. She loved the all-night philosophical discussions. She loved reading Nietzche, Sartre, Rand, Vonnegutt, and Camus. She did not realize until later that this late-teen period was only "the illusion of enlightenment." She was still trying hard to be a "good girl" — she was president of her sorority and active in Campus Crusade for Christ. She was still striving for approval and a sense of worth, so she followed the pattern of the times — MBA, the corporate ladder climb, the Yuppie trappings of success, the designer suits, the designer cars. She admits, "Things get blown out of proportion in terms of what's important, what's ignored, or what's pushed to the sidelines. The things that are given short shrift are relationships."

She laughs now that the book *Bobos in Paradise* was "right on" about overachieving Yuppies who went from "Make Love Not War" in the 1960s to "Make Dough and Drink Chardonnay" in the 1990s. She explains, "What we've been trying to do in our generation is have it all and pretend. There have been a lot of charades going on. It started in the Woodstock era, and we thought just loving each other and not having trappings was the answer. Then we went completely in the other direction, wanting to keep the trappings and buy the spirituality back by renting a house in Montana in order to feel like people in Montana — but not in winter — by having a big house on the mountain and then coming down to have a beer with the real people." She laughs at the analogy, and it's clear she knows the laugh is on her, too.

Angie began turning full circle with her marriage to Sam Allen, who was also a successful investor. They went into business together and loved working together. They selected an Episcopal church to attend in Atlanta that was highly involved in community outreach and had a diverse congregation. What was still missing in her life became starkly apparent when she took a Christian course called "Dynamics of Identity and Faith," taught by Dr. Jim Fowler. It was a breakthrough for her. It tied her past to her future. She more deeply understood the need to integrate her faith into her living. She decided her new vocation would be orchestrating a way for her contemporaries to connect their business and faith circles.

> "Lots of people think they are charitable if they give away their old clothes and things they don't want."
>
> — MYRTLE REED

Though it's still in the formative stages, she hopes Full Circle Living will provide the coaching for others to "give back." There will be workshops and training for a personal stewardship portfolio. The idea is to be intentional about living your faith, so your time and resources improve the world.

Some of her former business colleagues have teased that she has merely experienced "Success Remorse." But Angie knows what she has experienced is something deeper, something more lasting. "I've been peeling off the layers that have been building up and covered what originally was true spirit, a spirit that had gotten sidetracked by what the world was telling me I should be pursuing. I realized that I need to be a conduit, not a hoarder."

So Angie is leaning into life in a different way. What she wants to create is a more faith-based context for business success that will humanize capitalism. Like many others, she is uncomfortable with the kind of wretched excess that has resulted in huge compensation packages for CEOs who slash and burn employees. "When things have gone in one direction so long, we all begin to think that's normal, it's standard, unless people speak up that it's out of control." She agrees that the epidemic of corporate scandals might have been a wake-up call for many in the business world to reevaluate their lives. "There is more of a sense that Rome is burning and I've got to do my part and quit fiddling."

Her advice for those struggling is to find a mentor who can guide you through the process of clarifying your beliefs. In her case, it was a Methodist minister who was also a psychological counselor specializing in transitions. "She was always a step ahead of me, guiding me through various stages of disengaging from my business and dealing with the disorientation of going from something you know to something new . . . over time we do grow, but it does require continuing to apply yourself and being intentional about it."

Angie's own faith is growing to include a deeper appreciation of other belief systems. At some point, she says, you realize that everyone in the commonwealth of mankind is a neighbor who counts as much to us as our close family members do. She's decided the future of the world is finding the right answer to the question: "How do we encounter and treat difference?" We can begin by asking how generous, how hospitable are we to those in our family circle — and how generous and hospitable do we treat those who are not?

"There are three kinds of giving: grudge giving, duty giving, and thanksgiving. Grudge giving says, 'I hate to.' Duty giving says, 'I ought to.' Thanksgiving says 'I want to.' The first comes from constraint, the second from a sense of obligation, the third from a full heart. Nothing much is conveyed in grudge giving since 'the gift without the giver is bare.' Something more happens in duty giving, but there is no song in it. Thanksgiving is an open gate into the love of God."

— ROBERT N. RODEMAYER

Crochety columnist Mike Royko used to grouse that the motto of Chicago ought to be "Ubi mea?" — Latin for "Where's mine?" Indeed, it could be the motto of my baby boomer generation, which began with great promise but might have set the record for spending money we don't have to buy things we don't need in order to impress people we don't know.

It is estimated that the largest intergenerational transfer of wealth in U.S. history will occur in the next two decades because the members of the post-depression/World War II generation were such careful savers. Some philanthropy experts say as much as $10 trillion will move from the elderly, who invested in homes and stock for decades, to their children, who are baby boomers. What will the Me Generation do with this opportunity? Will they begin thinking of their legacy? Will they see this as a last chance to make a more positive dent in their neighborhood and in the world?

One of my favorite movie scenes is from the 1982 movie *Year of Living Dangerously*, which was about the 1960s political turmoil in Indonesia. It's proved remarkably prescient since the archipelago is still in turmoil and considered a magnet for terrorist unrest. In the movie, Mel Gibson plays an Australian journalist who is being shown around town by a go-between named Billy Kwan, amazingly played by Linda Hunt. The journalist is moved by the poverty he sees around him and expresses concern. Billy reminds him that in Luke 3:10, the disciples ask Jesus, "What then shall we do?" The disciples are told to give away what they don't need. Billy adds that Russian novelist Leo Tolstoy was so impressed by the Scripture that he wrote a book with the same title. In fact, Tolstoy was so upset by the poverty in Moscow that he went to the poorest section of the city and gave away all his money to the people. "He later realized it wouldn't do any good. It was a drop in the bucket," Billy said. What to do then? Billy tells the journalist: "Don't think about the major issues. Do whatever you can about the misery in front of you. Add your light to the sum of light."

And Billy was right. Do what you can. No one can resolve all the complicated problems around us, but everyone can do something. The advice in the movie resonates today as inequalities between the developed and undeveloped countries grow more pronounced. There is a disconnect between the haves and the have-nots of the world as well as a clash of religious cultures.

As the *New York Times* columnist Thomas Friedman warns, if you don't visit the worst neighborhoods, they will visit you. There is a pressing need for people of faith to reach out to one another. The Habitat for Humanity effort is a shining example. Started by Atlanta businessman Millard Fuller and his wife, Linda, twenty-five years ago, Habitat has recruited thousands of volunteers from churches and corporations to build homes for the poor. They've provided shelter for more than 500,000 people in more than seventy countries. In Florida, Habitat has provided houses for migrant farm workers. In earthquake-ravaged El Salvador, Habitat has designed stable homes. In war-torn Northern Ireland, Habitat brought together Catholic and Protestant volunteers to build shelter for one another. That success shows you can make it a better world, one family at a time, one volunteer at a time, one brick at a time.

In recent years, many believers have

> "The only gift is a portion of thyself."
>
> — RALPH WALDO EMERSON

begun investing their money in funds with a moral purpose as a way of doing good while doing well. There are now several dozen religion-based mutual funds. The holdings are screened to avoid companies involved in such things as pornography, birth control, bombs, giving benefits to same-sex partners and charging interest on loans — the mix depends on the religious leaning. For example, the MMA Praxis Funds, following Anabaptist Christian ideals, does not hold the stock of military contractors. The Maria Catholic Fund follows Catholic principles and the Noah Fund follows evangelic preferences.

There also are commonsense ways to pass along blessings. Heifer International was started in the 1930s by a young Church of the Brethren youth worker named Dan West. He ladled out cups of milk to hungry children on both sides of the civil war in Spain in the 1930s. It occurred to him that what the families needed was "not a cup, but a cow." He asked his friends at home to donate heifers, a young cow that has not borne a calf, so hungry families could feed themselves. In return, the family could help another family become self-reliant by passing on to them one of their gift animal's female

Aisha, the wife of the Prophet Muhammad related: "A poor woman came to me along with her two daughters. I gave her three dates. She gave a date to each of them and then she took one date and brought it to her mouth in order to eat, but her daughters expressed desire to eat it. She then divided the date that she intended to eat between them. This (kind) treatment impressed me and I mentioned what she did to the holy Prophet Muhammad. Thereupon he said, 'Verily God has assured her Paradise because of this act.'"

calves. The idea of giving families a source of food rather than short-term relief caught on. Thanks to Heifer, families in 115 countries and thirty-five states have enjoyed better health and more income — and the joy of helping others. For as little as thirty dollars, donors can provide a beehive for someone to make honey or for ten dollars provide a rabbit that can produce a steady source of protein and income. Now headquartered in Little Rock, Heifer has been chosen by *Worth* magazine as one of the one hundred best charities in the United States. Though it is rooted in the Christian tradition, Heifer joins with people of faith everywhere to work for the dignity and well-being of all people.

Whether your calling is to act locally or globally, the answer is the same. You must add your light to the sum of light. Soon.

TAKE HOME:

How then shall we give? Again, Tolstoy, the great nineteenth-century Russian novelist, was once asked by a beggar for some coins. The novelist replied with regret, "My brother, it pains me deeply to tell you that I have nothing to give you." The poor man consoled him, "But you have already given me more than any other person. You have called me brother."

That is the great message of the monotheistic faiths: that the family of man has mutual obligations. Judaism has expanded the acts of charity/ social justice called "tzsedaka" (*see-dah-kah*) into an even more noble category called "g'milat chesed" — acts of loving kindness. Rabbi Benjamin Blech explains that while charity is carried out with money, loving kindness must be practiced in person, spending time with the sick and needy. Charity usually is given only to the poor, but loving kindness can be shared with the poor and the rich, consoling those who are grieving and befriending the lonely. And last, while charity is dispensed to the living, loving kindness can be shown by helping arrange for a burial or tending to a departed friend's affairs. Even a poor person who lives off tzedakah should perform acts of tzedakah according to the Babylonian Talmud.

Maimonides, who became known as the Great Rabbi in Spain in 1190, brilliantly codified charity with a ladder of giving that holds true today. Each rung represented a higher level of virtue in giving:

The lowest rung is to make a grudging donation.

Moving up, the recipient might know the giver, but the giver would not know the recipient.

Up another rung, the giver to know the recipient, but the recipient not to know the giver.

The second highest would involve a giver who didn't know who had received his gift and a recipient who didn't know who had given him help.

The highest and most virtuous, would be for a giver to help a stranger by offering him a loan or helping him find a job so he would no longer need help.

Even in Medieval times, long before welfare reform, Maimonides knew that acts of kindness should preserve the dignity of the needy, not inflate the ego of the givers. He tried himself to cultivate gentleness, modesty, and an even temper throughout his life, believing that a life well lived was a tribute to God. And in the end, he wrote that the knowledge of God was "like a kiss."

In Islam, "zagat" is one of the five pillars of faith. It is usually translated as charity or the "poor due," but it literally means "to purify." Not coincidentally, there is a ritual of giving after the end of the fasting of Ramadan, which emphasizes our need to keep our appetites in balance. The material and sensual world can distract us from our primary mission to love God and our neighbor. The Qu'ran

> "You should each give, then, as you have decided, not with regret or out of a sense of duty; for God loves the one who gives gladly."
>
> – 2 CORINTHIANS 9:7

specifies that 2½ percent of one's holdings should be distributed to the poor (after expenses are subtracted). The Prophet Muhammad advised, "When a person dies, his actions come to an end, with three exceptions: recurring charity such as building a school or hospital, knowledge from which benefit continues to be reaped and the prayers of his pious children for him."

TEN

Working

"Work is love made visible. And if you cannot work with love but only with distaste, it is better than you should leave your work and sit at the gate of the temple and take alms of those who work with joy."

— KAHLIL GIBRAN

And now it's time to think about the *other* six days of the week. Because we spend so many hours and weeks and years of our lives earning a living or maintaining a home, how we go about our tasks should be a reflection of our beliefs, our character. We teach with our lives every hour of the day. We also learn from those around us, so we must choose our teachers well.

Many people can't openly profess their faith on the job — but they can still show it. As a daily presence on television, Diane Sawyer has become a highly visible role model. She's in our homes first thing in the morning on *Good Morning America*. In the months following the September 11 terrorist attacks, many gave the news anchor high praise for helping set a constructive tone while much of the country was on an emotional roller coaster. Publicly, she carried on with poise and professionalism while buildings fell before her eyes and as families broke down in tears in the studio. Although there were immediate concerns that Times Square, just outside the ABC-TV studio, might be attacked next, Diane was out on the street reporting and soon on her way to the World Trade Center site, where the hellish scene was like nothing she had witnessed before. Privately, she admitted, her faith helped her stay centered and on task as she interviewed rescue workers and witnesses.

In fact, in November that fall, country singing star Garth Brooks interrupted the boot-stomping fun on the *Good Morning America* set to applaud someone else: Diane Sawyer. He thanked her for playing a "huge part in the healing of this nation," for showing "class and cool" as well as compassion in the broadcasts since the terrorist attacks. The studio audience roared its approval. It was an unscripted twist, but a valid point. Covering the emotional explosions had called for daily grace under pressure. Although Diane probably didn't realize it, she was among those who showed the country how to carry on.

We talked one November morning in her office, which was crowded with white lilies and Emmy statuettes. Diane had changed from the sweater-skirt and high heels she had worn in the broadcast to some slouchy-but-chic khakis and a pink cotton shirt. Thinking back, she admitted that it took all of her professional discipline to keep from crying as she interviewed Americans at the center of the tragedy — the widows, the firemen, the nurses, the sailors at sea. She was on camera with co-anchor Charlie Gibson watching the live shots of the World Trade Center as the second airliner hit the tower. She reacted very humanly by gasping, "Oh, my God!"

She recalled, "I think we were doing what everybody in the country was doing simultaneously. You could hear this collective consciousness saying first of all, 'Well, it must have been a terrible accident, and there's another plane — maybe they're going to help.' Then, 'No, this can't be, no!' As Charlie has said, we were all in denial about what we were seeing initially. And then the minute the plane hit, you could feel the entire earth turn on its axis because you knew that it had to be deliberate and that everything is rearranged."

Only most people didn't have to deal with it on camera. Remembering her first night at "Ground Zero," Diane said, "I have been in war zones, I have been in sniper fire, I have rushed into scenes where bombs were exploding, and there was nothing to prepare you for the sight of that smoke-encased inferno the first night." But she refused to let herself cry until later, off-camera. "Much of the time, I've been on the verge of tears, and I've thought, no, they have a right to their tears, this is about them. And it holds me back."

She said the first time she cried was the weekend after September 11, when she got to spend a little time with her husband, Mike Nichols, and her stepchildren. "We decided to just drive out of the city and into the country. The first sight of the trees and the sun and the day that we were all getting to live together as a family just tore me up," she recalled.

The most difficult interview, she said, was with Lisa Beamer and Liz Glick, two of the widows from Flight 93, which had crashed into a field in Pennsylvania. "When Liz Glick said her husband had called and said to her, 'Just promise me one thing, that you'll have a good life and that you and our daughter will have a good life — that's all I want to know,' and then he put down the phone and went to take on the hijackers," she remembered, her voice breaking. She paused and added softly, "Your heart simply stops."

The emotions at such times "sneak up on you," she said. "You never know. You're talking to someone, and the eloquence of these great people just gets to you. That first night at Ground Zero, and half of the time you didn't know if you were talking to a fireman or a policeman, everybody was dust-encased. And the poetry of them, the courage and the valor of that moment came through every single one of them."

To be sure, the fifty-six-year-old morning anchor, a media veteran, can be as aggressive as they come. But it was telling during one show how she tenderly comforted several nurses who broke down while describing the victims they had treated. Diane patted them gently while they struggled to recover their composure. She told them, "It's OK, we're all in this together, side by side." It was an unusual step out of the orthodoxy that journalists mustn't inject their own feelings into the story. But it expressed what many Americans had been feeling as they watched the rescue efforts from across the country: that the class and wealth barriers that became so pronounced during the last affluent decade were melted as people pitched in where they could. Wall Street financiers stood on street corners with pin-striped lawyers and applauded as weary policemen and firemen walked by. It was a leveling the terrorists didn't plan for; recognition that any of us can disappear in a second, that our lives are interdependent, and that sports stars aren't really the heroes.

"When we were out on the carrier *Enterprise*, which had just returned from the Middle East, the admiral said to us, 'We went out to fight for freedom of the press, too, you know.' And we all laughed. And he said, 'No, I mean it, we did.' So I was talking to a kid later on the deck, and I said, 'I just want to thank you for what you did.' And he said, 'You be brave for us, and we'll be brave for you, and we'll all be brave.' And I thought, *Yes, we should all be brave for them, sometime, some way.*" She added, "You know the average age is nineteen or twenty for the people on those ships."

Faith and family are part of Diane's roots. She was brought up a Methodist, attending a church in Kentucky that her father helped build. "Our lives revolved around that church and the street where we lived," she remembered. Nowadays, she quietly slips into the back of Redeemer Presbyterian in Manhattan when she can. It's a fast-growing church that is drawing many of the young professionals who have come to make their fortune in New York. The services are held in the auditorium at Hunter College and the sermons by Reverend Tim Keller are always packed. Diane tries to keep a low profile when she attends, which not only preserves her worship experience, it doesn't distract from those around her. In the week of the attacks, she said she called Reverend Keller in an effort to deal with her emotions. "I don't remember what I said into his voicemail, but I hope it wasn't all babbling," she said. "Somehow it helped."

Like most journalists, she tries not to let her personal beliefs intrude into her work, but being human, sometimes they do. Whether you agree with the political tinge of a question or not, you can tell she is thinking, not just reading a script. On camera, she is sophisticated and stylish without being pretentious. She is always polite. Off camera, she is methodical and disciplined — before agreeing to our interview, she requested a half-dozen of my columns and apparently read every word, judging from references she made during our talk. And after I wrote an article about the interview, she wrote me a thank-you note. Judging from the warmth shown to her by her co-anchor, the cameramen, and her assistants, she is not the kind of prima donna whose ego gets in the way. Indeed, the most negative quote you can find about her is a description as the "warm ice maiden." Most tend to agree with the *People* entertainment critic that she "got to the top with a formidable blend of smarts, drive, warmth, and earnestness."

Indeed, Diane started her TV career as a weather reporter on a television station in Louisville, Kentucky, where her family had moved from Glasgow, Kentucky. She returned to her old neighborhood when she carried the Olympic torch for the 2002 Winter Games through Louisville. She pointed to the church at the end of the road and said "every house on the block had a welcome sign for kids" when she was growing up. There was a playhouse in the backyard that her father built with his own hands. And there was an upright piano downstairs, where her mother made her practice while her friends waited on the stoop. She checked the stairs — yup, the eighth stair still squeaked, which had made it tough to sneak in after curfew. And yes, there were still marks on the door showing when she reached 58½ inches tall.

Diane graduated from Wellesley and went from that first job in Louisville to work on the staff of Press Secretary Ron Ziegler in the Nixon White House. She left her post as a press aide to assist the former president with the preparation of his memoirs, then returned to broadcast news as a reporter in the CBS News Washington bureau. It wasn't long before she became an anchor and then the first woman on the super-successful *60 Minutes* news magazine. From there she jumped to ABC News to anchor *Prime Time Live* with Sam Donaldson. By the fall of 1994, she had signed a $7 million contract and became one of the highest-paid women in broadcast news. This seemed a far cry from the time I worked as a TV critic in the 1970s and

> "When one door of happiness closes, another opens; but often we look so long at the closed door that we do not see the one which has been opened for us."
>
> — HELEN KELLER

network TV executives regularly insisted that women would never be accepted as news anchors by audiences because their higher, softer voices lacked authority and they would not be taken seriously. Three decades later, we have attorneys like Cynthia McFadden reporting and anchoring. Lesley Stahl digs up the story on *60 Minutes.* Christiane Amanpour is all over the globe. And Gen X journalists like Ashleigh Banfield are reporting from war zones in Afghanistan.

Despite the pressures of live television and her high-profile schedule, Diane Sawyer seems to wear her fame lightly. On the set, she seems oblivious to the distractions of producers, equipment, and the countdown to airtime. During the breaks, she carefully studies her script or playfully teases her coworkers. In one segment, she interviewed eleven-year-old Mattie Stepanek, a pint-size poet with muscular dystrophy. When she asked about the unfairness of his illness, he answered, "Why me? Why not me? Better me than a little baby, a child without a lot of strength." Mattie confided that there had been times during his illness that he thought he had seen the angels. Diane thought just a second and closed the segment by saying,

"Maybe we just did, too." Her co-host Charlie Gibson gave a mock moan as he began the next news segment, "Great — I've got to follow that."

As we talked afterward in her office, she was more low-key but equally gracious. Given a series of words to respond to, she responded gamely:

Rival Katie Couric: "Irresistible."

Charlie Gibson: "A real salt of the earth, true-blue guy."

Bill Clinton: "Unusual brilliance."

Richard Nixon: "Fascinating and a study in Greek drama."

Her husband, Mike Nichols: A rippling laugh, a pause, and then a sexy, "Ummmm."

Her relationship with her seventy-year-old spouse is one of mutual admiration. On one Valentine's week show when all the anchors named their favorite romantic place, the others picked exotic locations: Diane picked being inside one of her husband's long-sleeved dress shirts, because it made her feel so close to him. Though they found each other at midlife and he had been married three times before, they seem to have a comfortable relationship. He need not feel overshadowed by her high profile because he is a superstar himself, having directed *The Graduate, Carnal Knowledge, Who's Afraid of Virginia Woolf, Silkwood,* and *Primary Colors.* Diane once told Peter Applebaum of the *New York Times* that just conversing with Mike is so fascinating that sometimes she feels she should be paying admission. She recalled the time that his former comedy partner Elaine May looked up at Mike during dinner and said, "You know what bothers me about God?" And her husband replied without a pause, "That he hates arrogance so much but doesn't seem to mind cruelty." And Elaine nodded, "Exactly." Diane said she just sat there with her mouth open, awed by his verbal agility.

Diane likes to organize games for their family gatherings at Thanksgiving — like treasure hunts where people have to answer the clue before they get to the next course. She said it helped regain a sense of normalcy to keep up those holiday traditions after September 11. She tried to maintain a similar sense of equilibrium on air, demonstrating tact and composure even as the anniversary of the attacks was observed a year later.

"You hesitate to say this is who we will be now, because the next thing you know we will be back to Jennifer Lopez outfits

> "Work is not primarily a thing one does to live, but the thing one lives to do. It is, or should be, the full expression of the worker's faculties, the thing in which he finds spiritual, mental, and bodily satisfaction, and the medium in which he offers himself to God."
>
> — DOROTHY LEIGH SAYERS

and we will have to eat our words. But I think some of the lessons will last. We have looked in the mirror and seen strength we forgot was there, and suddenly, we all knew that we weren't just a nation of ferocious consumers and giddy pop culture. We didn't have a palpable reason to feel that before, but now we do. It's a gift. At an awful price, but a gift."

She's reluctant to describe herself as a role model for others, but she did agree that there are moments when we can be guides for each other. She likes to close some of her speeches with a line from Goethe, that "some people are like the stars, just above the horizon" to make the point that everyone should strive to be like the stars above the horizon, so others will look up to find the direction to go.

It is a benediction if you can invest your work with meaning, but to be realistic, many people today are struggling merely to survive the demands of the workday. How do you deify your work in today's 24/7 world, where many people find themselves working harder and harder with less and less satisfaction?

That's the question the Reverend Rebecca Miles is wrestling with both as a minister and a mother. When I called her at home, she had barely answered the phone when she had to turn away from the conversation to answer a question from her husband: "I don't *know* where her pants and shoes are. She took them *off.*" With a three-year-old and an eighteen-month old, Rebecca has plenty of distractions from her work. Her work is studying how everyone else works. Rebecca is a "moral theologian" and teaches ethics at Perkins Theological Seminary at Southern Methodist University. At forty-one, her level of exhaustion might be higher than mothers who are younger, she admits, but it gives her an appreciation of the draining lives many Americans are leading. In fact, she is writing a book about rethinking work.

In a talk presented at SMU in 2001 called "Walking the Tight Rope," she told the audience about a sign that was posted at the university pool where she used to swim (back in the days when she still had time to exercise). The sign read, "There are three kinds of people in the world — those who make things happen, those who watch things happen, and those who wonder, 'What happened?' "

It's a perfect slogan, she suggested, for the changing work patterns in the United States. She explains that the sharp increase in work hours over the last three decades has placed tremendous pressure on workers as they try to balance their home responsibilities, particularly women. Though the time that parents spend with children appears to have held steady, work demands have taken time away from other interests — civic work, church study, socializing, caring for the poor, even basic personal activities like sleeping, eating, having sex, cleaning house, reading, and worshipping. In addition, numerous studies have shown that long hours are linked to weight gain, increased alcohol and cigarette consumption, and higher levels of stress-related illnesses.

We have become "Puritans without a purpose," she suggests, as we work punishing hours to afford consumer goods we

> "Three rules of work: Out of clutter, find simplicity. From discord, find harmony. In the middle of difficulty lies opportunity."
>
> — ALBERT EINSTEIN

do not have time to enjoy. At the same time, we could be called "Puritans without a Sabbath," because the work usually does not have an underlying sense of divine calling and there is less leisure time on Sunday. Today's workers usually are so busy, she says, that they have less time than generations before them to have long, emotionally fulfilling conversations about their inner life and fewer people to talk with because they haven't the time to keep up relationships.

Invariably, Rebecca gets a strong response from audiences. "I don't think I've ever done anything that hits home the way this does. It strikes a chord with people," she says. "If you look at the patterns of overwork in American life and the other patterns that go along with it, like overspending, if you keep asking questions about why, you get to the question about what did God make us for? What is ultimately important in our life? What is God calling me to do?"

"For a lot of Christians and other faiths, the impulse to work hard used to be so you can do more to serve. As a missionary kid and a missionary myself, I would ask myself, 'How could you ever work too much?' But it is a question of the kind of frantic pace that many of us have gotten ourselves into. It raises huge questions about what is ultimately important. If you look at our spending patterns, you discover we are spending in part as compensation for feeling so tired because we work so much. We feel we are owed."

Rebecca points out that Juliet Schor, who wrote *The Overworked Americans, the Overspent Americans,* discovered that people feel pressure to spend more because their reference points for what is appropriate spending have changed. While they previously compared themselves to neighbors who made relatively close to what they made, their reference today is to TV characters and celebrities, whose lifestyles they cannot really afford to emulate. The more they watch TV, she explains, the more exaggerated their idea becomes of what the average American makes, which brings us back to the questions of what we desire today and what that says about our faith. Spending becomes another way to find fulfillment, she says, "but objects, however important, are not going to do that. It ends up a form

> "Workaholics commit slow suicide by refusing to allow the child inside them to play."
>
> — DR. LAURENCE SUSSER

of idolatry. And that is at the heart of a lot of problems in American culture: the sin of idolatry, although we're too cool to call it that. You are not going to find a substitute that matches up with God, so it is always going to be a losing proposition."

Rebecca continues, "One of the wonderful things about American culture is that generally we have had a tradition of working hard; that is part of what made us great. And in Scripture, work is given a high value. So work is a good thing when you believe you are working for a higher good. If you are a 'Puritan without a Purpose,' however, you have the same desire to work, but without a sense of vocation and calling, so you end up feeling spent at the end of the day. You don't have anything left to give people you love."

Recent studies show several shifts that might alleviate a little of the pressure. One is that working fathers are spending more time with their children, although they still spend less time than mothers do. More men also are becoming full-time dads, although the percentages are still relatively small. And women are staging their careers in different ways in an attempt to balance family needs. As an example, Rebecca says, "I waited until I was thirty-eight to get pregnant. I was finishing my dissertation and was close to tenure, so I reasoned, why not wait until I get tenure? Once I got tenure, I wouldn't be under the same kind of pressure. I would be freer not to work the same kinds of extremely long hours I did before." Many other women are opting to stay home while their children are very young — according to the 2000 census figures, only a third of the mothers with infants under one year old have a full-time job outside the home. However, as the kiddos get close to six years old, the mothers start edging back to work. Nearly 75 percent of the women between the ages of twenty-five and fifty-five are working and struggling to do it all.

Because she is from a family of ministers in Arkansas who were almost always "on call" for their flocks, Rebecca knows that if you let it, your work can gobble up your whole life. Her husband, father, and brother are all Methodist ministers. When she talks to groups, Rebecca reminds them that faith can make a difference in your work decisions, not just your personal life. One is letting go of control. "A lot of people who are trying to juggle employment and children are trying to control every detail to get it all done. They might need to let go even if things are not done to perfection. There's something about trusting in God and being willing to accept forgiveness and be at peace with who you are. That can be an antidote to our hyped-up needs for control."

It is easy during the workweek to lose track of what ultimately matters in life. "So going to the synagogue and the church is a way of reminding us that all those little things we do every day have a relationship to the big things, like our relationship with God. Do we make time for God every day?"

Studies show Americans are working more than they did twenty or thirty years ago, more than people in other countries and even more than people in Medieval times. "We work longer hours than agricultural societies, who had lots of festival days and down-time during cycles," Rebecca said. "So we have to stop and ask ourselves, *who* are we working for? Ourselves? Some image of success? Or God?"

> "While I am busy with little things, I am not required to do greater things."
>
> — ST. FRANCIS DE SALES

There is a limit to what the human body can do, she reminded. "Our bodies will tell us that we are working too much and we will get sick."

She recommends that people insert more prayer into their lives at work and home. "I use something called ejaculatory prayers. Those are short prayers you can say over and over during the day, whatever the context, whatever you're doing, to just bring God along with you. That can be thanking God, asking forgiveness, asking to be faithful, asking help with the task at hand, asking God to be an interpreter between you and someone you are dealing with. Whatever the situation is, I do a lot of those short prayers during the day, either out loud or to myself. The beauty is that they can be done anywhere."

And many studies show that saying prayers with your children, or other rituals you observe regularly with them, can make a positive difference over time. "The kids will remember them as special times with you," Rebecca says. "It's a way to teach them how to approach life and respond to life. It's also one of the few times you are close and quiet together. You can't run around and multi-task when you are saying a prayer with your eyes closed."

She noted that one of the exceptions to the decline in civic participation in communities is that more people are being drawn to small groups in churches or synagogues, either study groups or account-ability groups, where they can meet to pray and talk about their lives. "That's a great thing, to have places to pray," she says. "Prayer before meals is also a very important thing for families. One thing that a number of studies have shown is that kids who sit down and eat meals with their families have lower levels of depression. It's a good indicator. Not only are there lower levels of depression, but those kids are more likely to be conservative sexually and more conservative about drugs and alcohol abuse. On one hand, all those problems seem so insurmountable. But on the other hand, something so simple as taking time to have meals around the table and to say prayers together can make a difference."

Reducing the stress of the week will take paying attention on a lot of levels, Rebecca advises, and our culture works against paying attention by constantly distracting us. "We have a hard time sitting still with all the noise around us, the e-mail, the fax, the cell phones, the radios, the TV — everything. It's hard to sit still. We have to give it extra effort, simply being in silence whenever possible, with regular attendance at religious services where you can bow your head and pray. The Quakers have a phrase — a 'way opening' — can happen at such moments. There might be an answer to a question you are asking in your life in the sermon. You have to listen in prayer and be attuned to what comes to you. You have to listen to the people around you. You might 'see' something by listening to them. All those little things can be part of a way opening where you can discern what God is saying to you."

Rebecca suggests that companies can do more by adopting life balance policies, with flextime, sabbaticals, and rewards for qualities other than merely working the longest number of hours. "The unhappiest employees are usually the ones who work the longest number of hours," she observes. "I am not against capitalism, but if we are smart, we will find ways to humanize it."

Workers can do their part by keeping their faith in their thoughts while they are on the job. The idea is not to separate prayer and worship on one side of our life and place work and play on the other, but to integrate them so all those things are a means to grace, a way to draw closer to God. The more we try to control our life by compartmentalizing God into one time square, the harder it is to keep the rest of our life in sync. We end up with what the Hopi Indians called "Koyaanisqatsi," or life out of balance.

> "The really important things in life can't be said, only shown."
>
> – WITTGENSTEIN

The Indians wisely knew that God was part of the everyday and everything. You will find that once you look for God in the ordinary, it becomes extraordinary with possibility.

You might say Linda Alvarado has built on her faith. She's at the top in a field that is the epitome of hard-hatted machismo: construction work. She is owner of Alvarado Construction Co., a commercial general contracting firm based in Denver, Colorado. It is one of the fastest-growing companies in the United States. Some of her trophy projects include the Colorado Convention Center and the new Bronco Stadium. Every day she supervises millions of dollars in construction and hundreds of workers. She also is the first Hispanic owner of a major baseball franchise as a partner in the Colorado Rockies. How did she get there, and how does she stay there? Positive thinking, which she learned from her parents and her faith.

She was brought up in Albuquerque, New Mexico, as the only girl in a family with five brothers. She had to compete to keep up. And she did. Her parents were very supportive and positive. They not only expected their children to go to church and to do well in school, they expected them to be able to tell what they learned. Each child was active in sports, and each child was expected to do something to help others in the community. "You could not just be a joiner, you had to be a leader," Linda recalls. And she was. When she went to Pomona College in California, she worked for a landscape company to help pay her way. She began as a day laborer, "Which was not bad, because I got to wear Levis to work, got a tan, and worked with some fun men." She felt comfortable in the construction environment because she had shared construction-toy sets with all her brothers and joined them in building forts. She began taking unusual classes for a woman: survey, estimating, and computerized scheduling. She moved into a project accounting position onsite, then into a support position to a project manager . . . then into project engineering function.

In the 1970s, the number of women in the industry was less than 1 percent. As Linda moved up in construction jobs, she was not always well received. Women were not encouraged by most men or accepted by other women. She was sometimes taunted with graffiti on the walls or crude pictures of her in various stages of undress. She shrugged it off. "It was one of the last bastions of male dominance," she says. "I don't say that in a negative way, it was just much slower to change than other areas."

Coming from an optimistic, competitive family, Linda was determined to show that women could succeed even in the most male-dominated field and still keep their femininity. People are still shocked when the owner of the company walks in and is not a burly guy, but an attractive, five-foot-six woman. Being different is almost a family tradition. Both of her grandfathers were protestant ministers — one Presbyterian and one Baptist — at a time when most Hispanics were Catholic. So Linda grew up knowing what it is like to be an outsider and with a keen awareness of "the commonalities in religion, whether you are Presbyterian, Catholic, or Methodist."

Though it was a time of prevalent discrimination against Hispanics, her parents had such a positive attitude, she never doubted she could achieve. And though they were of modest means, they scraped together the money to help her start her first company. She had presented her business plan to six banks. And she was turned down six times. Her parents mortgaged their home for $2,500 to get her going. Her mother, who had taken in ironing to support the family, told her "Don't quit — not now, not ever." She gave her a "dicho" (words of wisdom) in Spanish: *"¡Mijita, empieza pequeno pero piensa muy grande!"* ("My dearest little one, start small, but think big!") With perseverance and persistence, Linda got a small business loan. And with dogged hard work, she made her company a success.

She gets by on four and a half hours of sleep each night, so she can get up at 3:30 a.m. and start working. At fifty, she's determined not only to build a good company, but a country where dreams are raceless and genderless. Toward that end, she devotes many hours to community service and mentoring young people. When the Colorado Rockies played an opener at Coors Field, Linda treated 150 inner-city kids to tickets. Unlike some business leaders who simply donate the tickets, she showed up to personally give them a tour of the stadium, pointing out all the possible job opportunities if they stay in school, from sportswriter to trainer to even owner — for boys and girls alike. Determined to encourage more at-risk Hispanic students to stay in school, her company gives generously to scholarship programs, and she served on President Bill Clinton's Advisory Commission on Educational Excellence for Hispanic Americans.

She keeps her life with her own family private, to shield her children from publicity or pressure. And she is, by her own description, not an overtly open person about her faith, although she is a churchgoer and reads Scripture. "I am hopeful my actions will speak as loud as my words," she explains. She keeps a copy of the Ten Commandments by the telephone in her office as a quiet daily reminder. She joked that they aren't merely the "Ten Suggestions" and that the Lord was serious about the directives. "To use a construction analogy," she says, "it's a blueprint for Alvarado Construction's core values. It's how we work together as a team. It's how we work with our clients, subcontractors, and suppliers. I believe one can demonstrate faith and still have fun."

All her hard work has its rewards, she adds somewhat teasingly, like the fact that her brothers treat her a lot nicer now that she owns a baseball team. Linda also recently heard from a young girl who was dressing up like her for Women's History Month by wearing a hard hat and heels. And she received a letter from a woman in Peru who read about her baseball ownership and sent her a letter of admiration.

Does your "business blueprint" include core spiritual values? Terese of Lisieux said that Christ was present not so much in prayer "but rather in the midst of daily occupations." Kathleen Norris reminds us in *The Quotidian Mysteries* that cleaning and cooking "all serve to ground us in the world, and they need not grind us down." She says it is the "daily tasks, daily acts of love and worship that remind us that the Christian religion is not strictly an intellectual pursuit. . . . Christian faith is a way of life." Can you name three mundane activities in your workday or workweek in which your love of God is present? Do you

> "I long to accomplish a great and noble task, but it is my chief duty to accomplish humble tasks as though they were great and noble. The world is moved along, not only by the mighty shoves of its heroes, but also by the aggregate of the tiny pushes of each honest worker."
>
> — HELEN KELLER

feel filled by your labors at the end of the day or depleted? If you cannot change your job, how could you change your attitude toward your tasks each day? How do you treat women who must work at "menial" jobs out of necessity? How do you treat the people you work with or who work for you?

It's a real blessing when you can use your work to improve the lives of others. But you don't have to be a social worker or in a helping profession to do so. You just have to develop the attitude of service to those you work with. Companies can develop a competitive advantage by doing what's right for workers *and* the bottom line. As a result, their workers feel they are being served by the company leadership, not used. That's the concept developed thirty years ago by Robert Greenleaf in *The Servant Leader.* He believed that the test of leadership is the growth of those served, not the depletion. If we are to learn from the Enron debacle, the lessons should include better employee relations as well as better accounting oversight.

The Mary Kay Corp. stands out for having made *esprit de corps* its business blueprint. The cosmetics company not only excels at selling makeup, it excels at empowering women. Sherril Steinman was twenty-five when she went from feeling hopelessly stuck in the little town of Pigeon, Michigan — population four hundred — to an energizing career in direct sales. Sherril had married right out of high school and went to work so her husband could go to college. Then, while he was building an insurance company, she juggled raising their two young children with managing a florist shop and moonlighting as a wedding and funeral consultant.

Eventually, the stress of the nonstop busyness left her frazzled. Call it depression or call it burnout, she was drained. "I couldn't even make myself go out to the front counter anymore to talk to customers who wanted flowers," she remembers. She was at the end of her rope but hated to admit it, she says, because "I had been taught if you had time to cry, you weren't working hard enough."

Her husband suggested that she accompany him to an insurance convention in Nashville, Tennessee, for a "getaway" weekend. As she was unwinding, she confessed to a new friend she met there that she was "about to drop dead." The woman, who was a sales director for Mary Kay Cosmetics, suggested that Sherril might like to try makeup sales because she could work from home and it might provide a saner schedule for her.

At first blush, it didn't seem a good fit. Sherril recalls, "I didn't even wear makeup. And neither did most of the women in Pigeon. They only wore lipstick for weddings and funerals." Still, the friend urged her to give it a try, emphasizing that she would be selling the concept of skin care, not covering up with makeup.

So Sherril asked her mother-in-law to take over the florist shop while she began pitching skin care to her friends and neighbors. Her first goal was to earn enough for a winter coat with fur on it. She earned that. Her second goal was to get a Chevette hatchback. She got that.

How did she do it? By using what she had — her country friendliness and sense of humor — to put other people at ease. As she puts it, "Look at me. Red hair. German descent. I'm five foot seven inches tall and a size thirteen. I am pretty much an everyday woman, not thin, not fat, not too tall. I tell women, 'Look at me. If I can do this, so can you. Look in the mirror and I am you. I am your everyday, normal woman who loves her kids and loves her family and wants to do well by them.' "

Even though Pigeon was an hour and a

half from the nearest freeway exit, Sherril built her sales territory by hitting the road in her Chevette and recruiting new customers. She discovered she was not only selling cosmetics, she was motivating other women to improve their lives. And she was sharing the values of her faith. Many of the women needed help with self-esteem. They needed recognition that they were capable human beings. And they needed job skills they could integrate with family life.

"Women are good about putting into words that they are tired, upset, worried, or angry. But very few can say, 'Now what am I going to do about that?'" Sherril explains. She would challenge them, "How badly do you want to change? If you are willing to do something, you have to say, 'I am going to take charge of this' and be open to what it would take to change. That takes a lot of courage . . . found energy . . . faith . . . and humor.

"You build on who you are today," Sherril explains. "God willing, you are not going to be exactly the same next week, or next year, or five years. Say to yourself, 'I'm going to be an amazing, strong, courageous woman.' I believe you are going to get exactly what you imagine yourself to be, so please just don't think too small."

By thinking positively, Sherril overcame the limitations of a rural sales territory and became a national sales director at the age of forty-eight. Today, she is responsible for a million dollars a year in sales.

Her advice to other women is to laugh, support, and believe: "You have to get to a point where you are laughing at how ridiculous any situation is instead of letting it get you down. On my first sales trip on the road, a dog ate the fur collar on my coat. You have to laugh at yourself, but take your relationships seriously. Tell people in person and in writing and in voicemail how much you appreciate them."

Her faith has helped her deal with the rejection that goes with sales work and helps her deal with difficult people. "I don't look at that person as an irritation anymore. I pray on it and say 'Lord, show me why this woman is in my path.' Nobody is in our path by accident. Someone might be annoying, but her purpose might be to lead you to someone who was meant to be in your path. It's pretty awesome when you see those connections."

She is a Lutheran ("Of course — I'm from Wisconsin") and was raised in parochial schools. She says one of the best things about working for the cosmetics company is that founder Mary Kay Ash encouraged her employees to bring their religious values to work with them. "When we say 'God first, family second, career third,' we mean it," Sherril says. She pointed out that one of the other directors in Wisconsin is a nun. The nun's revenues are used to support her convent, Sherril said, so when she earned a pink Cadillac, the nun took cash instead for the sisters' household fund. Whereas talking about your faith might raise questions in another organization, in Mary Kay, nobody bats an eyelash about it. "I don't make a single phone call or walk into a single situation that I don't pray on it," Sherril revealed. "My purpose is clear when I talk to a person. If she tells me 'no,' when I walk away, I tell myself to say a prayer of gratitude that apparently God is protecting me from something there. It's not that you lost, but that the situation wasn't right for you. If you turn your life and work over to God and believe you are being led, you don't always get depressed over a negative thing. It just might not be part of the plan. You look on down the road. If there is something pretty dramatically disappointing, I'll say, 'Lord, I can't handle this. I'm going to give this to you. I don't have the skill or the words or the wisdom. I'm turning it over to you.' And that has made my life happier."

The organization is a "very tight girl network," Sherril says. It's common practice for the saleswomen to come to the aid of each other and their customers. When a woman struggling to care for her kids told Sherril she couldn't keep an appointment because she was sick, Sherril asked, "How sick?" and picked her up to go to the doctor. That feeling of sisterhood has led the corporation to adopt domestic violence as a corporate cause, providing substantial donations to shelters for battered women around the country. The company also funded a PBS documentary *Breaking the Silence* to demystify the domestic violence that is a silent epidemic throughout the country. The documentary was nominated for an Emmy and is now being distributed by the American Bar Association (www.abanet.org/publiced/domviol.html).

It is a worthy cause. The National Domestic Violence Hot Line (1-800-799-7233) receives more than five hundred calls a day from women being abused. In 2001, more than four thousand women were killed in their own homes. Every day in the United States, according to Jan

Langbein, director of the Genesis Women's Shelter in Dallas, eleven women are murdered by their husbands or partners. Yet only two out of the seven women needing shelter are helped around the country. Most of the young boys in prison for crimes committed between the age of twelve and eighteen are there because they were trying to protect their mother.

At Mary Kay, domestic violence is not just a cause for the corporate headquarters. Sales directors like Peg Percival, who lives in St. John's, Michigan, support the domestic violence cause in their own way. When Peg turned forty, she gave herself a birthday party, rented a hotel ballroom, got state troopers to help sell tickets, got the high school band to play, got the drill team to put on a show, got the jazz team to perform, and wrangled gifts from merchants and a hockey puck from the Detroit Redwings to auction. Half the proceeds went to a cancer foundation, because her parents had both died from cancer, and half went to a domestic abuse home.

With more than 500,000 sales consultants, the Mary Kay organization knows full well that many women have difficult home lives. The company's greatest contribution ultimately may be in exporting its motivation techniques to women in thirty-three countries, who often have discovered for the first time that they can make money for themselves and they can empower others. At Mary Kay's memorial service in November 2001, a letter was read from a seventy-eight-year-old woman who has been teaching English in Beijing for thirteen years with her husband. She had recently spotted a Mary Kay office and was told that there were now some 60,000 Mary Kay sales representatives in China. She said the Chinese saleswomen were so impressed with the motto of God first, family second, and work third — that more young women were coming to church "because they wanted to know why you thought God was so important." The woman said she hoped it would be an encouragement and blessing to the cosmetics CEO "to know you are being used in this remarkable way here in China."

In a similar vein, the *New York Times* reported on April 20, 2002, that a courageous woman named Anya Vanina, who had been trained to sell Mary Kay Cosmetics, has become a champion for civil liberties in Russia, fighting against corruption by local authorities. "Not taking action means accepting what I see around me," Ms. Vanina told the *Times*. "I cannot do that." What had impressed Ms. Vanina, a widow with children, was the respect for individuals that came with the pink packaging for the cosmetics. The company's preachings — financial independence and sisterhood — appealed to her. She eventually turned her beauty salon into a women's center. The American company had made a revolution in her life, she said, because it exudes a "tender care and value for people that amazed me." So she started fighting for teachers who had not been paid. And she fought the bureaucracy for a villager who had lost the roof on her state-owned apartment. Though Ms. Vanina is no longer selling the product, Mary Kay no doubt would be proud of her efforts.

As we get older, we realize that we paint a portrait with our lives that others can see much better than we can. By midlife, many of the brush strokes are in place, but there

> "Some women transcend categories. Their faces are beautiful forever, rather than pretty for fifteen minutes. They change the world (not the other way around). They write, they read, they do. They make us laugh. They seduce us into being more than we were."
>
> — J. PETERMAN CATALOG AD FOR SILK PANTS

is still time to find the highlight you would like to play up, time to add shadings and color that reflect the character we have learned. Sooner or later, we have to look in the mirror and pay attention to the image we present to the world. How does how you look and act reflect your values? If you were charged with being a Christian — or a Muslim or a Jew — would there be enough evidence of faith in your daily life to convict you? Does your business work allow you to model your ethics and values? How do you lift others up? How does what you do during the day lift you up? Perhaps you could make it

> "There are two things to do about the Gospel — believe it and behave it."
>
> — SUSANNA WESLEY

a goal to take at least one break for spiritual quiet and renewal during the day, to give positive feedback to at least one co-worker, and to do at least one "good turn" for someone you encounter today. Then, at the end of the day, when it is time to rest, you can ask yourself, "Who did I work for today?" and sleep well.

We have seen many public figures fall from grace in the glare of 24-hour media coverage. It might sometimes seem that there are few role models who manage to integrate their faith and their work. But you can find them if you look beyond the image. Often they might hold their religious beliefs close to their hearts as the one private treasure they have in the glare of public life, but you can tell by the arc of their lives what guides them.

Justice Sandra Day O'Connor, for example, does not speak often about her religious beliefs, but on many Sunday mornings, you will find her serving as a lay reader at the National Cathedral in Washington, D.C. When she was seventy-two, I asked her if she still did the readings, and she said emphatically, "Oh yes." Every week? "No, not every week. But often. Very often." She was gracious, as always, but didn't volunteer more. Perhaps she doesn't want her religious philosophy to complicate interpretations of her judicial rulings, which are held under a microscope by lawyers and legal scholars across the country. As one of the most influential women of the twentieth century, she has been continually observed since Ronald Reagan named her the first woman on the Supreme Court in 1981. Since then, she has conducted herself with impeccable rectitude on and off the bench. Having shouldered the responsibility of being the first woman on the highest court in the land, she has been conscientious in her work and circumspect in her comments. To be showy about her religious practices would simply be out of character.

Yet hers is a faith with deep roots in the harsh land she grew up in during the 1930s and 1940s. In her loving memoir of ranch life, *Lazy B*, she tells that her family didn't go to church on Sundays because it was too far to town to go. Her father believed that you didn't have to go to church to appreciate God's gifts. You just had to look around you. She remembers him telling her as a child, "It is remarkable to see how the clouds form and produce rain, which produces the grass and plants, which sustains animal, bird, and insect life, and which in turn sustains human life from generation to generation. It is an amazing, complex, but orderly universe. And we are only specks in it. There is surely something — a God if you will — who created all of this."

Sandra's character was shaped by the rugged environment of ranch life. What counted most were the qualities needed to keep the ranch running: honesty, dependability, competence, and good humor. "A basic instinct in both animals and humans is that of territoriality," she wrote. "We want to belong to a place familiar to us. If we have such a place, we are part of it and it is part of us."

It might surprise some, who have only seen photos of the justice lined up with her colleagues in their black robes like a dour choir, to learn she is a cowgirl at heart; what used to be called a tomboy. To her apparent delight, she was inducted into the National Cowgirl Hall of Fame in Fort Worth in 2002. For someone who is customarily impersonal in her public remarks, she was considerably nostalgic in her speech. She recalled that when she was a girl working on the Lazy B, she rode on the roundups and did everything the cowhands did. And now, she added, "I find myself riding herd on lower-court judges."

"At heart, I will always be a cowgirl," she confessed when speaking at the hall of fame event. Her story from cowgirl to Supreme Court Justice is a remarkable one. She was raised in an adobe ranch house with no electricity or running water. A family of skunks lived under the old screen porch, and Bobcat was the family pet. The ranch house was thirty-five miles from the nearest town, so at the age of six, she was sent to El Paso to live with her grandmother so she could attend a good school. She learned her lessons well, skipped two grades, and graduated at age sixteen.

At Stanford University, Sandra graduated magna cum laude in economics. She was third in her class in law school — future Supreme Court Justice William Rehnquist was number one — and she married a classmate from the law review, John J. O'Connor. The only job she could get was as a legal secretary. She kept on trying and found a job with the attorney general in Northern California. She later opened a small firm in Phoenix, worked as a state judge, ran for the legislature, and became the first female state senate majority leader in the country.

Along the way, Sandra took five years off to be a full-time mom to her three sons. She was serving on the appeals court bench when she was invited in 1981 to interview with President Ronald Reagan for the Supreme Court nomination. She didn't think she would get the nomination, be-

"When most all the other girls her age
Were learning how to dance,
She was out there with her dad,
Just helping out on the ranch."

— BOB E. LEWIS,
"The Cowgirl and Her Horse"

cause, well, no woman ever had. But the minute she was confirmed, she has said, states across the country started putting more women on their own supreme courts. "And it made a difference in the acceptance of young women as lawyers. It opened doors for them," she told Katie Couric in a rare 2002 interview.

Sandra always seems acutely aware of her role in history, as if everyone is watching what she says and does. Usually they are. She doesn't like to think she has ruled any differently because she is a woman. She told Couric, "It seems to me as other women on the bench have said from time to time, that a wise old woman and a wise old man will reach the same decision. I think that's generally true." She not only holds her own in questioning attorneys who appear before the court, she often sets the standard for proper temperament.

Occasional rumors surface in the capitol that the justice, who has survived breast cancer and other health problems, might step down during the Bush presidency to guarantee a conservative replacement. If she does, her legacy on the bench will be one of independent thinking and pragmatism — she has not been an ideologue, like her colleague William Rehnquist, not a showy intellectual like Antonin Scalia, nor as much of an overt feminist as the second woman on the court, Ruth Bader Ginsburg. She has simply tried to follow her conscience and be a reasonable reader of the law. In recent years, she has been an influential swing vote, part of a moderate-conservative bloc. She has opposed applying the death penalty to minors, favored equity for women in pension plans, opposed admitting homosexuals to the Boy Scouts, favored tough prosecution laws, favored narrowly tailored affirmative action, generally favored women's access to abortions but with some restrictions, ruled that men should be able to attend nursing schools, supported parochial schools, and helped set the boundaries on prayer in schools. It is a record grounded in her sense of ethics as well as the law.

Incredibly, she has lived out most of her life in the see-through shark-tank of politics and maintained an impeccable reputation. Her former law clerks describe her as authoritative, very much in control, dedicated, intense, a perfectionist — but also warm, down to earth, and optimistic. Shortly after taking her seat, she established a morning exercise class in the court gym for female employees. She has mentored many young women as law clerks and been a firm but friendly taskmaster, known for long days and seven-day workweeks. Still, Sandra knows when to break for fun, being particularly fond of popcorn, Mexican food, and white-water rafting. According to the Supreme Court Historical Society, when she was diagnosed with breast cancer in 1988, she fulfilled a speaking engagement at Washington and Lee University the day before her surgery and was back on the bench ten days later. Like many women who have been pathbreakers, she has spent much of her life proving she was capable. But she has also proved that the character you show in the process is just as important as any accomplishment.

When her father died, she climbed Round Mountain, dodging several rattlesnakes along the way, and placed his ashes in a rock cairn at the top, where all the ranch could be seen. It is a place, she wrote, "where the stars at night are brilliant and constant, a place to see the sunrise and sunset, and always be reminded how small we are in the universe but even so, how one small voice can make a difference."

"A dairy maid can milk cows to the glory of God."

— MARTIN LUTHER

TAKE HOME:

Many people might know that Shaker furniture is lovely, but might not know much about the religious movement that led to the simple designs. Even though the Shaker sect has dwindled to near extinction, many of the homespun practices of that movement still shine as worthy values.

The sect was founded by Ann Lee in 1772 in Manchester, England, as the United Society of Believers in Christ's Second Appearing and brought to the American colonies in 1774. The members were nicknamed the Shakers because they shook with emotion during services. The Shakers believed that God is both male and female and that Ann Lee, "Mother Ann," was the reincarnation of Jesus Christ. That was a difficult sell then and now. But thousands of believers were drawn to Mother Ann's teachings on the virtues of simple living, hard work, and serious worship. She believed that the purpose of life was to glorify God by living out the lessons of the Gospels. The hallmarks of Shaker life were pacifism, celibacy, common property, and absolute honesty in all business dealings.

Because the Shakers did not believe in

marriage or bearing children, survival of the sect depended on conversions and adoptions, which ultimately made it difficult to sustain growth. Today, just a few elderly Shakers remain, but their philosophy on work bears revisiting in today's "swim with the sharks" business climate. Mother Ann's motto was "hands to work and hearts to God." To the Shakers, work *is* prayer. The Shakers used the word *laboring* as their term for worship. No wonder the Shakers excelled in all manner of work — sewing, tanning, weaving, basketweaving, furniture making, and growing medicinal herbs.

Ingenious Shakers invented the circular saw and the clothespin. According to *Gifts of the Spirit*, by Philip Zaleski and Paul Kaufman, the Shakers believed that work was not merely a necessity to earn a living, but a sacred duty that should be used to elevate the soul, strengthen the body, curb

> "The streets are quiet — every building, whatever may be its use, has something of the air of a chapel. The paint is all fresh; the planks are clean bright; the windows are all clean. A sheen is on everything; a happy quiet reigns."
>
> — NINETEENTH-CENTURY DESCRIPTION OF A SHAKER VILLAGE FROM *GIFTS OF THE SPIRIT*

appetites, and bring order out of chaos. Some of the rules that governed their work include:

꩜ **Work must be practical.** Forget useless frills and artifice. Hence the simple, spare beauty of Shaker furniture.

꩜ **Work cannot be rushed, and the worker should strive for perfection.** Wood might need seasoning. It might take extra time to lay a brick properly. So be it. Shakers wanted their work to be of such quality that it would last for centuries. And they wanted their souls to be valued even longer.

꩜ **The worker never spares or promotes himself.** Quality speaks for itself. Shakers did not sign their creations because they believed everything belonged to God. And if you believe you work for God, you tend to do so with more attention, love, and care.

ELEVEN

Going and Doing

"What do you plan to do with your one wild and precious life?"
— FRANCIE COOPER, LIFE COACH

Today, women have more options than ever before. But too much of the discussion in the past has been about careers and not enough about calling. After all, you can be the CEO and still feel like a failure as a human being. You can be the best mom on the block and still want to make your life count in other ways. That's when you might find yourself asking the same question the disciples asked, "What then shall we *do?*" The three monotheistic faiths make it clear: Believers should be helping those in need. The three faiths that sprang from the patriarch Abraham were distinctive in that regard. Judaism, Christianity, and Islam all brought a passion for social justice into a world where only brute force had ruled before. They institutionalized the concepts of justice and charity. Two Hebrew words sum up the obligation of faith: *Tikun Olam,* "to fix the world." God wisely left the world unfinished and imperfect. That gives man and woman an ongoing, never-ending challenge to exercise our souls.

Remember at the end of the movie *Saving Private Ryan* when the young private played by Matt Damon visits the cemetery where his colleagues from World War II are buried? They had died saving his life because he was the last of five brothers in his family. Tears came to the private's eyes as he looked at the graves and remembered the words of his dying captain, who knew the private would get to go home and live to middle age and he would not: "Earn this."

Earn this. That's our challenge as well. Since September 11, more Americans have felt the urge to do something with their lives, something constructive. The ticking clock of terrorism registered deeply with aging baby boomers, who already were beginning to feel the tug of mortality as they moved north of forty. In particular, many women at mid-life, who might have devoted the first half of their lives to their families or building their career, have felt a desire to devote more time to putting their beliefs into practice.

How women choose might at long last provide the answer to Sigmund Freud's famous question, "What does woman want?" I discovered as I interviewed women for *What's Next?* and *What's Missing?* that what women want is really the same thing men want. They want to be respected for what they think and do. They want to be useful. To know love. To make their life count. They want to leave a legacy, a trace, some proof that they spent their lives on something that will outlast them. Their gift to the future will be to leave things a little better.

Each must find her contribution in her own way. Sometimes the contribution finds you. Phyllis Glazer thought she had found the perfect weekend retreat when she bought Blazing Saddles Ranch in the piney woods of East Texas in 1988. She bought it with her inheritance from her father and named it after the Mel Brooks comedy because her dad had the same sense of humor. She hoped the ranch would provide a serene, back-to-nature experience and thought she would use the peace and quiet to write a novel or children's book about animals. She loved animals, so she and her husband, Robert L. Glazer, stocked the ranch with rare horses, elk, llama, bison, emu, and miniature donkeys, creating their own wild game ranch. She thought it would be a peaceable kingdom.

It turned out to be more of a nightmare. She found herself drawn into a legal battle that would make Erin Brockovich proud. It turned out their gorgeous property was only a few miles from a deep-well injection site for hazardous waste. The closest residents had been suffering from severe medical problems for years. Most of them were descendants of slaves who had been freed after the Civil War, trapped in a cycle of poor schools and poor prospects. They had been complaining about the plant without getting any relief.

Phyllis was suddenly introduced to the problem in 1991 when she was driving her son Max to school one day. As they passed down the highway by the chemical plant, Gibraltar Chemical Resources, Inc., great clouds of reddish-brown fumes were spewing into the air. She saw workers fleeing from the plant, and she started to worry what was going on. She felt a burning sensation in her throat and mouth. A few days later, she was shocked to discover a hole had developed in her nasal septum. Tissue inside her mouth was shredded.

Later it was revealed that there had been an explosion at the plant when two chemicals were accidentally mixed. Horrified, Phyllis went to a town meeting to find out what was going on. She listened incredulously as company officials pooh-poohed concerns about the foul odors that wafted from the plant and about the possible contamination from tons of noxious chemicals that were being pumped into a mile-long shaft. A company official said that even if pollutants had leaked into the groundwater, the aquifer could be easily cleaned up. Phyllis surprised herself by jumping to her feet and blurting, "That's the most ridiculous thing I've ever heard!" It was the beginning of a totally new stage in life for her: environmental activist.

It would have been hard to find a more unlikely crusader. She later told *Time* magazine that she had been too intimidated to speak publicly most of

> "The world is full of lost people, motherless children and fragmented children who need our help. We can all participate in mothering, caring and nurturing. In such a way we fulfill our basic need to be needed, to reproduce ourselves in another by loving that person into the kingdom."
>
> — KARI TORJESEN MALCOLM

her life, but at the meeting she became a different person: "I felt I had to do something, and I felt I was born to fight this fight." Phyllis had been, by her own description, a pampered matron. "I was just a housewife before," she says. "I was happy to be a housewife." She had grown up in Phoenix, the only daughter of a Holocaust refugee. She had married a man her father picked out for her and had two children. When that marriage ended in divorce, she moved to Dallas in search of a father for her sons. Three months later, she married Glazer, a well-to-do liquor distributor, and they had a son together. It was a comfortable life. Her idea of a busy day was shopping at antique stores, having lunch with well-to-do friends, and going to art exhibits. You would never catch her without her diamond ring or without her hair done. Then she began her decade-long fight against pollution. She ended up spending millions of dollars in legal fees, but she was transformed in the process.

Phyllis learned that the nearby plant disposed of petroleum by-products and caustic materials such as sulfuric acid — some of it from as far away as Mexico. Some four hundred types of chemicals were recycled or pumped into an underground cavern. Her financial advisor told her she ought to sell the ranch property and get out. But by then, she had been to meetings of neighbors who felt powerless, and she had seen the children with horrible ailments, neurofibromatosis, Hodgkins Disease, and birth defects. "I was the only one with the [financial ability] to fight back," she told the *Houston Chronicle*. "What was I supposed to do, walk away?"

Instead, she put a large black-and-yellow warning sign from the U.S. Defense Department on her front door that read, "Caution: Hazardous Waste." She hired environmental engineers who found pollution in a local private water well. She hired epidemiologists to evaluate the birth defects. She hired a photographer to document the disfiguring ailments. And she hired some of the best environmental lawyers in Houston, Austin, and Dallas to take on the waste disposal company. She formed a group called MOSES — Mothers Organized to Stop Environmental Sins. After another explosion in 1993, the mothers picketed the gates of the company every week for seven months. They made black dolls to sell for donations called "Wasted Babies" in memory of the children who had died from peculiar maladies.

Phyllis took groups of residents and children to the state capitol and to Washington, D.C., to complain about the lack of regulatory action. Her favorite saying became, "I don't have heart attacks. I give them." NBC's *Dateline* program spotlighted her crusade and nicknamed her the "toxic avenger."

As you might imagine, the plant owners were not pleased. American Ecology Environmental Services, which had purchased the plant from Gibralter in 1994, complained she distorted the facts. They insisted in statements, "We didn't kill babies. We don't cause genetic mutations. We didn't stiff taxpayers. Those are untrue statements meant to force us to close the business. They're simply not based in fact." Townspeople who did not want to lose jobs and tax dollars said Phyllis Glazer ought to move out of town.

Even her own attorneys admit Phyllis can be dramatic to a fault. "There are times you want to strangle her," said Houston attorney Jim Blackburn in one news story. "But I have the highest personal regard for her. Phyllis does what it takes to open doors that would otherwise be closed. She's a brave woman."

At one point, Phyllis had to hire security

guards because of threats against her. Decapitated heads from dolls were ominously hung from the trees at her ranch. Her car was shot at. She's only five foot three inches tall, but people generally say she seems taller. A postal inspector who got involved in the fight tells that the first time he met her, she was highly agitated before an important hearing before the Environmental Protection Agency. A Methodist minister who was supposed to lead the group in prayer had cancelled at the last minute. Unable to find a substitute, Phyllis stood up before the group and sang the theme from the movie *Exodus*. It was an extraordinary moment. But somehow, with her deeply felt sense of justice, Phyllis pulled it off. Her flamboyance was the perfect antidote to the bland torpor of government bureaucracy. Most of the conservative Christians in the rural area had never had contact with anyone Jewish before, and certainly no one ever encountered anyone like Phyllis, who had a tendency to show up in a designer ranch outfit with a load of turquoise jewelry on. A black seamstress whose daughter had breathing problems and a skin disorder was skeptical at first, but after sharing personal stories with Phyllis, came to "love her to death." As they say in that part of the country, Phyllis might be a city woman, but she has a heart "as big as a washtub."

When we talked, Phyllis said she probably gets her determination from the Jewish value system she learned from her father. "There *is* a God," she said. "When I was a little girl I would ask my father how he could believe in God when he lost his whole family in the Holocaust, and he would say to me, '*God* didn't kill my family.' And he would tell me that when Jews throughout Europe were knocking on the doors of their neighbors begging refuge from the storm raging around them, they were denied protection. So I've always felt that when someone came to my door, I would have to help. I knew the sound, the knock. It was recognizable. I knew I had to answer the door."

More than four hundred of the town's five hundred-something residents ended up filing a class action suit against the company. The company fought back and filed a suit against Phyllis, her seventy-six-year-old mother, her husband, and her husband's company for conspiracy to interfere with the business. But in 1994, the company agreed to pay a $1.15 million settlement with the state for environmental violations. And in 1997, the company stopped accepting waste and announced the site would close.

The postscript for Phyllis Glazer, however, is not all sunny. At fifty-four, she became one of three Winona residents to develop brain tumors and has been recuperating. But she still has found time to fight the addition of a soccer field to a girls' school in her neighborhood that would have required the removal of 150 mature trees. And she regularly provides advice to people around the country on how to form grassroots groups like MOSES. "If you look around the country, you don't find hazardous waste in neighborhoods with affluent, white children," she observes. "There is no environmental justice. They do what they always do — deny, deny, and hope critics will go away — but the things never do go away, do they? They never learn that women whose children have been harmed will not go away quietly. We will fight to protect our children and our neighbor's children to the end."

Looking back, Phyllis said she is grateful she had the opportunity to do "something that a lot of people don't have the opportunity to do, a mitzvah (good deed)." But she observed, "I think many of us miss what we are here for. We have our families to raise, things to do. And sometimes there is something we need to do with our lives — maybe writing a book, maybe something else — and we pass it up because we're too busy with other things. I made myself un-busy. I had no idea how big a thing it was. I thought all I had to do was inform the government about what they did at the plant and they would close. I had no idea what I was in for, but I learned," she said. "I learned."

> "Knowing is not enough; we must apply. Willing is not enough; we must do."
>
> – GOETHE

As Phyllis discovered, going forth and doing disrupts your status quo. If you feel uneasy and unqualified and unsure about what you are being tugged into, that's okay. When God really loves you, they say, he disturbs you. Later you realize it was a good thing.

Jeanne Johnson Phillips felt some twinges about taking a presidential appointment — Ambassador to the Organization for Economic Cooperation and Development. Certainly, it was an enormous honor. A plum posting in Paris, a house near the Arc d' Triomphe, a prestigious chance to carry the American flag into decision-making circles. But her daughter Margaret was only eight years old. Her husband had his psychotherapist practice in Dallas. She had not lived anywhere else since she graduated from Southern Methodist University two decades before. It was such a leap of faith. Across an ocean. So, of course, she said yes.

No sooner had she arrived in Paris, jet-lagged, homesick, trying to learn the names of fifty staffers, than September 11 happened. "Suddenly, everyone in the foreign service knew they were in new territory, different territory," she said later. "We were all trying to do our part in our corner of the world. I immediately saw the goodness of the people who are career foreign service people. It was amazing. No one showed any fear, they just buckled down and did their jobs. It was humbling and made you feel really proud to be an American and able to serve. Three days after the attacks, the OECD community — the staff, the diplomatic members, and their families — had a memorial service. I had not even met many of my colleagues. September 11 was my second day in the office. The memorial service was my first official assignment. I closed with the twenty-third Psalm, which I paraphrased. I hesitated to do it, but something told me to go ahead. And I was amazed how many people came up afterward and said thank you so much for talking about that. Thank you for talking about God."

One of the immediate security concerns was the possible assassination or abduction of U.S. diplomats, so Jeanne suddenly found herself with bodyguards on her morning walk. Her husband, David, went with daughter, Margaret, to school and sat in the class with her. "I never felt afraid," Jeanne said, "as person of faith, I felt I was in good hands." She wondered at first why she was in that place at that time, but as the months went by, she could see more clearly how steps in her life had brought her there for a purpose.

In some ways, her upbringing had prepared her more to be an ambassador's wife than an ambassador. She was brought up as Jeanne Linder in Arkansas, where her father was a prosecuting attorney. She was a high achiever — cheerleader, student body president, president of her pledge class at the University of Arkansas. And she was a golden girl, with a mane of blonde hair, sky-blue eyes, and a welcoming smile that had a laugh not far behind. But her life of privilege fell apart when her father had severe business difficulties and sank into a drinking problem. Her dad later found help in the Alcoholics Anonymous program, resumed his law practice, and mentored others, but the interim struggle rocked their family. The experience steeled Jeanne. She calls them "those dark years," but her friends all say she became a stronger, even more empathetic person because of the experience. She transferred to Southern Methodist University and married a college classmate. They went their separate ways after five years, and she poured herself into building a public relations business. Her PR work led her to volunteer in George Bush's 1980 presidential campaign, the beginning of a loyal relationship that has lasted more than two decades. Pressed into fund-raising during the 1984 Republican convention, she immediately proved masterful — she raised $3 million from one luncheon and from then on, Jeanne was known as a fund-raising ace. She raised money for the Bush presidential campaigns in 1988 and 1992 as well as the gubernatorial campaigns for George W. Bush in 1994 and 1998. She could have taken a post in

Washington during the first Bush administration, but her heart told her to stay in Texas. She knew politics; having a family and children was more important to her. She realized she'd found the right guy when she met David Phillips. He wanted her to go to dinner one Sunday evening. She said she wanted to go to church at 5:30 p.m., so perhaps they could meet afterward. He said he'd like to go with her. She was impressed. They got married and along came Margaret, who almost immediately was trundled along with her mom to a hotel room in Austin while she orchestrated George W. Bush's gubernatorial inaugural.

Along with her fund-raising magic, Jeanne's organizational and motivational skills have become legendary. Not surprisingly, when it looked as if George W. Bush would be declared the winner over Democrat Al Gore, Jeanne Phillips got the call to go to Washington, D.C., and put together an inauguration. It was a formidable assignment: put together a celebration with fireworks, several concerts, big-name stars, a parade, and a half-dozen balls. There were thousands of invitations to coordinate, tickets, security passes, press requests. She had to raise $40 million immediately and find thousands of volunteers. And oh yes, one little detail: She only had thirty-one days to prepare, compared to the eighty-two usually available for inaugural preparations. And in the middle of all that, there were the Christmas holidays. And the Secret Service was warning of threats from terrorists and political protestors.

Some people would have hid under the bed. Jeanne just went to work eighteen hours a day. And made the inaugural a success despite sleet and snow. Was everything perfect? No, she admits, "but it was *exciting*." She used four guiding principles to put the inaugural together that ought to be a text for business schools:

∾ **Make every moment count.** Starting work in an empty building with no phones or desks, she told the assembled skeleton staff, "We only have thirty-one days to do this. Can you accept that? Then we won't mention it again." She convinced the staff that they would only have such an opportunity once in their lives. They would have to make every moment count. "I'm a great believer that we should enjoy the moment; the future will take care of itself. It's like when I am braiding my daughter's hair and I realize that I won't always get to do that. I want to enjoy that moment and make the most of it."

∾ **Elevate the mission.** She applied a lesson she learned from Dallas oilman Ray Hunt on major civic projects: Elevate the mission. As she explains, "This wasn't just A Big Weekend. This was not about rears on seats. It was about what we are as Americans . . . the peaceful passage of power with no tanks in the streets. Demonstrators, yes, but that's America. We were aware every minute of our place in history. We learned from the National Archives that it was the two hundredth anniversary of Thomas Jefferson's swearing in and that he was the first president sworn in Washington, D.C. That helped give us the foundation that America is still creating our stories and myths. We began to use positive language about the history, that we were creating a story that we would want to tell our grandchildren and they could tell their grandchildren. It became part of what we were doing psychologically."

∾ **Work as a team.** It was a humbling experience, she said, to pull together hundreds of people from various organizations in the capitol who probably weren't for George W. Bush. The election was a cliff-hanger that went into overtime, leaving a divided country. "We came in very humble," she said. "We saw the vote count." There were problems — they couldn't find a producer for the youth concert until a week before the event; they had to make snap decisions like spending a half a million dollars for police barricades. But she tried to convince the three hundred politically diverse staffers that their efforts would be stronger together than individually, so they would have to pull together quickly. "If we all win, we win big," she told them, "If we lose, we lose big."

∾ **Don't neglect the people in your life who help you.** Jeanne realized how grateful she was for the support players in her life: her sister, who took her daughter to school while she was gone; her husband, who spent most of the holidays without her; her friends, who pitched in to help. She encouraged her staff to thank the support players who were backing them up as well. "I began to consciously have good words for people," she recalled afterward. There were times when the phone man was the most important person in my entire life. I made sure to say, 'Great job on those phones. I appreciate your putting those in.' You discover that people are all alike. They want to be respected for what they do."

That's not a bad four-point program for any leadership book, and Jeanne would need it as she wrapped up her life in Texas, studied like a grind for Senate confirmation, and packed up her family for Paris, practicing her French all the way. It was telling that of many hundreds who worked on the presidential campaign, Jeanne Phillips was one of the very few who did not ask for anything in return. And because of that loyalty, President Bush made sure she got a Cinderella opportunity that turned out to be her biggest challenge yet. As Ambassador Phillips, she is bringing her own perspective to the two-year assignment. Her priorities: globalization, water, and education for women and children.

"The events of the last few months have made us all very aware that we live on a really small planet and we have to do more to see that people are not disenfranchised," she says.

She is looking at many of the global issues with an eye to how women and children are impacted. Indeed, studies are showing that living standards — family income, education, nutrition, life expectancy — all rise as women move toward equality and birth rates fall. One statistical model in Egypt showed that if mothers with no education had completed at least primary school, poverty would have been reduced by one-third.

"This is where having a woman at the table changes the dialogue," Jeanne said. "You can ask questions other people might not think to ask. They might know there are looming water shortages all over the world, but they might not think of it in terms of how many children will be made sick and die." That water problem grows more severe all the time, she added, pointing out that by 2050 a stunning two-thirds of the countries in the world will not have access to clean water. Part of the answer, she suggested, is creative partnerships like the "Living Water" program started by the Overseas Private Investment Corp. When OPIC finances a development project nowadays, she said, they also drill a well to provide fresh, potable water for a school or village. "It's a small thing, but it's the small things that add up," she said, pointing out that individual corporations or nonprofits could follow a similar approach.

Jeanne is particularly concerned about the impact of AIDS on children. Recent figures have shown that the number of children in the developing world who have lost at least one parent to AIDS will double to 25 million in the next eight years. "It's a scary situation. We are losing whole generations of people," she said. "We are looking at the situation in Africa with AIDS and how we as a major country can contribute to the solution. It is a significant opportunity for doing good."

Once again, she is calling on her staff to "elevate the mission" and realize that even

"The worship has ended. Let the service begin!"

— REMINDER IN THE SUNDAY BULLETIN AT ST. BART'S EPISCOPAL CHURCH IN MANHATTAN

their most mundane daily work is "not about visas or paperwork," but that they are on the front lines representing their country during a very challenging time. She admitted she feels like "Cinderella at the ball" sometimes. "I know it's going to strike midnight in two years and that's okay, because we feel so lucky to have this chance. It's an incredible gift because it stretches you to do things you never thought about doing or thought you could do. I'd like to be remembered as someone who was fair and did her homework and represented the president with honor and dignity. I also want to do whatever I can to make the world a better place, and there are certainly opportunities here. If this had happened to me ten years ago, I wouldn't have been ready at all. There really is some kind of divine plan for the right time, the right place, doing what you are supposed to do at that moment, and doing as much good as you can when you can. This is a teeny little spot on the planet, but it's sort of a multiplier effect. If everyone is trying to do all the good they can do when they can, pretty soon something *really* good happens."

One of the good things that has happened to Jeanne already is that her faith has been challenged at a deeper level as she has been moved away from all her familiar surroundings. "When you have to start someplace new, you really are challenged to think who you are at a deeper, different level. What do you really seek from God? Where are you going? You're not just going to church then because you always have to or because your friends do, you go because you need that anchor. I feel more intensely than ever that I am blessed by my marriage and my friendships and my child. So many people have reached out to us — my French driver said to me the week after September 11, 'You're so sad and we are so sad for you, but we are here for you.' Dozens and dozens of people have reached out to us. And you come to see those moments as opportunities to stand for your faith, to say something like, 'I believe God has his hand in this,' as opposed to 'Oh thank you, I believe it will work out.' I'm not sure I spoke up with my faith in every case, but I am acutely aware that I have an opportunity to gently reveal my faith. It's a fine line in government — you don't ever want to shove your beliefs on someone else, but you don't want to deny who you are, either."

Not surprisingly, when First Lady Laura Bush made her first solo trip overseas, she chose to speak in Paris at a special summit on education. The summit was organized by Jeanne Phillips and spotlighted the importance of early education in preventing poverty. As you might expect, it was im-

> "I never notice what's been done. I only see what remains to be done."
>
> — MARIE CURIE

peccably well organized — with great faith that everything would turn out fine.

One of the advantages of the twenty-first century is that women are finally moving into positions of influence where they can make a real difference. Case in point: Rep. Nancy Pelosi became the first woman to crack the "Capitol ceiling" when she was sworn in as Democratic Party Whip in 2002. Amazingly enough, in the 218-year history of the U.S. Congress, no woman has won a major leadership position or chaired a powerful committee. Until Nancy Pelosi. She moved another giant step up the ladder when her colleagues selected her Democratic Minority Leader after the fall 2002 elections. She became the most powerful woman on Capitol Hill and joked, "I've been waiting 200 years for this."

As a young girl Nancy had other ambitions — she thought for a time she would like to become a priest, had that been possible. Her mother wanted her to be a nun, she confesses, "but I knew not to go in that direction. It was clear to me even as a young girl that priests had more authority and more opportunity to do God's work. But in a way, I've had that opportunity here." She muses that allowing women to be ordained is a matter of timing. "Something about it is inevitable," she said. "Others think it is inconceivable. We need to shorten the distance between the inevitable and the inconceivable. The church would flourish and benefit."

The church and politics have been a part of her entire life. Her father, Tommy d'Alesandro Jr., and her brother Tommy III were mayors of Baltimore. Her father was one of thirteen children from Abruzzo, Italy, and worked his way up in America as a door-to-door insurance salesman. He went on to serve in the state legislature as a five-term U.S. Congressman and as the first Italian American and first Catholic mayor of Baltimore. The message Nancy heard day and night at home was: America is about opportunities. "My family always felt they were working on the side of the angels," she says.

Nancy grew up with politics like other kids grew up with the Mouseketeers. She remembers the first time her dad ran for mayor. She likes to tell that you could walk in her house and be handed a bumper sticker or brochure to distribute anytime but Christmas or Easter. She also remembers the people who would come to the door looking for help from her father. Often they'd end up having dinner at the D'Alesandro house because they were hungry. "That stays with you," she says. She learned how to refer constituents for welfare assistance or hospital care. She learned how to get some into housing projects and some out of jail.

And she grew up in the Roman Catholic Church. She remembers going to school at the Institute of Notre Dame in Baltimore and going next door to Mass at the Church of St. James. The nuns would give the schoolgirls hot chocolate afterward, *real* hot chocolate. She says, "I can still taste it." When it came time for college, Nancy went to Trinity College, a Catholic college for women that was just 45 miles away in Washington, D.C. That was as far as her parents would allow. After she married Paul Pelosi, they moved to New York, where he worked as a banker. Four of their five children were born there, and a fifth was born after they moved to California in 1969.

While her children were young, Nancy limited her politics to volunteer work. She became a powerhouse fund-raiser and then state party chair before jumping into elected office herself in 1987. The *Almanac of American Politics* rather drily observes that "She has the energy and shrewdness of one who has handled the most delicate political chores and the charm and unflappability of one who is the parent of five children."

When she was sworn in as Whip, *Washington Post* political maven Mary McGrory marveled, "Nancy Pelosi is this implausibly nice congresswoman from California who is about to be sworn in as Democratic Whip of the House. Chic and mannerly, mother of five, she is not one of the boys and conspicuously has not gone along to get along. . . . A Republican fan, Rep. Peter King of New York, describes her as '110 percent female and 110 percent tough pol.' "

To underscore the significance of her whip selection, Nancy hosted a luncheon before the ceremony for all the former and current female members of Congress. Out of some 2,000 members of Congress in U.S. history, 209 have been women and 117 of those are still living. Of the current 435 House members, sixty-two are women. That's up from nineteen two decades ago. In the 100-member Senate, the number of women since 1981 has risen from two to thirteen.

Nancy's theory about why more women have not gained more power on Capitol Hill is that their thirties and forties — the prime ladder-climbing years — are also the prime childrearing years. Most women do not feel right about leaving their families to live the one-dimensional and often solitary life of Congress. As a result, they usually lag ten years behind men entering politics. By the time they have gained any seniority, they are closer to retirement age than the men. But at sixty-one, Nancy doesn't look or act as if she's the retiring type, even though she's a grandmother and proud of it.

She was not a household word when she vaulted into the party leadership. But Americans are starting to learn more about her. Her home base is in Napa Valley, and she has represented the San Francisco area for eight terms. Her district is one of the most liberal in the country so, not surprisingly, so is she. Her critics call her a "latte liberal." She is pro-environment, pro-minimum wage, and pro-gun control. But she's not afraid to go her own way out of conviction. Like the more than 80 percent of Catholics who support abortion at some level, she is pro-choice, believing that it is not up to Congress to decide what medical procedures are allowed for women. She explains, "I believe God has given us a free will, with responsibilities that apply to each of us as individuals and that it should be up to the individual woman to make a decision about the size and timing of her family. It is up to her, her family, her god, and her doctor — not members of Congress." She also bucked union pressure to support NAFTA. And she broke with the Clinton administration to support human rights improvements in China.

As one Republican staffer admitted, "She's not just another pretty face even though she has a pretty face." She is the ranking Democrat on the Intelligence Committee and has been a prominent voice on the Appropriations Committee, where she has championed funding for AIDS research and assistance for New York City.

Her favorite saying is that the three most important issues today are "our children, our children, and our children." She explains that she believes her job is to "make the future brighter for the next generation," and that shapes her positions.

Her faith also has shaped her career. "We were raised in a very religious family, but I don't like to mix religion and partisan politics. It's a fine line, although there is no question that the values we have from our religion have an impact. I am inspired all the time by the Gospel of Matthew: 'When I was hungry, you gave me to eat. When I was homeless you gave me shelter.' The whole Gospel is an inspiration for trying to help people."

As she gets older, Nancy said she is finding that she is more and more interested in reading the Bible. "It goes in stages for me," she said. "Right now, I am fascinated again by the Bible." And she is trying to learn more about Islam. "We have to demonstrate a greater respect for the religions of other people if we want respect

"We shall some day be heeded, and . . . everybody will think it was always so, just exactly as many young people think that all the privileges, all the freedom, all the enjoyments which woman now possess always were hers. They have no idea of how every single inch of ground that she stands upon today has been gained by the hard work of some little handful of women of the past."

— SUSAN B. ANTHONY

ourselves. We can't simply say, 'I believe what I believe and you're incorrect.' I prefer, 'I believe what I believe and therefore, I respect your belief.' "

Ever the politician, she says she has never asked anyone to vote for her because she is a woman, but neither would she want them to vote against her because she is a woman. But when asked if having more women in office would empower other women, she doesn't hesitate a second to say with feeling, "Yes, yes, definitely, *yes*."

Those who think it has not made an appreciable difference to have women in elected office need only look at the changes that Sen. Kay Bailey Hutchison — a longtime Episcopalian — has helped make. When I covered the Texas Legislature back in the early 1970s, Kay Bailey was a state representative in her 20s. Setting a pattern that she would follow throughout her career, she built coalitions with women of all political stripes to change the law so women could hold financial accounts in their own names for the first time. And she pulled together the votes to bar the publication of the names of rape victims. Keep in mind that this was a time when it was still legal in Texas for a man to beat his wife with a stick — so long as the stick was no bigger than the man's little finger. To go against that engrained mind-set, Kay chose her battles carefully, built relationships with powerful members of the legislature, and worked harder than anyone else. After she was married to former Rep. Ray Hutchison, she gained a memorable ballot name that has proven unbeatable. She went on to become state treasurer and was elected to the U.S. Senate in 1993.

Kay didn't lose any time organizing a girl network in the Senate. And to encourage women of all ages to persevere through difficulties, she helped put together a book about the obstacles faced by the women in the Senate, called *Nine and Counting*. When she needed support calling for an investigation of the Tailhook scandal, most of her Senate colleagues were behind her, and when she adopted a baby girl and a baby boy, they understood the importance of that mid-life dream and threw a baby shower for her.

Just to show how Kay has made her time in Washington count, here are some of the changes she has championed that have benefited women: Passage of the Home-maker IRA, Passage of Pension Catch-Up,

Repeal of the Marriage Penalty, Reauthorization of the breast cancer stamp, Passage of antistalking legislation, Passage of the Afghan Women and Children Relief Act, and Introduction of single-gender school legislation.

It would be impossible to calculate how many women's lives have been touched by those laws. Kay is careful to point out it is not that men are against all those things, "they just had not thought of doing them." So she helped them think of doing them.

But there is much more

> "To keep a lamp burning, we have to keep putting oil in it."
>
> – MOTHER TERESA

work to do. Our laws have not kept up with the dramatic influx of women into the labor force. In two-thirds of all couples today, both spouses work. Unfortunately, tax laws and Social Security programs still penalize women who enter the labor market. It's going to take a lot of dogged hard work and votes to see that women are treated fairly in the fine print. Though the women in Congress are in small numbers, they tend to work together well and often cross party lines to support each other — Democrat Hillary Rodham Clinton, for example, teamed up with Republican Kay Bailey

Hutchison to push for the single-gender schools.

Women who think that politics is for others should think again. In recent years, women have come to Congress after being travel agents, college guidance counselors, advertising executives, and nonprofit volunteers. Betty Karnette was a teacher for two decades in California before she won a seat in the state senate, so she understands education issues. Kay Granger was a teacher before she served as mayor of Fort Worth. Now in Congress, she is trying to improve insurance portability. Probably the most dramatic transition is Carolyn McCarthy, who went from being a nurse to a champion of gun control in Congress.

Growing up in Long Island, Carolyn McCarthy was dyslexic and struggled with bookwork. She was shy, but she felt called to help others, so she became a nurse. She married an outgoing Irishman named Dennis McCarthy, who did well in the securities business in Manhattan, and they have a son, Kevin. But their suburban life together was not without its problems. They divorced during a stressful time but later reconciled and remarried. Then, on a cold night in December 1993, she learned her husband and son had been shot by a mentally disturbed man as they headed home from work on a crowded Long Island train. The *New York Times* reported that shortly after 6 p.m., "the gunman entered the train's third car and walked backward down the aisle, looking into the eyes of passengers as he shot one after another with his nine-millimeter handgun. As passengers screamed, diving to the floor, the man calmly emptied his gun, reloaded it, and began shooting again." When the doors to the commuter train opened at her local station, six people were dead and nineteen wounded. Police found Dennis McCarthy slumped over his son, Kevin, who was shot in the head. Doctors said the twenty-six-year-old son would never walk again.

That was the beginning of Carolyn McCarthy's metamorphosis. She rejected the neurosurgeons' glum prognosis for Kevin and declared, "He will live, and he will move." She personally supervised his rehabilitation, refusing to install ramps so he would be forced to stretch himself to become mobile.

"Vision is not enough. It must be combined with venture. It is not enough to stare up the steps, we must step up the stairs."

– VACLAV HAVEL

As she later told a British reporter, "I guess I was the kind of nurse who didn't believe in coddling a patient. I mean, if it takes two hours to comb your hair, then do it, and the next time it will be less." As a result of her care and prodding, Kevin recovered enough to resume work at the same investment firm where his father worked.

As Kevin became more independent, Carolyn became more active in gun-control efforts. To her chagrin, her congressman, a Republican incumbent, refused to endorse legislation banning assault weapons. So she decided to run against him on the Democratic ballot, although she remained a registered Republican. She won easily. The widow McCarthy became Congresswoman Carolyn McCarthy at the age of fifty-two. After she won, she visited her husband's grave and said, "Hey Den! My God, Dennis. Look at me now. Who would've ever thought?"

Since then, she has earned her Congressional colleagues' respect, if not their votes, for her hard work on the gun-control issue. Democratic leader Dick Gephardt called her a "citizen-legislator. She is exactly what this country needs." A TV movie, produced by Barbra Streisand, was made about her story.

The most dramatic moment in her career came in June 1999. Pressure had been building for Congress to do something about the easy availability of guns in the wake of the shooting at Columbine High School in Colorado. The emotional high point of the debate came when Representative McCarthy gave the speech of her life on the floor of the House of Representatives, begging the lawmakers to pass restrictions on the purchase of weapons at gun shows. It was 1 a.m., so most Americans didn't get to see the speech. Carolyn McCarthy, a petite figure in navy and pearls, walked up to the well of the House and told her hushed colleagues: "I am trying to stop the criminals from being able to get guns. This is not a game to me. This is not a game to the American people." She said the background check would only be an inconvenience to some people, a possible delay of three days, not a removal of anyone's right to own a gun. She implored her colleagues, "This is the only reason I came to Congress . . . I am sorry that this is very hard for me. I'm Irish, and I'm not supposed to cry in front of anyone, but I made a promise a long time ago. I made a promise to my son and to my husband. If there was anything that I could do to prevent one family from going through what I have gone through . . . then I have done my job.

"Let me go home," she concluded, with tears streaming down her cheeks. "Let me go home." And although her colleagues applauded her resoundingly, when the time to vote came, the measure failed. But the next spring, Carolyn was back at it again, trying to close gun show loopholes and require child safety locks on new handguns. "Things go slow," she admitted. "It doesn't look like it's time to go home yet."

To turn up the heat on the gun-control issue, Carolyn became one of the biggest cheerleaders for the Million Mom March on Mother's Day 2000. Mothers from around the country trekked to Washington, D.C., for a massive demonstration of concern about gun violence. Her goal is to convince more people that reasonable safeguards are needed, "because we lose 35,000 people a year and thirteen children a day to gun violence." Indeed, views on gun control appeared to be shifting after so many multiple shootings, with a poll that week showing 61 percent of Americans felt gun laws needed to be stricter.

Though she was targeted by pro-gun groups for defeat in 2002, she won re-election. Her efforts have made her a new kind of political role model for women. When the White House Project, which is trying to get more women involved in politics, did a study of the most believable messages in national politics, Carolyn McCarthy's message registered as more compelling than any other with young women who were interested in running for office. In focus groups, many said they were impressed that she did not start out as a politician and that she had taken on public service out of conviction, not raw ambition.

The irony is that although the United States has been a leader in promoting democracy around the world for two hundred years, a woman has never been elected to our nation's highest office. Only 1 percent of all U.S. Senators and 2 percent of all U.S. Representatives have been women. The goal of the White House Project is to get more women into the leadership pipeline so that women who represent the issues of concern to the majority of Americans can run viable campaigns for higher office during the next decade.

But in order for women to campaign on equal footing with men, to broaden the national agenda, there will have to be a greater number of women to take on civic life. Women will have to be mobilized from a variety of backgrounds to join the conversation about who can lead this country. They will need encouragement to envision themselves as county commissioners, state representatives, or as school board members instead of PTA presidents. But as Carolyn McCarthy and Nancy Pelosi and Kay Bailey Hutchison have shown, women can change the conversation when they put the values of their faith to work.

Could you envision yourself in public service? If the rough and tumble of partisan politics isn't for you, then you might still consider public service close to home, especially on the school board, the city council, juvenile board, or mental health board. Just do the best you can, leave before you're burned out, and then let someone else try. That's it.

We all tend to seek the safe and the comfortable; we want to settle down and be acceptable. But God calls us to comfort those who are not safe, who are not acceptable. He calls us, as Joan Chittister reminds, "to be signs of the age to come, models of belief, living witnesses, a gift of hope to the next generation."

No, we can't solve all the problems in the world, but we each can do something about our corners of the world. Is there some cause that gets *your* pulse beating? You might want to start small. But the point is to start. You might embolden others just by thinking outside of your comfort zone.

When uniforms were needed to help Afghan girls go back to school after the fall of the Taliban, an organization started by women in the United States — "Vital Voices" — found a way to provide them. They got the endorsement of First Lady Laura Bush, cloth donated by Liz Claiborne, and thousands of treadle sewing machines donated by a Florida company. Now the Afghan girls not only have uniforms, their families also have a way to make other clothes and a living. It shows how women's networking can have a multiplier effect. Vital Voices also is coaching women in Vietnam how to start businesses and is supporting international legal changes to crack down on the trafficking of one to two million women and girls in the sex trade.

It is a sign of the times that "Finishers Project," a coalition of more than 50 mission agencies, has been founded to reach baby boomers interested in doing mission work at mid-life. The first two conferences in 1999–2000 attracted six hundred participants who were wrestling with what to do with the rest of their lives. One of the speakers was Julie Soltis, a homemaker whose husband had died. She was intrigued by the idea of a second career as a missionary. Two years later, she was working with Bosnian refugees in Austria.

As you look for ways to pitch in, remember that there are many forms of service. You might be able to use dormant gifts — you might use your college language skills to translate for a relief group or you might try singing in the choir after years of sitting in the pew. If you took piano lessons as a child,

> "Someone will say, 'One person has faith, another has actions.' My answer is, 'Show me how anyone can have faith without actions. I will show you my faith by my actions.'"
>
> — JAMES 2:18

you might pass that training on to a child who needs mentoring after school. The artist hidden in you might tiptoe out to paint murals for a day-care center.

If you think you have no artistic talent, you could still pick up a hammer and help Habitat for Humanity build homes for homeless.

You could be one of those desperately needed Girl Scout leaders, helping young girls learn survival skills.

Or do reading for the blind.

Or gather books for inner-city schools.

Or donate clothes to a battered women's shelter.

Or you could serve as an election monitor.

Or . . . you choose.

TAKE HOME:

Women of faith have always led the way in the United States in making change. Probably the best-known advocate for women, Susan B. Anthony, was a Quaker who always identified herself as a Friend, even after her family switched to the Unitarian Church because the local Quaker congregation did not support the Anthony family opposition to slavery. When asked to lead the prayer at meetings, Susan B. Anthony generally preferred the Quaker way of giving thanks in silence. According to Lynn Sherr's treasure of a book, *In Her Own Words*, Anthony rarely missed services when she was home and called them "Sunday lift-ups." Her life also was influenced by the fact that many of her friends were ministers. Her life-long colleague Elizabeth Cady Stanton had an irreverent, rebellious approach to religion and even produced her own, antipatriarchal *Women's Bible*. But Anthony shrewdly knew she could not take on the church and the country at the same time. She was tolerant and counted Christians, Mormons, Jews, and nonbelievers among the suffrage supporters. Once, when asked if she prayed, she said, "I pray every single second of my life, not only on my knees but with my work. My prayer is to lift women to equality with men. Work and worship are one with me."

According to *Not for Ourselves Alone*, by Geoffrey Warm and Ken Burns, church Sunday Schools were the only source of education for many young girls when our country was young and mostly rural.

Women of the church were the leaders of

the fight against slavery — sometimes leaving the church behind. Abolitionists Sarah and Angelina Grimke were the devout daughters of a Charleston slaveholding family and left their home and the Episcopal Church rather than sanction the enslavement of others. Angelina wrote "An Appeal to Christian Women of the South," exhorting them that slavery was a sin and that "female slaves are our sisters."

Lucretia Coffin Mott was a Quaker minister, an agent for the Underground Railroad, and a founder of the first female antislavery society. Like many Quaker women, she supported temperance as well. The battered women of that era often were abused by drunken husbands, which fueled both the temperance and suffrage movements.

Likewise, social reformer Jane Addams came from a Quaker family dedicated to the antislavery cause. She went on to found Hull House in Chicago in 1886. The "settlement house" became the model for providing social services as well as cultural and intellectual stimulation under one roof. Hull House ministered to the poorest immigrants, Sicilians, Irish, Greeks, and Russian Jews, and the exploited workers in the meatpacking houses, the steel mills, and sweatshops. According to her biographer, Jeane Bethke Eishtain, Jane Addams believed that better selves come from helping others — and better cities, too. She went on to found the Women's International League for Peace and Freedom during World War I to spread social freedom to all members of the human community.

Dorothea Dix had the misfortune of growing up in a home with an alcoholic father who was an itinerant Methodist preacher and a mother who was not in stable

> "Then I'll be all aroun' in the dark. I'll be ever'where — wherever you look. Wherever they's a fight so hungry people can eat, I'll be there. Wherever they's a cop beatin' up a guy, I'll be there. If Casy know'd, why I'll be in the way guys yell when they're mad an' I'll be in the way kids laugh when they are hungry an' they know supper's ready. An' when our folks eat the stuff they raise an' live in the houses they build, why I'll be there."
>
> — THE CHARACTER TOM JOAD in John Steinbeck's *Grapes of Wrath*

mental health. She left at age twelve to live in Boston with her grandmother. By age fourteen, she was teaching in a school for young girls with a curriculum that emphasized the sciences and the responsibilities of ethical living. When a young clergyman asked her to begin a Sunday School class in the East Cambridge Jail in 1841, she accepted. She observed the inhumane treatment of insane and mentally disturbed persons, who were locked up with criminals. They often were unclothed, chained to walls, and flogged. She began a lifetime of documenting conditions and pleading for better care for the mentally ill of the country, a radical idea at the time. She played a major role in the funding of thirty-two mental hospitals and fifteen schools for the feeble-minded, a school for the blind, and training facilities for nurses. Though she had inherited enough money to retire, she continued her humanitarian work, saying, "I think even lying on my bed I can still do something."

TWELVE

Forgiving

"Only one petition in the Lord's Prayer has any condition attached to it: it is the petition for forgiveness."
— WILLIAM TEMPLE

Some of the best advice I've encountered on forgiveness was in a short daily reading in *The Upper Room*, the little devotional magazine that is distributed around the world. A woman from Perthshire, Scotland, shared three steps that you can take when you are finding it difficult to forgive:

First, you should ask God to enable you to forgive the person. It's too hard to do on your own.

Second, you should ask God to bless that person. Make that request every day, thoughtfully, not just once quickly.

Third, you should ask God to give you an opportunity to show kindness to the person. And when that opportunity comes, be kind, even if you have to grit your teeth at first. You'll get better at it.

Forgiveness is something that Mary Lou Redding, managing editor of *The Upper Room*, spends a lot of time thinking about and writing about. "If I had to choose the issue that people need more help with in the world, it would be forgiveness. That's something everybody needs help with. We could never publish enough about forgiveness. Everyone is deeply wounded along the road of life. The only way to leave behind the wounds, the way to freedom for people, is learning how to forgive and not waiting until people are sorry before we forgive."

So forgiveness is necessary, not just for the deep and deliberate wounds, but for the everyday slights. Mary Lou says, "Our grudges add up to the point that they are like an enormous green plastic garbage bag that we drag along behind us, in which we put all this junk. You know, all the mean things she said. All the times they didn't do *X*. We keep it bagged up and drag it with us the rest of our lives. Forgiving is very important because that is what empties the garbage bag. Somehow we have to decide to leave the bag and move on. It is a crucial and central issue because so many people just don't know how to do it."

Mary Lou's job is a daunting one. She is

responsible for supervising the editing, production, and distribution of the magazine for 2.1 million subscribers in the United States and more than 3 million readers around the world. The bimonthly publication features short devotionals submitted by readers from Boise to Brazil. Each page features a Scripture reading and prayer related to the day's theme. The magazine has built a large, loyal following. It is printed in forty-six languages and distributed to eighty-plus countries.

Yet Mary Lou wears her responsibilities with self-deprecating humor. She reads Dave Barry and Jerry Seinfeld as well as Henry James, and William Faulkner. She listens to Chopin and Linda Ronstadt and Appalachian groups. She jokes that she is either a Renaissance woman or a Jacqueline-of-all-trades — she bakes bread, makes clothes, watches *Star Trek* and plays racquetball. She's proud that she is from "hardy, Kentucky hillbilly stock." "Even though it reinforces stereotypes of my ethnic group," she admits in a personal sketch, "I am one of seven children and have more than fifty first cousins." She once told Amazon.com, "People in the South don't all see the world in the same way, but we all see it differently than those from other parts of the country. The South breeds people of eccentricity — and so we all learn to live with weirdness as a part of daily life. That takes its toll on us and skews our worldview. People who read Faulkner or O'Connor and think their characters are examples of extreme creativity have never lived next door to my relatives." She says her hillbilly heritage is a fierce independence — and she proved that by pulling up stakes with her daughter and moving from their home in Oklahoma to live and work in Nashville, Tennessee, where she lives now. She has taught writing on the college level, one of her loves, and has written several books, including *Breaking and Mending: Divorce and God's Grace* and *While We Wait: Living the Questions of Advent.*

It was in *Breaking and Mending* that she expressed the depths of her own struggle in the chapter on forgiveness. She went through a divorce after seven years of marriage. That experience not only rocked her faith, it left her in a sort of desert limbo for several years while she sorted everything out. Life was not what she expected it to be. She observed wryly that she has a mug with an appropriate saying: "Life. It's nothing like the brochure." But she admits,

> "Among Jesus' last words on the cross are words of forgiveness. Jesus — come to the fullness of humanity, the end time, the final moment — goes burned into our mind as a forgiver. Clearly, to be everything we can become, we must learn to forgive."
>
> — JOAN CHITTISTER

she found God in the struggle and discovered that life is a matter of relationship, not just rules, "Which is good, since keeping all the rules is impossible for me," she wrote. "I was and always will be deeply flawed. I will never be able to live up to my highest ideals. I will never be able to do everything correctly and make everything come out okay. That has always been the truth. That is why I need God's grace. I am grateful that God pours it out on me and on all of us."

Like many people who divorce, Mary Lou went through a series of stages. She felt she had to get out of her marriage, but as a believer, she anguished over the decision. She asked God to forgive her and asked the people she had hurt to forgive her. She also had to forgive those who had hurt her, starting with her spouse. Yet her first response was to pretend she was not all that deeply wounded, which was a way of avoiding truly forgiving and thinking about the things she wanted to forget. One night she was having dinner with a friend when her ex-spouse called, and she became angry enough about the conversation to hang up. Her friend observed that she still was not free if the relationship still made her that angry. She prayed about it and wrote in her journal about it. "I wasn't ready to forgive, but I asked God to make me willing to be made willing," she wrote in *Breaking and Mending*. Gradually, she was able to talk to her spouse and keep her emotions under control.

The old hurts still clung to her, however, disturbing her façade of composure and competence. She thought about her mother, who had stayed bitter about growing up desperately poor in the Kentucky coal-mining area. Her mother was critical and pessimistic about human nature the rest of her life, which had both defined and limited who she was. Mary Lou did not want to be shaped and limited by her own disappointments, so she talked to her counselor about it. She came to realize

"I hereby forgive everyone who offended or angered me or sinned against me."

— PRAYER ON GOING TO BED, from the traditional Jewish prayer book that her ex-husband was probably in as much pain as she was. She began to pray for him. She thought of the pain he must feel being separated from his daughter, and she prayed about that. She found herself praying for him freely, not out of any obligation. She was able to acknowledge the good things in their marriage. "When I was able to care about him and pray sincerely for God's best for him, then I knew I was truly free of the hurts that had built up over the years," she wrote in *Breaking and Mending.*

But there remained someone else to forgive: herself. She was still angry with herself for making a mistake in marrying. Then one day, while she was consoling a friend with a problem, she realized that she wasn't dealing as gently and compassionately with herself as she was with her friend. Now, she admits, when she is flogging herself mentally for making some mistake, she asks herself, "Would you treat your best friend this way?" Then she tries to be more loving to herself as a fallible human being. She came to believe "that God is continually guiding us toward forgiveness."

But what finally convinced her of that was a call from her ex-husband. He asked for her forgiveness — for the things he had done to hurt her during their marriage, while they were divorcing, and in the years afterward. He concluded, "I'm sorry, and I ask you to forgive me if you can." She was speechless. Then she told him that of course she forgave him and had done so years before. But what had happened to bring him to apologize? He explained that he had been participating in a prayer vigil when it entered his heart that although he had asked God to forgive him many times, he had never asked her to forgive him. After that, she

> "Everyone says forgiveness is a lovely idea until they have something to forgive."
>
> — CLIVE STAPLES (C. S. LEWIS)

says, the tensions that had dogged their relationship were gone. From then on, they usually were able to share events in their daughter's life and even meals without friction. Yes, she still might get annoyed with him, but about things of the moment, not the past. While the road to forgiveness might be long and winding, she wrote, "there is a wide, good place at the end. This is a gift of grace."

We forgive on many levels — we excuse someone for being late, for causing a wreck accidentally. We pardon or show mercy to someone who has committed a grievous offense against someone else. We forgive our children for breaking the lamp. We forgive the CEO who never says thanks for working late.

But someone always has to go first. The process starts when you give up any ideas of getting even. Real life is not like *The Sopranos*. You can't whack the people on your enemies list. You can place the matter in God's hands, though, and walk away to a freer life. The others might not see the error of their ways in your lifetime, but you should at least stop carrying that green garbage bag of hurts around as Mary Lou suggests. Get over it.

That doesn't mean you totally forget the incident — you might forgive someone and still be able to recall that you were once hurt. Forgiveness does take the sharp, saw-toothed edges off the memory.

Letting go is a struggle even for theologians. C. S. Lewis wrote just before he died, "I think I have at last forgiven the cruel schoolmaster who so darkened my youth. I had done it many times before, but this time I think I have really done it."

Judaism instructs that those who have wronged another must seek forgiveness from them. The wrongdoers are mandated to sincerely ask pardon and seek to correct the harm they have done. But after a certain point — after three sincere apologies from the offender, an attempt at restitution or an indication that the offender has had a change of heart — it then becomes the duty of the wronged person to forgive.

We are learning that harboring ill will is not only bad for the soul, it is bad for your health. In *Shoah*, a documentary on the Holocaust by Claude Lanzmann, a survivor of the Warsaw ghetto talked about the deep bitterness he still harbored in his soul for the Nazis, saying, "If you could lick my heart, it would poison you."

Hanging on to grudges can be toxic all around. Social scientists are finding that forgiveness can lead to physical healing as well as emotional wholeness. It releases the forgiver from prolonged anger and stress that have been linked to cardiovascular diseases, high blood pressure, hypertension, and even cancer. One study found a significant decrease in depression and

> "Then Peter came to Jesus and asked, 'Lord, how many times shall I forgive my brother when he sins against me? Up to seven times?' Jesus answered, 'I tell you, not seven times, but seventy-seven times.'"
>
> — MATTHEW 8:21

anxiety among elderly females who participated in a forgiveness program. Since more than 20 million women suffer from depression — nearly twice as many as men — alleviating some of those burdens could prove healing.

Theologian Lewis Smedes suggests in *Forgive and Forget* that you have to reinterpret the person who has wronged you, so the person is not reduced to a one-dimensional caricature. Try to think differently and seriously about the offender, Smedes says, who is "a needy, weak, complicated, and fallible human being like ourselves."

> "For if you forgive others their trespasses, your heavenly Father will also forgive you; but if you do not forgive others, neither will your Father forgive your trespasses."
>
> — MATTHEW 6:14–15

When you can find meaning in the pain you have experienced, you are probably on your way to healing. The full goal is for both sides to work through negative feelings, reconcile, restore the relationship, learn from the experience, and grow. Could you share a joke or a hug or a meal with the person? If not, you're probably not there yet.

The Bible is full of role models for forgiveness. Joseph forgave the brothers who sold him into slavery in the Old Testament. The father forgave his prodigal son in the New Testament parable. We not only must forgive others, we must also forgive ourselves — just as Paul had to forgive himself for persecuting Christians and pour out new love for them. We also must ask others to forgive us for our transgressions. The Alcoholics Anonymous 12-Step program tells those who want to recover that they must make a list of all those they've wronged and be willing to make amends to all.

And we must regularly ask God to forgive our mistakes, a central spiritual principle. Confession is a way you can learn to ask forgiveness from God — and in the process, gain understanding about the frailties of others. In one issue, *The Upper Room* suggested that readers say, "We confess our sins, knowing that through Jesus Christ, God forgives us and changes us." A few minutes are suggested for silent confession, then the prayer, "Forgive us, God. Change us so that, redeemed and renewed, we will serve you. Amen."

The Catholic and Orthodox churches still offer individual confession, but after reforms of the sixteenth century, Protestant denominations evolved away from private, personal confession to congregational confessions of a generic nature, kind of a blanket amnesty. The Apostles Creed that is often recited by congregations, for example, says only "I believe in the Holy Spirit, the holy Catholic Church, the communion of saints, the forgiveness of sins, the resurrection of the body, and the life everlasting." The Nicene Creed briefly recognizes, "We acknowledge one baptism for the forgiveness of sins."

> "Confession is nothing but humility in action . . . When there is a gap between me and Christ, when my love is divided, anything can come to fill the gap. Confession is a place where I allow Jesus to take away from me everything that divides, that destroys."
>
> — MOTHER TERESA

But a more personal admission of sin is more cleansing and therapeutic. The Anglican prayer book comes closer to the older Catholic ritual by spelling out the need to confess our "manifold sins and wickedness." The general Anglican confession is elegantly blunt: "Almighty and most merciful Father; We have erred, and strayed from thy ways like lost sheep. We have followed too much the devices and desires of our own hearts. We have offended against thy holy laws. We have left undone those things which we ought to have done; And we have done those things which we ought not to have done; And there is no health in us. But thou, O Lord, have mercy upon us, miserable offenders. Spare thou those, O God, who confess their faults. Restore thou those who are penitent . . ."

Some Protestant churches and small study groups are beginning to restore forms of confession. They have recognized that without a way to express their mistakes safely, many people trudge through life with a lot of covered up guilt. Without the regular confession of the church, the only outlet many people have is a hired counselor or psychologist. With fewer long-term, intimate friends and less reflective time to share innermost thoughts, most people have fewer opportunities to talk through their mistakes. If your denomination does not specifically in-

> "Pardon one another so that later on, you will not remember the injury. The remembering of an injury is itself a wrong: it adds to our anger, feeds our sin, and hates what is good. It is a rusty arrow and poison for the soul."
>
> — FRANCIS OF PAOLA

clude an opportunity for confession that allows you to feel heard and forgiven, you might wish to make it a point to add specific words of confession in your prayers at home and express those feelings out loud. It is cathartic.

It also might take practice to express your innermost feelings to others, to confess them informally. One of the things that Mary Lou Redding recommends is being part of a small accountability group, where you can talk about the zigs and zags in your life. One day a week, she gets to work at 7:30 a.m. for an accountability group she shares with several women co-workers. "Anybody who knows us says that's a miracle — to make a commitment to be dressed and in your right mind at that hour is quite a challenge. The paradigm for our group came out of the Emmaus movement. We talk about where we are challenged, where we have done well, and where we haven't done so well. Each of us has a personal mission statement, so we can hold each other accountable about how well we are living by our mission statement. Then we pray for each other.

"One of the things that is true about spiritual life is that people who are part of a small group grow more steadily than people who are not. The spiritual life is not meant to be an isolated life. It is a communal life. People have some accountability for their spiritual journey."

Mary Lou said one of her friends keeps a plaque in her office that reads, "A friend is someone who knows the song in your heart and sings it for you when your memory fails." And that's how the group functions for her. Mary Lou said that when she was going through her divorce and it seemed as if she could not connect with God for several years, her small group became the incarnation of God's presence for her. "They helped me to listen. For me, discerning God's will is a communal experience. If a single person listens alone, they can get some really weird ideas about what God is. If you are listening with a community of believers, they are a wonderful way to test out what you think you are hearing from God. I like to listen with my brothers and sisters of faith. They say we get two ears and one mouth so we should listen twice as much as we speak."

Mary Lou also journals as a way to express her ups and downs. "My definition of spirituality is learning to pay attention to God. One of the ways I attend to the presence of God in my life and the world is journaling. The question I ask myself in a million ways is Where have I seen God? Where is God at work? What do I see God doing in the world? Journaling is where I experience God. I have been journaling all my life. My daughter keeps asking me, 'Mom when you die, can I read your journals?' And I say, of course, they will belong to you. But if you read them before I die, you might die."

In the meantime, at fifty-two, she has found enjoyment in a new relationship. She simplified her life by downsizing and is trying to have more balance in her schedule by not staying in the office so much. But one of the projects she'd like to complete is — not surprisingly — a book about forgiveness.

"Some are reluctant to forgive because doing so seems to discount the seriousness of the wrongs that others do; actually forgiving says the opposite," she wrote in *The Upper Room* in the fall of 2002. "Forgiving requires first acknowledging that an act is wrong. If it were not, forgiveness would not be needed. When we forgive, we are saying, 'What you did was wrong, but I release you from its penalty.' " By forgiving, we release ourselves as well; we are no longer bound to the other by bad feelings. As Mary Lou points out, "Nursing hurts from the past takes energy, and forgiving frees us to use that energy to live fully and abundantly in the present."

We all drag many of our hurts along with us as we go through life — the critical teacher, the fickle friend, social rejection, setbacks at work. Are you dragging around anything in your green garbage bag that you ought to let go of? Was your faith tested by failure or rejection or disappointment this week? If you knew you only had a few days to

> "The sins of others are before our eyes; our own are behind our backs."
>
> — SENECA

live, would there be someone you would want to clear accounts with? Does it help to visualize that person as God might see him or her? Bishop John Shelby Spong tells us to "love wastefully." We each have to ask ourselves, do we?

TAKE HOME:

Forgiveness can be key to stopping cycles of violence. It hasn't made much news, but some of the family members of the September 11 victims are setting a powerful example of compassion. They have formed a nonprofit organization seeking effective alternatives to war as a response to the terrorist attacks. It's called "Peaceful Tomorrows," and it is an effort to stop the cycle of violence that now crosses oceans, destroys buildings, and blows up buses in the Holy Land. Peaceful Tomorrows favors the creation of an Afghan victims fund to match the outpouring of support for U.S. victims. Four family members even traveled to Afghanistan to meet with civilian victims of the subsequent bombing campaign to flush out the al Queda terrorists. One of the Americans involved lost her brother in the World Trade Center when he stayed back with a quadraplegic friend. Another lost his daughter on the United Flight 93, which crashed into the earth in Pennsylvania. Another lost a brother-in-law in the Pentagon crash. Rather than become bitter or angry at all Muslims because most of the terrorists were believed to be Muslims, the family members are choosing to extend a hand to Muslim families. Just like the victims in the United States, many of the Afghans simply were in the wrong place at the wrong time. One humanitarian observer reported seeing children arriving screaming at the hospital maimed by American cluster bombs, an inadvertent, but nevertheless tragic consequence of the effort to flush out al Qaeda terrorists. The effort to bridge that pain with compassion is not only commendable, but essential if we are ever to feel safe with each other.

Rabbi David Wolpe of Sinai Temple in Los Angeles often sees families torn apart, siblings who do not speak to each other, parents who cannot sit in the same room as their children, and ex-spouses who speak of each other with contempt. All know that forgiveness would be a helpful step, but they will not take that step. Rabbi Wolpe likes to tell a Hasidic parable about a king who quarreled with his son. In a fit of rage, the king exiled his son from the kingdom. Years passed while the father stewed and the son wandered alone in the world. Finally, over time, the king's heart softened. He sent his ministers to find his son and ask him to return. But when they found the young man, he said he could not come back. He had been too hurt, the wound was too deep, and he was still bitter. When the ministers brought back his refusal to the king, the king gave them another message to take to his son: "Return as far as you can, and I will come the rest of the way to meet you."

And isn't that a beautiful way of expressing the extra distance that forgiveness requires? Judaism teaches that God models forgiveness for human beings. When we fall short, we ask God to forgive us, and know that with the asking, we are forgiven. Our task is to grant others what we seek time and time again for God. Left unforgiven, Rabbi Wolpe says, "the grudge perches on the heart like a gargoyle on a parapet, looking out with an ugly countenance and growling at the world." He advises those harboring grudges to ask themselves, "Will this insult matter in thirty years, or even in thirty days? If you could fly and take an eagle's view of the crisis, would it still matter so much? In short, is what happened as grievous as it seems?"

We might not directly experience any immediate fruits from the forgiveness we grant, but it can be a force magnifier, unleashing other acts of compassion. The story is told about Walter Rathenau, a German foreign minister, who was murdered by three men. Two of the murderers committed suicide. The third, Ernst Technow, was captured and put in prison.

The dead minister's mother, Mathilde Rathenau, wrote to the prisoner's mother: "In grief unspeakable, I give you my hand. Say to your son, that, in the name and spirit of him he has murdered, I forgive even as God may forgive, if before an earthly judge your son makes a full and frank confession of his guilt . . . and before a heavenly judge repents." When Techow was freed from prison in 1940, he smuggled himself into Marseilles, where he helped more than three hundred Jews escape to Spain. He later told a relative of the Rathenau's that his transformation had been triggered by Mrs. Rathenau's letter and the great example she set by forgiving him.

"What God gave Adam was not forgiveness from sin. What God gave Adam was the right to begin again."

— ELIE WIESEL

THIRTEEN

Teaching

"A teacher affects eternity; he can never tell where his influence stops."
— HENRY BROOKS ADAMS

Her dad says Anne Graham Lotz is the best preacher in the family. Since her dad is evangelist Billy Graham, that's saying something. While her younger brother Franklin now directs the Billy Graham Evangelistic Association, and just about everyone in her family is involved in the ministry, Billy Graham's second daughter is emerging as one of the most influential Christian speakers in the country. Her popularity has picked up with the publication of *Heaven — In My Father's House*, just a few months after the September 11 terrorist attacks. It came out just in time to provide Scriptural answers to the existential questions that have been haunting the nation: Where do our loved ones go after death? How then should we live now?

In *Heaven*, Anne explains how God has prepared a place for believers. It's like the feeling of returning home, she says. Home to her will always be her father's house — "a log cabin nestled in the mountains of western North Carolina, with a light in the window, a fire on the hearth, and a welcome embrace at the door."

Her message was timely. Within three weeks, the book was on the best-seller list. "There are a lot of people out there who want to know what heaven is like or want to share that comfort with somebody, judging from the personal response I've gotten," Anne said when we talked the following May. "Everybody knows somebody who is dying — a parent or friend. I know a woman whose daughter just fell in a freak accident and was killed. Just to be able to send her that book and write her a little note was gratifying. You can be afraid for yourself about the hereafter, but for your child to die suddenly and not to know she is safe . . . if you're a Christian family, then there is a real need to understand that child will be in Heaven. So much has been said about heaven and we may think we know what it is like in our imagination, but the image we get from popular culture is just a cartoon picture. This book is based on the Bible, which I believe is true. It does answer all our questions and gives us enough of a glimpse so we will know where we want to go. I get letters and e-mails all the time from people who want to know more about heaven. One was from a woman whose son was murdered. The witnesses who saw it said the kid who did it was a drug dealer. The mother just couldn't get away from that scene in her mind of her son dying in the street by himself. But it is comforting for her to accept the vision that he didn't die alone, that Jesus was by his side. She said she had come across my book and when she went into the courtroom, she would be carrying the Bible and my little book. Praise God, praise God, for the comfort he has given her, to know where her son is, to give her peace."

About three years before, she pointed out, *Time* magazine featured a cover story on heaven and the statistics said that the afterlife wasn't something many Americans were concerned about, compared to other issues. "They weren't thinking about it. About 85 percent believe there is a place where God is when you die . . . and nearly 90 percent think they are going there. The vast majority thought that just being a good person would get you in. There is a great ignorance about the meaning of

Scripture, that Jesus is our living hope, that heaven is certainly the Christian hope that this life is not all there is."

Perhaps the reason contemporary Americans have not focused on where they are going after death is that life has been fairly cushy in the post–World War II era. "We've been so prosperous," Anne suggests, "Our life is more comfortable, easier for a lot of people. That's good in some ways. Maybe it's not like that for somebody in Afghanistan, who has been stripped of everything and might have more of an intense longing to go to heaven to escape this world. I don't know the exact reason heaven has dropped out of our thoughts, but we do need to know that every day we are stepping into eternity. On September 11, it didn't matter how prosperous the people were, or what age they were, what denomination, the only thing that mattered was their relationship with God."

She actually had started writing *Heaven* before September 11. Her brother-in-law had died of a malignant brain tumor and a family friend, who was like a second father to her, died suddenly of a massive heart attack. That started her thinking about the hereafter, and she gave a talk about it that her father heard. "He couldn't stop talking about it," she recalled. "Three months later when he was giving an interview in Florida, he mentioned it. I know he knows where *he's* going, but it made me think that if what I said could impact him and give him comfort and focus, then I better write it down. So I wrote it down in July and was looking for a publisher when September 11 happened."

As family members were interviewed about "losing" loved ones in the terrorist attacks, it reminded Anne that we often use the euphemism "lose" when talking about someone who has died, "but if you are a believer in Jesus Christ, you know where they are." Still, she says there is a lot of misunderstanding about how you get to heaven.

> "It has been more wittily than charitably said that hell is paved with good intentions. They have their place in heaven also."
>
> — ROBERT SOUTHEY

"In that *Time* magazine article, I think 87 percent said they believe they are going to get there just by being a good person and doing good works. A lot of people think they are going, but they are in for the shock of their lives. It was a wake-up call to me. They can choose to go to heaven or choose not to go to heaven, but I want the choice to be based on accurate information. It's totally distressing to me that so many people think they are going to heaven just because they are good. They have to place their faith in Jesus. How would you know how many good works is enough? Or too little? The wonderful thing is that God, in his grace and his love knows, that no one can do enough good works. That's why he sent his son Jesus. I believe it is only through faith in Jesus that we can gain entrance into heaven. People ask me if that is exclusive or fair — to me, the wonder of it is that God could have left us all in our sin with no way to heaven. He made a way. He has revealed it to us, and we can choose to go that way and be confident and sure that when we step into eternity, we will step into our heavenly home."

If there is good to come from the September 11 tragedy, Anne mused, it might be that God has a message for us and the world at large: "That you need to get serious about God, because every single one of you is going to step into eternity. And when that moment comes, where would you rather be? I'm sure if those victims could make one more cell phone call, they would say make sure you have done everything you can to ensure that you are going to spend eternity in heaven. You've made sure that you have insurance for your car and your house and your health; you need to get your insurance for eternity so you are going to be safe forever in my father's house. I have no question that they would urge us to be safe. That's the message to the world are large: that we are not important. That life is temporary. It doesn't matter in the long run if you are rich or poor or black or white, male or female, president of the company or not — it doesn't matter. What matters at that moment and in the long run is your relationship with God. People have to stop and think, *Where am I going to spend eternity?* With all our materialism and prosperity, we have not paid attention to the long run. For people like me who call themselves Christians, the message is to wake up and get serious about the Gospel of Jesus Christ and get serious about the world created by God, because you don't want to go to hell and be apart from God. People also forget to think that the flip side of heaven is that you will perish. It could be my neighbor, my child's teacher, my daughter's boyfriend, the clerk at the store, or all

"Hell is truth seen too late."

– ANONYMOUS

these people around me that I love — it's their choice. I don't want to push my choice on them. But I want them to be informed when they make their choice and know what I believe."

The September 11 attacks could just be a prelude to more attacks, Anne said. And the lessons learned from mourning the September losses might not keep the attention of Americans long. After all, there already had been bombings in the World Trade Center basement, in our embassies, and then the USS *Cole* before the crashes into the Trade Center and the Pentagon — not to mention the record-breaking floods, hurricanes, and fires that might have been another way for God to get our attention. "As powerful as we are, our power is weak in the face of nature. Everything we put such a high priority on is so fragile. We need to get right with God, repent our sins, tell God we are sorry, and quit shaking our little dust fist in his face."

Though that might sound like a sermon, Anne insists she is just a teacher, not a preacher. That's in keeping with the Baptist adherence to the admonition in 1 Timothy "as in all the churches of the saints, women should be silent in the churches. . . . If there is anything they desire to know, let them ask their husbands at home. For it is shameful for a woman to speak in church." Out of respect for that tradition, Anne did not pursue a theology degree or ordination as a minister. But she has been steadily drawn into the spotlight as a powerful teacher. She draws crowds up to 70,000 at her revivals. She fills stadiums like a rock star. And she is invited to speak all around the world. She has spoken in Amsterdam to 10,000 evangelists, the only woman on a program of three hundred. She was the first woman invited to speak to the famous Keswick Bible Conference in England. She was one of the key speakers for the Millenium World Peace Summit of Religious and Spiritual Leaders at the UN General Assembly.

But isn't much of what she does preaching? No, she maintains, she is not an evangelist who brings people to God, she is a teacher who addresses the second step of teaching people about God's word and God's promise. She doesn't want to be ordained, she says, because she does not feel called to "marry, bury, and baptize." She does feel called to teach Scripture. As is so often the case for women, when the rules are constricting, women of faith find a way to do what needs to be done and say what needs to be said. In Anne's case, the way is AnGeL Ministries, named after her initials. Her books have sold millions, and she is in constant demand to speak. She appears at some one hundred events a year but does not charge admission or take a salary herself. Most of those appearing on the program are volunteers. Just as her father has avoided the financial and personal scandals that have tainted many evangelists, Anne is trying to keep her ministry as "pure" as possible by not making money the object. Reaching and teaching people is the object, and it is a mission she seems to have been groomed for all her life.

At fifty-three, Anne is a striking woman, a feminine variation of her father's lean good looks. She is clearly her father's daughter in the pulpit, speaking with passion in a honeyed North Carolina accent. But she is her mother's daughter in other ways, following her mother's example as a devoted wife and mother. Because her father was often away, her mother Ruth watched over Gigi, Anne, Ruth, Franklin, and Ned. Being the children of the most famous evangelist in the world was not always easy. Anne and her sister Gigi once considered placing a toll rope in front of their house to charge the many visitors who made a pilgrimage to their neighborhood to catch a glimpse of their father. For a while, she considered becoming a model, but at eighteen her father introduced her to Dan Lotz, a former college basketball champion who was a dentist in the Air Force. Her father and mother sensed that they were ideally suited. They were. According to family lore, Dan phoned his mother after his first date with Anne and told her, "Mom, quit praying. I've found the girl I'm going to marry."

Dan and Anne have three grown children, who are all married and involved in the family's ministries. When they were youngsters, she says, being confined in a small house with "Small children, small sticky fingerprints, small clothes, small toys, and small words" became frustrating to her. After attending a conference in Switzerland in 1974, Anne invited a few friends to her home to share her faith. One cried, one was afraid, and one left. So Anne tried a less personal and more organized approach. She invited the Bible Study Fellowship to establish a

"Aim at Heaven and you will get earth 'thrown in'; aim at earth and you will get neither."

— C. S. LEWIS

class in Raleigh. What began as a pilot program in 1977 with 150 women grew to 500. Anne ended up the teacher until 1988. She rekindled her faith by teaching it. In the process, she has said, she became a "better mother." And that regimen of daily Bible study has formed the core of her ministry today, which is built around Scripture lessons and basic beliefs. She is a conservative believer: She is against abortion, opposes homosexuality, and favors the death penalty, though she went to the side of convicted murderer Velma Barfield to pray with her before her execution. Hers is more of a tough-love philosophy than a touchy-feely spirituality, and she does not bend her views to be more hip or saleable. Her approach is that she's telling timeless truths, not selling herself, yet audiences are drawn to both.

Early in Anne's speaking career, a group of men in the audience turned their backs to her, refusing to believe a teaching can come from a woman. But she continued speaking and says she believes God has commissioned men *and* women to share their personal testimony. Today, her revivals draw a lot of men. "I don't feel called just to women, I do feel called to the church primarily," she says. For the women who come to hear her by the thousands, she says, "I pray that they'll have a fresh touch from God, that through them his message will reach the family and the children and create a revival of the church."

She takes all her tasks seriously — her friends say she's the kind of person who makes her own piecrust from scratch. But she's known to have a funky sense of humor — her cat has two names, Xerxes, after the Persian ruler, and Tammy Faye, yes, after the long-lashed televangelist.

Her life has not been all peaches and Bible parties. After her marriage, she struggled with infertility and had a miscarriage. In recent years, the family went through a string of challenges: Their property was wrecked by a hurricane, Dan's dental office burned down, her son Jonathan was diagnosed with cancer at the age of twenty-eight, and both of her parents have needed medical help as they have aged. When her mother had to have back surgery and hip replacements, Anne took care of her. When her father needed treatment for Parkinson's disease, Anne went with him. She said later, "I haven't thought of it as a test, but it's true quite a few things happened in a two-year period that made the pressure and the stress and even the emotional suffering very intense. I just fell back on my faith. You lose everything else at such times, when you don't know the questions to ask, much less the answer. There are lots of times when I didn't even know what to pray for, I just fell back on what's most important in my life. God stripped away everything else."

She went through a period, she said, where going to church did not speak to her needs. "You know, for the post-modern man, we now have the post-modern church with videos and dramas and mimes and musicals, and I was just feeling empty and stressed out. Probably if I had gone to counseling they would have diagnosed me with depression. What I decided was *Anne, you've got to come to grips here.* I didn't want to leave the ministry, but I thought, *I can't handle all this with everything going on.* But you can't escape life. I think what God was doing in that period was giving me a cry for revival of my spirit, for me to step out into this ministry of revival. When I get up on the platform, I am not telling them what they need, I am telling them what happened to me and what I need. It makes a big difference if you can identify with people who, for whatever reason, feel un-satisfied, unfulfilled. There are many

> "In my Father's house, there are many dwelling places. If it were not so, would I have told you that I go to prepare a place for you? And if I go and prepare a place for you, I will come again and will take you to myself, so that where I am, there you may be also."
>
> — JOHN 14:2–3

people who feel a restless spirit, who have a heart's cry and can't articulate it."

She wrote the story of her struggle in *Just Give Me Jesus*, which also became the new theme of her revivals. Her candor about her ups and downs is a reminder that even high-energy speakers have low-energy days, even believers have problems, even teachers need to take their own advice and get back to basic connections to God. What feeds those who feed others? Careful reading of Scripture and quiet prayer. Her own regimen is rigorous: an hour of prayer and Bible study each morning and a three-hour study session at least once a week. It takes time to develop a loving, informed relationship with God, she reminds. "I'm sorry to say it, but a lot of Christians go to church on Sunday — and they're ten minutes late for that — and that's the sum total of their relationship with God. Then they're looking for another relationship to satisfy that hunger in their hearts," she told the Minneapolis *Star-Tribune* in 2001.

Anne often mentions in her interviews and speeches that Americans have taken too much of religion out of their lives, their marketplace, and their schools, so they have forgotten that the time will come when God will hold them accountable. Although many hearts are restless, she said, they won't find rest from the uncertainties of this world until they rest in God. "People think that the world is falling apart, but it's falling into place." She says she has hope, because of one word: "*Jesus.* And because I looked at the end of the Bible. I know how the story turns out. I know God has his plan and that when all is said and done, he's going to be there. He's the end of the story."

> "Teaching a Christian how he ought to live does not call so much for words as for daily example."
>
> – ST. BASIL THE GREAT

Getting that message out is her life's work now, and she acknowledges in *Heaven* that it often is a difficult path, with travel that takes her away from her family and the pressures of being on a public platform, scrutinized and criticized. She often spends hour after hour studying a passage of Scripture until it "breaks open" and she can relate it to her life and the lives of others.

Anne says she asks herself three questions when she studies Scriptures: What does it say? What does it mean? What does it mean to me? Using that guide, you can parse the Scriptures for yourself, as many have done century after century. The calendar changes, the cast changes, but the Biblical message stays the same. Understanding it is a lifelong labor, but then, that's the point.

Lifelong learning has become a driving theme of Janet Marder's work as a rabbi. Yet she did not set out to become a rabbi. She thought she would be a lawyer. She was from a family of lawyers in Southern California. But she was transformed when she took a course in Jewish history at the University of California. "I was fascinated by the miracle of Jewish survival, and I began to spend more time with Jewish student groups," she recalls. She was a senior when the Yom Kippur War of 1973 broke out. She suddenly realized how much it meant to her that Israel survived and the Jewish people survive. A month after graduation, she flew to Jerusalem to see and learn for herself. It changed her life.

Three decades later, she is becoming the first woman to serve as president of the Central Conference of American Rabbis. That's the organization representing the Reform branch of Judaism, which is the largest in the United States, with 906 synagogues. Judaism is not hierarchal like many other faiths, so the congregations do not report to a central authority. But serving as spokesperson for the Reform rabbinate will give Janet a unique opportunity to shape the reform movement and showcase the role of women in religion.

Women have advanced slowly but steadily in rabbinical roles since the first woman was ordained in 1972. Janet currently leads the Beth Am synagogue in Los Altos Hills, a suburb near Stanford University. Beth Am is one of the largest congregations in the United States, with nearly 1,300 families.

The percentage of women in charge of large congregations is still small, Janet says. That is partly due to choices women have made for part-time rabbinical work while their children were growing up as well as resistance from congregations. For example, Marcia Zimmerman, who now leads the large Temple Israel in Minneapolis, worked three-quarters of the time from 1994 to 1997 to help raise her three children. Janet's congregation is in the prosperous Silicon Valley, so she has benefited from the fact that the Beth Am congregation places a high value on innovation and was open to a female leader. The cantor also is a woman, which means the two most senior clergy at Beth Am are women. That is unusual. But so far, Janet says, no one has raised any concerns.

She understands the difficulties women have experienced in all three monotheistic faiths in winning the confidence of congregations. "Religion touches something very deep and visceral in people. We associate our religious environment with comfort. It's something that harkens back to time when we were children. So a reassuring presence is very important to people. It is discomfiting to some to see someone in the bema or the pulpit who is not a Big Daddy. The resistance comes from women as much as men." There is nothing explicit barring women from leadership roles in Judaism, she says, although there are limiting factors — women cannot serve as witnesses or judges in religious court.

Yet women, with their intuitive and verbal skills, have a valuable role to play in religion, she said. "Within our congregation, women are far more open already than men to the spiritual experience, possibly because we are not afraid to show our neediness. I think that impulse to reach out for God does not come when you are feeling on top of the world. Opening ourselves to God is a reflection that we are *not* all-powerful. That is a harder admission for men. The danger for women is that we get stuck taking care of everything and everybody around us and don't give ourselves time off for prayer or to read and have quiet time. It's a spiritual experience to be involved in the world and serving the community, but we often do that without reflecting."

> "The art of teaching is the art of assisting discovery."
>
> — MARK VAN DOREN

Teaching her congregation how to deal with the aftermath of September 11 has been a profound challenge, Janet says. Many people came to her in despair about the unrest in the world and what to tell their children. They needed to find a positive and affirmative message in the anxieties of this time. She said many of her congregants have begun looking at their lives in a more reflective way, many have returned to services, and others have affiliated for the first time. "I have heard this from other colleagues as well," she said. "When the world seems to be turning into a wilderness, it is imperative that people stand up for values that are true and right."

And at such times, the rituals of faith are comforting. Janet said more members have told her in recent months they are trying to re-incorporate the Sh'ma prayer into their lives, saying it in the morning and at night as they were taught as children. They have been feeling insecure because of the turmoil in the Middle East and the collapse of "dot-com" companies in Silicon Valley. "The blessings ask you to take note and appreciate the good things around you. That is particularly critical when you are in despair. A special blessing is said on Friday nights when the Sabbath begins. A cup of wine is lifted up as a symbol of joy, a reminder that we are to lift up and cherish all the things that are dear to us. It is also a tradition at that time for the man to say words of appreciation to his wife as a woman of value and for parents to bless their children, which is reassuring to them."

One of Janet's goals is to engage all of her members into some form of lifelong learning, "To make this place an even more warm and caring community. That we are so large is a particular challenge. We have to create smaller support groups, study groups, so everyone feels connected with people they know and care about. We have been very hard hit, for example, by the economic downturn for computer companies, so we have a professional networking group for those out of work right now. They meet every week with one of the clergy as well as a social worker. We ask them to study and reflect about what is it that *really* matters in life, you or your job? We look at the whole question of wealth. This has been a profoundly difficult time for many people. Their dreams have fallen apart. There are a lot of hard-driving type-A people in Silicon Valley, so Shabbat becomes an even more important time, to stop at least one day a week and devote that day to your soul and your heart and the people who are important to you. Also, this culture places a high value on intellectual achievement, so our religious values remind us of the inherent dignity of *every* soul, achievers or not."

A petite woman with short, dark hair, Janet tends to be hard-driving herself, and her eyes flash with intellectual intensity, like lightning in a bottle. The demands on her time have multiplied with the increased need for pastoral care. One of the times we talked in the spring of 2002, she had just returned from a meeting in New York and had appointments every hour until 10 p.m. that night. She was feeling pressured, she said, and had to remind herself to make regular time for prayer, to take a short break between appointments in order to breathe deeply, reflect, and prepare herself to focus fully on the next person she would be with. "My greatest passion is to be with my family, but I am finding it really important to exercise and take time to be outside and listen to music and read. When I don't do those things, I become depleted and don't have enough to give anyone else."

Janet and her husband, Rabbi Sheldon Marder, have two teenage daughters, so their life is full not only with congregational concerns, but pre-college activities as well. It's fortunate that her husband is also a rabbi, she said, because he understands the demands on her time. Likewise, she has learned from his ministry — he works at a Jewish home, where the average age is eighty-eight, so he encourages the residents to reconceptualize aging. "It should not be a time of devaluation and debilitation, but a time of harvest. People who have gained some measure of wisdom have something to share with the coming generations," she says. Her husband often assists in the creation of ethical wills, she said, which is a healthy process of reflection and life review. "It's an important step for anyone to reflect, have a sense of wholeness, and perceive the value in your own life."

Part of the lifelong learning she endorses is learning from ancient teachings. Often their lessons are surprisingly applicable to our contemporary world. Take the Jewish teaching on breathing, one of the most basic elements of life. The Torah tells us that in Genesis God breathed the breath of life into Adam. What is interesting is that the words for *breath* in Hebrew all relate to aspects of the soul: *neshamah* ("life breath"), *ruach* ("spirit"), and *refesh* ("soul"). Focusing on your breathing can be a way of focusing on the here and now. If you take a break from the hectic busy-ness of the day, close your eyes, and simply breathe in and out slowly, quietly. It is a wonderful way to decompress and calm the present moment. Likewise, a Hebrew morning prayer says, "Elohai neshamah shenatata bi tehorah hi." This means, "My God, the breath that you have given me is pure." It's a reminder that the breath of life is given to us each morning and should not be taken for granted, Janet says.

There also is a Jewish tradition of beginning every day with a prayer that means, "I am thankful." This Jewish teaching helps train generation after generation to be grateful. Learning to begin each day with gratitude is a proven antidote to the anxieties of the day or the age. You might be worried about your job, you might be worried about your health, you might be worried about tomorrow. Such prayers teach us to be thankful — for our problems and our blessings.

It has become both a problem and a blessing for Ingrid Mattson that she is one of the most visible Muslim women in the United States. She became the highest-ranking woman in the Islamic faith a week before the Sep-

> "Once a man came to the Prophet Muhammad and asked, 'What is faith?' He replied, 'When doing good makes you feel good and when doing bad makes you feel bad, then you are a believer.' The man then asked, 'What is a sin?' The prophet answered, 'When something bothers your conscience, give it up.'"
>
> — HADITH

tember 11 attacks. She had just returned from the convention of the Islamic Society of North America, the largest association for Muslims in the United States and Canada. They had celebrated the release of a new stamp commemorating the Islam Eid holidays. It was a symbol of their integration into America. She left with optimism, hopeful that American Muslims were beginning to contribute positively to public life while preserving their unique identity.

When she returned to her home in Hartford, Connecticut, and saw the images of the falling towers on TV, she was horrified and frightened. Then a voice in her head said, "It's over — all the work you have done has gone down the drain." Then the phone started to ring and e-mails started to come in. Men and women whose churches she had spoken in were checking to see if she and her family were safe. Students who had taken courses she had taught as a professor at Hartford Seminary were worried that Muslims would be scapegoats. Two calls moved her to tears. The first was from a minister, Rev. Don Larsen, whose son had died in a car crash just three weeks earlier. He was concerned by the anti-Muslim comments he was hearing and was worried about her well-being as a prominent Muslim. He invited her to read from the Qu'ran and say a few words at a prayer service at Grace Lutheran Church that evening. Then a friend called from the Congregational Church where Ingrid had given a talk on Islam the year before. She said she was thinking about having some women at the church wear head-scarves out of solidarity with the Muslim women who were afraid of being targeted.

Ingrid realized that all was not lost after all. She came to see that her work was all the more important. She was one of the first to call on other Muslims to condemn not only the terrorist attacks, but any violence done in the name of Islam. As she put it, "Who has the greatest duty to stop violence committed by Muslims against innocent non-Muslims in the name of Islam?" she asked. "The answer obviously is Muslims."

Since then, Ingrid has been interviewed on CNN, *The Today Show*, and National Public Radio. On a panel discussion at the American Society of Newspaper Editors, she emerged as the soft-spoken voice of reason after the other two panelists got into a testy argument about the Middle

East. While they jabbed and lashed at each other, Ingrid stayed serene. She has a grace about her. *The Christian Science Monitor* once referred to it as her "arrestingly calm demeanor." She says she was that way even before she converted to Islam. She was the sixth of seven children growing up in Canada. "What I learned was I could not out yell all the others, so I learned to make my point quietly because there was no other way to win an argument." She grew up in a Christian family in Kitchener, Ontario. Her father was a criminal lawyer, and her mother stayed home to raise the seven children. There was a spirit of social activism in the family — one brother became an environmental lawyer, another a labor lawyer, and another a criminal defense lawyer. So Ingrid grew up with a bent for social justice.

Always independent-minded, Ingrid decided to quit attending church at the age of sixteen. She had taken her faith seriously before, but she began to feel hypocritical because she didn't feel the same conviction. She didn't want to attend "just for show." When she entered the University of Waterloo in Ontario, she studied philosophy, which turned out to be good training for becoming a Muslim. She learned in philosophy that individuals are free to make choices in a seemingly meaningless world. When she came to study Islam, she learned that what you choose defines who you are in life — while your choices might be limited by your circumstances, there is always the opportunity to choose good. And it is your responsibility to choose right over wrong, which can give you a sense of peace, no matter what happens. Reading the Qu'ran, Ingrid felt the presence of God more than she had as a Christian. Her heart was touched. The readings brought her back to belief in God.

She met her husband, Amer Aetek, when she was just out of the university and working as a volunteer in a refugee camp in Pakistan in 1989. She was in Peshawar teaching young girls and trying to improve conditions for their families. Amer, an Egyptian engineer, was helping dig wells and construct housing. The refugee families — who had pitifully little themselves — were touched when they heard the young couple had quietly married and that Ingrid did not have a wedding dress. They pooled their resources and presented her with a makeshift bridal outfit — satin pants and a red velveteen dress with pompons.

Her husband is now a systems application engineer, and they have a daughter, Soumayya, and a son, Ubayda. Other than the fact they dress more modestly, they are a typical suburban family. Their son is keen on baseball, and their daughter is attending a school where she can follow her love of horseback riding.

In the months after September 11, Ingrid was on a planned sabbatical, working on academic articles. She was pulled away from her academic work to speak around the country about Islam and to help make interfaith alliances. "God knows the result," she sighed, "but at least I felt like I had a role to play."

She said she wishes she could see more acknowledgment by the U.S. government that Muslim American citizens were not tied to the attacks. "You know there was a lot of suspicion about the Muslim community at the beginning, that we were harboring terrorists or secretly trying to undermine the United States. One of the things we have learned is that the hijackers were not part of the ordinary Muslim community. They just came here for a certain purpose. With the continuing fear about the attacks, I think it is important that the ordinary American person is reminded about that distinction. There really is a community that is loyal and part of America that rejects violence and has nothing to do with those people who are undermining all of our security. It seems that after all the thousands of interviews and all the work of the intelligence services, they haven't found conspiracies within the Muslim community itself. There are still some who have been held for violating visa regulations, but so far, no internal conspiracy."

Ingrid expressed hope that the number of foreign students from Muslim countries will not be cut back, because one of the best ways to influence thinking in their home countries is to let them live here and get to know Americans, "so long as they are coming here for study and not some ulterior motive."

She thinks the debate within the Muslim community about the role of women in Afghanistan and other restrictive countries, like Saudi Arabia, has been healthy. Sometimes, she observed, people inside a culture need a prod from outside the culture to re-examine what's going on. But you must be careful not to prod too hard from outside, she cautioned, or the insiders might defensively rush to defend their community first and foremost against outside influence.

One of her initial goals as vice president, she said, had been to develop broader leadership within the American Muslim community. The Imam of a mosque in other countries simply serves the people who come to the mosque to pray. In the United States, the role is evolving into more of a ministerial role, with the Imam taking on responsibility for more pastoral and administrative duties, as mosques become more of a center for other activities. That trend to enlarge the role of the Imam virtually rules out a larger role for women in the faith, because only men can lead prayers.

But what women can do, Ingrid explained, is become chaplains, so their constituency is for everyone in the community, not just Muslims. "All chaplains have to deal with an interfaith environment — often the people they are called to help are not particularly religious but are in a crisis situation. Often they are not looking for an authority, as for someone to support and help them, someone who can help them find their way back into their relationship with God. So being a chaplain takes a different kind of skill, a nurturing, communicating skill a lot of women are good at."

Most chaplains in other faiths have a Master of Divinity degree, she says, so she has been working to develop a certificate in chaplaincy for those who earn a Master of Arts in Islamic studies. Adding chaplaincy programs to seminaries across the country would help Muslim women take on a more prominent role in their faith. It would be a way of showing that Islam is not isolated from the rest of American life. On college campuses, for example, she pointed out, Muslim students often are isolated. A goal for a Muslim college chaplain might be to expand interaction with other student faith communities so the college campuses are not Balkanized.

And as Ingrid has learned in her teaching, "Faith is so important in making it possible to be brave in challenging the things wrong in your community. The thing that often holds us back in doing that as women is that we are afraid of what other people might think of us, when we shouldn't conform to the notions that other people have of what you have to do to be a good Muslim, Catholic, Jew, whatever. You have to remember always that it all comes back to God. You have to remember that God has to be pleased with you first. Even if you are getting a lot out of your faith at the moment, with prayer and ritual, remembering that it is about God, not you, then God will give you the courage to make the kind of change in those institutions that is needed."

> "For thirty years I went in search of God, and when I opened my eyes at the end of this time, I discovered that it was really He who sought me."
>
> — BAYAZID BUSTAMI, D. 874

That's the kind of advice that's needed to strengthen moderate Muslim voices in this country. Other Muslim intellectuals have been trying quietly for years to improve the image of Islam in the United States and fend off the influence of radical offshoots like al Qaeda and puritanical branches like the Wahhabism in Saudia Arabia. The moderates are hopeful that a humane Islam — what they believe is the legitimate Islam — will prevail. But they will need help.

Women are playing an increasingly important role in most religions today. Some 70 percent of the people in pews are women, according to Diane Connolly of the Religion Newswriters Foundation. In most churches, women historically have been the Sunday School teachers, the volunteers for day-care, and the cooks for fellowship dinners. Today they are also likely to be the professors and preachers. According to the Association of Theological Schools, the number of women students increased from 30 percent in 1990 to 35 percent in 2000. In some denominations — Methodist and Episcopalian — the women are often half the seminary students. According to the Bureau of Labor Statistics, the number of women answering the church's call has tripled since the BLS began noting their presence in 1983. By the year 2000, there were 51,000 women working as clergy. That constitutes only 14 percent of the clergy overall, but the figure is more impressive if you consider that it includes some branches of the Jewish faith that do not ordain women and the all-male Roman Catholic Church, which is the largest denomination with 63.6 million members. The second largest denomination, the Southern Baptist Convention with its 15.9 million members, announced a moratorium on the ordination of women in 2000, declaring "The office of pastor is limited to men, as qualified by Scripture." Yet women are proving themselves as spiritual leaders for Episcopalians, Lutherans, Presbyterians, Unitarians, Methodists, and others. Even so, those women say, there is a "stained-glass ceiling" that makes progress slow and difficult. Women usually are assigned to small churches or to secondary positions in larger churches.

Some of those women are gifted preachers, but some are not, just like the men. Yet they all face a daunting threshold of acceptance. Some have taken on that challenge by using their feminine gifts of verbalizing and empathizing. Their ministries tend to be more laity-directed, empowering the congregation to participate in church management instead of being empowered by them as an all-powerful shepherd.

The Rev. Sheron Covington Patterson has had to overcome a double challenge. She not only was one of the few women in her theology classes at Perkins Seminary at Southern Methodist University; she was also a black woman. If her colleagues were surprised to see her there, she was surprised to be there. She had not intended to be a minister. While she was at Spelman College in Atlanta, she had majored in communications. She was editor of the school paper and had her own radio talk show. Her goal was to go into filmmaking and be the black Katharine Hepburn, a brassy lady who speaks her mind and still gets the guy. Her buddy Spike Lee, a film student at neighboring Morehouse College, was going to be the first black Steven Spielberg. They used to sit around plotting their Hollywood careers, Sheron says. But God had different plans for her. One day she was sitting in her dorm room and a voice spoke to her, saying, "Use your talent to glorify me, not yourself." She had never thought of a pastoral career before, but she knew the voice of God when she heard it.

Her parents worried that she had gotten caught up in the religious fervor of the 1980s. "It was a time when kids were running off and joining the Moonies and Rev. Sun Myung Moon's Unification Church. I had a neighbor who was at MIT and they got him. It made my parents really nervous. They thought maybe the Moonies had got to me, too," Sheron once told an interviewer.

She was a little uncertain herself about how to proceed, so when she enrolled at SMU, she applied for a joint degree in theology and communications. Being the only black woman was difficult, even for an outgoing, attractive "Buppie" — black upwardly mobile preppie. "They were polite and gentle. The whites ignored me, and the black men, though cordial, thought little of me or my abilities as a pastor." The first semester, she says, was like boot camp. "They weed out people because they make you study yourself. They can make or break you. All that self-reflection, while challenging, is also very difficult. You end up confronting demons you didn't know were there. But when you come out the other side, you are stronger and more understanding."

As part of her degree work, she began a singles ministry at St. Luke's Community United Methodist Church, a prominent African American church, and began specializing in male-female relationships. She was discovering that she had a real gift for no-nonsense counseling. And she was learning that something had to be done about the high number of absentee fathers and the cycle of teenage mothers in the black community. So when she was named associate pastor at Jubilee Methodist Church in Duncanville, Sheron started holding "Love Clinics," regular meetings at the church that dealt with relationships between black men and women, which she still continues today. She says that the men at the clinics often are nominally Christian. The women are usually very involved in their churches. The men usually will know one thing about marriage: Women should submit. "He doesn't know where it is in the Bible that women should submit to their husbands. (Ephesians 5) He doesn't know the context. He doesn't know that it also says men and women should submit to *each other*." Needless to say, Sheron introduces them to the full Scripture — and to the concepts like sharing family responsibilities and communicating.

She makes it clear she is not anti-male. She can point to her own marriage as an example of power-sharing. Her husband, Robert Patterson, is an investment banker, and they have two teenage sons. While he attends church and has a special interest in helping with a homeless ministry, he has his own career to look after and does not function as a traditional minister's spouse who tags along with the minister at every event. But he does help with the care of their boys — when Sheron's away on business, Robert does all the cooking. And she's making sure that her boys get the "New Faith" message that women are partners, not subordinates.

Sheron is currently the senior minister at St. Paul United Methodist Church, the oldest black church in Dallas. The historic church — with its picturesque woodwork and stained-glass windows — is just a few blocks away from the skyscrapers of downtown. Stop by in the summer and you'll discover the smell of pizza wafting out the door and hear the sound of children singing as part of church camp downstairs. Upstairs, Sheron is working on revisions for her book, *The Love Clinic: How to Heal Relationships in the Christian Spirit.* She also has a regular ABC radio show that is broadcast in 25 cities and a two-hour local radio show co-hosted with another minister.

She is a powerful preacher and engaging teacher. "When your praises go *up,* blessings come *down,*" she reminds a class. "Don't wait for the battle to be *over* to shout 'Amen!' " At forty-three, Sheron is a dynamic role model for the young women in the church. She's articulate, fashionable, and seemingly fearless. She's been compared to "Dr. Laura," but with more grace and love.

Her biggest challenge, she says, continues to be acceptance by black congregations who are accustomed to male preachers who are politically powerful patriarchal figures. When she got her first church assignment, she discovered that neither black men nor black women were prepared to accept a woman in the pulpit. The women were even less accepting than the men. "The men basically left me alone, ignored me. I thought the women would rally around me. They left in droves for churches led by male pastors. The ones who stayed didn't know what to do with me. Many of them had this attitude of 'Who took her out of her place?'" One older black woman used to park in the space marked "Pastor" just to defy Sheron's authority.

She began to observe the women in her congregation. She saw the effects of a male-dominated culture on their lives. She saw them suffering in their relationships with the men in their lives. She saw the lack of unity with other women. They had been taught not to challenge male leadership at home or in the church. They were unable to make changes in their lives. She decided she would teach them a *New Faith,* a faith of empowerment and real love. Putting those thoughts into a book, she wrote, "Girlfriend, as black, Christian, and female, you are awesome times three. But to bloom into the true diva that you are, you can't just go with the flow. Stop going along to get along. If you know it's not right, don't accept it. Move against the grain, counter the culture. Your authentic beauty won't shine through acquiescence."

In the same way that black men separate themselves from Scripture that supports slavery, such as the order in Colossians 3:22 for slaves to "obey in everything those who are your earthly masters," Sheron began encouraging women to reject isolated verses of Scripture that support the suppression of women. She was particularly horrified when church women who had been beaten by their husbands would call her. One of them showed up at work every Monday covered with bruises. She explained to Sheron that her husband was a nice guy most of the time, but when he got drunk he "got mean." She sobbed to Sheron, "He's my husband. He has the right."

But Sheron explained, "The Bible should never be used for abusing others. That is a distortion." Still, she often encountered abused women who believed passages written by the Apostle Paul justified "putting women in their place," particularly the passage in 1Timothy 2:11–12 where Paul wrote, "Let women learn in silence with all submissiveness. I permit no woman to teach or to have authority over men, she is to keep silent." Many times while counseling in cases of domestic violence, Sheron has had to point out that Paul's concern about decorum in the fractious early church has been too broadly applied. She reminds that Jesus was a gender equalizer throughout his life. "It is recorded that he interacted with women — such as Mary and Martha, the woman at the well, and the woman with the alabaster jar — and lifted them up as leaders and spokeswomen of the church." His multiple examples of empowerment far outweigh the suppression and domination that have been extrapolated from Paul's words, she says. Choosing the example of Jesus, she insists, is not changing the Bible, it is changing a modern interpretation that is at odds with the ministry of Jesus. Besides, she argues, if Paul wanted women to submit and live under the authority of their husbands, why did he declare that men and women were "equal" in Galatians 3:28?

She advises women that when they go back and read the Word for themselves, they will see that what they have been taught has been skewed. "They have been taught that women should suffer, take abuse, and be second-class citizens in the church. And that is not the truth," she says. "This untruth has spilled over and colored our relationships with our men." Changing is difficult, she says, because most women have been conditioned to being oppressed after hearing the Gospel from a male perspective decade after decade.

Women have been indoctrinated with hymns that are largely male-oriented ("Rise Up, O Men of God") as well as contemporary culture that condones rap songs dissing woman as "bitches" and "hos." Sheron says that generation after generation, women have gotten the message that they "had to accessorize the lives of men, get the attention of men using their clothing and make men love us." Men will love them in a healthier way, she insists, if they see women as partners to be respected, not just seduced. In the same vein, women will love in a

"Dear God, Open our eyes to the value we have in You. Relieve us of fleshly living. Help us to walk by faith and not by sight. Stop the maddening dance of money that we find so delightful. Let us walk as whole men and women with You. Amen."

— FROM *THE LOVE CLINIC*

healthier way when they see men as something other than a meal ticket or seducer.

Sheron is equally frank when teaching sex education to students. To break the cycle of pregnancy and poverty that has ravaged black families, she hosts summer Love Clinic camps that teach teens the destructive risks of sex and drugs.

The teenagers see a video of a childbirth. They learn about sexually transmitted diseases. They learn about birth control even though the primary emphasis is on abstinence. They're taught about drug and alcohol prevention, overdoses, and how a stomach is pumped. They hear testimony from repentant male batterers, visit a women's shelter, and hear from a representative of Mothers Against Violence.

One of the girls said after the first session: "I'm not having sex until I'm fifty." Usually, in the camps with thirty to forty participants, about twenty commit themselves to Christ and the majority make commitments to sexual purity. They say it's easier for them to resist pressures — from gangs, from drug dealers, from dates wanting sex — if they feel God is on their side.

The church should set the tone for respecting women, Sheron says. She preaches that women can do much more for the church than cook, clean, and keep the children. They can bring valuable working skills:

∾ **Participatory management.** Women will more often try to get to a win-win solution, collaborating rather than competing with others in the group. They don't feel their femininity is at stake if they ask for help, whereas men often do.

∾ **Concern for human relationships.** It matters to women how others feel about them; they are relational creatures and tend to form circles of support rather than hierarchal structures.

∾ **Ability to do many things at once.** Women are multi-taskers. "There is no shame to fixing dinner and preparing a Bible study simultaneously."

How do you start strengthening the role of women in the church? Sheron suggests that women begin by inviting their pastor to listen to them and by supporting the efforts of other women. Her vision is of a braver, wiser church where women will no longer be considered lesser-than or be content to be spiritually small. Her vision is women who can love other women as sisters. Her vision is young girls who understand that abstinence is not to make life dull; it protects young girls who usually get shortchanged in premarital relationships.

Sheron teaches women how to love their men without losing themselves. She advises, "Take a look at all of your relationships to determine if they are healthy and positive. If they are not, take action to change them or yourself." Her vision is a partnership marriage that insists on mutual respect. She coaches the men to say, "I'm sorry." She coaches the women to listen. She encourages the men to let their faith be stronger than their anger. She encourages couples to understand each other's sexual needs and to communicate their needs honestly. She encourages them to pray for each other and with each other. She encourages them to attend church together. And to please, model respect if the minister in the pulpit happens to be a woman like her.

Sheron Patterson, Anne Graham Lotz, Janet Marder, and Ingrid Mattson not only

> "Heaven goes by favor; if it went by permit, you would stay out and your dog would go in."
>
> — MARK TWAIN

teach about religion, they also teach with their lives about the ability of women to serve God in the twenty-first century. What is the role of women in your denomination? Do you agree with that role? Does it bother you to see women in the pulpit? Why or why not?

TAKE HOME:

Though there are some marked differences, the teachings in the three monotheistic faiths share much common ground about heaven. As *Newsweek* summed it up in a cover story in August 2002, all three faiths teach that "Heaven is the home of the one God, who is just and merciful, and at the end of life metes out rewards and punishments. Heaven is a perfect place, devoid of anger, lust, competition, or anything like sin. In heaven, you live forever."

In *The Lovely Bones*, a haunting novel that became a best-seller while newspapers were full of headlines about child abductions, a fourteen-year-old victim of a serial killer tells what her life is like in heaven — her paradise contains swing sets and puppies.

Have you ever given serious thought to

what heaven would be like? Or the dreaded flip side? The lack of contemporary focus on heaven until recently is in stark contrast to earlier cultures, where imaginings of heaven and hell dominated art and literature for centuries. Dante Alighieri took the prize for categorizing all the kinds of hell in the *Inferno* section of *The Divine Comedy*. He pictured heaven as a series of concentric levels with God at the center as a brilliant light. How close you get to God depends on your capacity for love and joy and how far away depends on the error of your ways. But it's worth remembering that Dante said the worst offense might be simply coasting through life, not committing to anything. He called those people who floated between good and evil, those who only lived for themselves, the "opportunists." They end up in "the vestibule of hell." As Dante memorably put it, those who followed no cause were doomed to "waving a banner through the dirty air — as they run, they are pursued by wasps and hornets which sting them and produce a constant flow of blood and putrid matter, which trickles down their bodies — and is feasted upon by loathsome worms and majors who coat the ground." The message is grisly but clear: One of the worst sins is not believing in anything but yourself.

In Islam, "Jannah" is the place where your soul is rewarded for listening to its "fitrah," or inner conscience. Those who resist their animal desires and "Shaytan" the evil one will find themselves rewarded in paradise. In paradise, the faithful will encounter a wall with eight gates. The gates will be named for practices such as charity, prayer, fasting, struggling against evil — and believers get to enter through the door of the activity they have been best at. Holy people and angels will greet arrivals at the door with "Peace be upon you! You have done well. Enter and dwell within." Within there will be seven layers, and the level where believers are housed depends on their goodness on earth and the amount they learned of Muhammad's teaching. Wine, not allowed on earth, will be allowed there, as well as guiltless sex. There will be plenty to eat, markets, shops, silk clothing — all in all, endless delight.

The Jewish faith embraces the idea of an afterlife, but the Torah provides few details. The emphasis traditionally has been how to live in this life. The Torah does contain images of a "Jerusalem of Gold." One hour there is considered better than all of earthly life. Hell also is recognized as a place where souls are purified of their sins. How long this takes depends on the life you lead, but twelve months is considered the maximum. That's why Kaddish prayers are recited for eleven months, to make sure the deceased gets support to see them safely through the process.

Sister Joan Chittister teaches that if you believe that heaven is a place with an admission fee, a strict merit system, you might focus on the arithmetic of this life and try to pile up points. But if you come to see that heaven is about grace as well as bookkeeping, you will try to live a life of union with God now; you will realize by loving more generously that we get to experience a little bit of heaven in our hearts, right here, every day.

> "And Jacob awaked out of his sleep, and he said, Surely the Lord is in this place; and I knew it not. And he was afraid, and said, How dreadful is this place! This is no other but the house of God, and this is the gate of heaven."
>
> — GENESIS 28:16–17

FOURTEEN

Soloing

"Nobody is perfect. Look for the good in others. Forget the rest."
— BARBARA BUSH

Aging has its terrors and heartaches for everyone, but it's really tough to age in rock and roll. Few do. Patti La Belle has. She has not aged gracefully. She has aged dynamically. At fifty-eight, she's still got great pipes and is drawing enthusiastic crowds as one of the super divas of pop music. At night, you might see her sequined up, singing her heart out on a new U.S. tour. During the day, you might see her on TV, endorsing hormone replacement therapy for women of a certain age.

"I think I've gotten better, stronger. More sexy — if that's possible!" she likes to quip. But in a more reflective mood, she acknowledges the secret of her longevity is not just new estrogen, but old-time religion. She started singing in church. She was a young choir member at the Beulah

Baptist Church on the south side of Philadelphia. Back then, she was known as Patricia Lee Holt — "Patsy" — and considered herself homely. She was so shy that instead of playing with other children, she would stand in front of the mirror and sing songs like "My Funny Valentine." Yet four decades later, she has recorded fifty albums, starred on TV and Broadway, and has received ten Grammy nominations and three Emmy nominations. Rather than slowing down, she is working on yet another album — a gospel album that returns to the roots of her faith.

In a way, her signature songs are an outline of her life. Her plaintive rendition of "Over the Rainbow" is a souvenir of her early days wishing for big-time success as she formed a series of girl groups. First there was the Elmtones, then the Ordettes, and then Patti LaBelle and the Bluebelles as she started coming into her own. Often the girls would sing five shows a day, seven days a week. Shy Patti had to be coaxed onstage for her first performance. She became the power singer in a bouffant wig, tight dress, and five-inch heels. Between tours, she married a high school principal named Armstead Edwards, who took over the management of most of the details in her life. They had a son, Zuri, and adopted two other sons, Stanley and Dodd.

In private life, Patti was a devoted wife and mother. On stage, she competed with Aretha Franklin and Diana Ross with torchy songs like "Lady Marmalade," a rock superhit about a prostitute who extends the invitation, "Voulez vous coucher avec moi ce soir?" — "Would you like to sleep with me tonight?" With her outrageous outfits and four-octave range, she began to develop a devoted cult following of fans. They would turn out even in subarctic temperatures to hear her.

It was Patti who suggested turning the Burt Bacharach/Carol Bayer Sager song "On My Own" into a wistful duet with Michael McDonald in 1986. It hit number one. And it anticipated the aching loss she felt when she and Armstead decided to divorce in the late 1990s. She was on her own for the first time since she was a young girl. Looking back, she says that her feelings had been dead for years. It took her a long time to admit it. "It hurt," she told me. "It was scary, but it was something I had to do for growth. I did it and I'm living and I am not afraid anymore. You get away from things you aren't comfortable with. For fifteen years out of thirty-one years of marriage, I was uncomfortable. It was necessary, it was tough, but God will see you through."

As she says in her book *Patti's Pearls*, she hung in with the marriage for a long time. She didn't want to hurt her son. "That's how I rationalized the happy marriage charade," she wrote. "That's how I handled everything — the loneliness, the emptiness, the pretense." Then she remembered advice she had been given years before by singer-writer Laura Nyro. At the time, Patti was trying to decide whether to leave the Bluebelles to go solo. Laura had advised her, "Many a false step is made by standing still." Patti realized that doing nothing was a choice in itself. And in her heart, she knew it was the wrong choice. When she split with the Bluebelles, she realized that even if she fell on her face by going solo, she would at least be going forward. And when she and her husband decided to split, even though her hands were shaking, she opened the door and went out on her own.

When she wakes up in the morning, Patti thinks of Isaiah 12:2 to get started without fear, hesitation, or doubt: "I will trust, and not be afraid; for the Lord Jehovah is my strength and my song; he also is become my salvation."

The divorce was not her only mid-life challenge. She lost three of her sisters and her best friend to cancer and her mother to diabetes. She discovered she has diabetes herself, which meant a drastic change in her lifestyle. She had always traveled with cooking utensils on the road, preferring to prepare her own soul food than eat out all the time. She is a talented cook, and those who shared her hospitality encouraged her to write a cookbook of her favorite recipes: Lasagna LaBelle, Burnin' Babyback Ribs, and Say-My-Name Smothered Chicken. The result was *LaBelle Cuisine.* Now that the butter and cream she slathered on everything are out of the question, she is writing another cookbook, this time for diabetics who also love to eat but have to be careful about what's on their plate. "My six-cheese macaroni is no longer a staple on my Sunday dinner table," she says with regret.

In the mid-1990s, writing her best-selling autobiography, *Don't Block the Blessings,* forced her to take a hard look at her life and make some sense of it. She says today she is more wary of "2F" friends — Fake Friends — who are there when they can benefit from your success and gone when they cannot. And she is more out-front about her faith. "Every day I'm out there, I say, 'God, I got through this one and it's because of you.' He's always on my side, and there is nothing I can't do, although I'll still complain I can't do it. I sometimes have to remind myself that there are people who can't do anything because of their health or wealth. I am a blessed child, and I tell myself I can do it ALL if I want to. The one thing stopping me is myself. That's when God comes in and starts pushing me to make me stand up again and take it like a woman. My faith has everything to do with my success and survival."

Yes, she says, there are those who question whether she can be a Christian and sing and dress the way she does at rock concerts. "Some people think I might be hypocritical for wearing short shorts or showing cleavage in a show, but so many other people are going through life hiding their failures and faults while they are judging others. I think God loves us no matter what our color or what skirt we

> "I think we've got to measure goodness by what we embrace, what we create, and who we include."
>
> — FROM THE MOVIE *CHOCOLAT*

wear. I don't do drugs. I don't do bad things to people. I live like the way I want people to treat me — I don't judge, I have fun. I try to do what feels good in my heart. And what feels good is respecting people and trying to take care of those who can't take care of themselves."

Patti is known as one of the most generous performers in show business and often performs benefits for causes like homelessness, AIDS, adoption services, Alzheimer's groups, cancer organizations, and diabetes research. "I sometimes do so much for others, I forget me," she admits. "But like I said, I am very blessed in so many ways, so I have a lot to give. Some people take that as a weakness and take advantage of it. But I'll pray for them. God will speak to them."

She was hurt when the minister of a church she had attended was asked to do an interview for a prime-time special. He refused to appear on camera. "I guess he figured I was singing for the devil," she said, noting that such judging and discriminating is what keeps people outside the church who want and need to be inside. "I deal with it," she said, "but now I just go to the church in my mind."

To some, she might not seem the picture

of a churchgoer. During a funky phase, she wore her hair in a sort of Afro-Mohawk. She reportedly has more than three thousand pairs of those five-inch heels. But for the cover photo for *Patti's Pearls*, she has her hair pulled back in a respectful chignon and is dressed in white pearls and a sophisticated white cocktail dress. She looks like a debutante. Her message is that there are many facets to her talent and many phases to her life — and she intends to experience them fully.

She shares her faith in her concerts, urging the crowd to remember their blessings and "pass it on." She also includes in her repertoire songs like "Oh People," with lyrics that say, "If we are all one big family, no one would have to beg to eat. If we live in a world of dignity, no one would have to live on the street." Another of her favorite songs is "When You Are Blessed," which says, "In a sea of haves and have nots, I survived the raging storm . . . I pray for the world where we all can be free . . . the day when the music of heaven will show us the way." She has been working on

> "Man beholds the face, but God looks upon the heart. Man considers the actions, but God weighs the intentions."
>
> — THOMAS À KEMPIS

a new rendition of "The Lord's Prayer" for her album of gospel music, which she admitted is hard to sing, even with her range. "It starts off a cappella and you have to be careful not to start too high," she explained, singing a few bars two different ways as an example. They both sounded pretty good.

Music reviewers often marvel at how much of her energy and herself she gives to audiences. She's also known for tending to friends who might be down and out. In fact, just a short time before we talked, she had been to visit a longtime friend in the hospital who was critically ill. She had heard he wasn't eating, so she took him food from one of his favorite restaurants in Los Angeles. When he saw her, he asked her to "Feed me." She didn't have any utensils, so she fed him by hand, bite by bite with her fingers. Three days later, he called her to say he had been regaining strength and was grateful that she had not let some of the difficulties in their friendship over the years keep her from coming. That made up for the fact that she got a bad review about her concert that evening because she talked too much about how moving it was to visit her friend in the hospital as part of her stage patter. "I knew I shouldn't go see him before the show, because it might mess me up to be thinking about how he might die," she said. "But I was so moved that I did talk about him in the show, and one of the critics said he didn't want to hear about my sick friend, he wanted to hear me sing. So I called the critic and said, 'You know, you're right. I did talk about it too much.' I'm very human. I get too involved. And I paid for it by getting a bad review. But you know, so what? It's like the song, 'We all fall down, but we get up.' I'll sing again. And I'll keep helping people in my own way because I think we have an obligation to help each other. At least I think I'm helping them. I lend my heart to them."

Helping others takes her mind off her own worries, like her recent decision to revamp her musical sound to keep from getting stale. To do so, she switched all of her backup musicians. "It took me a year to work my nerve up to say to them what I wanted to do. They are like family. But if somebody really loves you, they will let you go to try other things. My faith said I had to let go and let God take care of them and let them know that I needed to change to keep growing. What really pulls me through those kind of things is remembering how far I've come and that I can go even farther. For a long time, I didn't know who I was. Then finally I found out. God has been there waiting for me."

She still slips, she admits. She forgets to take her medicine. And she eats some things she shouldn't. She still has fears — like being afraid to fly. But she said she feels more "grounded" at this stage of her journey, thanks to the perspective gained from writing two books about her life and from learning how to cope on her own after her divorce. Her advice for other women, she says, is "Give yourself to God; you can be sure he will take care of what is his. That's all you need to know to live genuinely, joyfully, generously." The only thing she would add, she said, referring to another of her favorite sayings, "is that whenever times get hard, when you don't know how you got wherever you are, let alone how you're going to make it out — out of the pain, out of the heartache, out of the terrible sorrow or situation you find yourself in — remember that God never built a staircase to nowhere. And when you do what you can, he will do what you can't."

I was struck after talking to Patti — who is considered the most compassionate of the rock divas — that here was another talented, creative, independent woman who dropped out of the institutional church because of a negative experience with someone who represented the church. She felt disowned by her pastor, yet she was trying in her own way to be faithful. Sad to say, I ran across many other talented, independent-minded women while researching this book who also felt alienated from the institutional church. Either they had been turned off by a singular event in their lives, or they had felt too hemmed in by the limited roles for women in the church. The same month I talked to Patti, a documentary filmmaker in New York told me that she had felt so repressed by the strict nuns in her Catholic girls school as a teenager that she had stopped attending Mass, even though she has clung to the beliefs she learned all her life. She did not see the compassion, tolerance, and love for others she believed in being practiced by the church hierarchy. Likewise, a former astronaut told me that she could not identify with the narrow, legalistic approach to religion in the United States after she had the privilege of traveling around the world and learning about other faiths. She did not adopt those faiths, but she did respect their histories and faith traditions. Besides, she had worked very hard to earn respect as a woman in the business world; why should she settle for a religious culture that still treats women as second-class citizens?

It seems a shame that such talented women, who have much to give the church, are outside the established church. True, you can find God in your own way, in your own garden, on a mountaintop. But it helps you learn to be among a community of believers. As one Texas priest told writer Jan Jarboe in *Texas Monthly*, going to church is a "rewarded action" in itself. When people enter the Church, they leave the world behind and find a moment's peace. That gives them the courage to face the problems the world presents. At the same time, the church needs spirited people in its ranks to stay fresh and meaningful. These two opposing thoughts keep colliding in my head:

"There are many churches with people

"I wonder what becomes of lost opportunities. Perhaps our guardian angel gathers them up as we drop them, and will give them back to us in the beautiful sometime when we have grown wise, and learned how to use them rightly."

— HELEN KELLER

who are trying in good faith to heal the world."/"There are many churches with people who are so caught up in orthodoxy and personal agendas that they fail to be truly compassionate."

I can't reconcile them, but I think they are both true.

In fact, I recently met a writer in New York City named Wickham Boyle who also was a church dropout. Her book, *A Mother's Essays from Ground Zero*, had fallen into my hands, and I didn't get up until I had finished reading every single one of the beguiling little essays about what it was like for a family to live just a shout from the World Trade Center. A lot was written after September 11 about the people who worked in the towers and the people who tried to rescue them, but not much about the families who lived in the shadow of the towers. "Wicky" tells that family story well in her writings. She should. She's a Yale graduate, former Wall Street stockbroker, and former manager of the La Mama Theater. And she's a mother of two teenage children.

When the planes hit the towers, she jumped onto her bike and headed as fast as she could peddle to her son's school, P.S./ I.S. 89, a few blocks from the towers. It was right in the path of the collapse she instinctively sensed was coming next. Don't ask how she knew. Mothers just know. She pulled out an old press pass from her freelance days and forced her way through the crowds. The school was a beehive of confusion. She left her bike with her purse in the basket to search for her son. Even in New York City, you think of your son before you think of your purse.

She saw her thirteen-year-old son, Henry, with a bunch of friends and said, "Who's coming with me?" She took a dozen with her with the directions: "Stay together, hold hands. You will see people crying, screaming. Don't look back, keep moving forward. Listen to me and do what I say." By the time they made it across a nearby highway, a third of the youngsters were crying. She could see people flinging themselves out of the towers and wanted to shield the children. "Just look ahead!" she ordered. Then she looked back — the mistake of Lot's wife — and saw the south tower dropping in a cascade of smoke. She also had forgotten that if you tell kids not to do something, their instinct is to do it anyway. They did. They looked. They saw the people holding hands jumping from the top of the skyscraper to the ground.

Then they ran. They ran like hell, she says, until they got to her loft in TriBeCa. One kid was crying because his mom worked in one of the towers. Wicky kept saying she knew his mom was okay. She went out to the deli to get them some food. She's Italian, she explains, so in a pinch, you eat. "If I go," she reasoned, "I'm going maximum chubby."

When she got back, the remaining tower had tumbled and all the kids lost it. She turned off the TV. They watched *Charlie Brown's Christmas* instead of the news. She made sandwiches. One by one, the parents showed up. Even the mom from the tower. Her family ate pasta and toasted their good fortune to have each other. She wanted a bath. There was no water. The National Guard rolled by outside, and their landscape was changed forever.

Flash forward to the next spring. Wicky collected the essays she wrote and photos from that unique moment into a little book. All the proceeds would go to restore the schools in the neighborhood. "Lots of us in families, we try to teach our children how to cope with humanity's worst moments, but we don't always get to see them do it. We all stuck together as a family, and we decided to stay. We did not cower. We did not leave. We went out to the cars that were flattened in the street and put pink lilies in them. We could see the fabric of humanity around us, even when it seemed the most unraveled. We got to see the re-establishing of our neighborhood. It was a huge healing process."

Her son and daughter Willy were transferred to a "foster school" in another part of town for six months while their school was decontaminated. When they returned, the students were asked to make place cards for a re-entry ceremony. "My son's place card read, 'You're back. Don't forget to be grateful.'" She marveled: "This is from a thirteen-year-old boy, a wild, hard-hitting, bony-kneed boy.'"

He had terrible nightmares, afterward, like many of the students. News stories reported that nearly 90 percent of New York City school children had some symptoms of posttraumatic stress after September 11 and as many as 75,000 had severe problems. Wicky worried whether she should take her son on the trip they had planned for October. His friends all had bar mitzvahs at thirteen, so she was going to take him to the Arctic for his "bear mitzvah." They went anyway to observe the migration of the polar bears. When they got back, he told her, "Mama, nobody is jumping out of the window in my dreams. Now they are dropping through the ice." She checked with a psychologist who told her "pain does not just leave, but it can migrate, and if images change, that means your mind is healing and the pain will be diminished."

Her seventeen-year-old daughter, Willy, did not see the same horrific scenes, but she lived with the aftermath in their neighborhood and wrote her college application essays while watching the dust settle. She wrote that the community around them had been brought together by the events. She hoped that what her generation takes away from September 11 is the need for community spirit. (Mount Holyoke agreed and accepted her.)

Her mom marvels at what the members of her family have learned about themselves and each other since September 11. "All of us knew who was in there, inside of us, before September 11. Maybe we exercised that person a little more after that."

Ironically, Wicky was called to try out as a contestant for the *Survivor* TV series in the midst of all the rebuilding. She didn't make the cut. But to read her little book is to know she already won the real contest.

She knows what it is like to give her last bit of Scotch to the policeman on the block who just realized his partner didn't come out of the building. She knows what it means to fall into bed and cling to her husband, like spoons with feet intertwined, while sirens go on outside. She knows what it is like to hug your children close and smell the familiar smell of their hair as if for the first and last time. She knows what family means and what neighborhood means as never before. She knows how to love strangers with an open, nurturing heart. And that is a great gift.

"I loved you before you were born. I dreamed about how the world would be a better place because of you. I know what you are feeling, but remember life has a purpose. You can start over. Love, God."

– UNITED METHODIST CHURCH TV COMMERCIAL

We met for breakfast at a bustling little TriBeCa café called Bubby's to talk about her essays. Wicky said she is trying to teach her children to understand the ways of the world, just as her mother, an anthropolgist, used to teach her about the faith stories of the world. Her mother would say, "This is the story of the Navajos . . ." or, "This is the story the Jews tell . . ." She remembered, "I loved the creation stories. Like the one from Central America, I think it was, where God made cookies and they were burned. So he put in another batch and they came out whitish and underdone. So he put in another batch and they came out just perfect, a mellow tan-brown, so he put them in Central America. And that became their story."

Her mother was Italian Catholic and her father was Irish Catholic, so it was inevitable that Wicky would go to Catholic schools. But she was asked to leave with the suggestion that she would fit better in public school. "I made good grades, but I was too mouthy," Wicky recalls. "You know, asking the nuns why they didn't get married . . . trying to peek under the wimple . . . going in the boy's bathroom if the girl's bathroom was full. Terrible stuff. They would threaten that bad children would go to hell and talked about the good children going to heaven. I started thinking hell might be the better option because their idea of heaven seemed soooo boring."

She's gone her own way since. After a series of careers and loves, she now finds herself at fifty, settled in comfortably with her husband, Zachary, a life skills consultant for pro sports franchises. They live in a loft apartment and she is a familiar sight in the neighborhood, riding her bicycle to the grocery store, chatting up young people with tattoos at Bubby's café, or giving advice to the manager about his toddler's rebellions. There is a robust life force about her that is very compelling; people like to hug Wicky. Her blue eyes always seem to be enjoying some joke and you are welcome to share.

She's articulate: "I try to teach my children that intelligence is a gift not a weapon."

She's sentimental: "My son is such an innocent. For him, ice cream will be cold every time he tastes it."

And she's blunt: "Organized religion is just one way to respond to God."

I understood how she came to that conclusion, but I couldn't help but think what a lot of love and creativity the organized church lost when a few pushed her out. The round peg church has never figured out the square peg individuals, even though many of them have painted the paintings or written the poems or chal-

> "Drink is not your problem. What you need is something or someone to believe in."
>
> — TENNESSEE WILLIAMS, "Night of the Iguana"

lenged the civil rights of the time. Yet the church today could use more of their art for inspiration and more of the questioning that gets to the real heart of the matter. Asking questions is the way to enter our faith and truly be engaged in it; otherwise, it is merely a borrowed thing.

Toward that end, the Methodist Church has begun an interesting experiment in Dallas. The Reverend Diana Holbert, a fifty-one-year-old minister with a background in liturgical dance, has been given the unusual assignment of ministering to artists in the downtown area. With rather astounding carte blanche, she was told by her bishop simply to seek out the artists of the city and see what happens. So she went out on her own — no staff, no office, no phone, no sanctuary — to find the creative community and invite them to worship. All she could take with her was her own shining faith and a mischievous intellect. So far, she's drawn together a nucleus of dozens of creative types — writers, sculptors, and painters. Operating in a borrowed office with a patched-up computer, Diana draws them to the theater and to discussions at a late-night bakery. She has assembled a lecture series before Christmas on the depictions of Mary in religious art.

She's helped organize a new religious opera company. And she has danced for her new "congregation," which probably would not have felt comfortable in a traditional, four-wall church.

She calls her moveable ministry "Artspirit." The name is a reminder that the Holy Spirit speaks to us through art. Today's church needs artists to elevate its message just as today's artists need the church message to elevate their sights. The most nihilistic artist or most misogynistic rapper might have a painful space in their soul that a compassionate church could fill.

Writing an e-mail to her "Artspirit" colleagues, which is how she communicates with them, Diana pointed out that Sally McFague had written in *Models of God*, that "we feel the best when we are loving and being loved. It's not about sex or lust, it's about value. We want to be valued, to be delighted over, to be precious."

And of course, that's the root of many of our discontents, isn't it? We come into this world crying and wanting to be held and leave it the same way if we have not let ourselves be fully loved by God and are loving in return. Whether a soul singer in five-inch heels or the staid chalice bearer in a white robe, we share that drive to know and be known. The challenge for the church today is to see the child of God in the Mohawk haircut and say "Come in."

A remarkable nine out of ten Americans say they believe in God, but one half of them do not belong to a place of worship. At least 20 percent say they are "spiritual," but not religious. That means many people are struggling with the universal questions of meaning — Are we the product of chance or a loving God? — outside the church.

> "You must have things that you care about. Otherwise you are empty."
>
> — NEW YORK CABDRIVER

Many women who did not find empathy in the formal church have found it in let-down-your-hair talk sessions on TV shows like *Oprah* and *The View* as well as Lifetime and Oxygen cable networks. When the huge ecumenical service was held at Yankee Stadium on September 23 to comfort New Yorkers, who was chosen to lead the assembled, Christian, Muslim, Jewish, Sikh, and Hindu clergy? Oprah Winfrey. As the magazine *Christianity Today* noted, with a TV congregation of 22 million viewers, Oprah has become one of the most influential spiritual leaders in America.

After consoling mourners at the service that "hope lives, prayer lives, love lives," she offered the benediction, "May we all leave this place and not let one single life have passed in vain. May we leave this place determined to now use every moment that we yet live to turn up the volume in our own lives, to create deeper meaning, to know what really matters."

Oprah's core beliefs were shaped by the Baptist Church of her youth, where she first began public speaking. She clearly feels her calling is to help others. She keeps to a generalized spirituality on the air, although she refers unabashedly to "the Lord" or "blessed Savior" in personal appearances. Some evangelicals dismiss her as too much New Age and not enough New Testament. It's true, the guests on her show have included New Age voices like Deepak Chopra and Marianne Williamson, but they also have included Holocaust survivor Elie Wiesel, the Dalai Lama, and Richard Thomas of PAX-TV talking about real-life miracles. It's important to recognize that those weren't conversations you would have seen on shows with hosts like Jay Leno, David Letterman, or Conan O'Brien. Though she has been criticized for showcasing a Heinz 57 kind of faith,

Oprah Winfrey has done more than any other post-modern role model to make it acceptable to talk about faith publicly and comfortably. She has taken faith and put it smack in the middle of everyday life.

Oprah often challenges viewers to ask themselves basic questions: What do you believe? *Really* believe? And are you living a life that is supported by those beliefs? If you were plunked down on the stage with Oprah, could you answer those questions on air honestly? If you are trying to live a faithful life outside the church, when and where do you turn to God? What daily actions do you take to reinforce your beliefs?

No doubt many people could cite events or people that have turned them away from religion — sermons that droned on, ministers who did not practice what they preached, hypocritical believers who did not love their neighbor. Have events drawn you closer to faith or away from faith? If you are one of those who feels estranged from the established church, what do you think God would want you to do? Is there someone in your church background who you need to forgive? Nobody ever said believers were perfect. Often our faith has to survive the worst of the church, the humanness of it. Let's face it, the politics inside the church can be messy and disillusioning. Rev. Skip Ryan, a Presbyterian minister in Dallas, once compared the ugly side of church politics to the disorder inside Noah's Ark. As he put it, things probably were fractious and messy and awful inside that boat with all those different kinds of animals. But when it starts to thunder and rain, he asked, where would you rather be, inside the Ark or outside? Good question.

After September 11, the value of institutional religions was uplifted as millions who had strayed — or fled — returned to churches and synagogues and mosques. They sought comfort and answers. Some went to yoga class, yes, some went to bars, but most went to God's house. Perhaps more would if churches could announce a general, mutual amnesty — "You come back and really love us and we'll embrace and really love you."

TAKE HOME:

The tension between belief and doubt can trouble those inside the church as well as those outside the church. The discipline Mark wrote, "Lord, I believe; help thou mine unbelief." Martin Luther, who began the Protestant Reformation, described spiritual depressions when he felt he was fighting Satan's attacks. The German theologian Dietrich Bonhoeffer wrote poems of doubt and abandonment, even as he bravely conducted worship services and ministered to other prisoners in a Nazi concentration camp.

And when the letters and diaries of Mother Teresa were published in 2001, it was revealed that even she sometimes felt rejected by God as she struggled to care for the poor and dying of Calcutta. The excerpts appeared in an Indian theological journal called *Vidyajyoti* and were reported by the Associated Press. Her writings had been gathered by nuns and priests who were preparing a report for Pope John Paul II, who was considering Mother Teresa for beatification. Though she described tears of loneliness and sometimes felt abandoned, she never stopped writing of her longing for God and her desire to be used by him. And though she was discouraged, she never stopped her work. The order she founded in 1946 expanded to more than one hundred countries by the time of her death in 1997.

She confessed in her writing that she

sometimes was unable to pray. Some of her most agonizing thoughts came in 1959–1960, apparently a deeply despairing point in her life. She wrote, "Now Jesus, I go the wrong way. They say people in hell suffer eternal pain because of loss of God. In my soul, I feel just the terrible pain of loss, of God not wanting me, of God not being God, of God not really existing. Jesus, please forgive me the blasphemy — I have been told to write everything — that darkness that surrounds me on all sides. I can't lift my soul to God: No light, no inspiration enters my soul." But in time, her search for understanding led her to feel closer to Jesus and to understand joy. By the 1990s, she wrote, "I have begun to love my darkness, for I believe now that it is a part, a very small part, of Jesus' darkness and pain on earth."

With good humor, she later would even joke, "I know God won't give me anything I can't handle. I just wish he didn't trust me so much."

At times she was criticized for only tending to the immediate needs of the poor rather than changing the social order that created the poverty. She could tend nine thousand needy a day — a remarkable logistical accomplishment. But that was only nine thousand out of more than 3 million poor in Calcutta. And the city doubled in size during her lifetime. What then should she have done? What should we do? As teacher Beth Moore tells her classes of women in Houston, you do the best you can in life to reach out to the few you have been directed to help. Do you quit because you are surrounded by unanswered need? No, you do what you are called to do.

Beth Moore observes that Mother Teresa was also criticized for tending to the dying, when there was nothing more that could be done to save them. But, she explains, Mother Teresa wisely would "sit with them and pray with them, so that people who had nothing, would awaken to everything. . . . They would shut their eyes to the pain and the emptiness and open them to a mansion."

> "People throughout the world may look different or have a different religion, education, or position, but they are all the same. They are the people to be loved. They are all hungry for love. The people you see in the streets of Calcutta are hungry in body, but the people in London or New York also have a hunger which must be satisfied. Every person needs to be loved."
>
> — MOTHER TERESA

Mother Teresa knew that darkness draws us closer to God and that closeness in turn leads to joy. Perhaps that's why she wrote so often about joy: "Let anyone who comes to you go away feeling better and happier. Every one should see goodness in your face, in your eyes, in your smile. Joy shows from the eyes, it appears when we speak and walk. It cannot be kept closed inside us. It reacts outside. Joy is very infectious."

It's important to remember when you are trying to change the world, that it happens one person at a time. It's a start to find the like-minded and create shimmering centers of belief. People will want to be part of that warmth instead of soloing.

FIFTEEN

Enjoying

"For many people, life is a struggle. At its worst, it is a struggle to survive, at its best, a struggle to become totally true. In its essence, joy celebrates triumph."
— SISTER WENDY BECKETT

God reminds us time and again that he wants us to be happy. Rejoicing is expressed by a variety of terms in the Old Testament: joy, gladness, merriment, a ringing cry, leaping, exulting, jubilation, shouting. We are encouraged to find joy in nature, in our relationships with others, and in our place in time. Night cometh, yes, but joy comes in the morning.

Today we live in a time where people work like plowhorses so they can afford leisure. But joy still eludes them. We are beguiled by the Madison Avenue mirage of happiness — a faster car, a thinner Swiss watch, pointy-toe Via Spiga shoes that cost more than a village income — only to discover T. S. Eliot was right about the hollow people who come and go. What is joy? Why does it seem like the phosphorescent moon glow you try to scoop from the ocean waves at night, only to see it slip through your hands? Perhaps we can begin to define joy by examining what it is not.

Joy is not constant, like the cheerfulness we affect. But just knowing it is possible, now and then, helps us face whatever life might throw at us.

Unlike the high from booze or drugs, joy is not something that will give you a hangover. You don't regret real joy. There's no remorse the next day. You pay a price with overeating and overspending in pursuit of pleasure. You don't pay a penalty for the taste of contentment.

It's not an escape from your problems, in hopes they will magically disappear while you're out of town. It's facing your problems with the confidence that someone on high is cheering for you to rise to the occasion. Just imagine your mom ahead of you in the swimming pool saying, "You can make it!" and holding out her arms to receive you. And as you struggle ahead, the wise parent eases back a step or two, calling you forward with the words, "You're almost there, come on." And when you make it — joy!

It's not something that gets boring after a few tries. Real joy is the song in your attitude, a way of looking at the world that helps you see the aspidistra growing through the asphalt.

It's not something done at the expense of someone else. Real joy never leaves someone else feeling worse or used.

Is joy possible in this lifetime? You bet. Like butterflies. And snowflakes. Joy alights. Frederick Buechner says that happiness turns up more or less where you'd expect it to — a good marriage, a rewarding job, a pleasant vacation. "Joy, on the other hand, is as notoriously unpredictable as the one who bequeaths it." We can't fully fathom God, so perhaps we can't really fathom joy. But we can pursue that sense of fullness, rightness, aliveness, and purpose with the assurance that, like Anne Graham Lotz, we know how the story turns out, a room is waiting for us. Buechner also points out that in the Gospel of John, Jesus sums it up by saying, "These things I have spoken to you, that my joy may be in you and that your joy may be full." It was his last supper with his disciples. And he wished them joy. One of the odd things about joy is that when you are wishing it for others with a sincere heart, you probably have it, too.

There is a visible difference in people who have known joy and want to share it with others. Beth Moore, a Houston Bible teacher who is one of the most engaging speakers in the country right now, says that people who are graced by faith are *graceful.* "The picture we get at the end of the New Testament is of a church where people are having a *blast,*" she says. "They broke bread together in their homes . . . and had glad and sincere hearts." Glad, she explains, means to sing songs and to dance. These were people who had a good time. "The vision of the church (in the Book of Acts) is not dry and lifeless. It is a word-centered environment of great fellowship, fulfillment, miraculous, with the presence of God to distinguish it."

Beth Moore is a good example of someone who seems to be plugged in to God and, as a result, is illuminated. To see her speak at one of her giant rallies is an unforgettable experience. When she takes to the stage, she drops to the floor, on her knees. Bent over, a little curved heap of a human being, she prays with a passion that is absolutely riveting:

"I *praise* you Lord. You are so far beyond anything we can even imagine. *God,* we ask you to keep *stretching* us, to keep *teaching* us, Lord, to help us think *beyond* ourselves . . . to *risk* learning things of you that might make us uncomfortable, that might not be the things, Father, that we have always believed. We pray to be able to — Lord! — break out the shells of *sameness* and really *know* you. Oh, how I *pray* that, Father! That we will break out of the little shackles, Father, of just what religion offers and begin to know the God of the *word*, the God of the *truth*. We are desperate to know *you*, Lord, not just to know religious *things* and not just to practice religious *actions*, Father, but to *know* the God of all creation who spoke and it *was*.

"I pray, Father, that something in every single one of us today will *quicken*, that it will just come to *life* through your Holy Spirit this morning, Father. That even if we have heard this kind of plea *100 times* in the course of coming to church through the years, that today it will *stick* and take root and we will *respond* to it. Oh Lord, *bring us to life! Bring us to life!* If we begin to know the true life of the spirit and the power that is released through your word, God, what *magnets* we would be. If we just *get* it, there would not be an *empty* seat in that sanctuary, Lord, our lives would be so *magnetic,* people would want to come where we come and do some of the things we do. God, help us. We are your people. We desperately need to get it. We just praise you, Lord, for your *patience,* that you continue to *strive* with us. Lord, you keep pulling us along, and *dragging* us along at times. We come here to today, Father, to proclaim that we are thankful. We ask you to speak, Father, and let it get to us. Let us hear with spiritual ears and have the courage enough to respond. In the sweet, wonderful and awesome name of Jesus, Amen."

Then, rising to her feet with her microphone, Beth asked the audience to turn to a Scripture, in this case, Psalm 19, and she got right to work, parsing every sentence to find the meaning that might otherwise be missed. Two things make Beth's teaching ministry powerful and wildly popular: First, her talks are heavily scriptural, with lots of Bible quoting and word study, something audiences are apparently hungry for. Second, she is delightfully funny. She's good evidence that you don't have to be square or dull to be a believer. When some women

> "Happiness depends on what happens; joy does not."
>
> — OSWALD CHAMBERS

were fumbling to find the right chapter in the Old Testament, she reassured them, "It took me *years* before I discovered what all that paper was before Matthew."

Women all over the country are scribbling their way through Beth Moore's Bible study workbooks because the studies are down-to-earth and do-able. Her talks are chock-a-block with references to Hebrew and Greek meanings. Words are important, she hammers home. She often instructs her audiences to "camp" on a word while she explains the original usage and meaning. In one talk, she reminded the women that it takes self-control to avoid being *mastered* by our desires, and explained the Greek word for mastered is *exousiazo*, which means "to be ruled by or be under the power of, to be in bondage to." By the time she got to the third definition, the picture was clear that to be mastered by your desires is like the adage that "first you take the drink, and then the drink takes you." Later, the question came up, What does it mean when the Bible refers to "gentleness"? She went to the Greek word *praotes*, which means "meekness, mildness, forbearance." She described it as "inward grace of the soul" and the calmness toward God "when we quit *fighting* him."

Beth also teaches with personal stories and irreverent observations, putting audiences at ease with "girlfriend" chat. At an early morning workshop for women at Second Baptist Church in Houston last year, she pointed out that once one of her daughters had chided her when she was being cross, "That's not very *Christiany* of you!" As women, she admitted, "We can just be meaner than snakes. We can use our tongues to literally *kill*. But it is never too late to ask forgiveness and to remember when we get ourselves stressed out that our husbands and kids are not looking for perfection. They are looking for *authenticity*."

At another session, she held up a Superwoman costume and told the crowd, "We all know who this one is. This is the woman who is busy, busy, busy. She is happiest not only controlling her life, but the lives of those around her. This is the woman with the bumper sticker that says, 'God could not be everywhere, so he created me.'" And the crowd roared with laughter at themselves.

> "I tell my kids, if you don't think every day is a great day, try going without one."
>
> — CAROLINE HITE

In Revelation, she observes, believers are told they will be given the dress to wear for being reunited with God. She warns that believers "must be ready by the active pursuit of purity, growing and progressing in the sight of God." Then she puts the audience squarely on the spot by asking pointedly, "*What* are we doing to make ourselves ready? Here's our tendency as women: We want to get everyone *else* ready. Here's advice for Mrs. Fixit: You are fighting a losing battle to get your husband ready. You can't be his Holy Spirit. You have not been called to change your man. You should just love him and forget sanctifying him. That leaves you free to love them and live the kind of life that they will want to emulate."

Too often women are trying to do what they think others want them to do, so Beth advises: "You've got a crowd in your head. You brought a crowd in your head with you today. Don't you want to say sometimes, 'Everybody sit down!' "

She likes to use her husband, Keith, as a foil, always being careful to compliment him before telling a funny story about him. "Keith is the neatest guy. We are tight as thieves because we have been through so much. But I tell you, if he can afford it, he has it." He likes to tease her, she says, that she only got into teaching because she was rejected by the handbell choir. It's true, she says. When she first moved to Houston, she applied for the handbell choir at First Baptist Church, but there were no openings. So she began teaching a church aerobics class . . .

. . . which led to the invitation to teach a Sunday School class . . .

. . . which led to standing-room-only sessions in the sanctuary . . .

. . . which led to workbooks . . .

. . . which led to bestselling books . . . to audiotapes . . .

. . . then to videotapes in the Holy Land and Greece.

All the while there were trips across the country to speak to thousands of women at a time. So now, she says, when they are sitting in church and the handbell choir plays, Keith nudges her and whispers, "Baby, that could have been *you!*"

Actually, Beth's journey to teaching involved tears as well as laughs. She calls her organization "Living Proof Ministries" because she says

"Life need not be easy to be joyful. Joy is not the absence of trouble but the presence of Christ."

— WILLIAM VAN DER HOVEN

she is living proof of God's grace. And she is. At forty-four, she is transforming ministries to women. She fills churches, stadiums, and ballrooms with women hungry to hear someone talk to them about Scripture in a real-world way. But a decade ago, Beth was stopped in her tracks by depression and anxiety as she struggled to deal with memories of childhood abuse. She doesn't go into detail because she doesn't see herself as a "victim speaker." But she sometimes alludes to her problems in the past, because it shows she understands suffering and she knows healing. She has said that the abuse came from outside her immediate family and that she repressed the trauma for many years.

She felt a call to serve God while she was in college and was taking a group of sixth-grade girls to a church summer camp. She remembers waking one morning with the sense that God had told her, "I have chosen you; you are mine." She committed herself to ministry but did not feel called to seminary. She decided to leave herself open to other ways to serve and began looking for the right way. After some trial and error, teaching appeared to be her calling. She threw herself into studying the Bible, not only catching up, but racing ahead.

Then, in the early 1990s, the wounds from her childhood surfaced. It threw her off track. Thanks to her maturing faith, counseling, and the encouragement of her family, she steadied herself. She emerged an even more persuasive, powerful, and empathetic speaker. Now when she talks to audiences about being in bondage to sin, she can admit she was once addicted to sin herself and used to chastise herself, "Act right, act right!" Again, she doesn't elaborate what the stronghold on her was, other than to say that she had a destructive pattern in her relationships. "I have had so much shame in my life. It was not enough that I was victimized, I had to go and make the world's stupidest decisions."

You can tell by the tone in her voice that she has indeed been there and done that which she wishes she had not done. "I am a tremendous work in progress. I was blind and now I see. I was a very emotionally handicapped person. I dressed it well. Any number of people would not have known, if they didn't know me well. I kept my distance. I knew how to make it work. I knew how to fix the thing so it didn't show."

She now says, "God and I worked extremely hard" to overcome those problems. She turned to Scripture with new intensity, replacing what had been a submerged "victim" attitude with a stronger overcomer attitude. She asks her audience, "What is most secret to *you?* God already sees it. You know the closet with the lightbulb in the top? You need to be tall enough to reach up and pull the chain and turn on the light in that closet. It is the darkness in the closet that is keeping it a stronghold. When I reached up and pulled the chain, it was not a pretty sight. But there's not a person in here who can't be set free. . . . If we confess our sins, he is faithful and he will purify us and restore us. Too often the problem is we don't believe God. If we *really* believed God, our behaviors would change. We don't believe our sins are forgiven. We do not accept forgiveness and repent. Just remember: Though I have fallen, I will get up."

It's hard to picture this attractive, articulate woman "in the ditch with sin." She looks like a sorority girl with a few years on her. But she sounds believable when she tells audiences, "You cannot out-sin me." And she sounds believable when she promises "Believe what I say is *true.* God loves you. So we give an answering love in return, loving him first and others second. If God doesn't have an unlovely person in your life for you to love, then you are not getting out enough. We are called to do a few things for God, not a thousand. He will fill the canteen for us. If we will just try to do a few things for the absolute glory of God and do it with excellence. We are called to be light. To be joyful, to be filled with the spirit. So ask the question, What several things are a priority in my life? What things have I been called to do in this season of life? We have got to find ways in our busy life to get some more Sabbath moments."

Beth has had to make an effort to keep her life from becoming too busy as her ministry becomes bigger and more international. Her travel schedule has taken her to Canada, the Philippines, Minneapolis, Chicago, Denver, Nashville, Fort Worth, Greece, Turkey, and France. "When I felt called to the ministry," she says, "my social life went into the toilet. My kids are my social life. All of my 'B' friends went down the drain." Hers is a peculiar life now, she admits. She speaks on the weekends and concentrates on running her ministry, studying, and writing on weekdays. She and her husband agreed that she would only speak out of town every other weekend while their daughters were young, so she faithfully restricted her travel schedule. She usually leaves Houston on a Friday and hurries back home Saturday night. She throws herself "body and soul" into her speaking, so that sometimes, after back-to-back sessions at workshops, she feels like she can't even lift her hand by the time she gets to the airport.

But the quick turnarounds are worth it, she said, to keep the equilibrium in her marriage and family. "I wanted to raise my own children. I *loved* the role of mother-hood," she says. Her ministry grew as her children grew. Somehow she has managed to keep a "real life" that is enriched by her spiritual life — and vice versa. When we talked, she seemed very much at ease even

> "You will always have joy in the evening if you spend the day fruitfully."
>
> – THOMAS À KEMPIS

though one of her daughters was getting married in just a month and she had only recently returned from taping a video in Israel. At the same time, she was debuting a new book, *When Godly People Do Ungodly Things*, and she was producing a new Internet ministry, lproof.org, so she will be even more accessible to women around the world.

Why does she think her ministry is

spreading so dramatically? The growing demand for Bible literacy. "I'm convinced that we are part of what is happening worldwide. There is a growing appetite for the word of God. Any Bible-based ministry is seeing it. God is teaching lay people how to love him and be in communion with him through the Word. It is a lay movement, not just the church leadership."

She says the best part of her ministry is watching "the light come on for someone," but she tries to downplay her own abilities. She says she connects with people when the "spirit of the Scripture" flows through her. She maintains that her primary focus will continue to be women, even though men often attend her classes. She has been able to strike a diplomatic balance between her call to teach and the tenets of the conservative denomination, which says the office of pastor was limited to men. Beth says she prayed about that concern and consulted with church leaders before venturing on. She felt a reassurance from the Holy Spirit to the effect of "Go ahead. You worry about what you're going to say, and I'll worry about who hears it." So now, she says, "I don't seek a male audience. If a man seeks the class, it's because he chooses it." Many of her sessions are labeled "For Women Only," she says, "because that's our deal. If men come to the class and stand in the back of the room, that's *their* choice." It's a smart, workable strategy.

She tackles the role of Christian wives in her book, *To Live Is Christ,* which surveys the writing of the Apostle Paul. Her interpretation of Paul's instructions in Ephesians that women should "submit to their husbands" is that it does not mean that women are under the authority of men in general. It does not mean inequality. It does not mean wives are to treat their husbands like God. And it does not mean slavery. It *does* mean that married partners have mutual obligations, she says. That requires a lot of give and take on *both* sides. God is good and loving, she emphasizes; therefore, he would never give approval to meanness or abuse by a spouse. Her position stands in clear contrast to those who have used Paul's words to advise women to tolerate domestic abuse from their husbands.

That kind of commonsense scriptural doctrine is drawing not only Baptist women by the thousands to her classes, but women from many other denominations as well. Even though the crescendo in her ministry has increased the demands on her, she seems determined to hang on to her naturalness and normalcy. She has a gift not only for interpreting Scripture, but for savoring the moment she is in. In her audiotapes, she reveals that one day when she felt particularly pressured, she just dropped everything and went to the zoo by herself. Once when she was out on a walk and got caught in a downpour, she decided to just raise her arms up and enjoy it.

It is that very zest for life that makes her talks so appealing. "Some of you have your soul on a diet," she tells her audience. "You've got yourself on a diet with God and on a binge with the world!" Instead of compartmentalizing God as something only for Sundays or only for difficulties, she says believers should understand that God is like an on-going dance. It's a compelling image: God as a dancing partner, just within reach if we open our arms and listen for the music.

In her workbook *Living Beyond Yourself*, Beth points out the Greek word for joy is *chara*, which also means "rejoicing, gladness, enjoyment, and bliss." So in many ways, she says, *chara* means "to celebrate." Celebrate what? Perhaps that we are not orphans in the universe. That we belong to

God. That he wants us to be around him. So that we can proclaim his blessing to others. The generosity of that plan is stunning when you stop to think: Who are we that God watches us so closely? How does he hear our softest prayers in the vastness of the universe? Why does he want to share the music — the fugues and the arias — with us? We come to realize we are embarrassingly small and inadequate and fortunate and blessed.

Joy, it seems, can be both a moment of clarity and a process of illumination. To be "surprised by joy" is to know the "ah ha!" moments when we see how it all really does fit together. Then we begin to understand that the power of God is with us in all our tribulations, not to spare us, but to help us bear on. Eventually "abiding joy" comes from the realization that although the branches must be pruned, they will be the better for it.

> "People from a planet without flowers would think we must be mad with joy the whole time to have such things about us."
>
> — IRIS MURDOCH

Beth Moore cautions that if you can't feel joy, you probably are exhausted or tuned out or centered only on yourself. You must refuel. Go back to the basics of

Scripture and prayer or confer with a spiritual advisor. You eventually learn there is joy when you are alone, as well as the exhilarating mountaintop moments. "If you've lost your joy, it's right where you left it," she says, "in his presence."

She suggests you can refresh your joy by relating to someone outside your circle of comfort. "Ask God to make you sensitive to those who are lonely," she advises. "Step out in faith and draw them in. Dear friend, how boring and mediocre our lives would be if we were surrounded only by the stereotypical persons with whom we feel comfortable. Branch out! Make friends and relationships of different colors, different economic persuasions, different backgrounds, even different denominations! Go ahead! Live a little! The body of Christ comes in all shapes and sizes. Take some risks. They will become your joy."

Her point is that sharing multiplies our joy. Too many people, she says, make the mistake of thinking that having "stuff" will bring them satisfaction and joy. "So much of what we accumulate, what we crave, and what we *have to have* is an attempt to meet a *soul need*. It's much more than what we need around the house or need to get to work. It's not the car, it's the *prestige,* the *soul need,* of being identified somehow with something that is *fine.* You know, I need to dress a certain way because I have a *soul need* that isn't met. That we need prestige, that we need to accumulate, that we need so much of what we have and what we're unwilling to let go of, is because of a *soul need.* I want to tell you God distributes, God gives wealth. But he means for none of us to hang onto it." Believers will find more joy, she teaches, if they try to fill their soul with God instead of things.

Beth observes that many people who are beat down by their problems either believe that they are not worthy of joy or not likely to receive any during their lifetime. She chides: "If you believe delight belongs to someone else — then *change!* Please! You'll be so glad you did." She believes people should anticipate joy, expect joy, and seek joy. Too many women live a sacrificial life, she says, thinking the fun is on the outside of church, or for later in heaven. *"This is the life,"* she emphasizes. "There is fullness of joy in *this* life. There is *delight* to be had in *this* life. Right here in the land of the living. Right *here,* that his joy would be in us and our joy would be full."

"For crying out loud," she tells audiences, "enjoy God! We keep partaking of the sins of the world because we think it has more to offer us. Christians are not supposed to enjoy anything. Something is wrong with that. There is *delight* in Christ. There is *joy* and great *pleasure* in Christ."

It's not that Beth does not ever have low-energy slumps. Once she admitted she had to be reminded by a co-worker as she wearily left her office to "Party on." She can get worn down like anyone, but she knows the way back: Open yourself to God again. Make joy for others. Breathe joy. If there is no passion in our faith, she reminds, why on earth would our neighbors or children want to be that way, too? The thing young people dislike the most about organized religion, she points out, is inauthenticity. If Christianity is such a great deal, why don't those pushing it seem to be enjoying it? If there is no joy in your life, she tells audiences of church women, *what* are you waiting for? She advises them to work toward that place in their faith where they can say honestly to God, "I want you to be the greatest delight of my life." Then you are able to smile at your surroundings more and laugh at your predicaments more. Faith is good therapy.

When Beth Moore finishes speaking, she invariably gets a standing ovation. Audiences cheer for more. They would listen for several hours more, but she usually has to get home to her family. She has become "living proof" not just of God's grace, but how very magnetic a believer of sincere conviction is. Her sheer certainty is compelling. Her effervescent good humor is contagious. When you leave the presence of someone who is as high-powered as she is, you are energized, too. But what then? What to do after you drive out of the parking lot and back to life? How do you keep joy alive from one day to the next, like the Olympic torch being carried from one small town to another? How do you become a transmitter of joy?

Perhaps you can start by traveling lighter. If you have pain that you just can't see around or get past, you should try writing it down, suggests the Rev. Mark Craig at Highland Park United Methodist Church. He counsels that you should put those problems in a "God box" and leave them, trusting that God in his wisdom will work out what is best for you.

Rev. Craig says that most of the people who come to him feeling despondent are looking for a sense of purpose in their lives, a way to make their life count. He recommends five steps:

1. Ask yourself every day what you can do to be more helpful to others — then do it.

2. Write, phone, or e-mail someone each day and say how much you appreciate that person.

3. Ask what you can do to help the elderly, the sick, or the abused — then do it.

4. Commit yourself to a single act of kindness in your family, your school, or your workplace before the day is done.

5. Think of someone you have not forgiven for something. Forgive them this day.

That's a good prescription for finding the *joie de vivre* that the French celebrate, or what the Costa Ricans call *pura vida,* the good life.

To keep your moorings, you also will need to become more Biblically literate. As Beth would put it, do you know what all that paper is in "the Good Book"? The goal should be to make an A in living rather than an A in Bible study, but deeper intellectual knowledge of Scripture can lead to transformation of your heart. Fortunately, there are several time-honored approaches to Bible study that can help that transformation from word to heart.

The oldest is called "divine reading" from the Latin *lectio divina,* which was practiced by the monks as far back as the fourth century.

ᕒ **First, there's the reading:** Read several verses of Scripture or paragraphs of a study book once quickly, then again more slowly and deliberately. Look for key phrases that are repeated or have special meaning to you.

ᕒ **Then, there's meditating on the words:** Look away. Let the words sink into your head and heart. For example, read the Lord's Prayer that you have been saying by rote all these years. Think about the words "Thy kingdom come, thy will be done." What does that mean to you really? Do you *really* believe God's kingdom is coming? Or are you just saying so? Think about Psalm 23 for the same reason. "The Lord is my shepherd." Notice the "my." Where are you being guided? Look for new angles and shades of meaning, even in time-worn verses.

∿ **The third step is praying over the scripture:** Pray your response to the ideas that surface. Ask God to show you how to apply what you have read to your life. Ask God to give you a tender heart, as Beth Moore suggests, a transformed heart.

Another method for studying Scripture is called Ignatian reading, after Ignatius of Loyola, the Spanish priest who founded the Jesuit order in the sixteenth century. In his "Spiritual Exercises," he suggested that you imagine yourself as an observer in the background as Scripture stories unfold. Use all your five senses. Imagine the taste of the fishes and loaves Jesus shared with the crowds. Would it be like rough seven-grain bread and sardines? The idea is to make the Scriptures three-D and real. Then it is easier to see how you might have acted or reacted, or how the event applies to you today. Imagine you were Phoebe hosting a Bible study in your home in the earliest days of the church. Are you a leader, or do you always leave the leading to others?

Another method is called Franciscan

reading, because it tracks the qualities of the Assisi saint: delight in creation, praise, beauty, and love for all creatures great and small. You might turn to Scripture, for example, and read Proverbs 27:19, "It is your own face that you see reflected in the water and it is your own self that you see in your heart." Look in the mirror at your own face — do you see kindness and peace or worry in your eyes? Contrast what you see with the fruits of the spirit in Galatians 5:22–23 — love, joy, peace, patience, kindness, goodness, gentleness, faithfulness, and self-control. If your story were in an A&E *Biography* profile, which of those qualities would be shown? The technique is only the beginning. Writing those qualities into your life is where will and grace come in. Read some verses every day. The result from the effort is a quiet joy that comes at its own slow pace, perhaps without your even noticing at first, like the green springs of grass that emerge in your lawn before you even realize that winter is over.

> "Joy is peace dancing and peace is joy at rest."
>
> — FREDERICK BROTHERTON (F. B.) MEYER

Sometimes a period of correction must occur before joy can enter our lives; more room must be made in our thoughts and days for the spiritual. The years 2001 and 2002 might go down in history as a convergence of corrections. Just think of all the individuals and institutions that fell from grace in 2001 and 2002: Enron, Worldcom, Tyco, RiteAid, Christies, Sothebys, FBI, CIA, the Catholic Church bureaucracy, Martha Stewart.

The message at the beginning of the millennium has been that the laws of gravity get to everyone sooner or later. Remember how we used to speak of "correcting" our school papers, putting in the right answer, not just criticizing what's wrong? On Wall Street, a "correction" is the market's way of humbling an artificially inflated stock. Something overvalued falls until its true value is settled. People with inflated egos or misplaced values might find themselves smacked by a reality check as well. Writer Michael Franzen might have presaged the wave of public humblings with *Corrections*, his award-winning novel about a dysfunctional (of course) family.

In Katherine Leary's case, her correction turned into a good thing. She grew up in the church in New Jersey, then "spent twenty years far from it," as she says, a familiar cycle. She had taught elementary school for a few years, but didn't want "to die in the teacher's lunch room." She decided she needed to go out into the big world and see what she was made of. She went to business school just as the high tech boom was building. She became the CEO of a software company called One Touch Systems in New York City. In 1996, she cashed in and went to Silicon Valley to do it again. She started a distance-learning company called Pensare and put her heart and soul and twenty-four hours a day into making it golden. Harvard Business School adopted the system for graduate education. The hip *Mother Jones* magazine featured Pensare as a shaper of high-tech style. But when the tech bubble burst in 2001, Katherine's company was one of the young firms that did not have the resources to last through the economic slump.

So Katherine started over with a new twist: She began a ministry for dot-com refugees at Menlo Park Presbyterian Church. She had become a committed Christian while working in New York. She had attended Redeemer Presbyterian, which became a magnet in Manhattan in the 1990s for young professionals. When she moved to California, she began attending Menlo Park, a progressive church in the Stanford area. She had hoped she'd make a bundle of money at Pensare so she could donate bigger bundles to help others. But when Pensare crashed, she realized that she could help others with a work-life ministry instead. She began counseling cyberholics on how to pour more of their spirituality into their professional life. Many of the Silicon Valley strivers did not feel a spiritual need when they were on the way up because their physical needs were being so handsomely fulfilled. Just before the century turned, there were more than 250,000 millionaires in the Valley. Church attendances was a curiosity. But then the unemployment rate went from 1.7 percent to 7.8 percent. Now the parking lots are crowded for Bible studies in the evening, according to *Christianity Today*.

"One of the things so many people are struggling with is the differences in integrity between their beliefs and the worldview and the practices of corporations. They seem in conflict," Katherine says. "What I am trying to put together is how we can support each other on those issues and start some initiatives to effect change."

She explains that the contract between employers and employees has become confused in recent decades. "If you ask someone about the implicit meaning of that relationship in each decade, you would get a totally different answer from the employee and the employer in terms of what is owed for a day's pay or what is deserved in terms of loyalty from management. The expectations have gotten really jumbled from the era of my father's generation. There was much more beholdenness then. They used to think they owed the company their life. Now it's more like What have you done for me lately? on both sides."

When she talks to Christians in the technology sector these days, she observed, they are likely to say they just want to find a good company environment. "No one ever says they are in one," she underscores. Often when she is counseling with a group on careers, she asks them to raise their hands if they have ever been in a healthy corporate environment. "There are few hands," she said. "So the real question is How are we going to get this environment that we all say we want to work for next? Is it going to fly from the sky? I've been trying to challenge them on that. The answer is not just sitting there. So what are we going to do to create it? We have to take the initiative. It's really not productive to always be comparing against a standard of a dream company that might turn out to not be healthier. If this (downturn) is all a bit of a message, then what can I do to effect change? How can we start building a business community based on some more mutually satisfying, common values?"

Servant leadership is part of that, she agrees. CEOs must see their roles as more than a casino sweepstakes where the game is rigged so they win. They must establish an emphasis on human dignity and integrity in the business place from the top. MBA whiz kids must be taught to value the dignity of others and conflict resolution as well as spreadsheet skills.

> "When someone does something, applaud! That will make two people happy."
>
> — SAMUEL GOLDWYN

Is there a way to bring more spiritual principles into the corporate workplace without blatantly shoving Scripture into people's faces? "Oh yes," Katherine says. "For example, in conflict resolution, when I was CEO I would advise someone who wanted me to fix a problem they had with someone else, that I couldn't talk to them about it unless they had spoken to the person themselves about the problem. If the two of them couldn't resolve it, then the two of them could come in and talk to me together."

There are also things that believers can learn from the Silicon Valley culture, she points out. "I went back to business school in my early thirties, just as the doors were opening in technology, so I feel so happy to have enjoyed some pretty interesting times. To be able to be part of that was not all bad. We are talking now about the excesses of Silicon Valley, but there also was some incredibly great stuff inside those companies in terms of innovation, establishing a meritocracy, and an energy level and people feeling like what they did every day *mattered*. There was a convergence of academic and business disciplines. There was multiculturalism that worked. If we could export the mentality of the best Silicon Valley companies to the churches across America, I think they would jump alive. They know me around the church for saying 'If we can get *that* excited about *technology*, don't you think we can pump people up a little more about *God?*' Who's going to *really* change the world?' "

That's the real challenge — how can we

get more of the spiritual values into the corporations and more of the market energy into the church?

Painful as the "corrections" have been, Katherine said, they might have been necessary. Some in Silicon Valley have even used a forest fire analogy, suggesting "we were having a burning because we needed that for the rebirth, the excess growth needed to die down so we could be reborn stronger."

> "A person's true wealth is the good he or she does in the world."
>
> – MUHAMMAD

As a result of that "right-sizing," some of the Silicon Valley CEOs have gotten religion. According to *Christianity Today*, Silicon Valley Fellowships is hosting sessions with former Microsoft executive John Sage, who has founded Pura Vida Coffee, which uses proceeds from its high-quality coffee beans to support ministries in Costa Rica. Greg Slayton, the CEO of ClickAction.com now keeps his kids' artwork on the walls of his office to remind him not to forget his family. Chen Wen-chi, CEO of Via Technologies, has instituted prayers before strategic decision meetings at company offices worldwide and Bible studies and praise sessions are available. The company helps with community water treatment and sponsors engineering scholarships for the needy. Even the chips have been given Biblical names — Joshua, Samuel, Ezra — to remind employes how God has led the company through its struggles.

Katherine Leary suggests that more thought will have to be given in the future to work-life balance. "You get the tone that people are working as slaves, as opposed to working with a joy that you are thrilled about. You need a Sabbath. God certainly set the pattern by showing that we should enjoy what we produce for six days and then take a Sabbath. It was not that he got caught up in drudgery for six days and then took a rest to do what was *really* important in life. It's *all* important. We need theology in our work, and we need rest to reflect on our theology. I certainly didn't have time the last six months that Pensare fell apart. It was hard enough to have prayer time to hold my shoulders up and go in every day, swimming upstream. I think a lot of the answer

> "We are all crowded togther on a very small planet. A difficult family. A collection of close relatives. Let us be kind to one another."
>
> — PAM BROWN

is having a vision for your life, to care what your life is about, to view your life as your vocation and your job as a critical part of that, but not the *whole* part."

Katherine suggests that grafting spiritual values to the free enterprise system could lead to deeper thinking by business leaders on the environment and how God might be calling them to do business in a way that is healthier. "Faith also would help workers transcend the ups and downs of their daily jobs. The key is that joy won't be delivered to you by your paycheck. Whatever happiness and joy we receive is not delivered to you by the world. It is between you and God and the people that God blesses your life with," Katherine said.

At Redeemer Presbyterian, she said, she will focus on small groups for her workplace teaching. She's developing a set of questions, such as "Do you even think about God during the day?" The idea is to encourage believers to connect to God as they work, not just on Sundays. So many professions and industries have turned work into an Iron Man Triathlon, she said. "The only way to get out of this bruising lifestyle we've created is to *humanize* it."

Some new generation companies, like

ExciteAtHome, the fourth-largest Internet portal, are now trying to bring their spiritual values to their business plan. ExciteAtHome has supported restrictions against pornography and adult chat rooms. Others are encouraging employees who used to sleep in their offices while in hot pursuit of a breakthrough to go home. They are discouraged from staying at work past 7:30 p.m. and from coming in on Sunday, so they can enjoy their families and rest in their faith.

> "When I was going through a very difficult time, someone called me up and played piano music for me on my answering machine. It made me feel very loved, and I never discovered who did it."
>
> — AN EDITOR AT CONARI PRESS

Katherine Leary says she prays that the current humblings are the beginning of a wider workplace movement. She says, "These are opportunity moments. I think some Christians are still reluctant to say or do something in the workplace, however. They think they should not be evangelizing, or they think they don't have the gift. But the most powerful persuader can be a lifestyle witness. Evangelize with your life. Let's take it to a whole new definition of what work looks like. Why are you doing your job? Can you bring some meaning and hope and joy to it that is distinctive?"

She also might start a secondary ministry to unmarried women in New York, as "an unmarried woman who would love to be married, but nonetheless feels you can have a joy-filled life." She explains that often women who don't find a meaningful marriage or children feel like work is second best, but it's all they have so they try to make up the difference there by devoting all their efforts there. "I can imagine making up the difference in another way," she says. "I think there's a way to get more faith and joy into that equation."

Are your work and faith compartmentalized into separate worlds that seem unrelated? Could you list three ways that your faith could bring more joy to your everyday duties? Do you pray for

"Happiness and narcissism are not synonyms. Self and selfishness are not the same things. The narcissist never gets enough affirmation. The selfish person never gets enough of anything to be satisfied. The happy person, on the other hand, has a sense of adequacy that no amount of lack can destroy, a sense of possibility that no amount of effort can dampen."

— JOAN CHITTISTER

everyone in your workplace in your prayers? If you are a homemaker, are there ways to lighten your tasks with faith? How does your family find joy together? As you have gotten older, has your definition of happiness changed? How would you define "the good life" today? What gives you contentment and a sense of purpose? If there is a spiritual awakening occurring, are you involved? Or are you watching and waiting?

TAKE HOME:

Several factors seem to be driving the current upsurge of interest in spirituality:

∾ The aging of the baby boomer generation, who are realizing that they need to work on their spiritual balance sheet.

∾ The increasing numbers of women who are moving into positions of influence in religion.

∾ Hundreds of thousands of women are being drawn to mega-revivals around the country like "women of faith."

∾ The looming terrorist threat of September 11, which has moved many Americans to confront their own mortality and what really matters in life.

∾ The dehumanizing elements of today's faster-paced global economy — cut-throat businesses, lonely cities, temporary neighborhoods, fractured families, and libertine culture — are driving many people back to religions that offer a structure to life and a sense of community.

Could this be a "great awakening" like those America has experienced three times before?

Robert William Fogel, author of *The Fourth Great Awakening*, definitely thinks so. His book has brought renewed attention to the history of religious waves in the United States. The First Great Awakening, which began in 1730, provided the ideological foundation for the American Revolution. The colonies were settled by religious stalwarts, he reminds. God was in the details as George Washington and company put their beliefs into democracy.

The Second Great Awakening, which began in 1800, introduced many of the social reforms that humanized our rough-hewn country, including the abolition of slavery, women's rights, temperance, public education, and Indian assistance.

The Third Great Awakening, which lasted roughly from 1890 to 1930, emphasized social injustice and produced the beginnings of the welfare state that grew after the depression. Child labor was abolished, elementary education was made compulsory, and labor pressure brought the reduction of hours in the workweek for many industries. The power of the robber barons was challenged.

Folger contends that the Fourth Great Awakening actually began in the late 1950s. It's true, concerns about the corporate pressures on the "man in the gray flannel suit" and concerns about civil rights began trickling to the surface of middle-class life. But the "Fourth Wave" might have been manifested more dramatically during the 1960s in the "Make Love Not War" movement that also celebrated environmentalism and meditative Eastern religions. Then the spiritual wave seemed to go subterranean as the country

> "I think that a good many people, here and everywhere, have a feeling in their bones that some sort of large-scale reawakening is in the cards for humanity."
>
> — E. B. WHITE
> *One Man's Meat*

struggled out of Vietnam and through Watergate in the 1970s. Americans were preoccupied with charging ahead on their credit cards in the 1980s. And in the plush 1990s, the moral debate deteriorated into whether oral sex was adultery or not. But just as the new millennium got under way, September 11 happened. The world trembled, the status quo was shattered, and more people looked up from what they were doing.

SIXTEEN

Hoping

"You're braver than you believe, and stronger than you seem, and smarter than you think."
— CHRISTOPHER ROBIN TO POOH

Over the years, I've asked women I've interviewed what their favorite Scripture is. I've been amazed how many mentioned Jeremiah 29:11–13. "For I know the plans I have for you, declares the Lord . . . plans to give you hope and a future. . . . You will seek me and find me when you seek me with all your heart."

Why Jeremiah 29? It has fascinated me that so many women selected that verse instead of the teachings of the New Testament ("Do unto others") and even the comfort of the Psalms ("The Lord is my shepherd . . ."). I noticed that Jeremiah 29 was cropping up on coffee mugs, plaques, greeting cards . . .

Why do the words of Jeremiah seem to provide such comfort for this generation?

Why such fondness for a book of the Bible that every scholar admits is choppy, patched-together, and almost impossible to read?

Why this respect for a prophet whose predictions didn't come true until four decades later? And who hated having to deliver the bad news?

In a word, the answer is hope.

At a time when many people are searching for clarity, Jeremiah offers hope that someone really is listening.

That someone cares.

That someone has a plan for us.

He says so directly. And without a flicker of doubt.

In some ways, Jeremiah was the Andy Rooney of the Old Testament. He told people with cranky bluntness when they were doing something dumb. Or wrong. Or sinful. He warned the people of Judah that they better change their ways before it was too late. They didn't listen. They were conquered by the Babylonians in 586 B.C. and taken into captivity, their temples destroyed.

Jeremiah's name is enshrined forever in dictionaries with the word *jeremiad* — a prolonged lament or complaint. But don't write off Jeremiah as merely another doomsayer nagging, "The end is near." The "weeping prophet" has become a perfect symbol for the twenty-first century of faith. It was Jeremiah who promised most explicitly that God wants to know us as individuals, that we are part of the story. It was Jeremiah who explained how the "new covenant" would be different from the "old covenant" given to Abraham: God would put his law inside the people instead of on tablets or in temples; he would write it on their hearts. They would all know him, from the least to the greatest. And he would forgive them for being so predictably human.

There was a lot to forgive then. As there is now. Jeremiah warned about the sins of the people who sacrificed their own children to find favor, who were wantonly promiscuous and worshipped other gods. But at the same time, Jeremiah predicted there would be mercy in the end. He described a loving God who would tell his wayward people, "I have loved you with an everlasting love; therefore I have continued my faithfulness to you. Again I will build you, and you will be built." He promised that "The steadfast love of the Lord never ceases, his mercies never come to an end; they are new every morning . . . ."

That Old Testament message resonates today: God has plans for us, not just rules. The God of Jeremiah promises, "I will turn their mourning into joy, I will comfort them, and give them gladness for sorrow."

Even in this Prozac nation, those who have given up hope, those who are depressed, those who feel abandoned can take heart in the example of Jeremiah, who was ridiculed, cast out, thrown into a cistern to die, and locked in prison. While he was in captivity, he sent detailed instructions to his clerk on how to buy a plot of land for him. He was banking that God would bring him home. That's hope.

Hope is hard to come by in this anxious age. Most people are starving for it.

They need hope that their strained marriages and rebellious kids will turn out okay.

They need hope that they can earn a living in a time of layoffs.

Hope that they will not face an old age alone without dignity.

Hope that their plane flights will land safely.

Hope that their country will be livable for their grandchildren.

That's where people of faith come in. When we are down, believers remind us whose children we are. That our lives have a purpose. That we have a job to do: fixing the world. They remind us that stars come out of chaos.

After the September 11 attacks, First Lady Laura Bush showed the nation what faith looks like during chaos. While others were wringing their hands and canceling their flights, she stayed admirably calm. She went on *Good Morning America* and *Oprah* to reassure Americans that they could and would survive this challenge. Hug your children, she reminded TV audiences. She exuded quiet confidence that this, too, would pass. All her friends often say that Laura Welch Bush is the most well-balanced person they know. I agree.

"A woman of valor, who will find?"

— PROVERBS 31

I've watched Laura from the sidelines since the early 1990s, when the Bushes attended the same church in Dallas as my family, Highland Park United Methodist Church. Her husband's father was in the White House then, and her husband, George W., was managing partner of the Texas Rangers. She seemed determined to have as much of a normal upbringing for her twin daughters as she could, carpooling grade-schoolers Barbara and Jenna to church choir in the family Suburban, bringing cupcakes when needed for Sunday School parties. She had a quiet strength even then, standing back just a little, observing, listening more than talking. After George W. became governor, I watched with fascination as this former teacher and librarian steadily grew more poised in public. During his first campaign, she spoke rarely. She would glance down at notes, unaccustomed to putting herself in the spotlight. By his second term, she had become a more practiced speaker, traveling around the state to push with passion for early education. And when it came time for her to speak at the GOP convention in Los Angeles in the summer of 2000, she demonstrated a flawless, poised delivery.

In a provident way, she had learned her lessons well. She met the press and held her own. She was prepared to step forward when the September tragedies struck. When the country needed reassurance, she was there as "First Mother" and "Comforter in Chief," as some headline writers described her. When the planes hit the World Trade Center's twin towers, she had just arrived at the Capitol. She was there to testify about early education, and it was to be her crowning moment, but the hearing was cancelled abruptly. Even as she was being escorted away to a safe location, her first thoughts turned to the nation's children: "Parents need to reassure children everywhere in our country that they are safe," she said.

The next day she visited injured Pentagon workers at the Walter Reed Army Medical Center. And again, her thoughts were protective: She cautioned parents to shelter young children from the troubling images of death and destruction on TV. She was concerned about the psychological impact. She also visited a blood bank adjacent to the

"A leader is a dealer in hope."

— NAPOLEON BONAPARTE

White House and thanked employees for donating blood. Two days after the attacks, she wrote two open letters to America's children about the tragedy, one for younger elementary students and one for middle and high school students. "When sad or frightening things happen, all of us have an opportunity to become better people by thinking about others," she wrote to younger children. "Be kind to each other, take care of each other, and show your love for each other."

At a funeral service commemorating the lives lost in the hijacked jet that crashed in a Pennsylvania field, Laura was composed and properly grave as she talked about the calls made by the Flight 93 passengers to loved ones in their final minutes. She quoted from poet Kahlil Gibran: "Love knows not its own depths until the hour of parting." She told about the last good-bye of one passenger, who promised his family that he would see them again. "That brave man was a witness for the greatest hope of all," she said, "that hope is real and it is forever." She said that at such times people learn that their faith is an active faith. "They learn that they are called to serve and care for one other, bringing hope and comfort," she said. And for the next weeks, she did just that.

The First Lady made a very visible display of traveling at a time when many were afraid to fly. She traveled around the country to visit classrooms and recruit volunteers for Teach for America. Even when Capitol Hill was being evacuated because of anthrax threats, she kept up a visibly busy schedule. I was impressed when Laura agreed during those anxious weeks to make time for an interview. We gathered in her pleasant office in the East Wing, which is as feminine and unostentatious as she is. When she walked in and sat down on the sofa, the strain of the last month showed a bit in her eyes and voice. But she could still laugh as her frisky Scottish terrier, Barney, scampered in behind her. The chunky little bundle of black fur, she pointed out, does bear a certain resemblance to those automatic shoeshine machines with big bristles on both ends. Her sense of humor has been a saving grace along with her faith. She had been evacuated into the White House bunker twice the week of the attacks, once as a precaution and once during a tornado alert, but she was spunky enough to apologize to the Secret Service for wearing "the same outfit" — she had on a makeup smock and house slippers because she was in the middle of getting dressed both times.

> "Where there is life, there is hope."
>
> — JERUSALEM TALMUD

When the attacks occurred, she told me, she immediately started checking on members of her family, who were all in different parts of the country. Her husband was on *Air Force One*, her daughters were at their colleges, and her in-laws were stranded in

Minneapolis, all possibly in jeopardy. So what did she do? She called *her* mother. "I told my mother I called to reassure her, but really I called to hear her voice to reassure *me*."

How had she kept her composure while having to speak at the emotionally wrenching memorial services? "I really don't cry very often, I really don't," she said, adding with a chuckle, "on the other hand, my *husband. . . .*" But just to make sure she could keep her focus at the memorial events, she said she practiced reading her speeches over and over.

Still, she had to dab her eyes at the Pentagon memorial service when the sea of 15,000 people spontaneously began singing "The Battle Hymn of the Republic" and waving small American flags. When she and her husband saw an African American woman stand up in the back with her flag, she said, they stood up, too. That prompted the rest of the crowd to get to their feet. And then, the families of the victims, who were seated right in front of her, rose to their feet. It was difficult, she said, to keep from weeping as she saw them all stand, but as news photos showed, she wiped away her tears with a tissue and carried on.

Immediately after the attack, she said, many of her young staffers, who had been evacuated with her from the Capitol, had been crying all day. So the next day, she met with them and told them that even though they might have expected a lot of excitement when they signed on at the White House, she understood that they could not have expected anything so tragic. But, she told them, since they were all there, it was an opportunity for them to show how to be constructive at such moments.

"If there is a silver lining, or something really good that can come out of such a horror, it is that everyone suddenly realized what really matters is the people we love, our faith, and our freedoms, which we really took for granted in our country," she said.

Like a teacher who urges her pupils to stay on task, she said she would keep urging parents to read to their children, which is not only reassuring to the children, but also to the parents. In fact, she said she had been reading more herself since the attacks as a way of staying steady. And she was trying to exercise regularly and get enough sleep so she could cope with the increased pressure.

It had been particularly comforting, Laura said, to share meals and prayers with family members on the weekends at Camp David. Her voice broke as she remembered that during the prayer requests after the attacks, her husband's brothers had asked the minister to please "pray for the president" — and she realized that they meant *her husband.* But she moved on, returning her focus to the interview at hand.

Where does she get that strength, that calm faith, I asked her. "From my mother," she said quickly, surely. "My mother was a Methodist, and we went to church every single Sunday when I was little. My mother taught Sunday School. My father was a religious man, but he usually did not go with us. Mother and I went off to church every Sunday." As a result, she said, she had always felt secure in her beliefs. Indeed, her faith has been a consistent thread in her life. Laura sang in the church choir and attended church camp when she was growing up. She chose a Methodist college — Southern Methodist University in Dallas. In 1977, she and George got married in the same church where she was baptized. And during the early years of their marriage, after he had decided to quit drinking, they attended a couples Bible class together. Today, she said, she and the president say prayers together and say blessings with their dinner.

On the Sunday after the attacks, they both were struck by the Bible verse read at the Camp David service — Psalm 27:8, 13: "Thy face Lord, do I seek; I believe that I shall see the goodness of the Lord in the land of the living!" The Scripture was so positive, so reassuring, that she decided to include it on the family Christmas card because it would bring a message of hope to the nation. She had started putting a Scripture verse on the family Christmas cards when George W. was elected governor and she chose Texas artists to do the illustrations. I asked her if she remembered the verse that she selected for their last Christmas in the governor's mansion, just as they were leaving for Washington, D.C. She nodded her head and recited: "And you will seek me and find me when you search for me with all of your heart."

"Jeremiah 29," she added. "It's one of my favorites."

Of course.

I mentioned as I was leaving that I would love to talk to her mother sometime about the importance of mothers sharing their faith with their children. But there were busy weeks ahead for Laura: She became the only First Lady ever to substitute for her husband in one of the Saturday radio addresses to the nation, publicizing the plight of the Afghan women. She went a daring step further and invited eleven women who had been exiled from Afghanistan to visit the White House, her way of supporting the inclusion of women's rights in the post-Taliban government. She then kept up her support on Radio Free Europe/Radio Liberty, urging the women of Afghanistan not to "stand on the sidelines," as decisions are made, saying, "You have a big opportunity and a lot at stake."

With all that going on, I was surprised when the First Lady's press secretary, Noelia Rodriguez, called and said she had not forgotten the interview request and she was still trying to schedule a session with Mrs. Bush's mother. And she did. On a spring morning while her mother was visiting the White House, we sat down to talk, one West Texan to another, one Methodist to another, one mother to another. At eighty-three, Mrs. Jenna Welch's steps are a little unsteady. She has grown more fragile in the last few years, and the First Lady is very protective of her. She calls her mother several times a week at her home in

Midland, Texas, and brings her to the White House or to the family ranch in Crawford as often as she can. Whenever her mother is in the audience at a public event, Laura Bush always proudly asks her mother to stand and share the spotlight.

If you have ever wondered where Laura Bush gets her calm, commonsense demeanor, just look to her mother. A trim, pretty woman, Jenna Welch has the open, accepting smile of someone who would invite you to come in and have some pie if you stopped by her house. During our interview, she sat with her hands folded gingerly in her lap and looked slightly embarrassed to be talking about herself. But she was game to try. She said she grew up mostly in El Paso, Texas, but as a young child she lived in Taylor, near Austin. She was named Jenna Louise Hawkins in honor of her two grandmothers. Her father's mother's name had been Jenny, she explained, so he changed the spelling to Jenna for her. "And I liked that better," she said. "It was different." She remembered that they went to the

> "Each second you can be reborn. Each second there can be a new beginning. It is choice. It is your choice."
>
> — CLEARWATER

Methodist Church in Taylor, but the German family next door was Lutheran and sometimes she would go to church there. "When it was your birthday, they would call out your name in church and you got to go to the front and get a blessing. I *tripped* going up the aisle." She laughed a little at the memory, "I still remember *that*."

She was eight years old when they moved to El Paso, a bustling border town of around 100,000. She loved the mountains that framed El Paso and remembered, "There was a mountain right behind our house." It reminded her of the Psalm, "I lift mine eyes up to the hills."

She went to college at the Texas College of Mines and Metallurgy, which later became the University of Texas at El Paso. With a nod my way, she said she studied advertising and journalism, thinking she might like to work for a newspaper. But after two years of college, she went to work full-time. She worked for the Popular Department Store, "the biggest dry goods store downtown," writing ad copy and radio copy. It was an imposing, seven-story stone building and quite grand with marble floors, she recalled. "I learned more there than I did in two years of college," she said emphatically. A co-worker kept telling Jenna that she wanted her to meet her husband's boss and said he was "around thirty." Jenna, who was twenty-two, wasn't interested until her friend pointed him out on the street: He was tall, dark, and good-looking. So she agreed to go on a blind date. Harold Welch turned out to be twenty-eight and nice. They went for dinner and dancing across the border in Juarez, Mexico, a popular destination. "El Paso was a *fun* town to grow up in," she said. They went to the Tivoli restaurant where there was "a lovely floor show and orchestra," she remembered, and had a good time. The next day there was an item in the newspaper: "Jenna Hawkins and handsome escort seen having dinner in Juarez." She smiled a sort of pleased, girlish smile at the memory, and for a minute, you could see on her face what it must have been like in that corner of her youth, dancing with the exhilaration that this was someone special.

Harold Welch went into the Army, so the rest of the courtship was by mail, she said. They got married during one of his leaves in 1944. What was he like? "Well, he was six feet tall, *really* handsome, with wavy hair — he later turned bald, but he had wavy hair then — pretty blue eyes, and a *terrific* sense of humor. He was a very funny, sweet man. Easy to know."

He served overseas for two and a half years, she said, and endured several bitterly cold winters in the field. When Germany surrendered, he came home to his wife. He went to work for the Universal CIT Credit Corp. in Midland and built houses on the side. She pointed out proudly, "He built every house we lived in." Moving to Midland, away from her parents, her job, and those mountains, was an adjustment. There were no mountains in Midland, just flat land and blue sky as far as you could see. But she learned to love the spare beauty of wide-open prairie. Her daughter Laura later wrote that the people in West Texas "don't live on or off the land there; they live with it — and thrive." And she's right. There is a frontier spirit in such isolated spaces that brings people closer together. Like the Nebraska prairie that Willa Cather wrote about in *O Pioneers!*, the flatlands of West Texas can be harsh — hail one day, tornadoes the next — but that only seems to strengthen the will of the people holding on.

Growing up in nearby San Angelo, I often thought the stretch of sky in West

Texas had the effect of an open cathedral. You sensed the presence of God because the heavens were so pronounced. On a clear night, people used to spread quilts in their front yards, lie there on their backs, and look up at the amazing ocean of stars. I asked Mrs. Welch if she thought the rugged geography and Big Sky inspired faith and she agreed, readily, "Oh yes!" But, she added, her own faith was always a part of her life. "I always went to church when I was little and I later taught Sunday School. When Laura was in the fourth or fifth grade, she said to me, 'You've never taught in our department.' So I did." With a bookkeeper's precision, she noted that it took twelve minutes to drive from their house on Humble Street to the church on Main Street. "I timed it," she said. She still attends, she said with a twinkle in her blue eyes, "only I am now in a class for women of 'mature ages.' "

She was a typical housewife in the 1950s, except that she also kept the books for her husband's construction company. She insisted on doing the accounts at home so she could be there for young Laura. Though she had little formal training, she did all the company's accounting until her husband's death in 1995 after Alzheimer's disease. Later, when bankers checked her books, she said with some pride, "They said, 'Mrs. Welch keeps very good books.'"

In photos from those early married years, she looks like Margaret Anderson, the wife on *Father Knows Best*, in that she was slender and neat as a pin in her shirtwaist dresses. Judging from the descriptions of her life back then, she sounds like a 1950s version of the Proverbs 31 woman. She wanted to please her husband, so she cooked three meals a day. She dutifully served as a Girl Scout leader, and when Laura worked on her bird badge, she developed a keen interest in bird watching and learned everything she could. According to Antonia Felix, author of *Laura*, a biography about the First Lady, Jenna Welch was something of a self-taught naturalist, having talked often about wildflowers and birds with her own mother, who grew up on a farm in Arkansas. She joined other women in forming the Midland Naturalist Group, which put out a monthly publication called *The Phalarope* about local flora and fauna. The women had se-

> "Rejoice in hope, be patient in suffering, persevere in prayer."
>
> — ROMANS 12:12

lected the name with some tongue-in-cheek daring, since the phalarope was a water bird that runs off on errands of her own and leaves the male to care for the young. Jenna showed her spunk by stirring things up as a naturalist herself, working to improve the Midland environment.

Jenna had her share of disappointments in life, but she does not dwell on them. Like many women of her generation, she believed that you didn't brag about yourself or complain about your problems. She would have liked very much to have other children, she said. But, she explained, "We lost three babies after Laura." You could sense a world of hurt in that one simple sentence. Three miscarriages. It was a "great disappointment," she said, but she put those feelings aside to care for her husband and daughter. Her church and friends, she said, gave her "something to hold on to." She made her home into a place where Laura and all her friends would like to gather — drinking Cokes and singing the lyrics to Beatles' songs. She passed along her love of reading to her daughter, who pored over *Little Women* and her favorite Nancy Drew books. When they would drive the hundreds of miles from Midland to El Paso or to Lubbock to visit grandparents, Jenna and Laura would pass the long stretches of time and highway by taking turns reading aloud to each other.

They are still that close, though life has taken her daughter miles away to 1600 Pennsylvania Avenue. Asked if she is proud of her daughter, she says, "Oh, yes," but it is implicit she was proud of her daughter all along. On September 11, when her daughter phoned, she said, "I knew it was Laura's ring." Though her daughter has said she needed the comfort of her mother's voice, her mother predicted Laura would "do fine." She said, "Laura is very steady . . . calm under pressure . . . she's always had that gracious quality."

Spending some time with Jenna Welch was a reminder of the genteel way women of her generation have. They say things like "I'll carry you to the store," when they mean they will give you a ride. They are likely to say they are "tickled" to see you. There is a sweetness to their attitude toward life that is often missing in conversation today. It would be a mistake to idealize the world of the 1950s that they knew, because there were downsides to that time as well. But it would be a worse mistake to ignore the good aspects of that time, particularly the efforts of women to transmit their values to their families, values that were uplifting.

Regardless of what happens in the Middle East, tomorrow's generations will need a moral architecture to hold their lives together. They will need guardrails. A compass. And confidence that their lives will be worthwhile.

As Beth Moore points out to her classes, the Hebrew word for "hope" is *Tikva*. It means "a cord," as in an attachment. It's what God gives you to hold on with. We are to grab it. Walk with it, like the rope they give kindergarten children to cling to so they won't get lost or stray as they walk together. Like the rope that ties together mountain climbers; if one falls, the others can help him up. As it says in Hosea 11:4, "I led them with cords of compassion, with the bands of love, and I became to them as one who eases the yoke on their jaws and I bent down to them and fed them."

> "Everything that is done in the world is done by hope."
>
> — MARTIN LUTHER

We might try to run away from God at times, because it seems born into us to be bent toward temptation and to make foolish mistakes. But God promises he will still be there for us. Remember the children's book *The Runaway Bunny*? In Margaret Wise Brown's tale, a little bunny teases his mother that he will swim away like a fish. "If you become a fish in a trout stream, I will become a fisherman and I will fish for you," the mother teases back. He tries again, saying, "I will become a rock on the mountain, high above you." Then, says his mother, she will become a mountain climber and climb to where he is. So the bunny says, he will just have to be a crocus in the hidden garden. Ah, says the mother, "I will be a gardener. And I will find you." But what if he becomes a bird and flies away? "Then I will be the tree that you come home to." Finally, he suggests that he will become a little boy and run into a house. And the wise mother says, "Then I will become your mother and catch you in my arms and hug you."

Playwright Margaret Edson brilliantly used that bunny catechism at the close of her Pulitzer Prize–winning play, *Wit*. In the play, an aloof, agnostic English professor who has devoted her life to teaching the theologically intricate works of poet John Donne lies dying in a hospital bed of cancer. In the last scene, an old friend, her former supervisor, comes to visit and comforts her by reading the children's book, which she was taking to her grandchildren. The irony is that the children's book is as brilliantly simple as Donne is complex. It is essentially Psalm 139 writ small:

> *"Lord, you have searched me out and*
>   *known me;*
> *you know my sitting down and my rising*
>   *up;*
> *you discern my thoughts from afar. . . .*
> *Where can I go then from your Spirit?*
> *Where can I flee from your presence?*
> *If I climb up to Heaven, you are there;*
> *If I make the grave my bed, you are there*
>   *also.*
> *If I take the wings of the morning*
> *and dwell in the uttermost parts of the sea,*
> *Even there your hand will lead me*
> *And your right hand holds me fast."*

When I'm feeling uncertain, I return again and again to Psalm 139. Sometimes it is reassuring to read it out loud.

It's one of the things I want to put in my "ethical will" to pass along to my sons, along with the advice from Genesis that Naomi Rosenblatt gives her children: *"Go forth"* and *"fear not."*

For every generation must begin the

learning process all over again, and we must show them the way with our lives. Eventually, we learn that the best way to bring people to faith is not to cram our beliefs down their throat, but to try to behave in a way that would not embarrass Jesus, Moses, Muhammad, Paul, or your mother if they were watching. That takes a concerted effort, and it requires that you keep growing in your faith all your life. You can't just store up some knowledge, score some brownie points and then say, "I think I've got it now, I'll just take a nap." If you don't do anything, you fall down before you know it. As Paige Benton, the director of the women's programs at Park Cities Presbyterian Church, puts it, life as a believer is like climbing up an escalator every day that is going down the other way. To move up, you have to be intentional. It takes some effort to stay in place, much less make progress. She explains that it's like Gene Kelly's advice that "If you're dancing and not sweating, you're not dancing."

But as the women in these pages show, the struggle to please God is worth it. It is the one true thing. Faith is not just an optional part of life, it is what we need to be a whole person. Faith gives us a purpose —

healing the broken world — that is larger than ourselves. Faith gives us a way of connecting and communing with others. Faith is where we feel at home. Faith gives us the comfort that when we are in a boat in a scary storm, someone is in the boat with us,

> "Be strong and bold; have no fear or dread of them, because it is the Lord your God who goes with you; he will not fail you or forsake you."
>
> — DEUTERONOMY 31:6

that when we are wheeled into that hospital room, someone is by our side and in that room with us. "Certainly I will be with thee" God promises in Exodus 3:12. There's no equivocation there.

Hold on, then. Believe big.

The truth is, our wobbly world needs you, your example, your prayers, your service. It's like the scene at the end of Alfred Hitchcock's movie *Foreign Correspondent.* When the lights go out in the radio studio during the blitz air attack on London, Joel McCrea pleads into the microphone, "Hello America! Hang on to your lights! They're the only lights left in the world."

You must let your light shine, dear friend. It is for this that we were lovingly made. Hold on to that thought. Let your light shine. And if you can, pass it on.

TAKE HOME:

God was wise when he made time an arrow that only goes forward. We must go on. We cannot stay in the past; we can only look back and learn, not just from our mistakes, but from the positive examples of women of faith. Anne Dudley Bradstreet was one of the Christian women who came across the ocean with the Massachusetts Bay Company to the American colonies in 1630. Anne was eighteen. She had been married two years earlier to her childhood sweetheart, Simon Bradstreet, a Cambridge University graduate and minister's son. She was well educated herself, and transplanted to the rough and rugged colonies, Anne became a woman of station and intelligence. Both her husband and father became Governor of Massachusetts, so she was part of a political dynasty not unlike the Kennedys or Bushes of today. But it is her own writing and great faith in the face of challenges that makes her life relevant today.

Anne Bradstreet became the first English poet of the new colonies with the publication of her book *The Tenth Muse* when she was thirty-eight. At the time, women were chastised for pursuits that did not conform to domesticity. Anne noted with typical humor that "They'll say my hand a needle better fits." And indeed, the book of poetry begins with notations from men who seemed to apologize for her gender.

The aphorisms she penned for her son more than three centuries ago are full of common sense: "If we had no winter, the spring would not be so pleasant; if we did not sometimes taste of adversity, prosperity would not be so welcome." Her theology is practical: "The reason why Christians are so loath to exchange this world for a better is because they have more sense than faith; they see what they enjoy; they do but hope for that which is to come." Her love for her family shows in many of her poems. When her beloved son Simon returned from England, she wrote that her fears had been turned to joys, her sighs to song, her tears to smiles, her sad to glad, because "He's come for whom I waited long." Her thoughts are not the dour and guilty stuff we might imagine from the dark-clad Puritans; she is very human and warm and caring.

Even more remarkably, she is brave. She rejected the intolerance of her father and husband who helped persecute the Quakers. At the time, the Quaker brethren were being branded as heretics. Some were hanged, some had their ears cut off, many were lashed with 650 stripes. Her husband was magistrate when the Quaker Mary Dyer was hanged from a great elm in Boston Common. Anne had begged him to spare the woman. As she heard the crowd riding back from the lynching, she wrote, "The hoofprint of every horse falls right upon my heart."

There is no monument, no grave marker, no surviving portrait of Anne Bradstreet, as there are for her husband and father. Researchers like Jeannine Hensley, Ann Woodlief, and Catherine Salmons have pieced together these fragments about her life. But her thoughts live on in her poems, thanks to a brother-in-law who had them published. We learn from her writing that when she was fifty-four, her house burned down in the middle of the night. And what did Anne Bradstreet do? She found some loose paper and wrote a poem to God. She wrote that when she heard the call of "Fire!" and "Fire!" again, she cried to God to strengthen her in her distress. When she could no longer bear to look at the flames that consumed her dwelling

"Barn's burnt down. Now I can see the moon."

— MASAHIDE

place, the hearth where she had raised "eight birds in one nest," she still blessed the name that "gave and took." All her "pleasant things" were in ashes; there was no roof left to share with guests, no table to eat, no candle to shine. But she wrote with certainty that God would be sufficient. That architect, she wrote, would provide a permanent home for her, already purchased at great price. "There's wealth enough, I need no more, Farewell, my pelf, farewell my store. The world no longer let me love, My hope and treasure lies above," she wrote. There is not a word of self-pity in the poem. It is the thought of this woman sitting by the ashes of her home, writing about hope, that catches the heart. Her last poem in 1667 closes, "Lord make me ready for that day. Then come, dear Bridegroom, come away." She died a few years later, confident that there was a place waiting for her.

Bibliography

BOOKS:

Arbel, Ilil. *Maimonides: A Spiritual Biography.* The Crossroad Publishing Company, 2001.

Armstrong, Dale. *The Battle for God.* Ballantine Books, 2000.

Armstrong, Karen. *A History of God: The 4000-Year Quest of Judaism, Christianity and Islam.* Alfred A. Knopf, 1993.

———. *Islam: A Short History.* Modern Library Chronicles, 2000.

———. *Through the Narrow Gate.* St. Martin's Press, 1981.

Batchelor, Mary, Compiled by. *The Doubleday Prayer Collection.* Doubleday, 1992.

Beckett, Sister Wendy. *Meditations on Joy.* Dorling Kindersley, 1995.

———. *Meditations on Love.* Dorling Kindersley, 1995.

Brown, Margaret Wise. *The Runaway Bunny.* HarperCollins, 1970.

Brueggeman, Walter. *Praying the Psalms.* St. Mary's Press, 1993.

Buber, Martin. *Tales of the Hasidim.* Schocken Books, 1991.

————. *The Way of Man According to the Teaching of Hasidism.* Citadel Press, 1994.

Calaprice, Alice, Ed. *The Expanded Quotable Einstein.* Princeton University Press, 2000.

Canham, Elizabeth J. *Heart Whispers: Benedictine Wisdom for Today.* Upper Room Books, 1999.

Cather, Willa. *O Pioneers!* Penguin Books, 1989.

Chittister, Joan. *The Friendship of Women: A Spiritual Tradition.* Sheed & Ward, 2000.

————. *Gospel Days: Reflections for Every Day of the Year.* Orbis Books, 1999.

————. *Heart of Flesh: A Feminist Spirituality for Women and Men.* William B. Eerdmans Publishing Company and Novalis, 1998.

————. *Illuminated Life: Monastic Wisdom for Seekers of Light.* Orbis Books, 2000.

————. *Life Ablaze: A Woman's Novena.* Sheed & Ward with Benetvision, 2000.

————. *Living Well: Scriptural Reflections for Every Day.* Orbis Books, 2000.

————. *A Passion for Life: Fragments of the Face of God.* Orbis Books, 1996.

―――. *The Psalms: Meditations for Every Day of the Year.* The Crossroads Publishing Company, 1996.

―――. *The Rule of Benedict: Insights for the Ages.* Crossroads, 1992.

―――. *The Story of Ruth: Twelve Moments in Every Woman's Life.* William B. Eerdmans Publishing Company and Novalis, St. Paul University, 2000.

―――. *There is a Season.* Orbis Books, 1995.

―――. *Wisdom Distilled From the Daily: Living the Rule of St. Benedict Today.* HarperSanFrancisco, 1990.

Collins, Judy. *Singing Lessons: A Memoir of Love, Loss, Hope, and Healing.* Pocket Books, 1998.

―――. *Trust Your Heart: An Autobiography.* Houghton Mifflin Company, 1987.

Craughwell, Thomas J., Ed. *Every Eye Beholds You, A World Treasury of Prayer.* Harcourt Brace & Company, 1998.

Day, Dorothy. *The Long Loneliness.* HarperSanFrancisco, 1980.

Demers, Patricia. *Women as Interpreters of The Bible.* Paulist Press, 1992.

Ellsberg, Robert. *All Saints: Daily Reflections on Saints, Prophets, and Witnesses for Our Time.* The Crossroad Publishing Company, 1997.

Falk, Marcia. *The Book of Blessings: New Jewish Prayers for Daily Life, the Sabbath, and the New Moon Festival.* Beacon Press, 1996.

Felix, Antonia. *Laura: America's First Lady, First Mother.* Adams Media Corporation, 2002.

Fogel, Robert William. *The Fourth Great Awakening and the Future of Egalitarianism.* The University of Chicago Press, 2000.

Ford-Gradowsky, Mary, Ed. *Sacred Voices: Essential Women's Wisdom Through the Ages.* HarperSanFrancisco, 2002.

Fox, Matthew. *One River, Many Wells: Wisdom Springing from Global Faiths.* Jeremy P. Tarcher/Putnam, 2000.

Gandy, Dottie Bruce. *30 Days to a Happy Employee: How a Simple Program of Acknowledgement Can Build Trust and Loyalty at Work.* Simon & Schuster, 2001.

God's Little Instruction Book II. Honor Books, Inc., 1994.

God's Little Instruction Book III. Honor Books, Inc., 1997.

Goldstein, Rabbi Elyse, Ed. *The Women's Torah Commentary: New Insights from Women Rabbis on the 54 Weekly Torah Portions.* Jewish Lights Publishing, 2000.

Granfield, Linda. *Amazing Grace: The Story of the Hymn.* Tundra Books, 1997.

Green, Arthur. *These are the Words: A Vocabulary of Jewish Spiritual Life.* Jewish Lights Publishing, 1999.

Hensley, Jeannine, Ed. *The Works of Anne Bradstreet.* The Belknap Press of Harvard University, 1967.

Hooks, Bell. *Salvation: Black People and Love.* William Morrow, 2001.

Horner, Mary and Vinita Hampton Wright, Compiled by. *Women's Wisdom Through the Ages: Timeless Quotations on Life and Faith.* Harold Shaw Publishers, 1994.

Huffman, Margaret Anne and Gary Wilde. *Simple Prayers & Blessings.* Publications International, Ltd., 1998.

Jones, Carolyn. *Every Girl Tells a Story: A Celebration of Girls Speaking Their Minds.* Simon & Schuster, 2002.

Keating, Thomas. *Active Meditations for Contemplative Prayer.* Continuum, 1997.

Keith, Kent M. *Anyway (The Paradoxical Commandments: Finding Personal Meaning in a Crazy World).* G. P. Putnam's Sons, 2001.

LaBelle, Patti. *Patti's Pearls: Lessons in Living Genuinely, Joyfully, Generously.* Warner Books, 2001.

Lawrence, Brother. *The Practice of the Presence of God.* Whitaker House, 1982.

Lotz, Anne Graham. *Just Give Me Jesus.* W Publishing Group, 2000.

———. *Heaven: My Father's House.* W Publishing Group, 2001.

Manser, Martin H., Compiled by. *The Westminster Collection of Christian Quotations.* Martin H. Manser. Westminster John Knox Press, 2001.

McBrien, Richard P. *Lives of the Saints: From Mary and St. Francis of Assisi to John XXIII and Mother Teresa.* HarperSanFrancisco, 2001.

Miller, Kathy Collard. *Women of the Bible: God's Word for the Biblically-Inept.* Starburst Publishers, 1999.

Moore, Beth. *Praying God's Word: Breaking Free from Spiritual Strongholds.* Broadman & Holman Publishers, 2000.

———. *Things Pondered: From the Heart of a Lesser Woman.* Broadman & Holman Publishers, 1997.

———. *When Godly People Do Ungodly Things, Arming Yourself in the Age of Seduction.* Broadman & Holman Publishers, 2002.

———. *Whispers of Hope.* LifeWay Press, 1998.

Moore, Beth and Dale McCleskey. *To*

Live Is Christ: Embracing the Passion of Paul. Broadman & Holman, 2001.

Mother Teresa. *The Joy in Living.* Compiled by Jaya Chalika and Edward Le Joly. Penguin Compass, 1996.

———. *Meditations from a Simple Path.* Ballantine Books, 1996.

Nathan, David. *The Soulful Divas.* Billboard Books, 1999.

Newson, Carol A. and Sharon H. Ringe, Eds. *Women's Bible Commentary.* Expanded edition. Westminster John Knox Press, 1998.

Noonan, Peggy. *Life, Liberty and the Pursuit of Happiness.* Random House, 1994.

———. *When Character Was King: A Story of Ronald Reagan.* Viking, 2001.

Norris, Kathleen. *The Cloister Walk.* Riverhead Books, 1996.

———. *The Quotidian Mysteries: Laundry, Liturgy and "Women's Work."* Paulist Press, 1998.

Panati, Charles. *Sacred Origins of Profound Things.* Penguin Arkana, 1996.

Patterson, Rev. Dr. Sheron C. *The Love Clinic: How to Heal Relationships in a Christian Spirit.* Perigee Books, 2002.

Patterson, Sheron C. *New Faith: A Black Christian Woman's Guide to Reformation,*

Re-Creation, Rediscovery, Renaissance, Resurrection, and Revival. Fortress Press, 2000.

Poniatowska, Elena. *Here's To You, Jesusa!* Farrar, Straus and Giroux, 2001.

———. *Tinisima.* Penguin Books, 1992.

Redding, Mary Lou. *Breaking & Mending: Divorce and God's Grace.* Upper Room Books, 1998.

Remen, M.D., Rachel Naomi. *My Grandfather's Blessings: Stories of Strength, Refuge, and Belonging.* Riverhead Books, 2000.

Rosenblatt, Naomi and Joshua Horwitz. *Wrestling with Angels: What the First Family of Genesis Teaches Us About Our Spiritual Identity, Sexuality, and Personal Relationships.* Delacorte Press, 1995.

Rosenblatt, Roger. *Rules for Aging: Resist Normal Impulses, Live Longer, Attain Perfection.* Harcourt, Inc., 2000.

Saddle Your Own Horse. National Cowgirl Museum and Hall of Fame. 2002.

Schiller, David, Ed. *The Little Book of Prayers.* Workman Publishing, 1996.

Schmidt, Joseph F. *Praying with Thérèse of Lisieux.* Saint Mary's Press, 1992.

Shanahan, John M. *The Most Brilliant Thoughts of All Time (In Two Lines or Less).* HarperCollins, 1999.

Shannon, Ashley, Collected with an Introduction by. *Irish Blessings, A Photographic Celebration.* Courage Books, 1999.

Sherr, Lynn. *Failure is Impossible: Susan B. Anthony in Her Own Words.* Times Books, 1995.

Smith, Dennis E. and Michael E. Williams. "New Testament Women." *The Storyteller's Companion to the Bible.* Vol. 13. Abingdon Press, 1990.

Smith, Huston. *The Illustrated World's Religions: A Guide to Our Wisdom Traditions.* HarperSanFrancisco, 1994.

———. *Forgotten Truth: The Common Vision of the World's Religions.* HarperSanFrancisco, 1976.

Smith, Robert Lawrence. *A Quaker Book of Wisdom: Life Lessons in Simplicity, Service, and Common Sense.* Eagle Brook, 1998.

Spiritual Formation Bible, Zondervan Publishing House, 1999.

Tolle, Eckhart. *The Power of Now, A Guide to Spiritual Enlightenment.* New World Library, 1999.

Walmsley, Lesley, Compiled by. *C. S. Lewis on Faith.* Thomas Nelson Publishers, 1998.

——— , Compiled by. *C. S. Lewis on Joy.*

Thomas Nelson Publishers, 1998.

———— , Compiled by. *C. S. Lewis on Love*. Thomas Nelson Publishers, 1998.

Ward, Geoffrey C. and Ken Burns. *Not For Ourselves Alone: The Story of Elizabeth Cady Stanton and Susan B. Anthony*. Alfred A. Knopf, 1999.

Williams, Michael E., "Old Testament Women." *The Storyteller's Companion to the Bible*. Abingdon Press, 1993.

Wright, Wendy M. *The Time Between: Cycles and Rhythms in Ordinary Time*. Upper Room Books, 1999.

Yancey, Philip. *Soul Survivor: How My Faith Survived the Church*. Doubleday, 2001.

Zaleski, Philip and Paul Kaufman. *Gifts of the Spirit: Living the Wisdom of the Great Religious Traditions*. HarperSanFrancisco, 1997.

TAPES:

Chittister, Joan D. Heart of Flesh, A Feminist Spirituality for Women and Men. Call to Action, 1997 Keynote Address. Benetvision, 1998.

———— The Heart of Religious Vocation (Two Tapes). Credence Cassettes, 1995.

———— Retreats International Conference

Keynote Address. January 20, 2002.

Moore, Beth. About Temptation. Living Proof, Inc.

———. A Blameless Heart On The Battlefield Of Home. Living Proof Ministries, 2001.

———. Blessed are Those: A Fresh Look at the Beatitudes. Living Proof, Inc.

———. Dealing With Thieves of Delight. Living Proof Ministries, 2001.

———. The Endless Benefits of Being Steeped in Scripture. Living Proof Ministries, 2001.

———. The Light of God's Grace. Living Proof Ministries, 2001.

———. A People Belonging To God. Living Proof Ministries, 2001.

———. A Pleasing Sacrifice. Living Proof, Inc.

———. A Sense of Center. Living Proof, Inc.

———. A Virtuous Woman. Living Proof, Inc.

"Reshaping Our Spiritual Lives" #2. UTA Women's Forum on Spirituality. Presented by UTA Womens Studies Program & The Damaris Project. March 28, 2002.

VIDEOTAPE:

Chittister, Joan D. Discipleship for a Priestly People in a Priestless Period. Benetvision, 2001.

PAMPHLET:

Address, Rabbi Richard E. "Making Sacred Choices at the End of Life." Jewish Lights Publishing, 2000.

Brener, Anne. "Taking the Time You Need to Mourn Your Loss." Jewish Lights Publishing, 2000.

Cardin, Rabbi Nina Beth. "Mourning a Miscarriage." Jewish Lights Publishing, 2000.

Chittister, Joan D. "The Heart of God: A Call to Forgiveness." Benetvision, 2000.

———. "Living in the Breath of the Spirit." Benetvision, 1999.

———. "Way of the Cross, Gateway to Resurrection." Benetvision, 1999.

———. "Women's Role in the Church." Sheed & Ward, 1993.

Cowan, Rabbi Rachel. "Coping with the Death of a Spouse." Jewish Lights Publishing, 2000.

Dinkin, Roxane Head. "Living with Cancer, One Day at a Time." Jewish Lights Publishing, 2000.

Eilberg, Rabbi Amy. "When Someone

You Love Is Dying." Jewish Lights
Publishing, 2000.

Flam, Rabbi Nancy. "Yearning for God."
Jewish Lights Publishing, 2000.

Friedman, Rabbi Dayle A. "When
Someone You Love Needs Long-Term
Care." Jewish Lights Publishing, 2000.

Lamm, Rabbi Maurice. "Jewish Hospice:
To Live, To Hope, To Heal." Jewish
Lights Publishing, 2000.

Lew, Rabbi Alan. "Looking Back on
Divorce and Letting Go." Jewish Lights
Publishing, 2000.

Weinberg, Rabbi Sheila Peltz. "Easing the
Burden of Stress." Jewish Lights
Publishing, 2000.

Weintraub, C.S.W., Rabbi Simkha Y.
"Finding Spiritual Strength in Pain or
Illness: Reaching In, Reaching Out,
Reaching Up." Jewish Lights
Publishing, 2000.

Wolpe, Rabbi David. "Finding a Way to
Forgive." Jewish Lights Publishing,
2000.

WORKBOOKS:
Moore, Beth. *Breaking Free, Making
Liberty in Christ a Reality in Life.*
LifeWay Press, 1999.
———. *Living Beyond Yourself, Exploring*

the Fruit of the Spirit. LifeWay Press, 1998.

———. *To Live is Christ, The Life and Ministry of Paul.* LifeWay Press, 1997.

———. *A Woman's Heart, God's Dwelling Place.* LifeWay Press, 1995.

About the Author

Rena Pederson, author with Dr. Lee Smith of *What's Next?*, is Editor at Large at the *Dallas Morning News*, the largest newspaper in the Southwest. She has been a finalist for the Pulitzer Prize and currently serves on the Pulitzer Prize Board of Directors. Pederson has been a featured guest on *The Oprah Winfrey Show*, and *Texas Monthly* named her one of the "Most Powerful Women in Texas."

HAPPY ENDING

Francesca Duranti's first novel, *The House on Moon Lake*, was a stunning literary debut, winning the Bugatti Prize, the Martina Franca Prize, and the City of Milan Prize. It was translated into many languages. Ms. Duranti has a law degree from the University of Pisa, and has translated novels from French, German and English. She lives in Milan, Italy.

Also by Francesca Duranti

The House on Moon Lake

FRANCESCA DURANTI

HAPPY ENDING

Translated from the Italian
by Annapaola Cancogni

Minerva

A Minerva Paperback
HAPPY ENDING

First published in Great Britain 1991
by William Heinemann Ltd
This work was originally published in Italy
as *Lieto Fine* in 1987
by RCS Rizzoli Libri S.p.A., Milano.
This Minerva edition published 1992
by Mandarin Paperbacks
Michelin House, 81 Fulham Road, London SW3 6RB

Minerva is an imprint of the Octopus Publishing Group,
a division of Reed International Books Limited

Copyright © RCS Rizzoli Libri S.p.A., Milano, 1987
Translation copyright © Annapaola Cancogni 1991

A CIP catalogue record for this title
is available from the British Library
ISBN 0 7493 9993 7

Printed and bound in Great Britain
by Cox & Wyman Limited, Reading, Berks

For Gregorio and Maddalena

HAPPY ENDING

1

Tried phoning you all day. Lavinia arrives tomorrow. Dinner 8:30. Come.

—Violante

WHITE STATIONERY. Clean-cut edges, no fraying. Large letters, traced with a fountain pen. Dark blue ink. Like an idiot, I sniff it. Unscented.

I take note of every detail with the complacency of someone finding everything as expected. Once it would have been different. I would have eagerly delved into that message, taking it apart, analyzing each of its elements, treasuring every one of them.

This until ten, fifteen years ago. And then, I came to understand that things were more complex than I thought. In other words, I realized there was no such a thing as the "right thing"—the right stationery, the right tone of voice, the right clothes. It was not a sudden revelation, I got to it gradually. But when I did, what a joy. I became more self-confident, less defensive. I gave myself a break.

Still do. I put Violante's note down on the desk and, with a thrill of transgression, slip into my purple silk pajamas: so rich, sleek, and luxurious, so far beyond mere garishness. Voluptuously, I stretch out on my monumental bed.

Since the right thing does not exist, why give up the luxury of occasionally yielding to the wrong one?

Once I had complete faith in vicuna overcoats and Mauritian valets; now I smile at my former innocence with paternal indulgence. Of course, I still have both, the overcoat and the valet: the first, sprinkled with naphthalene, is safe in its plastic bag, while the second, having laid out the purple pajamas on the bed—arms and legs spread, like a corpse floating on the pale blue bedspread—will soon usher in a new day by preparing my breakfast tray.

Indeed, even the Arnolfina is not exactly the right thing, which, however, does not prevent me from being delighted with it. My house is an architectural curiosity, an exception to the rural style characteristic of the Lucca plain. Built in white stone—like the Romanesque churches of the city—it started out as a small convent for a few nuns. The parish archives still contain documents concerning this religious community until 1318, when the archbishop forced the sisters to close up shop and return to the city "for reasons of decorum."

Later, the building was turned into a farmhouse, after which one has to rely on hearsay. It is said that one of its owners was the very same Arnolfini whose portrait, painted by Jan van Eyck in 1434, can be seen at the National Gallery in London. It is said that Arnolfini used the building as an olive press driven not, as has always been the custom in Tuscany, by water, but by the wind, like a Dutch mill. It is also rumored that the press never worked, which does not surprise me. When I bought the Arnolfina, I found no fixtures that might have suggested an olive press—no millstone, no press—but the tower was there, and still is. Thirty-four feet tall, its truncated cone looks extravagant, worse, incongruous in this landscape, and yet so attractive. Without vanes—if it ever had any—and with four large windows on the top, facing the four cardinal points, it rather resembles a beacon or an observatory.

My bedroom is right at the top of the tower.

After going to bed, I switched off the light, but could not fall asleep. So, I got up in the dark, and have come to sit on the large swivel chair—the only token of modernity in my entire house—by the window that overlooks Violante Santini's villa, where I have been so imperiously invited to dinner tomorrow evening. The park, laid out in a semicircle as if to hug the base of the hillock on which my Arnolfina rises, basks in the luminous July night: the large plane tree, the majestic curve of the driveway, the rose garden, the maze of hedges, the swimming pool, and the three houses. They are commonly known as Villa Grande, Villa Piccola, and Limonaia. The first, a three-story Renaissance structure, is where Violante lives, while her younger son, Leopoldo, lives with his American wife in the second—inferior in size as well as age, it being a *settecento* villa with an open gallery on the second floor. As for the third, the lemon house, it was renovated over twenty years ago for Violante's older son on the occasion of his wedding with Lavinia, but it was abandoned barely two months later when Filippo died, and the young widow went to live with her mother-in-law for a few years, and then left for Milan. She comes back every summer, but always as Violante's guest, unable as she is to outgrow the endless adolescence which allows her to be taken in, cared for, supported, and fully relieved of any responsibility even though she has a twenty-year-old son and a few silver threads in her blond hair. Seen from the Arnolfina tower, the three houses—large, medium, and small—resemble those of the three bears: Goldilocks is arriving tomorrow.

Right below my window, in the shady niche formed by the juncture of the tower and the façade of the house, the gardenias are in bloom. Eyes closed, I deeply inhale their scent, a magic ritual that immediately takes me back to what I consider the real beginning of my life.

5

I was only thirteen, but already tall and strong enough not to hang around when a German raid was expected.

I knew all the parks of the villas around Lucca, having visited them on numerous occasions, albeit always by stealth. The one near the church of Saltocchio was my favorite. Because of the war, some of the parks had been neglected and had turned into thorny thickets from which it was impossible to extract anything useful. Others were so well tended—like the Santini park, the very one I now dominate from my tower—that they put me ill at ease when I snuck in to loot them. But the one closest to the city, the Saltocchio park, only partly neglected, was eminently accessible, and full of nature's bounty: a true paradise. Hidden among its ancient trees, I fished for pike in its pond, gathered firewood, mushrooms, chestnuts. There, I discovered the fruit of an exotic tree whose name still escapes me, as I was never to encounter it again in any of my travels. It must have belonged to a very rare and probably now extinct species. Its fruit were green, shiny, oblong, and filled with a creamy pulp that tasted of cosmetics.

I would get there at dawn, hide the bike in a ditch that ran alongside the park, and climb over the wall. I knew that nobody would show up for another hour or two, and that I had the time to gather all the things I needed and pile them up by the gate; after which I would slip them one by one through the bars, climb back up the wall in the opposite direction, get my bike, and load my booty into a large straw bag.

I never left that garden empty-handed, nor did I ever find in it a definitive—or at least lasting—solution to the problem of survival for myself and my mother. I had to go back every day—whether there or elsewhere—trusting in my luck, keeping on the lookout, avoiding dangers. Was that life as it should be? It certainly was life as nobody wants it to be. I believe everybody's aspirations tend toward a definitive accomplishment

6

that does not have to be repeated every day, and in this my hopes are not different from the rest of the world's. But I am also sure of another thing: throughout that entire period, when every morning brought a new struggle and the stakes were life or death, I tasted a few moments of happiness such as I have never again experienced.

The day I heard people talk of a possible surprise attack, I climbed over the park wall around nine in the evening. Far off, I could hear the German trucks rumbling through the country-side. It was very hot: the summer of 1944 was torrid, at least in Tuscany. All the shutters of the villa were closed because of the curfew, but the panes of the five large French windows off the gallery were wide open. As I emerged from the bushes and crossed the lawn, getting closer and closer to the house, I could hear the sound of voices mingled with the melodious tinkling of crystal and silver: supernatural sounds, like those of magical bells, that seemed to have nothing in common with the opaque clatter produced by the crockery at home. I quietly climbed the steps that led to the gallery, and approached one of the shutters where a partially collapsed slat let through a shaft of light.

There were eight people sitting around an oval table: two men, two young girls, and four women. I never knew their names: they came into my life that evening, left their mark, and disappeared.

A very old servant went silently from one to the other, hold-ing out platters, pouring wine. The lady who sat at the head of the table was also ancient, and, in spite of the heat, wore a white fur stole on her shoulders. I thought she might be ill, unless old age, beyond a certain point, was itself an illness. Across from her, at the other end of the table, sat a white-haired, skeletal man, whom I assumed to be her husband. These were the only three characters, all in their advanced eighties, along with the two girls—whom I respectively placed in the first and last year of elementary school—whose ages I could guess: as if at the

7

beginning and at the end of life nature had the upper hand over statistics, and time engraved its signs according to universal laws I knew.

The other man must have also been past his prime to be dining peacefully while the Germans were combing the countryside. And yet, he was so polished and clean-shaven, with his hair slicked back against his skull à la Rudolph Valentino, that he looked like a young man. Among the other three women— all cool and mellow, and apparently forever fixed at the same ideal age—I intuited blood ties that involved gaps of twenty or thirty years.

Protected by the night, I saw without being seen, very close to them and yet totally extraneous to them. It was like being at the theater, with the stage lit in front of my eyes, offered to my appreciation, except that in this case, the characters were real people unaware of my presence.

I delighted in every detail. The young girls' dresses—identical, aqua-colored and full-length, with their white lace-trimmed collars; the braided uniform of the old servant; the crystal chandelier; the women's hair; the four large still lifes on the walls; the peach-colored tablecloth. Their voices—like the sound of the glasses and the silver—were airy and musical.

I was suffused by a joy that affected all my senses; the last one to be aroused was that of olfaction, which suddenly became alert to a paradisal fragrance—as limpid as water and yet as rich as an Oriental perfume—issuing from a large gardenia bush at the other end of the gallery. In the nearly total darkness, the green of its leaves looked black, and its flowers stood out like haloes of immaculate light. Entranced, I watched the meal all the way to its end, and moved only after everybody else had departed, leaving the old servant to clear the table alone. But I did not move from the gallery. I fell asleep on a wicker armchair and woke up at dawn. Assuming that the danger of a raid was by then over, I went back home, not, however, without first having gathered all the gardenias to bring to my mother.

I was an only child, and my father had been reported missing in Russia. We were never actually told that he was dead, but he never came back. I remember him as a meek man, with few resources. The fact that he was missing did not greatly alter our situation: in our case, poverty had been aggravated by war, not by the absence of the head of the family. My mother treated me like some mythical, miraculous child, the product of an immaculate conception, a rain of fire, a fecundating lightning. In her eyes, I was marked by a lucky star, and destined to do great things.

She spoke of what would become of me in a nebulous but inspired manner. Her prophecies were either infinitely vague or minutely detailed, always leaving the middle ground open. She spoke of "your future" as if it were written in capital letters. "You must never stop thinking of YOUR FUTURE, Aldo, not until it is well under way." Or, shuddering at the long shriek of a recalcitrant kitchen drawer, she would say, "This table will be the first thing we throw away the moment you have a position."

I had no inkling as to what radiant future I was destined for until the morning I went back home carrying that bunch of gardenias. She met me in the kitchen, wearing one of my father's jackets over her nightgown, and we sat at the table drinking barley coffee. Between us, the white flowers floated in a bowl of water.

I was telling her what I had seen through the crack in the shutter, and as I spoke, she placed her knotty hand over mine and squeezed it, hard, almost leaning on it with the full weight of her body. She listened to me with a hungry look on her face, as if my lips were about to drop a choice morsel which she was ready to catch before it touched the table.

Thus prodded, I went on talking, not daring to stop for fear of disappointing her. When I no longer knew what to say, I paused, painfully convinced that my awkward tale had failed to re-create for her what my eyes had seen.

9

My mother drank the last drop of her coffee, then, resting her elbows on the table, raised her cup, and held it midway between her eyes and mine. It was a white earthenware cup with a green rim, the sort of green that seems deliberately chosen to lend an additional touch of squalor to what—whether public or private—is already clearly poor: the painted wainscoting of the seediest taverns, the doors of drafty schoolrooms, the rusty fly nets covering scanty, unsavory victuals. It is the color of indigence, but for a while, immediately after the war, it became oddly fashionable under the name of "penicillin green." It was as if we could not believe we had the right to shun the greenish memory of military trucks and uniforms. And indeed, for a short while, that color strayed away from its natural habitat to find its place among the first "rich" objects to pop up from the rubble: V-necked woolen sweaters, the armchairs and ottomans of tailor shops, and even the first products of the reborn postwar automobile industry.

But on the morning I drank barley coffee with my mother, back in 1944, penicillin green had not yet become a fad and was still—as it is again today—the trademark of poverty.

"Look at this cup," she told me. A triangular chip on its rim tailed off into a thin, dark, diagonal crack. "Look at it carefully, and don't bother to look at anything else. Everything in this house is like this: my shoes, your mattress, the bicycle, the floor, the ceiling, your father's life, mine, yours."

Despite her words, I cast a quick glance around myself, but the awkward proportions of that room—long and narrow, with a long and narrow window poorly centered on its narrowest wall—immediately discouraged me with their ugliness.

My mother put her cup down and extended her fingers in the air like a pianist who is about to tackle a difficult piece. Then, with her hand, she drew a respectful curve a couple of inches above the bowl of gardenias, as if, not daring to touch the flowers, she had to content herself with caressing the perfumed air around them. She skipped the other half of the metaphor

10

and did not say that there were shoes, mattresses, bicycles, ceilings, floors, and lives like gardenias. She sighed.

"I will not rest in peace," she said, "until I see you all dressed in white, behind the counter of a pharmacy." Her eyes already shone with the brilliance of the snowy smock; the glimmer of vials, jars, and bottles; the glow of the shop windows with their Latin inscriptions, in gold letters on mahogany frames.

Something in the depths of my soul wriggled like a fish caught in a net; but it was so far below the surface that I was only aware of a slight undulation.

Beneath the firm determination and fervent will to fulfill my mother's dreams or die in the struggle, something stirred in the darkness. Maybe it was already the suspicion that the voice which had seduced me that night would call me forth to a whiteness, a brilliance, and a fragrance that had nothing to do with surgical gauze, stainless steel bedpans, or the scent of eucalyptol.

I have been sitting in my armchair for a long time, contemplating Violante's garden. I have left the cracked cup and the horrible kitchen of my childhood far behind me. My mother had the time to see me live, and briefly share with me, a life of gardenias. I look around myself in the circular, moonlit room, and feel profoundly satisfied with every object my eyes fall upon.

I like to spoil myself. Whenever I desire something, I make a point of paying double its worth. The extra money I spend is like flowers, clusters of gardenias on my mother's grave.

I turn my eyes back to the quiet, expectant park. Lavinia is arriving tomorrow.

2

''IT IS NOT BECAUSE of *it*,'' Lavinia repeated.

"It isn't?!"

"No. It is because of the awful vulgarity of the entire situation."

"Right," Sandro answered. "That, and maybe also because of the idiotic way in which I dissipate myself."

Lavinia strangled the receiver. Why had she blundered into that discussion? Why couldn't she learn to be quiet when there was no point in talking? Why didn't she stop falling in love with men like Sandro?

"Because you see, my dear," he said with the composure of someone who is obviously not in pain, "the truth of the matter is that you fly off the handle because of *it*. Why, in your heart of hearts you can't even imagine that I might desire another woman. How could you possibly accept my decision to spend the holidays with her without making a scene?"

It was the sacrosanct truth, but for some reason or other she didn't feel like admitting it. She wanted to tell him that his behavior was immoral and indecent; instead, she said weakly,

"That's not true, you know it . . . all I ask is that you be civil to me, and honest."

Sandro snickered. "Sure. I should have told you that a lady had invited me to sail around the Cyclades with her. Indeed, I should have also added that the lady in question has a very enticing mouth—soft, pink, and rather small—and a sizeable yacht equipped with all the comforts, and tons of polished brass. And, to conclude, I should have also told you that it is my intention—a most reasonable intention if I may say so—to take advantage of both, the small mouth and the large yacht. Lots of kisses and hugs and see you at the end of the summer. I would have been civil and honest, but you would have raised hell all the same."

Lavinia curled onto the couch, pulling her legs up so as to cradle the aching spot at the center of her body. Three suitcases were lined up by the door; she had already called her mother-in-law to inform her that she was going to spend the entire summer with her in Lucca.

It was too late now to change what had already been decided, first by Sandro when he had announced that he was going away with that woman for a month, and then also by her, when she had realized she would not be able to keep him from leaving. So she had called Violante. "I am coming to stay with you." That last scene was perfectly pointless, and would only make her feel worse.

Fortunately she could count on Violante.

"Come whenever you please," she had answered. "Your room is always ready for you."

That's when she came up with the idea. Why not, after all.

"What about letting me reopen the Limonaia? Everything should still be in order."

That idea had never so much as crossed her mind in the last twenty years. When she was in Lucca, she always stayed at her mother-in-law's. Her bedroom windows overlooked the Limonaia, but she did not see it, nor did she ever think of the two months of her marriage and what they had meant to her.

"I would like to spend the summer in my own house," she had told her. She would throw a few parties, her old Tuscan friends would court her. Most of all Aldo . . . Aldo, whom she so stubbornly refused to take seriously, though he had all he needed to deserve her love.

She would have to move the living-room sofa. She seemed to remember that its present location made the room look smaller. It was a beautiful room, square, with two large French windows opening onto the gray stone patio. She would plant flowers in the big terra-cotta pots that had once been used for the lemon trees—she could already see their color: the hottest pink, carnal, flashy, in a fluid profusion of blooms, nothing stiff, only long stems drooping under the weight of their redolent clusters.

It was not a bad idea. Sandro could do what he pleased.

"In that case, good-bye! Go to your whore with the small mouth and the large yacht," she said.

"That is exactly what I intend to do. A big hug, and I promise I will get in touch as soon as I am back. But now I am hanging up."

Lavinia redialed his number knowing that he would not answer. She clasped the receiver to her aching belly and let the unheeded ringing draw her into his apartment: the darkened rooms, the closed shutters predicting a long absence, his things—each of which was, to Lavinia, a secret fetish—obediently in their place. Sandro had extraordinary authority over inanimate objects, not to mention living creatures: so much so that it seemed as if the world around him—his friends, his work, his home, the passing days—spontaneously organized itself so as to protect him against any setback, disappointment, humiliation, trouble, shame—the basic ingredients of her own life, her daily bread. Lavinia clasped the crowing receiver tighter against her lap.

"The upholsterers have arrived," Margherita announced, opening the door and sticking her head into the room. Lavinia started and hung up.

"What upholsterers?"

"No idea. But you should know. They are unloading a bunch of stuff from a van."

"May we come in?" a voice asked. The maid moved away from the door and two men walked into the room carrying a huge roll of white fabric.

"Good Lord!" Lavinia exclaimed. Margherita turned directly to the older upholsterer. "What's going to happen now?"

"We have come to do the job." He turned to Lavinia. "You said it was very urgent . . . have you changed your mind?"

"No, no." She remembered now. One day—which now seemed long ago—she had envisioned herself surrounded by a different living room—white linen, no pictures, no knick-knacks. She had even quit smoking, for a few weeks, since that was also part of the new program of life inspired by a crystal-clear, minimalist style. It had happened in the spring, when she had first guessed the real nature of the relationship between Sandro and the woman who owned a collection of contemporary art—the same one who had now conjured up the yacht and the tantalizing mouth that had lured him away from her. Lavinia suddenly remembered clearly when she had decided to redo the living room, and also why: twenty years of analysis had not helped her get better or make fewer mistakes, but they had made her constantly aware of what was going on at the deepest levels of her consciousness.

So, she had envisioned herself in a dazzling, aseptic frame; and upon this vision she had immediately based a plan—because there was nothing more comforting to her than setting up a plan. It meant that the future was not just a flaccid continuation of an awful present but something new and quite different.

She remembered how she had begged the upholsterer to

break all other commitments and rush to the rescue of her living room. Then she had completely forgotten about it.

From the balcony, Sigmund started scratching the door to be let in.

"I'm coming, dearest," Lavinia shouted in his direction. She placed an ashtray brimming with butts into Margherita's hand. "Here, take care of it. And, please, let the dog in . . . My God, my God . . . Coming!" she shrieked at the balcony.

Sigmund burst into the room, and immediately started gnawing the leg of a table.

"Time is money," the upholsterer said.

"I'm going to leave you the keys so you can take care of it while we are away," Lavinia proposed. Back from her vacation she would find the stage readied for a role whose cues she had already forgotten. Actually, only part of the stage would be different: the white upholstery. The rest would still be the usual mess: the marks of Sigmund's teeth everywhere, cigarette butts, bills, receipts in empty flower vases, empty ballpoint pens, a whole life full of mistakes, missed opportunities, guilt, a life that no amount of reupholstering would ever set straight. Besides, it was going to cost her a fortune, and, as was often the case, she would have to ask Violante to help her pay for something that no longer interested her.

Margherita was walking back into the living room with the clean ashtray. She stopped by the door, right behind the upholsterer, shaking her head and gesturing silent messages of disapproval to Lavinia. "I could stay until they have finished the job," she finally suggested. Sigmund had started barking at the roll of white fabric. By now the sun was at its highest; they would have to travel in the worst heat.

"That's impossible," Lavinia whined. "As I already told you, this year we are not staying at Villa Grande: I have asked Violante to get the Limonaia ready for us. Who is going to help me if you stay in Milan?"

Her nervous gastritis was knotting her stomach; the dog was

going crazy; the heat was getting worse by the minute; the upholsterer, his helper, and Margherita were looking at her reproachfully because she was the one who had created the mess and wasn't doing anything to clear it up.

"Sigmund, shut up!" she screamed. She handed one of the suitcases to the upholsterer. "Please, help us get out of here," she said. "Take your time, and when you are done, leave the keys with the doorman." As the two men left carrying the luggage, she tried to reassure Margherita. "Should anything belonging to you disappear, I'll take full responsibility for it," she whispered in her ear. "Don't worry, and let's go."

"My color TV . . ."

"Don't think about it. Get that beast and let's go."

It was a horrible trip. The heat was asphyxiating. Sigmund kept vomiting, Margherita kept obsessing about her beloved belongings abandoned to the dubious honesty of a stranger. "My calf-length beaver fur, my snakeskin handbag, my color TV . . ." The doleful list went on and on. Lavinia kept telling her that she was ready to take full responsibility for everything herself, but her words only elicited a smile full of bitterness, sarcasm, and spite. Margherita had been with Lavinia for twelve years, and, all things considered, was fond of her, but she still saw her as a middle-aged child and not as a reliable adult.

"My silver frame, my cashmere *princesse,* my Valentino suit. . . ."

Meanwhile, Sandro's plane—Lavinia had furiously checked the schedule—had landed in Athens and, at the terminal, Rosy-lips was triumphantly waving to him from beyond a glass partition.

The car sped out of the last tunnel. Lavinia saw the Alpi Apuane on her left and smelled the sea in the air.

"Yes," she said. "I'm going to fill the patio with shocking-pink flowers."

3

I DON'T NEED A STUDY in the city. The paintings I buy to resell I keep at home. Since my business, though large in value, is small in size, it requires a minimum amount of administration and I don't have to have a secretary.

All I need is a quiet room, a table, and a telephone on the ground floor of the Arnolfina—on the ground floor and toward the back, otherwise my curiosity regarding the Santini family would keep me away from my work, my eyes glued to the navy binoculars that I bought as an absolutely indispensable instrument the very day I moved into my new abode.

Today the temptation is stronger than ever. I would have noticed the excitement in the park even if I had not received Violante's note: I have to force myself to go down to my study.

The painting with the kingfisher stands in the middle of the room, in full light, leaning against a sturdy scaffolding. It was brought to me two years ago by a ragman who had found it in an unauthorized dump, one of the many fouling up our beautiful city. Painted on three panels, somewhat warped and roughly held together, it represented—when I first saw it—two blond women sitting at the foot of a tree, of which only the trunk was visible, its foliage vanishing beyond the upper edge of the painting. The ground was stony and bare but for a tuft of bullrushes growing out of the lower right corner. Perched on one of these, its wings barely raised as if about to take flight, was the kingfisher.

The painting—in terrible condition—was simple but full of grace. As I had paid very little for it, I was immediately pleased with the deal; little did I know that, once the painting was cleaned, the entire scene would take on a new meaning that would mark the beginning of one of the most exciting professional ventures in my life.

On what I had at first mistaken for a tree trunk appeared, right at the upper edge of the painting, two nailed feet; and the two women—whose clothes and general shabbiness I had also misinterpreted—were not sitting but kneeling. In other words, I was no longer looking at an Arcadian scene but a religious painting, the lower part of a crucifixion. Given the quality of the style—neat but quite primitive—I was sure that the painting must have come from a poor country church, but which one? It did not look Tuscan, not even Italian; but I couldn't believe that such a modest, and at the same time bulky, work could have been carried across the Alps, or even moved from one region to the next: it made no sense.

And it had the oddest proportions. Even though mutilated, it was incredibly long and narrow, and it was obviously missing at least three or four more panels representing the body of Christ, and maybe a strip of sky above the cross. Such dimensions couldn't have befitted any of the old churches in the region, except perhaps one—now somewhat dilapidated but still bearing the traces of some ancient, rustic beauty—in a small village of the high Val Freddana that had grown out of a lansquenet camp around the sixteenth century

It was by sheer chance that I thought of that church, but the moment I did everything fell into place, including the northern characteristics of the painting. I combed through the entire area:

not just the ruins of the old church but houses, stables, neighboring villages. I found fragments of ancient murals, painted boards, and an entire wardrobe decorated with hunting scenes. Like a trademark, the blue-green bird appeared in all my finds. Everything pointed to the existence of a local sixteenth-century painter, of obvious Germanic origin, who signed his works with a small kingfisher in the lower right corner.

I have spent two years on the subject and now all I've left to do is to write a definitive draft and publish it.

Silvana has just brought me a cup of coffee, as she always does when she sees I have started working. All the Mauritians of the area are related: Sonny, Fatima, and Chris, their father at Villa Grande. Through them, news travels quickly from one house to the next. But Silvana is the one who gathers all the rumors up, and every morning delivers them to me while pouring my second cup of coffee of the day.

"This summer Signora Lavinia will be staying at the Limonaia," she tells me.

"How come, after such a long time?!"

Silvana sighs. "And yet it feels like yesterday."

For me, instead, it is as if centuries had gone by. What now? Now everything should start anew, but in a different way, I hope.

So, Lavinia is again going to take over what, twenty-three years ago, had been her home for just a few days, the length of her tragic marriage with Filippo, Violante's eldest son. I hadn't yet bought the Arnolfina. I was renting a handsome flat in the city, and Violante was only a client who hadn't yet accepted me among her friends. But I knew her sons well, even though Filippo was a little older and Leopoldo much younger than I. Already then, Lavinia responded to my adoration by confiding in me about her heartaches, of which her own marriage was most prodigal.

I saw her often, ran to her side at the merest snap of her fingers, and sent her huge baskets of flowers, while she—in just a few months—went through that entire terrible event, from the short engagement to the absurd wedding, Filippo's desertion, his tragic death, Nicola's birth.

She lived at Villa Grande, where she had sought Violante's protection just a few days after their return from the honeymoon. The Limonaia was closed, and closed it stayed.

Violante took care of the child. Lavinia enrolled in the university, dropped out when she was only halfway through, tried other things to fill her days. She moved to Milan right at the time when I bought the Arnolfina. Nicola remained with his grandmother, which was a reason for Lavinia to come to Tuscany quite often, though always as Violante's guest.

I take the reopening of the Limonaia as a favorable sign. Nothing, not even cannon shots, could keep me away from my tower right now. I immediately return to my room and try to interpret this last portent while, with my binoculars, I watch the two hired farmhands take care of the cleaning.

It is Nives, in her blue uniform, who orders them about. Her voice reaches me loud and clear. Nives has been my last article of faith. Indeed, she is the real right thing. Unfortunately, she can't be acquired, nor copied. No counterfeiter could imitate her satisfactorily, as I soon learned. Naturally, it was a bitter discovery, but as I was making it, I felt a certain gratification. I told myself that having the subtlety necessary to understand it was already something.

It happened on the occasion of Violante's seventieth birthday party. My book on the Master of the *Virgin in Red* had just come out. In other words, I was not exactly a nonentity; nevertheless I overflowed—literally—with gratitude for that invitation. I was even afraid that it would show, maybe in the form of some embarrassing liquefaction which the lady of the house would surely fail to appreciate. Just one week earlier, following an auction sale of Chinese porcelain, I had briefly stopped to chat with her and a few other people. Among them was a loquacious and somewhat fanatic woman who had been raving about a new book. "It drips with blood and tears," she had said. At which, Violante, barely raising an eyebrow, had replied, "I disapprove of anyone oozing organic fluids in public."

Is gratitude an organic fluid? I wondered as, not without some apprehension, I climbed the steps of villa Santini on the evening of Violante's birthday party.

As usual, a servant stood by the door to welcome the guests. I had recently summoned one of his brothers from Mauritius to come and fulfill similar functions at the Arnolfina. It was a special evening, a real reception, with women in full-length gowns and so on and so forth; but the most discreet and yet unmistakable sign of the exceptionality of the gathering was the presence, next to the servant—or rather, three steps behind him, toward the drawing room, in an intermediary position between him and the lady of the house—of a new character, who had just stepped out of the darkness, but who obviously had long been part of the house. Dressed in a long black gown, elegant but simple with the appropriate neckline, she accompanied the women to the cloakroom, where she undoubtedly provided them with all they needed: brushes, needles and thread, news, bits of advice. She also marked the clear-cut and insurmountable division between Violante's more recent acquaintances and her ancient, inherited friends: the latter addressed the black-clad figure by name—Nives—and hugged her, while, bestowing a very special smile on them, she inquired about their children and distant grandchildren.

Her presence in that house seemed an established fact. In a flash, two parallel genealogical trees appeared in front of my searching eyes, the witnesses of a slow progress, as slow as the establishment of any true nobility. Maybe Nives's mother, if not her grandmother, a rustic creature with smooth apple cheeks, had been the first to come down from her native mountains to work as a maid in the house. By and by, in the course of each individual life and through generations, the role had grown in prestige—from maid, to housekeeper, to governess—

22

until it had become something special, a beloved, irreplaceable figure, connected to the house by bonds stronger than blood.

A painting can be bought, as can a precious stone—not to mention a vicuna overcoat, I thought as I entrusted mine to the boy whose tanned face so resembled that of my Sonny. How could I have believed it really meant something? It could be bought with money, but Nives could only be inherited.

All this I merely intuited that evening, in a flash of clairvoyance; but I had time to put order to my thoughts during the following days, when Violante was ill—nothing serious, just a long, ugly flu. Like a good neighbor, every morning on my way to the city I stopped at the villa to inquire about her health, and asked to speak with Nives. She received me in a small parlor next to the vestibule: an ironing board, a desk with a telephone, a file cabinet, two armchairs, a television set. From this room, she governed the house and oversaw the execution of Violante's supreme instructions.

She would offer me a cup of coffee and speak to me of the lady, with great concern at first, while I affectionately reassured her: "But my dear, she is such a strong woman she will bury us all." Then she gradually grew more hopeful and serene, until at last one morning she met me with a smile. "I think you may pay her a short visit."

She accompanied me into Violante's room. The old lady was in bed, leaning against three pillows. She offered me a hand that looked as withered and crinkled as a bird's foot.

"I'm really fed up with being sick. Tomorrow I'm getting up."

"No way," Nives retorted.

And the two women started bickering—though that is not the right word, evoking, as it does, petulant sounds, whereas theirs was like a cooing of doves, which I eagerly took in, stunned by the joy of being allowed to witness an expression of such a long intimacy.

After which I did not find peace until I provided myself with a convincing simulacrum of Nives in the guise of a married couple in their fifties, on whom I had had my eye for quite a while before finally hiring them.

In the past, Piero and Silvana had respectively been the gardener and the cook's helper in Violante Santini's house; then they had married and taken over the tobacco shop in their village. For the next twenty-five years, they had lived in two small rooms right above the shop. My proposal reached them at the right time, when their son, having just gotten engaged, was waiting to find a job and a home before getting married. So, Piero and Silvana left him their apartment and their business and accepted the lucrative job I had offered them along with totally independent living quarters above the garage.

From that day on, until I was sure I had done everything in my power, I relentlessly worked on them with the same expertise—I would even say genius—with which, at the beginning of my career, I had upgraded so many common kitchen cupboards into "credenze Veneziane": in six months, Piero and Silvana came as close to being a couple of old and faithful servants as they possibly could. All the holes were filled with money, all undesirable protuberances were rounded off and smoothed down with daily applications of kindness and respect—ingredients I can use liberally since I am rich and my soul is naturally kind and respectful.

I don't think Piero and Silvana ever quite understood the real meaning of my enterprise. But they immediately figured out the precise extent of its aspirations, and, having made sure that the idyllic landscape that had been proposed to them as the locale of our relationship was exactly what it seemed and hid no traps, they helped me speed through the various stages of solidarity and affection, and in less than a year granted me what only a few servants grant to only a few masters during a lifetime spent under the same roof. In return, they received what is generally proffered in such instances, from the generous check for the newborn grandchild, to an affectionate tolerance for their whims—"So long, old boy," I would hastily say, shaking influential hands. "This evening I can't be late for dinner. My Silvana would never forgive me if I made her miss a single word of *Dynasty*."

4

VIOLANTE DECIDED TO SEE for herself. She glanced at the watch. She had all the time in the world. On the phone, Lavinia had said that she would be leaving early to travel during the cooler part of the day, but that was the sort of thing she always said and—for some reason or other—never did.

She took the shears, the basket, the gloves. She went through the vegetable garden where there was an area devoted to flowers for the house. While she was gathering them, she resolved to send a basketful to Lavinia every morning to avoid the havoc her daughter-in-law generally wreaked on the flower beds of the garden: brutally tearing off the stems, treading on just about everything, and usually abandoning her droopy, warm booty at the foot of a statue, on a bench, or on the roof of a car, where it would just lie, dying. She was unable to measure the duration of her passions: she would enthusiastically start something new, only to quit midway, discouraged by the most obvious and predictable difficulties.

On the other hand, Lavinia was unable to measure anything. Everything she owned was inevitably either too large or too small, she always did things either too early or too late, to say nothing of the way she spent money. When Nicola was born, everybody thought it was a blessing, albeit in the middle of a great misfortune, that Lavinia—barely twenty years old and eager to start anew after her terrible experience with Filippo—couldn't wish for anything better than to entrust her child to his grandmother.

Nicola: Violante felt the same pang she had felt when she had first held him in her arms. He had been such a quiet baby, never causing any trouble, as if he had wanted to apologize for being in the world. Then, he had become a good child, and now, at twenty-two, he was already a sensible young man, studious, kind, patient.

Her shears snipped the long stem of a brick-red zinnia. Still, one had to know when to quit. Everything had to be put back in its rightful place: feelings, blood ties, priorities. By the end of the summer, everything had to be in order, so that she would have a chance to see it with her own eyes.

It was strange that she so often dreamed of Nicola and Lavinia as if they were brother and sister, and both her children. Indeed, as she got older, something still odder happened to her even when she was awake: she saw the characters of the family portrait, of which she herself was part, take each other's place, overlap, split in two. In her memory, the two men who slept side by side in the country cemetery—her husband and Filippo, her older son—fused into one person, a beloved spouse who had died tragically, leaving her a whole array of children, including, besides the two sons to whom she had actually given birth, Lavinia and Nicola.

In that family portrait, only Leopoldo and Cynthia were at their rightful places. Leopoldo, her second and last son: Violante loved him with a will, as if to make up for never having loved him quite as much as his brother. And then there was Cynthia, the other daughter-in-law, the providential American who, with her dollars, had rescued the paper mill and restored the family finances.

Leopoldo had been so madly in love with her when he first introduced her to Violante. It was in the summer; Cynthia, with her white gloves and not one hair out of place, looked so irrepressibly and intimately clean—so much cleaner than anything else around her—that Violante had wondered whether she had received all the appropriate vaccinations and would be able to survive in a Latin atmosphere. She too had looked very much in love, despite her Anglo-Saxon reserve.

Something had gone wrong even in that marriage: politely, without tragedies. Nobody had confided in her—nor, surely, in anybody else—but she knew that even they were not doing well. "Doing well": Violante was much too reasonable to make plans of happiness either for herself or for others, but she felt it was her right to wish that her loved ones were at least "doing well."

She didn't have much time left. Everything cohered in her plan, but whereas she knew some of its elements well—all those relating to Lavinia and Nicola—she still had no clear terms for those concerning Leopoldo and Cynthia. What on earth was wrong with those two?

The French windows of the Limonaia were wide open. A great deal of furniture had been stacked upside down on the patio. Helped by two farmhands, Nives brushed, dusted, polished. Seeing Violante approach, she stopped and smiled at her.

"We are almost done," she said. "All we have left to do is to put this stuff back in, and that's it."

She went into the house to get two crystal vases; she filled them with water at the garden faucet and placed them on the stone table in the center of the patio. "While you prepare the vases, we are going to carry the furniture back where it belongs."

The vases were absolutely right for the flowers she had picked. Violante started dipping the stems into the water one by one. Nives kept ordering the men about, striding up and down the patio with a sure step. Her voice rang with a lively Emilian accent.

You will never abandon them, my old friend, Violante thought. Then, out loud, she said, "They have never lived here in the summer. I wonder whether it will be too hot for them."

Nives interrupted her work for a while and stood by Violante, staring at the open windows with her. The two women sighed. The newlyweds had only spent a few days in the Limonaia, after which Lavinia—crushed and forlorn—had sought shelter in the villa. Shortly thereafter, Filippo had forever untied the knot of that impossible marriage by driving off a highway viaduct.

Everything had been so brutally convenient, it was outright horrible.

"It's very sunny," Nives noted. "But when the awnings are up, it should be all right." Together, they walked into the living room just as the men were placing the sofa back onto the freshly polished brick floor. "I have done everything as you told me to, aside from Nicky's stuff. After all, we have time to think it over until Saturday."

"I have told you I have made up my mind. Nicola will live here with his mother."

She could not reveal her plans to Nives, and show her the diagram. She would have looked at it with her usual skepticism. There were times when Nives's good sense was depressing, and this was not the moment for her to lose confidence. Everything had to be organized according to her deepest convictions, as if it were a precise ritual with its own ineluctable laws whose logic and validity no one would ever dream of questioning. In this particular instance, the ceremony was the abdication of an old queen.

"You can at least start by having some of his stuff moved in—his stereo, for instance. Whatever you want. Then we'll think about the rest."

5

THE FURNITURE was authentic, but smothered under such a profusion of lace, velvet, and satin that the room looked like the dressing room of a chanteuse. Fatima—thin, dark, and dressed all in white—walked in with the breakfast tray. She placed it on Cynthia's knees and stood by her bedside.

"Madame Lavinia arrive aujourd'hui," she said.

Cynthia yawned. "I know. I was at my mother-in-law's yesterday, when she called."

"On m'a dit qu'elle habitera la Limonaia."

"Out of the question."

"Mais oui, madame. Nives et les hommes sont déjà là pour préparer la maison. Madame Violante a apporté les fleurs."

"I don't believe it. Is monsieur still in?"

"Oui, madame."

"Then go fetch him for me, quick. No, wait. I'll go myself. Hand me my robe."

She swooped down on him in a cloud of pink chiffon. He was already at the door, about to go out.

"Hold it," she said, threateningly.

"What is it?"

"Not here. Let's go into the library."

Leopoldo sighed. "All right. But I have only a few minutes." They walked into the library, but he held her back by the door, refusing to sit down. "I'm listening."

"Lavinia has reopened the Limonaia."

"So?"

"Did you know?"

"No, I didn't."

"Fatima just told me."

Leopoldo remained silent, waiting for her to go on.

"Did you hear what I said?" Cynthia asked after a while.

"What?"

Cynthia sighed. "Of course not. You haven't understood a thing. She is arriving in one hour and I have just heard about it from Fatima. From my maid, who heard it from Nives. In other words, I find out what goes on in this family through the servants. Now do you understand what I am talking about?"

Leopoldo did not understand. His wife's grievances had almost always seemed to him both perfectly justified and totally absurd. They were like her hair dryers, her blenders, her toasters, and all the other supermodern gadgets she had brought back from America: wonderful but inoperable on the Italian electric outlets, at least without the intermediary of a transformer.

"I knew nothing about it either. Why should you care to know what Lavinia is doing in advance?"

"I don't believe you," Cynthia sighed.

"I've got someone strong and fair/ who is waiting for me there/down in Santa Fe," she mentally recited. Oh, if she could only ditch that bunch of snobbish parasites, if she could only humiliate them by showing them how much happier she could be elsewhere—among clear, open faces, loyal hearts, simpler rules, and impeccable sanitary facilities, in other words, in Columbus, Ohio. But what would happen to her, far from all these people, things, trees, streets? Leopoldo's aquiline profile, dark

31

hair, and long thin hands; Lavinia's drawl; the flutter of the wind in the olive trees; Violante sitting at the head of the table during one of her dinners; Nives scolding Nicola for bringing home another stray dog; the old paper mill that had belonged to the family for three centuries and was still plugging away next to all the other new plants; the wardrobes full of linen sheets and towels; the Ferragosto procession winding its way through the garden . . . She would miss it all. She could leave, but she would come back, if only for the sake of discipline. Here was a world that was about to end and they, its legitimate children, didn't even notice. Maybe, by now, it was only a wax museum, but even if that were the case somebody had to see to its upkeep—with good will and respect.

"Come on, come on. No point getting into a tizzy over such nonsense," Leopoldo said. Then he added, "I won't be back for lunch. I'll see you this evening. Don't forget we are having dinner at Villa Grande."

"You don't keep me informed about what's going on in the family because you don't see me. It's as if I were invisible. I am no longer in Columbus, Ohio, but I am not here either. I am nowhere."

She pushed the door wide open and yelled, "Fatima! I'll be waiting for you upstairs."

She strode past Leopoldo and rushed upstairs, a hand clasped to her heart, her pale skin flushed by anger, her porcelain eyes shining with tears. She let herself drop onto her bed, face up, her fists denting the pillow on each side of her head, and did not move: she looked like a newborn princess in a frilly baby-gown on the day of her first public appearance.

She kept her eyes fixed on the velvet-ribboned tulle canopy, focusing them on the very point where the folds, converging, formed a sort of vortex. I am all alone, and maybe he no longer loves me. Could it be he no longer loves me? These were the rearguard of melancholy thoughts that gradually scattered and vanished into the darkness at the end of the huge, empty hall she was cleaning up. Following her doctor's instructions, without turning her eyes away she started concentrating all her attention, memory, and intelligence on just one point, letting her mind pucker into a sort of navel, like the one formed by the tulle of the canopy above her. At this point, she was ready to begin one of the mnemonic exercises of self-hypnosis, it made no difference which one. She liked to make up lists of names.

"Asher, Benjamin, Dan, Gad, Issachar, Joseph, Judah, Levi, Naphtali, Reuben, Simeon, Zebulun." She articulated every name syllable by syllable, breathing deeply after each one. Her fists began to relax. "How I love him," she said. Now she could think about it without suffering. She did love him, even though her love had little to do with that glorified emotion that was supposed to be at once compact and yet miraculously multiform, and to consist of elements whose proximity seemed to her both impossible and profane—crude lust and pure tenderness (of the kind she felt for Leopoldo), the most revolting physical prurience and the most angelic spiritual impulses, all at the same moment, all inspired by the same person as one total feeling. Was it possible? Either the entire world was privy to a colossal lie or it was the truth, in which case she lacked whatever it was—a gland, a humor—that could metabolize everything into a homogeneous compound.

Fatima entered the room and, with controlled, harmonious movements, started preparing the apparatus for the physiotherapeutical morning ritual, during which, without scenes or complications, both Cynthia's elementary libido and the sophisticated requirements related to her personal care were simultaneously satisfied. Among aromatic oils, white linen towels, rubber tubes, and shining bowls, a light flutter, like the flapping of diaphanous wings, would eventually occur somewhere within Cynthia's bowels, assuring at once the rosy smoothness of her Anglo-Saxon complexion, the regularity of her intestines, her muscle tone, and the proper irrigation of her scalp.

Cynthia never even wondered whether Fatima was aware of the side effects of her treatments; the expressions of her pleasure were so subtle that she herself almost forgot them the moment they were over and she could abandon herself to the neutral contentment of a well-tended baby.

6

HE CARRIED a rolled sleeping bag slightly askew across his shoulders—a simple affair, without the metallic frame used by today's hitchhikers. He held it in place with one hand while, with the other, he waved a red-willow stick on the tip of which he had left a tuft of silvery leaves. He wore tight jeans whose hue, like that of the shirt, was worn down to an indefinable sheerness which the eye of the observer could color as it pleased. His were the exact opposite of the emperor's clothes: real, but easily transformed or eliminated by the imagination. I am saying this because seen from a distance, the slender limbs of the boy suggested total nudity, whereas his entire figure—his raised arm, the oblong object resting on his shoulders, the stick, and the general impression of lightness and luminosity—reminded me of one of my earlier forgeries, a Mannerist *Good Shepherd* that I arbitrarily reinvented some thirty years ago by deftly connecting the few crusts of color left on an old canvas. That work had marked the beginning of a new era, since that's when I first got the idea of executing, in addition to the fake an art dealer had commissioned, a duly aged fake of the fake itself. I sold the latter on my own to a rich German merchant who had

35

come to Montecatini for the baths, and, much to my surprise, it brought me twice as much as the art dealer had paid me for the other canvas. After that experience, I set up my own business, and even made a few memorable deals—of which, of course, I can't yet speak freely, not even after thirty years. But the luckiest of them all—even though I did not realize it until later—was that the more I forged great art, the better I got to know it, so that I have now become a world-renowned expert on the subject, and definitely the highest authority in all that concerns Italian painting.

I spotted the boy who looks like the Good Shepherd a few minutes ago from my tower: I was getting dressed to go downtown while keeping an eye on the intense activity around the Limonaia. He was coming up the road that skirts the walls of Violante's park.

He walked slowly; I went downstairs, started the car, drove down my driveway and out the gate in the time it took him to reach the top of the climb and find himself right in front of me.

With his hand he signals me to stop.

"Excuse me . . ."

"Yes?"

"I'm looking for Nicola Santini."

"He is not here, he is in America. He should be back in a week."

He does not seem too disappointed. He shrugs his knapsack back in place. "In any case, this is where he lives, right? I mean, his family has a house around here."

I have already recognized him as a member of that immense freemasonry of young people who travel around the world visiting each other and do not hesitate, when they need a place to sleep, to call on their friends' parents, or friends of friends, dropping in on people they have never met before, without references to speak of but always ready to be turned down and go knock on the next door.

"Yes," I tell him. "His house is right inside this park. If you

36

follow this wall, you'll find the gate right around the next bend. There are three houses: Nicola's grandmother lives in the largest one, his uncle in the second largest, and his mother in the smallest."

The boy smiles, lowering his head and looking askance at me; the shadow around his eyes is light blue, almost silver.

"Like the three bears," he says. This is exactly what I thought last night while gazing at the Santini park from the top of my tower; but coming from him, the observation sounds so unbearably quaint that I pretend I haven't heard it. This boy inspires me with the sort of diffidence I immediately feel toward anyone who is trying to please me. I see him as one of those professional seducers who are unable to utter the simplest sentence without assuming a persuasive tone of voice and repeatedly batting their eyelashes. I can't believe he is a friend of Nicola's. Nicola is tall, strong, diligent, loyal. He is naturally kind to everybody, but doesn't worry about the impression he makes on others.

I leave the globetrotter on the dusty edge of the road and head on toward Lucca. I try to remember how I was at his and Nicola's age: I was very different.

In those days, I was swimming against the tide, with all my might and the will my mother had bestowed on me as if it had been a material asset, a family treasure to bequeath to one's offspring. I knew what I wanted to leave behind—the ungracefully oblique kitchen with its opaque sounds and the smell of poverty—just as I knew, with increasing clarity, that my goal was not a pharmacy counter; but it took me several more years before I actually knew what it was. A school diploma, a "proper" job, and a reasonably comfortable life as one's highest aspirations seemed to me even sadder than a chipped cup with a greenish rim.

Oddly enough, what was supposed to be a very humble means to a precise end—a sort of piggy bank to break open, empty out, and throw away—instead turned out to be the road to the realization of my mother's and my dreams. It was the inheritance left me by my father—a little man with the soul of a loser—that finally led me to fame and fortune.

That little man, of whom I have so few memories, had a small laboratory with the most elementary equipment, where he fixed pottery. My mother had always helped him, and therefore was fairly well acquainted with the trade. At the end of the war, she resumed working even more intensely than before since the antiquarian market, then in full upswing, permitted it and my studies in pharmacy demanded it. I studied a great deal, but had enough time to help her, and pretty soon started to lend a very personal touch to our activity.

It turned out I had an artistic hand. I quickly moved from pottery to enameled furniture, from that to the restoration of paintings, and from restoration to forgery. I crossed this last threshold the day a Roman art dealer asked me to clean up the portrait of a woman by Artemisia Gentileschi. It was a beautiful piece, but impossible to sell because the woman in the painting held a skull in her hand. As a result, people loved to look at it but did not dare buy it, no doubt put off by that macabre touch.

"A mere brushstroke," the art dealer kept saying, "would do the trick."

So, without bringing any alteration to the rosy arm and the position of the hand, I turned the skull into a mirror: it took only a couple of brushstrokes, the faintest tampering, and the art dealer sold the painting for the price he wanted.

At first, I had some qualms, somewhat shared by the art dealer, while my mother, who as a rule was a moralist, had none. According to her, the aim of a painting was to provide pleasure to the eyes: any painting fulfilling this requirement was, in her mind, honest and authentic.

"They are not blind. If they buy it, it means they like it, don't you think? Stop worrying and follow your nose."

Then there was the stratagem of the *Good Shepherd,* after which I started working on my own. At twenty-three, though I had only a few exams to go, I quit pharmacy. The university degree that's hanging on the wall behind my desk was not earned the usual way: it is *honoris causa* and was awarded to me last January, by the department of art history at the University of Perugia in appreciation of my work on the Master of the *Virgin in Red.*

Since I quit the profession of forger at the age of thirty, I have been simultaneously an art dealer and a scholar. I like to think that this change of activity has helped create two images of me that reciprocally enhance each other: the more garish and rascally aspects of the forger are somewhat upgraded and ennobled by the sound scholarship of the dealer, while the professorial grayness of the latter is lent gloss and color by the former.

I am sure, as I get out of my Volvo and place its keys in the hands of the garage attendant, that I have come a very long way since the crooked kitchen of my early youth, and that I can now definitely say I have arrived: indeed, today, I am very much like one of the people seated at the table I observed through the crack in the shutter, in the summer of 1944.

7

THEY ARRIVED at four, exhausted by the heat.

"Mrs. Santini is resting," Nives told them. "She left word to call her. Anyway, she generally wakes up around this time," she added, glancing at her watch. "Then, when you are ready, you can go to the Limonaia. We have straightened it up and the key is in the door." She took Margherita to her parlor and let Lavinia go to Violante's bedroom by herself. Filippo's widow was at home there, and did not need to be announced: this was what the governess had wisely left unsaid, Lavinia thought as she crossed the living room. And yet she did not feel at all as if those rooms belonged to her; rather, she felt that she belonged to them, worthless as she was and so totally unfit for anything. Twenty years earlier she had been unable to deserve Filippo's love, and now, here she was, late as usual, perspiring, unhappy, her belly all twisted up and swollen, dragging herself under the suspicious eyes of the portraits decorating the walls.

"Darling!"

"Did I wake you up?"

"No. I was reading. I am so happy to see you. Come sit next to me." Violante had always felt a great tenderness for that tall, clumsy child; and then Filippo—her firstborn, and only true love—had started treating her so obnoxiously that even the most natural movements of her heart were overcome by pity. Confronted with such abominable behavior, she had been unable to take her son's side, but she couldn't have remained neutral either: she had felt compelled to make a choice, and she had chosen Lavinia. She had taken her under her roof and had treated her like a sick kitten. She had also ordered all the doors of the Limonaia bolted for fear Filippo might come and carry out his evil practices right under that poor child's nose. Filippo had not come back; indeed, she had never seen him again, not even the little that was left of him after the accident. And she had never been able to get rid of the thought that he might have sped off that viaduct precisely because she had taken her support away from him, even if with reason. With reason? Can one speak of reason in such matters? And yet, at the time she had felt she had done the right thing; and since her choice had been so hard, she had even considered it noble, a behavior full of ancient virtue, worthy of a Roman matriarch. It had taken her years to realize that it was all wrong, that there are natural bonds that go beyond mere reason.

But that's what had happened, and she could not go back. The only thing that she could do now was to go all the way: if she had traded Filippo for Lavinia, then she might as well love her as a daughter.

Violante looked at Lavinia, trying to find something in her appearance she could say something flattering, encouraging about; but she found nothing. Her blond hair was hanging limply on each side of her long, white face. Lavinia, whose color could be either silvery or ashen, depending on the angle of the light, and whose long limbs could appear either sensuously fluid or awkwardly angular, occupied, on the scale of feminine beauty—and according to Violante's secret opinion—a variable place somewhere between Botticelli's *Primavera* and the bony spinsters of some English novels, first and foremost David Cop-

41

perfield's great-aunt Betsey Trotwood. A trifle was enough to make her shift in either direction, and today she was definitely closer to Betsy.

Violante gave up the idea of complimenting her. "Filippo's friend died," she said instead. "We knew she was old, but try to guess how old she actually was."

"Dead?" It was such a long time since Lavinia had given a single thought to the woman who had so atrociously humiliated her that, to her, she could have been dead for years. When Filippo had driven off that viaduct, it was as though he had left this world clasped in a deathly embrace with his permanent mistress, the very one Lavinia had been unable to supplant if only for one day, though she was only twenty—and she had counted on this as an unconquerable weapon of seduction—and Filippo already thirty-five.

Literally, not even for one day, since immediately after the marriage ceremony they had left on their honeymoon and, with no explanation, he had decided to stop after only nine miles, in Pisa, where they had arrived around two in the afternoon. That is where Filippo had fulfilled his marital duty, as if it were some minor office surgery. Neither of them had fully undressed, and the whole thing had happened so quickly that their bodies had barely rumpled the burgundy-and-white-striped bedspread they had not had the time to remove.

The previous summer, Lavinia had often gone dancing in Versilia, where Peppino di Capri sang and played the piano while standing—like someone who is only passing through and, having other pressing obligations, doesn't even bother to take a seat. Somehow she thought of him while her new husband, whom she really found somewhat ripe and out of breath—the very reasons that had made her hope he would love her tenderly and forever—was settling his debt with her, and decided that if anyone ever asked her how she had made love the first time, she would say, "Like Peppino di Capri."

Having done his duty, Filippo had left her alone in the hotel

42

and had not reappeared until the following morning. Then, after a few depressing days on Elba—which he had spent mostly on the phone—he had confessed, or rather, had voluptuously thrown in her face that he had spent their wedding night with Mafalda, who had deflowered him when he was eighteen, and had always been and would always be his mistress and his love, something everybody knew except, ironically enough, her, Lavinia. "How could you have ever imagined"—he had stared at her with the cruelest eyes—"how could you have fooled yourself into believing that I would ever love you?" And then had added other terrible things that she had tried desperately to forget and hadn't even been able to repeat to Violante.

"She was only three years younger than I. Can you believe it? Of course, I was a very young mother for Filippo—just imagine, I lost two of my milk teeth while I was expecting him. Still, it is unbelievable that he could have so totally lost his head over a woman who was almost his mother's age. But maybe not, maybe it isn't at all unbelievable. Les amours des autres, who's to say!" Then, with a coy smile, she added, "Besides, let's not forget that Filippo was an inveterate mamma's boy. Anyway, what about your own love life? How are things with your sociologist?"

"Ghastly," Lavinia sniffed disconsolately. "He's off on a cruise with someone else. I caught a glimpse of her last winter. Nothing special, believe me. At times I feel so disgusted that I'd do anything to get out of it . . . at least, emotionally. You see, I'd like to be able to see him as a man I like and with whom I don't mind spending an evening now and then."

"That's exactly what you should do."

Lavinia leaned back in her armchair and turned her eyes to the chandelier.

"I know, I know. On the other hand, you see, these other women come and go, whereas he has been with me for over three years. And there are times when it is all so perfect, and

43

he seems so . . . how shall I put it . . . so close and devoted. . . . Oh, I don't know."

Violante snorted. "The problem with you, Lavinia, is that you are like those poor little maidens, so common in other times, who seemed destined to be robbed of all their savings by their suitors. There were thousands of them, and those rascals could smell them a mile away. One could not let them out of one's sight, not for a second, they couldn't be allowed out by themselves, they had to be treated like children, and even that did not help. They always ended up the same way. They used to worry us sick, Nives and me. You should ask her sometime, she knows something about it."

Lavinia crossed her arms over her belly trying to still the cramps. "If that's the way I am, and you may be right," she replied petulantly, "then I might as well stay with Sandro. Otherwise I will be treated exactly the same way by someone else, someone I might not even like as much." She tilted her head sideways; her intelligent gray eyes started smiling, then, suddenly, her whole face lit up. "In any case, I am delighted to be here, and quite curious to see if I can survive on my own at the Limonaia."

"I think that was a very wise decision."

They could hear Sigmund barking at the butterflies on the lawn. Cicadas filled the air with their consumptive chant.

"I'm going to leave Margherita here with Nives," Lavinia said. "She'll join me later. But now I am sneaking out of here to take possession of my home by myself."

8

THE HOUSE, WHERE THE LEMON TREES in their terra-cotta pots had once wintered, was on a level with the large stone patio. When Lavinia and Filippo were about to get married, Violante had let them choose which of the other two buildings in the park—Villa Piccola or the Limonaia—they wanted to inhabit. In fact, they could have also chosen the Arnolfina—which had not yet been sold to Aldo and had no name—an abandoned farm which, owing to its odd cylindrical tower, occupied a very privileged position right beyond the park walls.

Lavinia had been the one to choose the Limonaia over Villa Piccola, which should have naturally come to her as the first-born's wife, as well as over the Arnolfina, which, being situated outside the park, was the most independent of the three and, as a result, the best suited for bringing up one's own family, touched by, but not directly exposed to, Violante's maternal radiance.

She had chosen the Limonaia—or so she thought then—precisely because she liked the way its arched windows opened directly onto the patio. "I love the fact that there is hardly any distinction between the inside and the outside," she had said.

"An environmental continuum," as architectural journals called it, and that year architects reigned supreme. Indeed, they were the ones who decided whether or not someone had the right to be happy, depending on the structure and the furnishings of one's habitation. Since the newly built villas looked like lemon houses, Lavinia thought that to live in a real one would give her a better chance at happiness.

"It will rain inside the house, and the water will seep in through the doors," Filippo had predicted. That was probably the only time they had behaved like most other couples: they had quarreled for a while about a practical issue concerning their future together.

When Filippo gave in, she congratulated herself for her victory. Obviously he loved her so much, he was so enthralled with his young fiancée that he was ready to satisfy her every wish. This is what she told herself. Indeed, she even liked to think that her choice had been totally illogical—a whim, a quirk—as it made his capitulation still more flattering to her.

It didn't take her long to realize that Filippo's acquiescence meant something quite different from what she had hoped. He wanted an official wife, a legitimate heir, a socially acceptable façade, no question about it, but not a conventional marriage, not a daily intimacy involving the sharing of common territory. Since he had no intention of giving up his essentially celibate program of life, it was hardly worth his while to get involved in long discussions concerning the appropriateness of the conjugal domicile.

The arched windows appeared right around the bend. Unless, Lavinia thought, she had chosen it unconsciously, not so much to satisfy an aesthetic fancy but because she felt that to live in that sort of summer tea house was a way of remaining connected to the main house. The Limonaia was so obviously an annex of Villa Grande—fragile, almost temporary, the sort of place that could be abandoned at a moment's notice in favor of a real house. In fact, more than Filippo, she had wanted to

46

marry the family—this was one of the many useless things she had found out in the course of her analysis—first of all Violante; then the old, paternal *Ingegner* Santini, who seemed to be one with his paper mill; then Leopoldo, her coeval, still a university student who liked to flirt with her, innocently, like a big affectionate puppy; and finally Nives, the servants, the farmhands—that entire, closed world that had so miraculously opened up to let her in and welcome her home, at last, she who since birth had felt doomed to be forever and everywhere a stranger.

She tore off a flower and started crumpling it in her hands. Everywhere, except in that garden, people seemed to be able to reach levels of intimacy among themselves which she could never even hope to attain with anyone. Allusions to past events, references to absent characters always baffled her: they were generally events and people she knew—as she, unheeded, inevitably hastened to assert—but always somewhat obliquely, never as closely as others seemed to. Where on earth was she at the magic instant of those fateful occurrences that had had the power to cement friendships, found undying memories, and, ultimately, confer on one that right of appurtenance that she would never possess?

Lavinia sat down on a stone bench whose back sunk into a thick, perfumed bush of angelica. What was the reason she always arrived everywhere late, when the chips were down and the polls were closed? Everywhere except in the blessed embrace of that garden. That was why it was so comforting, now and then, to go back to Violante's kingdom. What she had realized a little earlier as she was crossing the rooms of the villa was absolutely true: it was not the kingdom that belonged to her but she who belonged to the kingdom . . . yet it was such a comfort, if not to possess, to belong. To belong as intimately as she belonged to that family. With a shiver of deep satisfaction, she became aware of her undisputed superiority over Cynthia—the prom queen from Columbus, Ohio, former head

47

cheerleader, all sequins and paper pom-poms, the darling of country clubs, and, even today, after ten years of exile, the proud recipient of tons of air mail—who, in the Santini microcosm, was still somewhat of an incongruity, a precious but poorly set stone, with a different refraction index and the wrong sparkle.

Lavinia left her perfumed niche and resumed her walk toward the Limonaia. It was a one-story building, but rather large, as it comprised, beside the lemon house, the former horse stable as well. Renovated, it had easily accommodated a living room, a dining room, four bedrooms, and staff quarters.

The sky-blue plumbago, long relieved of its climbing duties, grew and spread in the flower beds between one window and the next. The door was wide open; amidst the vine shoots of the chintz-covered couch slept a young man. A tall glass, still containing a bit of milk, stood on the floor next to a plate with two peach stones and a few bread crumbs.

"Hi there!" Lavinia said. The young man opened his eyes and smiled. He had dropped a folded sleeping bag and a knapsack on an armchair: obviously he was not a farm boy who had come to help straighten up the house and had fallen asleep on the job. The tennis shoes had left two dark traces on the couch. His eyes were blue, and his fine, soft, black hair exuded a silvery glow that made it look very light and almost transparent. His curls, not long enough to coil, looked like a halo of diaphanous question marks around the tall forehead.

"You must be Nicola's mother," the young man said, sitting up. "I was with him in the military service."

In that case, he was not so young. He must be at least Nicky's age, twenty-two, even if, like him, he had decided not to defer doing his civic duty to finish his studies.

"You're out of luck. My son is still in America."

"That's too bad." His smile disappeared, and his face expressed a heartfelt, almost childlike disappointment.

"I'm sorry," Lavinia said. And she really was. Several years earlier, as she was about to leave for Paris right on Christmas day, Nicola had looked at her with exactly the same expression on his face. It was odd how she had quite forgotten it until now. In fact, she hadn't paid much attention to it even when it had happened. Of course, she had thought, children always wanted to have everything right there and then: their mommy, their granny, their nanny, their dog, their teacher, the sea, the mountains, their friends, their teddy bear, the snow, the grass, TV, potato chips. But there were times when they could not. This is what she had thought then, while placing a kiss on that small, disappointed face, which she now believed she was seeing again, poor love.

"Do you need anything?" she asked him. "Are you hungry?"

The young man curled out of the sofa like a cat. He was not very tall, but his movements were those of a long-limbed person. "I have already helped myself. The fridge is full." He didn't apologize for his brazenness; instead, he asked her, "Would you like some coffee?"

"What? I'm not sure there is any."

"Yes, there is." He started walking toward the kitchen. "So, would you like some too?"

"Yes, thank you."

Lavinia followed him. Only now did she realize that she had walked through the garden very slowly, stopping here and there, wasting time, putting off as long as possible the moment when, after over twenty years, she would again cross the threshold of the Limonaia. She was afraid she might be assailed by memories so unbearable that she would, as usual, flee back under Violante's wing. But the young man's presence had changed her script, dispersing the shadows of the past, starting up a new chain of events and emotions.

There were flowers in the vases and bottles on the cart. Even in the kitchen, nothing was missing, and in the bathrooms there would certainly be the usual bars of soap, the same ones Violante had been buying for years by the case, from a very old factory that seemed to stay in operation only to supply her—and the bubble bath, the talcum powder, the toothpaste, all of them bearing the brand name of another venerable firm Violante alone knew and had patronized for almost half a century. Such comfort, such pleasure. A special attentiveness, as sweet as a caress, and as steady as a rock.

And now, smack in the middle of the picture, a new figure had appeared from a completely different species. A child who had come to play and eat a snack with his little friend.

"What's your name?" Lavinia asked him.

"Marco."

No last name. Maybe the use of a knapsack had replaced that of a last name. Lavinia felt the need to say something to plump up such a spare answer.

"I like Roman names. My name is Lavinia, also Roman."

Marco had filled the coffee maker with great dexterity. He must have been used to taking care of himself. "This house has been uninhabited for years," Lavinia added. "A few things may no longer work."

"Everything is fine in the kitchen," Marco answered. "The bathroom too seems to be OK." As soon as the coffee was ready, Marco placed the machine and all the other requisites—the sugar bowl, the milk jug, a white linen doily—on a silver tray; then he preceded Lavinia into the living room. He didn't speak much, but his silence didn't seem to bother him. Indeed, nothing seemed to bother him, not even the fact that Nicola wasn't there. Lavinia began to suspect she might have imagined the disappointment painted on his face. Had he rummaged through the entire house? He certainly behaved as if he was at home. . . . Maybe I should throw him out, Lavinia thought. But since she knew she wouldn't be able to do it, she said, "You hoped Nicola would be here, didn't you?" If he did not care, it was up to her to find a justification for that unexpected visit, and the impertinent ease with which he moved through the Limonaia. I should throw him out, she thought again. Otherwise she had to act as if everything were in order. "He is coming, of course, as usual, but a little later. School is over, but he has decided to spend a few weeks in New York—a friend has left him his apartment. You thought he was already here, didn't you?"

"Right."

They remained seated—she talking and he silent—until Violante showed up, followed by Nives and Margherita. Lavinia felt as if she had been caught red-handed in a compromising situation.

"This is Marco, a friend of Nicola's," she hastened to explain. "He was with him in the military." She couldn't have said when or how she had started noticing it, but she was aware of an underlying cockiness in Marco that went way beyond a mere excess of youthful casualness. In front of those three eminently respectable women, she felt ill at ease for having been his accomplice in refusing to put him in his place. She did not have the courage to tell them that she had found him peacefully installed in her house, and preferred to let them believe she had invited him.

9

I HAVE ASKED MY BARBER to come up to the Arnolfina to give me an impeccable shave. I have repeatedly noticed that women do not dislike hairy men, and that the excellence of a close shave seldom elicits from them the sort of admiration men expect. On the other hand, I have always behaved absurdly with Lavinia, like a silly Sisyphus who is doing his damnedest to be appreciated while knowing from the very start that his efforts will be in vain.

When I met her for the first time, she was a tall fifteen-year-old wearing a kilt, blue knee socks, and a disgruntled expression on her face which suggested that she was being dragged along against her will by her parents who did not know where to leave her, and were certainly old enough to be her grandparents. They wanted to sell me their last family treasures: two tempera paintings by Massimo d'Azeglio, a drawing by Ingres, and a wonderful battle scene which, with a bit of authority—such as I already had at twenty-eight—could easily have been palmed off as a work by Salvator Rosa.

Their exceedingly young daughter seemed to cause them more embarrassment than anything else. As if because of her, and very much against their will, they had been compelled to tarry on this earth beyond their natural date of extinction—a delay that explained the ashen color of their skin, and the vague smell of chrysanthemum and dust that enveloped them.

Next to them, Lavinia looked like an orphan, which, I think, was precisely what struck me from the very start, and made me ardently wish to take care of her. Though, in fact, that was not at all the way she herself looked, despite the long face and blue knee socks, but the way they made her look. In other words, I fell in love with something that was quite extraneous to her, emerging as it did out of her contiguity to those parents who looked like two exhausted players forced to put in extra innings on this earth.

Lavinia's hair was blond, fine, straight, brushed back and held in place by a tortoiseshell band. Her hairline was shaded: from the forehead and the temples, an almost imperceptible peach fuzz gradually turned into long threads of pale gold. It was the first time in my life that I had happened to notice someone's hairline, but I immediately realized how aristocratic that continuity between face, hair, and the surrounding air actually was. Casting a dismayed glance at the Venetian mirror above the console table in my waiting room, I felt uneasy and unusually unhappy about my physical appearance: I suddenly saw myself as someone wearing a brown mohair cap, a tawdry, insurmountable barrier against the dispersion and desirable blurring of the animal flesh and blood that constitute a face. My terrestrial brutality was there, perfectly visible and ineluctably confined within its dark boundaries. I felt as if I was all teeth, tongue, lips, nostrils . . . an indecent cluster of damp orifices in front of that adolescent who, instead, seemed to be evaporating upwardly, in a perpetual ascent.

From the vestibule, where I had met them, I led the way to my study. I held the door open for them to pass, but Lavinia shook her head and, with an almost imperceptible smile said, "I'm going to wait here." Clearly, in that family money was not a subject to be discussed in front of underage children; but I understood it a little too late, after I had already made the mistake of waving my arm and hinting at a triple welcome with my eyes.

I bought the paintings for a price that was far above their worth, only to realize immediately after that I had made another mistake, which, in their eyes, must have characterized me as little better than a gangster with a great deal of money but not enough culture to give a correct estimate of a work of art.

Five years later, when Lavinia, who by then really was an orphan, married Filippo, and, as a wedding present, I offered her precisely one of those paintings—the battle scene which I had never resold—I again had the feeling I had done something terribly wrong, a feeling that made me break into a cold sweat at the very moment when, according to my calculations, the delivery man must have reached the door of the squalid apartment that Lavinia was about to leave forever.

Only when it was too late to back off did I realize that the value of my present was vulgarly excessive, and that its choice was irreparably inappropriate. I had meant it as a kindness, true, but it was an awkward, inopportune kindness . . . in short, I duly lashed myself for it.

Lavinia's reaction to that sensational present was very gracious, if sibylline: she thanked me with a very affectionate letter, but she never gave me any indication of having recognized the painting—and I still don't know whether it was because she had quite forgotten it, or because she did not want to acknowledge the awkwardness of my gesture.

So it is without faith, but conscientiously, that I have let myself be shaved, refreshed, and massaged, and have decked myself out in an expensive white linen suit to attend Violante Santini's dinner. The fact that Lavinia is staying at the Limonaia might well be a point in my favor since it could alter the usual course of events, if nothing else by providing a different setting for our first meeting.

Fortunately, the shortest way to reach Violante's villa from the Arnolfina leads into the park through a small secondary gate, and borders the patio of the Limonaia. I am so shy with Lavinia, even in the silliest matters, that I relish the opportunity of walking by her house pretending—only with myself since there is nobody else in sight—that I have only just realized that the Limonaia is open and inhabited. As I am crossing the stone patio, I slow down, then, assuming an expression of pleasant surprise, I stop. "Lavinia!" I exclaim. I walk up to the door and pull the bronze bell. "Anybody home?"

Her voice answers me from within. "Is it you, Aldo? Come in, I'll be right there."

As I walk in, she briefly appears at the other end of the room, beyond the open door leading to the bedrooms. She is barefoot, and, with her elbows raised above her head, is reaching behind her back to zip up her dress.

"Coming." She disappears, while her voice, now muffled, tells me about the weather in Milan, and the awful trip: the sort of thing one talks about when meeting again after an absence. There is something conjugal to the scene: I, all dressed up and waiting for her in the living room, and she, almost, but not quite, ready to go out, speaking to each other through a wall.

I feel a pang of regret for not having condescended to marry one of the young women—quite a few—who would have been glad to have me; while she goes on talking, I think of the daily gestures of couples, their expressions of love, their closeness, and for a moment am sure that any marriage would have been better than none.

"Are you coming to Violante's?" Lavinia shouts.

"Yes, I am."

"Well, then we can go together. Pour yourself something to drink."

She reappears wearing shoes and carrying a sweater and handbag.

Seeing her in full light is enough to rekindle my feeling—

whether madness or obsession: that disease which I have nurtured for almost thirty years—and let it burn, if not with the roar and ravenous flames of times past, with a slow but steady and lasting fire. No, no other woman could have given me anything worth regretting.

She pecks me on the cheek as she hastens to the front door and leans out. "Sigmund!" she shouts. "Pour me a drop too," she goes on without turning, still apparently addressing the park and the dog barking in the distance. "Everything you need is there. When I got here, that house looked as if it had never been closed up. Violante is phenomenal, and Nives too. Come, schatzerle, you can't carry on like that all the time."

Sigmund bursts into the room like a shot, leaps up onto the sofa then down again, and starts careening through the room, crumpling the rugs, his tongue hanging out, his ears thrown back, his mouth wide open on an ecstatic smile.

"This is too much!" Lavinia cries out with a plaintive voice suggesting weary distress, and the bewildered—maybe a little shortsighted—look of one who has just forgotten something and is about to lose something else in an uninterrupted chain of minor catastrophes caused by aristocratic ineptitude—very Myrna Loy, very thirties, including the dog and the dress, loosely draped on her slim figure in elegantly démodé folds. "Das ist ganz ausgeschlossen!" She often speaks German to the dog. "Enough, dearest. Margherita, help! Come get this devil and put him to bed."

The maid appears, grabs the dog, places him under her arm, straightens the rugs out with the tip of her shoe, and then withdraws. The balmy evening air suddenly fills the room like a rippleless lake. Lavinia slumps into an armchair.

"Sigmund is so happy in the country that I'm always afraid he might die of a heart attack."

I pick up the conversation where we left off. "You were telling me about your trip."

"Horrible, dreadfully hot."

56

"And what about you, in Milan?"

"A disaster. My much-esteemed sociologist is addicted to infidelity, neither more or less than if he were a drunk or a junkie. He can't do without it, nor does he care where he gets it."

Now, I know, we'll be able to talk calmly, without interruptions. Lavinia can devote herself entirely to her interlocutor only when speaking of her love life; otherwise, any conversation with her is doomed to crumble into innumerable fragments, none of which will ever reach a conclusion, being inevitably interrupted by the next one, and so on and so forth to exhaustion. In part, it is Lavinia who constantly interrupts herself to scold the dog, call Margherita, go look for cigarettes; and in part it is the exterior world that seems magically provoked into interrupting her: the phone, the Mormon with his leaflets, and, on one occasion, in Milan, even an earthquake, as if she had ordered its delivery just in time to protect the randomness of our conversation.

But her favorite subject is her love life, and when she gets going, nothing can distract her. She talks about it with me, with Violante, with Cynthia and Leopoldo, not to mention her official psychoanalyst and all the auxiliary ones, her innumerable Milanese friends who share the same privilege.

She does not do it because she needs to get it off her chest, or wants to see things a little bit more clearly, or, least of all, because she seeks advice. Besides, she already knows what I would tell her: get rid of that jerk (and the previous one, and the next one) and love me.

But this is not what she wants: she wants to speak of her beloved, and utter his name as often possible to have the illusion he is nearby, caught in a relentless web of words, bound to her by an endless verbal leash.

"He is desperately scared of death, you see, and infidelity—that is to say, duplicity—provides him with an alter ego, a second chance, a being elsewhere . . ."

Predictably, she drowns me in psychobabble. And, as usual, I feel an irrepressible urge to bring her back to earth with the crassest common sense, because if it is true that I have loved this woman for almost thirty years, it is also true that no one in the world can irritate me as much as she.

"If you like him," I tell her, "keep him as he is; otherwise get rid of him. If you want to know my opinion, I think you should do the latter."

"Oh! You think it's easy!" she sighs with a dejected smile.

"It's the easiest thing in this world. I don't believe in this constant need to analyze people—yourself as well as others. I don't think it's healthy, in fact I am sure it is bad."

"Violante told me the same thing this afternoon."

"It doesn't surprise me. She is a very wise woman."

"I know, dear, you are wise too. But this is a different game. . . . You, she, and all the people around you, in this part of the world, you live in a universe that has never been touched by psychoanalysis: a sort of national park full of deer and antelopes in their natural state. You speak a different language and think differently. Believe me, things are much more complex than they seem to you."

She looks at me affectionately; her eyes are full of melancholy wisdom. Maybe she is expecting me to jump from one piece of furniture to the next to confirm my true nature as a protected species.

I glance at my watch. "We are late," I tell her. It is not true, but I like to be on time, and I know Lavinia.

"I must change," she sighs. "Let me finish my Scotch and I'll go."

"But you have just changed. You were putting that dress on when I arrived. You are beautiful as you are."

She slips off her sandals, draws up her long, slim legs, and cuddles on the sofa like a fluid spiral, a wisteria shoot, too tenuous not to bow under its own weight.

"Esther Williams will be wrapped in a fuchsia satin gown and a pastel mink stole. I must keep up with the Joneses."

Like a schoolboy, I'd like to kneel at her feet and tell her 'I love you.' Instead, I say, "I like Cynthia. I even find her elegant in her Columbus, Ohio way. As for you, my dear, you are a snob."

This time she breaks into a genuine smile. "But I like her too, you know. My snootiness means nothing." Her smile grows larger. "I'm sure she does the same thing with me. I guess there is some mutual rivalry."

"Over what?"

"Oh, I don't know. Violante's love. Primogeniture: she is the wife of the current head of the family and I am the older son's widow. . . . All this sounds terribly outdated, but it isn't, not here, as you well know."

"You hold the winning hand: you are the heir's mother."

"That's true."

In the end, she does not change her dress. It was just a pretext to delay things, a habit of hers, and above all, to bring the talk back to Sandro. We arrive at Violante's late: I, terribly embarrassed; she, as if it were nothing.

10

THE TABLE IS SET under the dog rose pergola; a little further back, the Mauritian servant is passing around crackers and white wine to the guests seated around Violante in a crown of easy chairs. Besides Cynthia and Leopoldo, there are two American sculptors, husband and wife, representing the local Anglo-Saxon colony; Violante's Milanese publisher (she writes cookbooks); and Nicola's friend, the young man I spoke to earlier this morning. At Violante's, symmetry reigns supreme over even the smallest family dinners; I suppose the publisher was invited to reach a perfect balance between ladies and gentlemen, which has now again been thrown out of kilter by the unexpected arrival of the ephebe. The conversation seems to revolve around the particular qualities of cities throughout the world; but to judge from the last, weary exchanges, the interest must be flagging.

"Then, of course, there is Zurich," the American sculptress concludes.

"Zurich? Why Zurich?" the publisher inquires. "There are hundreds of cities in the world I like better than Zurich."

"But it is so reassuring. To us, I mean, to all those who live here. One has to have one's teeth cleaned now and then, don't you think?"

The ephebe's light blue eyes glower at the sculptress, his red lips already gathered in a pout. I wonder whether he is shocked by the woman's tactlessness or simply bored because he doesn't know English and therefore cannot understand what she is saying. It is Cynthia who comes to the rescue of her adoptive country.

"My dear, I really don't think you have to go as far as Zurich to have your teeth cleaned. Here they already had dentists when the Zurichers—not to mention our own ancestors—were still walking on all fours."

Violante catches the eyes of the Mauritian servant and stands up. "Let's have dinner," she says. "Our cuisine is even better than our dentists."

"I didn't get your name," I tell the young man as we walk toward the pergola. The crickets are chirring, the gravel crunches under our steps.

"Marco," the young man answers.

"Where did you meet Nicola?"

"In the military." His hair is slightly wet.

"You've gone for a swim in the pool?" I ask him.

"Yes."

He's not much help. His monosyllables plop like drops of opaque liquid among the evening sounds. Without regret, I leave him to his silence, glad that the seating arrangement spares me from having to entertain him.

Violante sits at the head of the table and I at her left, followed by the sculptress, Leopoldo, and finally Marco. The sculptor is sitting in front of me, with Lavinia on his right, then the sculptor and, last, Cynthia. A bowl of sweet peas is replacing the missing guest at the other end of the table, opposite Violante. Marco's beauty and youth are like Hermaphroditus's and find an apt symmetrical reflection in Cynthia's plump and tender femininity.

The conversation continues in English.

"I'm afraid your young guest doesn't understand a single word," I whisper in Violante's ear.

"I don't know. He pulls the same face even when you speak to him in Italian. He doesn't seem to be willing to do anything harder than just sit there and look young. He is not like our Nicola. You know," she went on without pausing, "I may need your help." Maybe she wants to buy or sell a painting. "Nives is awfully smart and full of common sense," she goes on, "but I don't think I can count on her in this particular instance."

Nives? Obviously it has nothing to do with a painting.

"I am at your disposal," I assure her.

"Thank you. At first you might find my project somewhat abstract, but you'll soon realize that it's the right way."

I try to make her tell me what it is all about, but to no avail. "This is not the right moment," she says and, looking around the table, changes the subject. "Look at that boy. Who would have ever thought that he would be the life of the party?"

By and by, the quiet little idol has become the center of attention. Everybody—except Violante and myself—is paying court to him with courtesies, witticisms, and all sorts of worldly charm. They are no longer speaking English, now; even the two American sculptors struggle with an Italian that twenty-some years among us have done little to improve. They are all as excited as children who have just been given a puppy, while Marco—just like a sleepy, indifferent puppy who submits to the games and caresses of his young new masters—sits quietly in front of his plate, a hint of a smile barely curling the corners of his mouth, his light eyes shifting from one interlocutor to the next with a look of utter aloofness.

After dinner, Cynthia gives him a tour of the library, and later, Leopoldo takes him to the cellar to look for a bottle of white wine. Around midnight, I ask Violante, "Where is our little prince sleeping tonight?"

She looks surprised. "In his own home, I suppose. Why?"

"Because I don't think he lives around here. This morning I met him while he was walking up the road with a knapsack on his back. His home must be elsewhere. Someone will have to offer him a bed."

"Well, . . ." she says. She tilts her head slightly to the side while her birdlike pupils dilate as if at the sight of some juicy worm. "He is a friend of Nicola's: Lavinia will have to take care of him."

This is new. As a rule, whatever concerns Nicola is Violante's province; in the very rare instances when there is some obstacle—as when she was ill—the task is passed on to Lavinia, Nives, or Cynthia, indifferently, depending on which of the three is most available at the moment—something Lavinia seldom is. On those occasions, the person in charge acts exclusively as Violante's representative. I have never heard my old friend abdicate—even if only in words—her guardianship of her grandson.

I gaze at her perplexed, wondering whether I should consider the sentence as a declaration of her future plans, and whether—in this case—I should express my opinion in favor of Lavinia, if nothing else with some fairly banal remark—the only one that crosses my mind—concerning the fact that, after all, she is the boy's mother.

I say it. "After all, your daughter-in-law is Nicola's mother. She'll take care of it."

From the very day the child was born, I have always had great difficulty defending Lavinia's maternal rights, partly because she has always seemed very, very far from wishing such a thing. Set side by side, the bed where she lay after having given birth and the white cradle of her child seemed to contain two equally defenseless creatures, more than willing to let the efficient lady in the pastel linen suit nourish, clean, and generally take care of them according to an extremely clear and comprehensive plan—hospital file, feeding schedule, and two weight charts, the first marking Nicola's progressive growth and the second, Lavinia's gradual return to her former self.

A few years later, the young mother found a small apartment in Milan (via Cappuccio) and a nice job at Olivetti; while the child, barely out of kindergarten, was secured a very costly, if precautionary, place at Harvard.

The child's bedroom, on via Cappuccio, was soon devoted to other uses. The day Lavinia first crossed her legs behind her new desk at Olivetti—two weeks before the opening of the Scala—Nicola, in a white frock with a blue bow, was sitting at a school bench some two hundred miles away. It had been decided that he would stay in Tuscany with his grandmother since his mommy, in her new role as career girl, wouldn't have the time to enjoy his company during the week. She would, however, bravely join the general weekend exodus to go spend Saturday and Sunday with him.

During the previous six years, in Lucca, Lavinia had tried other options: the university, a boutique, painting. She and the child lived at Villa Grande. The Limonaia was saturated with sad memories and, anyway, it seemed a useless hassle to have to reopen it when Nicky was so comfortably settled in the bedroom next to his grandmother's, and Lavinia in two handsome rooms with bathroom on the second floor—rooms that seemed particularly right during her artistic period, as they both faced north.

The job at Olivetti was followed by a rare-book store, which Lavinia had opened with a friend. Meanwhile, the child was growing up in the balmy country air—it would have been madness to move him to the noxious fogs of Lombardy; besides, Lavinia's supersmart and centrally located little bookshop took up so much of her time that she would have never been able to take care of Nicola as well as his grandmother.

Soon enough it was time to think of high school: Lucca's *liceo classico* had been, and probably still was, one of the very best in the world, a breeding ground for politicians, philosophers, writers, artists. Nicola was much better off where he was.

Then he went through military service. "No exemption. You'll do like everybody else," Violante had decided. And now he is in an American college. Nicola's bedroom on via Cappuccio has long been used as a wardrobe; when he goes to visit his mother in Milan, he sleeps on the sofa, in the living room.

I said the only thing I could say. I repeat it: "Lavinia should take care of it."

Violante casts a rapid glance across the room, where Marco is still quietly weaving his spell. "The more I look at him the less I like him. I doubt he is really Nicola's friend. Though," she adds, "he is all too easy to please. You have no idea what kind of boors he has brought home."

"He has a soft spot for strays of all sorts, whether animal or human."

"True. One would think all the dogs and cats of the area had heard about him. Even when Nicola is away, there isn't a single lost and hungry fleabag within a radius of I don't know how many miles that won't show up at my door expecting—and with reason—to be welcome."

Marco is now sitting in an armchair next to the empty fireplace, his ankles crossed, his hands clasped in his lap, his head erect, his eyes serene. Cynthia and the publisher are involved in a lively conversation, but rather than addressing each other they seem to be addressing him, like two court actors reciting a dialogue for the amusement of the heir apparent.

"I'm afraid," Violante continues, "this little angel might have something similar in mind."

"You mean, to be adopted as a house pet?"

"To spend his holidays with us. To settle in, while waiting for Nicola. He is not a dog or a cat. Humans are much more dangerous. What do we know but that he is here with the intention of killing us all in our sleep and taking off with the silver in his knapsack?"

"You really don't like him," I observe.

"Not a bit. He makes me uncomfortable. Look at him. He sits there like someone who has decided that no amount of torture is going to pull his secret out of him."

"Or someone who's trying not to show the profound disgust he can't help feeling."

"Right. He sits there and watches. It is inhuman to conceal one's thoughts so thoroughly. Unless, of course, he doesn't think. Maybe he is sleeping with his eyes open."

Lavinia approaches us, bends over Violante, and kisses her on the cheek. "I'd better go. I'm very tired, and I still have to make Marco's bed."

Cynthia has also stood up and, grabbing the boy's hand, has pulled him out of his armchair.

"Up you go!" She takes him by the arm and drags him after her sister-in-law.

"We are all leaving. I can prepare his bed if you are too tired. Marco, would you mind staying at my place?"

"Whatever," the boy answers.

We take our leave of Violante and walk out. In the distance, a light is visible at one of the Limonaia's windows.

"I am not that tired," Lavinia says. "Besides, it looks as if Margherita is still up. Don't worry, Cynthia, Marco is staying at my place."

"OK."

I've the feeling that a small battle has just been fought and Lavinia has won it. Or am I imagining things? What could have happened during the evening to justify my taking the indefinable excitement I have sensed in the air seriously, and interpreting it as the surface reflection of a subterranean struggle among the adults to attract the youth's attention?

In fact, nothing has happened. Violante and I were sitting to the side and could only hear the others' voices without distinguishing any of their words. As we say good-bye to the American sculptors and the publisher, and watch their cars drive away

66

down the gravel path, I almost convince myself that I imagined everything.

Lavinia, Cynthia, and the others, I tell myself, were only involved in a lively conversation, as is normal in society; as for the boy, he looked so Olympian and expressionless not because he was at the center of some sort of pagan rite in honor of youth and beauty but simply because he was bored and was in fact sleeping with his eyes open, as Violante suggested. Lavinia's and Cynthia's exchange was a courtesy contest, not a midsummer conflict over the graces of a pageboy.

We all walk toward our respective homes, the boy in front between Cynthia and Leopoldo, Lavinia and I a few steps behind them. In the middle of the sky, the moon is a white as chalk; we are steeped in a silvery light that seems to emanate from the garden with the scent of the flowers rather than coming down from above.

Lavinia tears off a shoot of honeysuckle, passes it under her nose absentmindedly, and then starts crushing it with her fingers.

"I envy those who have no emotions, and are able to arouse them in others without feeling anything themselves," she sighs. The tone in her voice is at once pained and elegant—but, as usual, more elegant than pained—and I again wonder, as I have for a lifetime, whether one should trust a sorrow that's expressed with such distinction.

"We don't know him well enough," I answer. "Maybe he seems so impermeable because he is shy."

Marco is walking lightly ahead of us; the two figures at his sides look heavy and dense in comparison. "How can we possibly judge someone like him?" I continue. "We don't even know what he does, all we know is that he wears tennis shoes, sleeps in a sleeping bag, and turns to strangers for a meal and a place to stay. He belongs to a different race. We have no terms of comparison for someone like him."

"Oh, him. Actually, I was referring to Sandro." To hear that

67

Lavinia's thoughts have been, as usual, converging on her un-faithful sociologist comes as such a relief to me that I can't help but acknowledge the fact that throughout the entire evening I have been jealous of Marco.

"Oh, him," I echo her nonchalantly. Better a lion in the Sahara desert than a flea in my bed, or, more to the point, better a charming sociologist in the middle of the Aegean sea than a petty seducer in the guest room at the Limonaia.

"Yes, him," she giggles nervously. "I can't think of anything else, believe me. And that is precisely what infuriates him. I can't help whining and being suffocating. A fatal tactical error. And I always feel it coming, you see, as if it were an approach-ing storm I can do nothing to stop. Careful, I tell myself, you are about to do something very stupid. And so I do, without fail. And all the while I can see myself, in total clarity. I look horri-ble: my face sags, I get pimples, a bellyache, bags under my eyes . . . you can't even imagine what I look like."

I refrain from letting her know what I think: that no man deserves as much suffering, least of all Sandro, the sociologist—an unbearable quack who puckers his lips and casts bewitching glances like a silent movie star. Nor do I cite myself as an example to follow, as I could: 'I also know the pain of unre-quited love, for you, but I do not let it destroy me.' Instead, I put my arm around her shoulders, gently draw her toward me, and place a chaste kiss on her temple.

We greet Leopoldo and Cynthia, who turn away in the direc-tion of their own house. After a few more steps we reach the patio in front of the Limonaia. Margherita has already gone to sleep; the light we saw from Violante's pergola is the one we forgot to switch off in the living room before leaving. We stop in the large yellow arcade reflected onto the gray stones of the patio.

"Would you like something to drink?" Lavinia inquires.

I decline. Marco sits on a wicker chair. "I would like an orange juice," he answers.

"I don't know if there is any."

"Yes, there is. I saw it in the fridge. In the lowest door shelf, with the other bottles."

Lavinia gives me a kiss. "If you don't want anything to drink, I'll let you go to bed." She pushes me toward the dark path that leads up to the Arnolfina and hurries into her house to get the orange juice. The back of the wicker chair in which Marco is sitting fans out into a series of whorls that look like a sort of wide, golden filigree halo surrounding his head. He sits there, not sprawling all over as most boys would, but enigmatically, almost orientally, composed.

He has settled in that chair like some god, and is now waiting to be served; I bet he won't even get up to help Lavinia make his bed.

From the deep shadow of the trees into which I am about to disappear, I turn one last time to steal a glance at him and am seized by an ever-growing, and now more than reasonable irritation.

I once stayed at Lavinia's in Milan, on my way back from Amsterdam. I had forgotten to reserve a hotel room and arrived in the middle of a fashion fair that had filled the center of the city with Japanese buyers. The Germans and the Americans had found lodgings in the adjoining areas, followed, along a series of concentric circles, by the other various ethnic groups in a decreasing order of efficiency and foresight, with the French and the Spaniards last, in the area around Bergamo, and last of all, myself, out in the streets.

It was a Thursday evening, Margherita's day off. Lavinia had welcomed me very warmly—I even imagined that she had not gone out in order to be there when I arrived—but when it was time to go to bed, she showed me how to open the sofa bed, handed me a pile of immaculate sheets, pillow cases, and blankets, and then withdrew to her room. Inwardly, I immediately decided that that was exactly how it should be, and that I was happy that way, though I had secretly wished to see her fuss over me like a mother hen.

We were both traditionally unfit to consider domestic chores as falling within our sphere of competence: I as a man, and she as a member of the upper class. In my milieu, women made beds; in hers, servants. So, if one of us had to adjust, why shouldn't I be the one since, after all, it was my bed that was in question?

As I reach the top of my tower, I do not switch on the light. Instead, I lean out of the window overlooking the Limonaia with my navy binoculars. I'm stirred by jealousy and a sense of deep injustice, along with an overwhelming need to know, and to watch. I am sure Lavinia will make that rascal's bed, and I want to witness the entire scene.

Up there, away from everybody, cloaked in my own voyeuristic darkness, so far from them and yet so close thanks to my lenses' magnifying power, I am, still and again, a thirteen-year-old boy lulled by the scent of gardenias and the music of mellow voices and tinkling crystal—the brush, like an angel's kiss, between a porcelain cup and a silver teaspoon—but also, as if forty years had elapsed in a second—a middle-aged man rich with money and success, perched like an old crow on the stones of a tower, surviving on the same ancient and unrequited love.

There he is, in his wicker shrine, with a glass of orange juice in his hand, while Lavinia, whom I can see perfectly through the open French window, is fluttering around his bed, spreading out a sheet, shaking it in the air, tucking it around the mattress, smoothing it out with her hands. Sigmund keeps coming and going as if busy conveying messages between his mistress and the boy sitting in a wicker chair on the patio.

The bed has been made, and now Lavinia, a glass in her hand, steps out of the house to go sit next to Marco. I don't think I would hear them if they were talking, but they seem to be silent. Indeed, they seem to be suspended in a pause, as if the author of the unfolding story had stopped writing to wonder what to say next. All the possible continuations hover around their heads like ghosts, "things" beyond words, primordial, not created by men through language.

Later, when one of the ghosts has shooed away all the others and assumed a concrete form, turning from hypothesis into fact, then, calmly, I will be able to tuck everything back into the Procustean bed of signs, and recover the certainty that there is nothing beyond words, and that the threatening shadow I see from the corner of my eye is only bad digestion.

11

REPLACE WALNUT SECRETARY w. directoire bureau in tulip room; bring wal. sec. to pol.; fix ext. leg on oval dinner table.

Violante closed the notebook and placed it on the nighttable with the pen. Those were all marginal details in the grandiose plan on which she was currently working and to which she would return the following morning, but not while in bed. Some sort of very intricate blueprint was gradually taking shape on the large sheet of drawing paper she had tacked to her worktable.

Luckily, she did not have to write a will, which simplified things considerably. Succession laws were wise, and her heirs—Leopoldo and Nicola—were both legitimate and full of reciprocal devotion. Besides, she had very little to bequeath. Nothing on the side of her own family—her father had been a penniless music teacher, and her husband had died before the passage of the law granting the status of heir to the surviving spouse. She almost forgot her only real possession—the literary estate consisting of nine published cookbooks—as if it were of no account, something silly, like the gold tinfoil medal earned at Sunday school, or the bouquets of violets from an unexpected admirer. And yet, every six months, her books, and particularly the last one—*Wheat, Corn, and Spelt in Mediterranean Cuisine,* translated into several languages—brought in a royalty check whose amount varied but was always more than what she expected. Violante's mind complacently lingered—but just for a second—on her writing activity; then skimmed over *The French Cook's Recipe Book* by Elisa Baciocchi, which she had found in some archive and whose publication she meant to undertake—if she had the time. Then, she dutifully returned to the tangle she had the sacred obligation to unravel before it was too late, straightening out each stem in its ideal direction, not going against nature but rather lending it a hand in avoiding dead ends and useless turns, so that everything might continue growing in a satisfactory manner.

It was a grandiose plan. Even the furniture to be polished and the plants to be replaced in the garden were part of it, minor expressions of the general equilibrium. At its center were the relationship between Leopoldo and Cynthia—including the child that should be born within the next three years, at most—and Lavinia's emotional stability. At the center of the center, however, was Nicola, who had to be given back to the person who had physically given him birth, not so much to provide him with a mother—at twenty-two they are no longer necessary—as to provide Lavinia with a son, at last. But though these were the essential points, the true grandiosity of the plan—of which she herself at times, almost overwhelmed, lost sight—lay in the simultaneous presence and mutual interdependence of so many heterogeneous elements that were so tightly bound together by their own ineluctable gravitational law that nothing, not the slightest thing, could be neglected: the gardener's retirement plan, the distribution of the three houses so that their recipients would find themselves in the place best suited to their roles, a complete overhauling of Villa Grande's heating system, and, of course, Nives's employment after Violante's death, since almost everything depended on that.

73

On the other hand, she had absolutely no power over Nives's decisions: at least not directly, since she could not acquaint her with her plan or convince her to accept it. Nives always refused to go along with her in the geometry of her programs: Violante had known this for a long time and no longer tried to involve her in them. "My dear madam," she would have told her, "this is not like gardening—seeding, uprooting, transplanting, fertilizing, all the while knowing that the results will somehow correspond to our expectations! This is not a flower bed, this involves people's lives!"

She could confide in Nives—as she had done for years—as long as she was unable to see things clearly; but the moment she had all the elements in hand, and started working with them as if she had a geometry problem to solve, she had better go at it on her own. Nives disapproved of strategies. She thought it more human, and maybe even more moral, to play it by ear, trusting equally one's good will, the mood of the moment, fantasy. "We'll do our best," she would say. "If they are roses, they will bloom."

What would she have said had she known that the two curves that lightly grazed each other in the complex diagram tacked on Violante's desk represented Lavinia and Nicola, and that if everything worked out according to Violante's plans and the two figures came in direct contact with each other it would mean that she had succeeded in tearing a son out of her heart to return him to the woman who had given him birth? Could Nives accept the idea that such a cataclysm could be planned by drawing curves on a sheet of paper?

Violante clasped her hands on her chest and closed her eyes. How much time did she have left? She did not mean how many more years to live: true, she had already felt death's first stirrings within her, but she knew it could go on for a very long time. It had not taken some new infirmity to prod her on to put her things in order, but rather a sudden opening up of her

74

awareness that one day she would also die, like everybody else. She was as fit as a fiddle and could go on for ten, maybe even twenty more years.

It was the others' opportunities that were wearing out, and then it would be too late. She couldn't just sit and wait for her own death, and let them fend for themselves. She had reigned too long and too well to simply up and leave.

What did they know? How much did they understand? They thought she ordered the soap and the toilet paper, bought wedding presents for her tenant farmers' children, took care of the garden, called the plumber, the upholsterer . . . they saw her do each of these things, and many others besides, but always one by one, separately, without ever realizing that all of them taken together—and what's more with an extraordinary sense of duty, as if they were all her responsibility—meant "to reign." They couldn't even imagine—and Nives, who could, did not want to—that if another queen was not there ready to take over when she was gone, everything would disintegrate in less than a year. Each of them would grab his or her favorite morsel and hide away to eat it in watchful solitude; and the barbarity . . . Why on earth had she come up with such a big word?

Indeed, what would happen if one day there was no longer anyone who knew how many *panettoni* to buy for Christmas? What relationship was there between the survival of civilization and the certainty that every Christmas for as long as they lived the parish priest, the two tenant farmers, the gardener, and all the others, including Bruna, the visiting nurse, would keep receiving the same semicircular cardboard box with the picture of the Milan cathedral? How could a panettone, itself a product of lemming logic, stave off the senseless accumulation of waste, the mad flight of a present without memory and without hopes—and what use was the little reserve of good will and good education accumulated during her reign, if . . .

The subject and the predicate kept moving farther and farther apart until they almost lost sight of each other across a sea of words, words, words . . . it meant that she was falling asleep. The mere thought of it woke her up.

What they needed was a national park, a sanctuary, a circumscribed, well-protected area within which no law would be allowed that said that novelty is in itself a value; a small territory that wouldn't be strewn daily with the refuse of the previous day and recklessly suffocated under heaps of cadavers—the putrefying carcasses of ideas, songs, characters, books, all the things that kept being dished out in haste and sloppiness to be trashed the next day.

It had been much simpler for her husband to leave the paper mill, itself an ancient kingdom that had belonged to the same family for three hundred years. And yet, Filippo, the designated heir, had risked spoiling everything by dying three years before his own father. He was to manage the mill when the time came, while Leopoldo, who was still only a boy—there was a difference of fifteen years between the two brothers—would have to spend a number of years learning the ropes under his older brother's supervision.

Instead, oddly enough, Filippo's sudden disappearance from his post in the firm had gone practically unnoticed. Everything had immediately adjusted to his absence. Leopoldo had returned from Canada, where he had been sent for a period of training in the cellulose plant of one of their oldest suppliers, and had effortlessly taken on all the responsibilities that had once fallen on his brother—including the chess game with his father every Monday evening.

Then he had married Cynthia, and when, only three years later, the reins of the business had been passed to him, he had straight off done an excellent job. His wife's dollars had certainly helped him survive the crisis which had affected that entire economic sector in those years, but they had not been crucial.

And yet, the paper mill—that allied kingdom in which Violante had never dared poke her nose but which she had watched prosper for years right next door—seemed so vast and difficult to govern . . . ceaselessly fermenting, teeming with workers, employers, clients suppliers, unions, banks, laws, plants. But of course, each of them knew what his function was—it was even spelled out in the contract—and that was a big advantage. The brief three years between his brother's mad flight and his father's death had actually been enough for Leopoldo to get ready to wear the crown.

Lavinia, on the other hand, didn't even know there was a crown to wear. If there was no time for Violante to change things, she would let it roll into a ditch as if it were an empty can of tomatoes.

Suddenly, Violante became aware of the smell of goats and oriental spices; she heard the call of a muezzin. The water that ran in the middle of the road dragged the crown away, tossing it right and left on the paving stones with a dismal clatter.

Violante let go, and glided slowly into sleep.

12

CYNTHIA TURNED OFF THE LIGHT in the entrance hall and started walking upstairs. Once home, while Leopoldo was bolting the front door, instead of proceeding immediately to her bedroom she had stopped in the library. There she had kicked off her sandals and had cuddled up on the red velvet sofa, tucking her legs under her body, closing in upon herself, she thought, like a tender little pet that can be picked up in the palm of one hand and stroked on its tiny head with a big, gentle index finger. That moment could have been the finest of the day: the two of them, alone, he would have brought her a glass of milk and would have sat next to her, repeating the words and gestures of their engagement days and the first months of their marriage—she still missed those times, while he had forgotten them who knows where, at the bottom of his memory. Instead, Leopoldo had quickly peeked into the room to wish her good night, and had gone upstairs, where each of them had a personal bedroom and bathroom, two separate planets whose orbits never crossed.

On the other hand, she had married Leopoldo precisely because she had understood that he would be able to "respect" her, a verb she had first learned when she was sixteen, during her grand tour of Italy, from an old maid at the Villa Silvestri pensione in Florence. Cynthia was happy to have a chance to practice her Italian, and poor Dilva wanted nothing better than to tell her about that extraordinary young man—a handsome, distinguished accountant—who showered her with attention and yet knew how to "respect" her. "I wonder what he sees in me," she would sigh with a blissful smile. Only when the handsome accountant disappeared with all the jewels and money from the pensione's safe did one understand what lay behind all his attentions and respect of poor Dilva.

But, of course, to Leopoldo "respect" meant something different. It meant that he intuited—without her having to defend herself—the precise point where, for Cynthia, physical contact turned from sweet intimacy into something nauseating that she was utterly unable to bear. Though they had never explicitly agreed on it—the mere mention of it revolted her—Cynthia had always been sure that even after their wedding he would not dare impose such a disgusting violence upon her; and since he "respected" her, he wouldn't force her to reject him, knowing that even that would make her die with shame, as it would clearly acknowledge that there had been a request, and before it, a sickening desire.

Before meeting Leopoldo, she had already been in love, and therefore knew the feeling and how it evolved, from beginning to end. At first, there was the sweetest emotion, as if the heart were about to overflow with tears of tenderness—a nearly unbearable happiness. Then, suddenly, everything degenerated into a disagreable confrontation: the face of the beloved became a bestial mask hovering over her—each dilated pore in the foreground—while the moist, animal warmth of his breath enveloped her hair and face in a viscous web . . .

The first time, millions of years ago—he was a schoolmate, and his name was Buddy—she had screamed, had run out of the car, parked right behind the ballpark, and had vomited right on the edge of the road. Then, she had kept on running, nonstop—she had even lost her shoes—until, filthy, her stockings tattered, she had locked herself up in her dorm room. She had stood under the shower for hours, unable to stop washing. Later, Marjorie, her roommate, had pulled her out, dried her off, comforted her, tucked her in bed.

Afterward, she had been able to organize her love life the way she wanted it, enjoying the part that she liked for as long as it lasted: the sweet, sweet languor, the soulful sighs, the skipped heartbeats and furtive kisses, the accidental grazing of hands, her head resting on his shoulder—that lovely vale of tenderness through which one could hear the other's life flow, like the sea in a conch.

That was as much physical closeness as any man could expect from Cynthia Timmis. She had learned how to prolong that moment of supreme happiness and how to recognize the warning signs of the horrible metamorphosis; that's when she fled, full of disgust and regret. The object of both feelings was the same man, except that, to her, it was as if an axe had dropped from the sky and divided him into two different persons: a dead beloved and a living beast oozing animal humors, eager to contaminate her with his own turpitude.

Then she had met Leopoldo—as ancient, refined, and weary as the Europe he seemed to incarnate—endowed with a surprising sensitivity that could only be compared to the subtlest musical ear. He might, in the distant future, offend her, or deliberately wound her—Cynthia sensed this immediately, indeed, she foresaw it as if a sudden flash of clairvoyance had torn the amorous mist that enveloped her—but would never, ever, disgust her with unintentional coarseness.

So, she had loved him without fear, knowing that he would never do anything to break the spell: neither intentionally, because he loved her and did not want to lose her, nor by mistake, because he did not make that sort of mistake.

During the very short engagement, Leopoldo may have

thought that Cynthia was only a staunch puritan and that, after the wedding—as soon as the thing was officially sanctioned by law—she would willingly submit to that infamy: it was possible, but she had quickly dispelled even this last doubt by refusing to linger on it.

To marry him without first putting all her cards on the table wouldn't have been fair, and to behave unfairly would have been like reneging on a deeply ingrained tradition, something that was hers by birth, like a Thanksgiving turkey with chestnut stuffing. On the other hand, she couldn't give up Leopoldo—since she had first laid her eyes on him she had been in love as never before and the mere idea of losing him panicked her.

After the wedding, when he had understood—the slightest trifle had been enough for him to understand—nothing dramatic had happened, at least not outwardly. He had gone on loving her—indeed, more than ever—and she had adored him. She had thought that everything was marvelous and that there was absolutely no reason for anything to change, until, suddenly, everything was over: Leopoldo's love had drained out, like water in an unstoppered bathtub.

The bedrooms on the first floor—Cynthia's to the right, Leopoldo's to the left, and in the middle the one for the children who had never come—opened onto the gallery. A jasmine in bloom swathed one of the columns that supported the arches. Sandals in hand, Cynthia entered her room, turned on the light, threw the window wide open to let in the scented air. In Leopoldo's room, at the other end of the gallery, the lights went off immediately, as if by agreement. Cynthia went barefoot to the parapet, tore off a sprig of jasmine, raised her eyes to the moon. Then she rushed back in, and, fully dressed, threw herself onto her frilly bed and almost burst into tears. But she didn't. Instead, she breathed deeply a couple of times, went to the bathroom, placed the jasmine sprig into a glass of water, took a shower, removed her makeup, brushed her hair—twenty-five times with the right hand and twenty-five with the left—took a sleeping pill, slipped under the covers, and turned off the light.

Through the open window, the scent of the jasmine also entered Leopoldo's room with the pale light of the moon.

Leopoldo sighed with fatigue. He was too old to indulge his erotic fantasies the way he had during his lunch break. Besides, Marisa was not his type. He hoped that, in spite of his brilliant performance, she wouldn't call on him again. Otherwise, she would force him to ditch her as quickly, if as gently, as possible. But he ran no risk: those two hours of strenuous acrobatics must have been as painful to her as they had been to him. "Good Heavens, what a bore!" Who sang that line? Maybe Don Bartolo. Unfortunately, boredom is more contagious than love. In ten years of marriage, he had been unable to infect Cynthia with his love and pull her out of her prudish, infantile terrors. And yet she loved him, poor dear; but had he, her gentle prince in a golden armor, dared graze his princess's lips with a kiss less light than the flight of a butterfly, in her eyes he would have immediately turned into an ugly toad. Indeed, his incredible conjugal adventure was only a comic parody of the famous fairy tale.

His American tamer with her invisible whip had made him jump as high as he could, as a lewd gorilla trained to obey. And, like an enslaved animal, he had ended up sharing Cynthia's revulsion with fierce voluptuousness. Bothered by the memory of how basely he had wallowed in his feeling of inferiority, Leopoldo lit a cigarette: his stifled desire had seemed to thrive on the fact that it was unrequited, and had kept growing in a soil amply fertilized with self-loathing.

This state of affairs had gone on for a few years. In that period he has filled his life with complicated love affairs. He had magnified every adventure into a passion, and had done his damnedest to be obsessed by it. He had tormented his mistresses with his jealousy, and had abandoned them, only to take

82

rich refugees—went back to their city, whether Milan or Genoa. Some of them must have died, others must have aged beyond recognition. The villa, with its gallery, is still there—I drive by it whenever I go eat game at Moreno's—but it too has become unrecognizable: bought and sold three or four times since the war, it is now divided into various apartments, each with its clothesline, rabbit cage, and the inevitable garage with a corrugated plastic roof.

It is as if the image of that night had flashed in front of my eyes like an ectoplasm, barely long enough to show me the way to my El Dorado and cling to my mind as a constant term of comparison. Cold, cold, lukewarm, warm, hot. Burning! I got it, I am right in the middle of it. I still can't believe it.

At times I wonder, not without some dismay: will I ever get used to it? When is doubt going to give way to the belief that I am not dreaming, that I really belong to this world, and that this world belongs to me—since I not only can see and hear its inhabitants as if I were spying on them through a crack in a shutter, but am also seen and heard by them as a guest at their own table. What happens to someone who no longer has anything to strive for? What stagnant pool will reflect the vision that is now offered to my eyes—two perfectly manicured hands buttering a toast, Meissen china on the tray, the silk bedspread, the Charles X chair, the sun-streaked rug, the furniture, the curtains, the white cashmere cardigan dangling sideways like a chimp, one sleeve nonchalantly looped around the coat hanger, the other dragging on the floor? What will become of me? What is the punishment for those who have reached the aim of their lives: restlessness? boredom?

I carry the tray back to the dumbwaiter and walk to the window. In the Santini park, Violante is pulling up weeds from among her dahlias. She is wearing jeans and a blue and white striped T-shirt—a small woman in her late seventies crouching like an Arab among her flowers. She pulls out tufts of couch grass, shakes off the earth that's clinging to the roots, and then

abandons them, as it were belly up, under the sun's withering rays. They are the same necessary, ritual gestures—devoid of both cruelty and compassion—with which a farmer wrings a chicken's neck.

I put my binoculars down and start getting ready, now and then strolling back to the window, while Violante, having weeded her border of dahlias, is pushing her wheelbarrow toward the toolshed. The gardener, carrying a shovel on his shoulder, meets her midway. They are almost the same age. They stop to chat a while, nod—showing, even at a distance of six hundred feet, a deep, mutual understanding—and then they part ways.

I should write all this down. But I can only write about painting, otherwise I should make it my duty to put down, in black and white—whether in the form of a novel, a play, or better yet, a musical comedy—something involving the characters of my secret theater. As it is, what will happen to them the morning when, waking up without being surprised by my surroundings—not by the silver bell, or by the Shiraz rug, or the T'ang horse—I forget to rush to the window to see what they are doing? What will become of my dear characters the day they lose their only spectator? They might have to turn off the spotlights, fold the backdrops, hang up their costumes, and then put their own bodies away in the equipment trunks.

Watching Violante from my window, I tell myself that everybody should have the right, if not to immortality, at least to a decent embalming. This is what my musical would do. It could be titled *The Taxidermist.*

Naturally, I would start with Violante, a tough customer, I'd venture, even for a real writer. So limited and yet so Olympian. And not a bit picturesque. A perfect house, a famous table, her cookbooks translated all over the world. Not to mention the garden. And the way she keeps a tight rein on everything, disregarding all that remains outside her pale. The time lapse between action and reaction must be short, the possibility of

interference from outside factors must be foreseeable, if not exactly controllable. And when things don't go as planned—aphids eat her roses, her favorite son stages a tragedy and concludes it with his abrupt death—she doesn't blame anybody, doesn't tear her hair out. Instead, she cuts off the nibbled stems, buries her son, and gets back to work.

As I wash, shave, and dress, shuttling between the window and the bathroom, Leopoldo has come out of the house and driven off.

The machines in the paper mill keep on running, running, day and night, all week long, but as a rule Leopoldo does not go to the plant on Saturday and Sunday. And since his mistresses are usually married women who devote their weekends to their husbands, if he has left early, on a Saturday morning, it must be for something other than work or love. More likely—his attire confirms my assumption—he has decided to go visit his old group of friends—a history professor at the University of Pisa, a bookstore manager, a lawyer, an elementary school teacher—with whom he shares a passion for the mountains.

They are all inveterate bachelors or disillusioned husbands. They bask in an atmosphere of fervent celibacy, the sort of misogynistic and slightly bawdy harmony—barely tinged with unconscious and puritanical homosexuality—that seems to flourish in the provinces. For a period of four or five years after marrying Cynthia, Leopoldo, unable to tear himself away from her, gave up his walks in the Apuane mountains. Instead, he invited his friends home for dinner, trying to impose on them a new form of social intercourse that would also include women, thereby hoping to salvage everything, the confederacy of bachelors as well as his conjugal idyll. This state of affairs went on for a while thanks to the desperate good will of all involved, then it collapsed, a casualty of the law of gravity as well as of the oppressive boredom of those evenings.

I was invited also, with Lavinia when she was around, or with some other, temporary flame. I sacrificed myself with unremitting zeal, mindful of the rallying cry that echoed throughout the city: do your damnedest to make the American bride feel at home and avoid Leopoldo's defection.

Even Cynthia did her damnedest to make sure that everything was simple, sportsmanlike, Italian, and male. She served tortelli with meat sauce and steaks instead of her usually fanciful and exotic dinners, told the maid to take the evening off, and waited on us herself, around a checkered tablecloth.

Nevertheless, their guests inevitably fell on either side of what seemed to be a natural, and inexorable, dividing line: half of them appeared haughty, affected, worldly, the other half rustic, old-fashioned, coarse. As I could not see myself, I don't know which side I was on; but I also shared in the general dreary feeling that I was getting bored for no purpose, and that I was projecting the worst possible image of myself.

But the most grievous part of it all was that, since the dividing line passed straight through Leopoldo, in his effort to get along with everybody the poor man felt compelled to smile affectedly on one side and laugh coarsely on the other, with the result that he resembled a court jester in a bicolored costume.

Much to everybody's relief, that sorry enterprise was soon abandoned. Leopoldo's fondness for his old friends, whom he now only sees occasionally, has remained unchanged though fraught with a deep nostalgia, as if they were all dead. He still performs a certain number of rituals—the Monday morning call to discuss the soccer play-offs, the twelve bottles of wine from his own farm for Christmas—with the regularity and compunction of one who is paying a visit to his loved ones in a cemetery. As his relationship with Cynthia has steadily deteriorated, for reasons my binoculars have allowed me to guess, Leopoldo has gotten involved in a number of extramarital adventures but has never resumed his mountain excursions; nowadays, the mournful rituals that have replaced his conjugal love involve his devoting the entire weekend to his wife.

On the other hand, from my tower I have noticed that this

Saturday morning Leopoldo has left in his mountain outfit, which means that he must have revoked his sacrificial offer. I do not know the meaning of this new event, nor can I guess what its consequences will be. However, in my solitary existence as the observer of other people's lives, I have noticed that very often human relationships behave like broken, old radio sets which no rational intervention seems able to fix and which suddenly start working again after a well-placed kick—all too often and for no apparent reason, a sudden jolt manages to fix human situations that seemed absolutely beyond repair.

14

SIGMUND BURST INTO THE ROOM, followed by Margherita. She placed the breakfast tray onto Lavinia's knees, went to the window to open the curtains, and then back to the bed to switch off the light on the bed table.

"There is some young man asleep in Nicola's bed. He's naked." She announced. The total lack of inflections in her voice betrayed disapproval. "The door was open," she added.

Margherita did not like young people. She saw them as sloppy, insensitive, always ravenous, and dirty: a lot of work and no tips. "Provided there are no children," she had specified when she had started working for Lavinia. Had she liked children, she would have stayed at Fabbriche di Vallico, would have married a woodsman, and would have given birth to her own children, three or four of them. Just like her sister, who worked twelve hours a day cutting vamps for a clog factory on her kitchen table, and who, every time Margherita went to visit her driving her own car and wearing her fine clothes, looked at her without even bothering to hide her admiration, as if she were a movie star.

Only later had Margherita realized that, in fact, there was a child, a ten-year-old boy. She was tempted to quit on the spot, but she liked working for Lavinia, besides which she had learned that—for some mysterious reason—the child did not live with his mother in Milan but with his grandmother, in Tuscany.

Shortly thereafter, she had met Nicola, who had come to spend two days with his mother.

It was the long All Souls Day weekend, but the weather had been so dreadful that it felt like winter. Nicola's grandmother had accompanied him to Viareggio to catch the six-thirty-three train. He had traveled alone, like a good little man who is no burden to anybody. He had gotten out of the train, had taken a cab, and Margherita—who had gone to open the door at the first ring—had found him, standing on the doormat, holding an Alitalia bag with one hand and a bunch of anemones with the other. "I am Nicola Santini," he had said. "Is my mother up?"

Nicky had been the sweetest child and was now a dear young man. But who was the fellow sleeping in his bed?

"I closed the door," Margherita added.

Lavinia sighed. She had had an awful dream. She was carrying her old elementary-school satchel, with the drawings she had made with her crayons inside. She was wearing her white frock with the pink bow, buttoned in the back; but underneath she wore nothing and therefore had to be very careful how she moved. Sandro and a tall blond woman who looked like Anita Ekberg sat facing each other on two gilded armchairs like the ones used by archbishops in cathedrals. Lavinia had to show them her drawings, one by one, first Sandro and then the woman. Every time she turned toward him she had to make sure that Anita Ekberg could not see in between the buttons that barely closed the back of her frock, and vice versa. So, as she pulled out a drawing with one hand, with the other she immediately covered her back with her satchel. But suddenly, with a horrified shudder, she realized that she was wearing braids and that, even if she could cover the gap in her frock, she could do nothing to cover the strip of bare skin on her neck where her hair parted, and which everybody could see, unbeknownst to her, since everything that happened on that side was beyond her control.

She had woken up in a cold sweat and had rung the bell, not so much because she wanted to have breakfast, but because instinctively she felt like clinging to that sort of alarm handle hanging right within her reach. She had a terrible headache. In fact, she would have liked to sleep a few more hours, sink into darkness without a thought in her mind. In Greece it was already ten in the morning. The sun shone high on the Aegean sea. His dark, hairy, naked body—muscular belly, sinewy limbs—was lying on a brightly colored air matress. Rosylips, also naked and glistening with suntan oil, was next to him. The boat floated with a faint rustle, sails to the wind, engine turned off. Later they would swim, fish. They would stop in a deserted cove, the shore rimmed with white pebbles and rosemary bushes, to eat what the sailors had prepared. Then they would withdraw to their cabin: the sea breeze, the smell of the sea, the glare of the sun on the water would pour in through the open porthole. He was like a wolf, nervous, spare, fiery. Lavinia could see his every gesture as if she were there, with them, forced to watch and suffer.

"He is a friend of Nicola's," she said.

"How long is he staying?" Margherita inquired.

"What?"

"How long is he staying?" Margherita inquired.

"What?"

"How long is that young man going to stay? Just for my information."

"Actually, I don't know. He didn't tell me. I imagine he'll leave today. He certainly can't wait for Nicola—he won't be here for another week."

"The dog is already full of fleas," Margherita noted with a reproachful tone. One would have thought she suspected the boy sleeping in the next room of having brought the pests into the house.

A cramp twisted Lavinia's stomach. Splotches of light danced on the ceiling of the cabin. Their hushed voices uttered the sweetest obscenities. Some tea might do her good. She poured herself a cup. Better take a pill too.

"He must have gone after the sheep," she said. "Yesterday he wasn't around all day. Besides, we know he is crazy about the shepherd's bitches. . . . In any case, you didn't try to hold him back either," she added sassily.

"In any case, it is not a tragedy," Margherita retorted. "As usual, Mrs. Violante will find a way of getting rid of the fleas and will get him a collar. But I would like to know what I should prepare for lunch and for how many people."

This was definitely not what Lavinia had been looking for when she had grabbed the bell: reproaches, questions, problems. Marco, the dog, the fleas, lunch.

"Nothing, don't get anything ready. We'll have lunch at the villa."

"In that case, I'm going to lend them a hand. I can pick the vegetables in the garden." That was one thing Margherita liked to do; thank God she was in a good mood again. Lavinia swallowed another pill with a sip of tea.

The phone on the night table rang: Cynthia.

"I have decided to have a picnic around the swimming pool, is that all right? I have even invited your admirer."

"My admirer?" That word unexpectedly stirred her interest. Something in her thermostat clicked and raised the temperature a few degrees. Had Cynthia noticed something strange in Marco's behavior? Such a handsome young man, so enigmatic . . . Actually he didn't seem to be particularly interested in anybody, but if Cynthia thought . . . "Who would that be?"

"Aldo, of course!"

Aldo, of course. The best, nicest, most predictable man in the world.

"Oh, him. OK to the picnic, then," she sighed.

"Great. Get Marco on the phone. If he is still asleep wake him up. We agreed I'd call him."

Lavinia signaled Margherita to remove the tray and slipped back under the sheets, huddling around the pain in her innards.

"Please wake the young man and tell him to pick up the phone in his room."

The splotches of light quivered on the tanned, naked torso. The long, lean muscles darted with the rhythmic movement. On deck, the metallic notes of some ancient stringed instruments pelted out of the sailors' Japanese transistor like hailstones. White sea foam caressed the sides of the boat. Everything was wonderful, as usual, when she was not there: from the fathomless depths to the farthest star, the entire universe was an unperturbed sphere of pure crystal.

If only she hadn't had the silly idea of going back to the Limonaia. How could she have thought it might help? And how could she have forgotten what she was going to miss by taking leave of Violante's roof—even if she was only a few feet away, she was in a separate house, out of Violante's direct influence. Otherwise she could have run to her . . . had she been in the villa she would have done so immediately, as she was, barefoot, in her nightgown. By now Violante's outdoor tasks must have been finished: she would have found her taking care of her correspondence or working at some new cookbook.

With her hand pressed against her belly, Lavinia got up and started dressing.

15

THE BELOVED FERRARI, the European myth Cynthia had most enthusiastically endorsed, was reserved for fast highway driving. For shopping downtown, the old *cinquecento* was much better. She could squeeze it in between two plane trees at the edge of Piazza Grande, in a tiny little spot that was not marked by any "No parking" sign and yet was always free—just for her, one would have thought—maybe because it was a sort of no-man's-land, a one-dimensional threshold between the street and the square which the Italian drivers—for all their imagination, individualism, and know-how—did not seem to have noticed. It had taken someone from Columbus, Ohio to see it.

She stopped in front of the Limonaia, honked a couple of times, opened the door on the passenger side, and waited, letting the engine idle. She was prepared to wait, sure that Marco would be late; instead, he appeared after only a few minutes, but dragging his feet like someone who has all the time in the world. He smiled lightly, a perfectly harmonious creature, without a care. He stopped to pick up a scarlet geranium and then turned toward the car. Before climbing into it, he tucked the flower behind his ear, among his short curls.

Downtown, Cynthia bought a few things for him: pants, T-shirts, swimming trunks, a pair of Indian sandals. They walked up and down the streets, crossing and recrossing their own paths—cigarettes, bread, shoes, groceries; up and down past medieval buildings, the Roman amphitheater, the Art Nouveau shops, the marmoreal façades; as if in a time machine shuttling over two thousand years in just a few hundred feet. Cynthia, the foreigner, knew every stone of her adoptive city and proudly showed them to Marco, while proudly displaying to the city the handsome boy who followed her quietly with a red flower in his curls.

She bought all the necessary ingredients for a hearty but simple lunch: everyone knows that twenty-year-old boys have a huge appetite and little imagination.

Leopoldo had gone before she got up, and had left word to tell her that he wouldn't be back for lunch. "Il a mis les bottes de la Garfagnana," Fatima had told her. In fact, not only were the boots missing—Cynthia had immediately checked—but so was the knapsack with its mythical vial of antisnakebite serum which Leopoldo would have never been able to use, but which he always brought along to underline the adventurous atmosphere of those excursions: no women, clean air, few words, true friends.

True friends: they were her real rivals. At the thought, Cynthia felt a pang of jealousy. Forget women. After all, what were women to Leopoldo? *Those women*—the ones he met in the *garçonnière* on via Fillungo, officially the guest quarters of the paper mill and therefore partly her property, since she was one of the major stockholders. Besides, it had even been furnished with their things, all the stuff she had discarded when she had redecorated her bedroom and the third master bedroom, known at one time as the children's room and now, quite as platonically, as the guest room. In fact, it was a room where, for as long as she had been married, nobody had ever slept, since the social life of the family was entirely absorbed and administered by

Violante. Even her own sister, when she came to visit her from the States, was a guest at Villa Grande.

She had decided to change the furniture that she had found in those two rooms because it had struck her as gloomy, indeed, quite sinister. It was probably very valuable, but so what, if it depressed her? Massive dark wood, handwoven linen, and raw silk were fine for a library, Cynthia thought, or for a man's bedroom. She knew that Violante wouldn't approve of her choice of furniture—and Lavinia even less—but she didn't let that intimidate her. She had redone the entire thing in pastel colors, laquered wood, tulle, velvet, and wall-to-wall carpeting. And when it had been necessary to furnish the apartment on via Fillungo, she herself had reminded Leopoldo of the old furniture they had locked up in a storage room. "You should use it for the guest quarters," she had suggested, pretending she believed that was indeed the purpose of the flat. Mere common sense since he would have done it somewhere else anyway, so why spend more money buying antiques when they had all that fine stuff moldering in some attic?

The last thing she bought with Marco was the whipped cream; then she loaded all the packages into the *cinquecento*, pulled it out of its niche between the two plane trees, and drove home.

Marco, prim and quiet in the passenger's seat, gazed straight ahead without talking.

"Did you like Lucca?"

"Yes."

"You don't talk much. Are you shy?"

"Shy?" To answer her, Marco turned not just his head but his entire body toward her. It was as if he had wanted to show himself to Cynthia rather than look at her.

"Or, maybe, you don't care," Cynthia went on. "Maybe you prefer to let others take care of things."

"Take care of what?"

"Of everything. Of talking, for instance."

Marco turned back without answering, the corners of his lips curled upward slightly, like two imperceptible commas that could easily be taken to suggest mild irony at a statement too stupid to deserve a reply.

"I come from Columbus, Ohio," Cynthia hastened to add. Marco gave no sign of having understood or even heard. Once Leopoldo had seemed to delight in the naive propriety of her code of behavior: gracefully keeping a conversation rolling, going to church regularly, wearing gloves even in summer. She saw herself, reflected in his eyes, just as she was, as she had been taught she should be, and as she wanted to be: clean, fresh, healthy, like an apple just picked from the tree, or a Christmas present in its foil wrap: the perfect American girl. Then, without warning, after four wonderful years, there had been a sort of click, as from a light switch, and the situation had changed: Leopoldo had started looking at her with maliciously weary eyes, and since her only other alternative was to become a pathetic imitation of something she could never be, she had preferred to hold on to herself with tenacity and devotion, the way one watches over a work of art, or defends a flag.

They drove out of the city walls and past the brief periphery.

"I come from Columbus, Ohio," Cynthia repeated in a different tone of voice, "where it is considered very important to chat amiably with the people one meets in society, as important as washing one's ears." They were driving by a vacant lot covered with all sorts of trash. A big rat crossed the street and disappeared into a ditch. "Where I live, some things are decent, others aren't. That's all." There *was* a connection, no point denying it. That relaxation of values—Lavinia's chronic lateness, Leopoldo's lazy sarcasm, Aldo's snobbishness, everybody's indifference toward religion—was directly responsible for the accumulation of trash and rats. Not to mention inflation, unemployment, bombs, cholera.

. . .

Lavinia was the only one missing. Aldo was in the water, leaning with folded arms on the edge of the pool; Violante, lying on an easy chair a few steps away, in the shade of the pergola, now and then raised her eyes from her book to exchange a few words with him.

And—incredibly—Leopoldo was back. In his swimming trunks, thin, dark, bent over the barbecue grill, spreading out the coal with a shovel, he smiled at his wife and the young man approaching with the grocery bags.

"I bet you bought steaks!" he shouted.

It was Marco who answered. "Right you are!"

Cynthia said, "You took all your mountain gear. I thought I wouldn't see you until tonight."

He was back, he was back! Cynthia was almost moved to tears. Now that he had given up his mountain walk with his friends, she saw it as such an innocent passion that she almost wished that he—dear love—had gone. Her heart swelled at the thought of his big boots, and that old knapsack with the anti-snakebite serum which had remained untouched at the bottom of his closet for so many years.

"I changed my mind," he was telling her. "The farther I drove, the sorrier I felt to miss a Saturday with my family."

They really looked like a family, Cynthia thought: two handsome young parents with a postadolescent son, minding the barbecue surrounded by various friends and relatives.

Leopoldo was fussing with the air vent. "It's stuck . . . look at the rust. We haven't used this thing for centuries."

"You've got a big black smear across your cheek," Cynthia said. She pulled a small pack of Kleenex from her purse. "Come, let me wipe it off." She held his chin with two fingers, as one does with children, while she removed the smudge from his cheek. My husband, she thought. His receding hairline, the aquiline nose reddened by the sun, his deep-set blue eyes. The mere thought moved her: her husband.

"It is one o' clock," Violante shouted. "And, of course, Lavinia's nowhere to be seen."

Aldo started to pull himself up onto the edge of the pool, but Marco preceded him. "I'll go get her."

On his way he met Fatima, who was carrying a basket full of plates and silver. They smiled at each other. "Dans une demi-heure j'apporterai les lasagne," she announced.

16

LAVINIA ALWAYS wore soft clothes. She loathed the stiff, rustling fabrics Cynthia seemed to favor. That woman did not look dressed but rather packaged, like a piece of candy. Indeed, she gave one the impression that, under the wrapping, she was made of some edible substance. One could even guess her taste, quite vividly: sweet, tart, a touch artificial. And the consistency as well: Cynthia's flesh was no doubt chewy, resilient, homogeneous. Like mozzarella, or one of those brightly colored American gelatin desserts known as Jell-O.

Lavinia knotted her belt, gathering the pleats of the light Indian cotton dress around her slim waist. Had she been able to achieve the desired pre-Raphaelite effect, or was she only a gangly female with a droopy face and a limp dress? One more question: why was it that whenever she came to Lucca she could not help competing with Cynthia, whom, after all, she even liked, and who, in any case, totally vanished from her thoughts the moment she was back in Milan?

The mirror did not tell her anything about the nature of her antagonism toward Cynthia, nor in which of the numerous layers of her consciousness it had nestled—like a small speck inside an oyster, but one which, she knew, would never produce a pearl. Instead, the mirror reflected back the image of a gangly female with a droopy face, but decidedly pre-Raphaelite.

For a short while after Nicola's birth, she too had worn only clinging clothes—similar to those Cynthia wore, though, of course, not cut from those unbelievable American materials. Violante had accompanied her to Florence as soon as she had left the hospital and, together, they had chosen some lovely fabrics. She could still remember her bottle-green princesse: she could squeeze the entire dress in her fist. Naturally, the colors were sober—after all, Lavinia had recently lost her husband and had just given birth to a posthumous child—and the styles were simple, but so close-fitting she could hardly breathe.

Violante had been intelligent enough to refrain from objecting in the name of good taste: she had understood. Lavinia's deformed belly had disappeared; her bosom—it had been decided that she would not nurse her baby—had recovered its original dimension. "Tummy gone, tummy gone," as the character in a commercial sang happily upon waking up from a nightmare: Lavinia knew exactly how it felt. The nightmare was over; now she could forget the entire affair: everything that involved Filippo, including her horrible pregnancy.

Of course, there was a baby, but he was awfully well behaved and Violante was so eager to take care of him.

Lavinia had registered at the university, and could easily convince herself that only one short summer had elapsed between her high school graduation and her first class in Pisa— instead of those grotesque and tragic fifteen months during which she had been in turn a fiancée, a bride, a widow, and a mother.

That entire period had been erased. It was dropped, like a digamma—a letter that was once part of the Greek alphabet but had disappeared before any poet could use it. "See," the teacher used to say, "this is where the digamma was dropped and was replaced by 'rough breathing,' " a tiny mark with an unpleasant name, a negligible entity.

The fifteen months poisoned by Filippo had also been dropped, and all that was left, though rough, was merely a breath, invisible, immaterial. Her figure, outlined by her new clothes, was as slender as before. Her classmates at the university considered her one of them.

Lavinia spun around on her feet to see how the skirt swung around her legs and whether the pleats fell as they should. Was it really true that her classmates had considered her one of them? She drove to school from Lucca in her white *cinquecento* instead of taking the train; she dressed better than anyone else; she took it easy, seldom attending the lectures, and showing up for just two exams a year.

She would wait in front of the classroom door in silence, while everybody else seemed to have so much to talk about. On second thought, she realized that those had been crucial years for most students, and that, for the first time in her life, she had been at the right place at the right time rather than, as usual, arriving when the party was over; unfortunately, she had not realized it then. She had noticed that there were more people, more policemen, more posters, but she hadn't even come close to imagining that she was witnessing the passage from one era to the next. A few months earlier she had set up a boutique, she had other things on her mind. She had been shuttling back and forth between Pisa and London, buying clothes on Carnaby Street and reselling them in Italy.

Unfortunately, Biba's and Mary Quant's brilliant ideas were already known all over the world and copied everywhere: the clothes Lavinia brought back from England were identical to those one could already find in Italy, but they were more expensive and more poorly manufactured. In her first commercial venture, Lavinia had again respected the most fundamental law of her life: she had punctually arrived too late. As usual. She had started by being born late, and from that day on had always been out of phase.

As a child, in the chilly drawing room, under the mournful eyes of a maudlin Mlle. Morot, she used to leaf through her parents' photo album. The snapshots depicted elegant youths leaning against the parapets of luxury liners; her grandparents on the steps in front of their Fiesole villa; her eighteen-year-old mother in a long white skirt carrying a tennis racket, some-where on the Isle of Wight, and then again, just a few months later, during her honeymoon on Mount Lavinia, on the island of Ceylon. . . . She adored that album, it was a real fetish for her, but looking at those photos hurt her, physically: even then she could feel a pain in the center of her body, like a burning finger marking that point as her eternal barycenter, a needle pinning a butterfly down on a sheet of white cardboard, with a Latin name underneath.

How wonderful her parents' life must have been before she was born, during those twenty long years blessed by her ab-sence! What evil spell had transformed that young man in his cashmere sweater leaning against an elephant into that spent, worn old man who went to buy his chicken liver in person for fear the maid would pocket the change?

And this wasn't true only of her parents—everybody else seemed to have done great things in her absence! Milan had been quite a city before she got there! The friends she had made there kept telling her of a golden age, when everything was happening. Not to mention her men, whose past lives always seemed to have been far more exciting than the one they shared with her.

Lavinia listened to them with a smile that she hoped was enigmatic, or, at least, sufficient to mask the true expression on her face, the one she felt inside, as her tongue had felt the seven stitches which, invisible from the outside, had been applied to the inside of her cheek when as a child she had fallen down the stairs. Similarly, her true, pathetic face was turned inward, invisible to all, but exceedingly ridiculous to her, since she knew what it looked like: the face of someone who arrives at the party out of breath and full of hopes, only to find heaps of trampled confetti and crumpled streamers scattered dismally on the floor.

The sandals with the characteristic leather strap across the big toe were also Indian. The flat soles—of a color that would soon be matched by the tan of the foot—were to give the impression of someone walking barefoot, thus emphasizing the general suppleness of the gait and, hopefully, minimizing the fact that she was always one head taller than anyone else, with the exception of Aldo who, fortunately, was also quite a beanpole.

The poor dear, he was also quite nice, and intelligent. . . . Maybe she should have met him when he was a forger: adventurous, something of a crook. Looking at him now, no one would have believed he had had a shady past. She brought her face to the mirror and looked herself severely in the eye: "Why is it you don't like honest people?" she asked.

A voice coming from the French window brought a sybilline answer to her question: "The lasagna will be ready in half an hour."

Marco entered the room, welcomed by Sigmund. "Are you ready? Everybody's waiting for you."

He had stopped behind her; raising her eyes to meet his, Lavinia addressed him in the mirror: "Do you always sneak into ladies' bedrooms this way?"

She had given him an opening to answer her with a compliment: "It depends on the lady"; "Only when the lady is beautiful." Instead he said, "The window was wide open."

Imagine that! What was the matter with him? Naiveté? Laziness? Unfathomable wisdom? Who knew, Lavinia thought, whether he was really Nicola's friend.

"You haven't gone for a swim yet?"

"I went downtown with Cynthia. We have scarcely had time to get wet: the little Indian is already setting the table." He held out his hand to her. "Shall we go, madam?"

He seized the tips of her fingers and drew her toward the window. After crossing the threshold with her, he stopped and held her close to him as if, walking through the woods, he had silently wanted her to listen to the song of a bird. They stood still a while, gazing at the garden; then his hand rose above her elbow, stroking her arm, her shoulder, stopping at the nape, his fingers crawling through her hair.

"Your eyes are driving me crazy," he said, and at once, Lavinia was absolutely sure that he didn't even know what color they were. Maybe, she thought, he feels he has to pay me back for my hospitality.

His hand brushed against her throat, proceeded down to her breasts, and roamed randomly all over Lavinia's body, without purpose and without meaning. His face, now turned toward her, did not express any recognizable emotion. The entire scene seemed so irrelevant that it didn't even warrant her pulling back and removing that hand from her body, unless, that is, she wanted to make an insufferably virtuous statement. On the other hand, as she stood there letting him caress her, she felt she had to carry out her part of the agreement according to the habitual sequence of erotic events, and so, without even realizing it, she offered him her face and lips, acquiescently, seeing how she had already acquiesced to so much.

He did not kiss her. Instead, he said, "We picked up some steaks." With a somewhat feline fluidity of movement, he moved his hand barely enough to quite change the meaning of the scene. Now he was simply escorting a lady through a garden full of flowers, inviting her, with deference, to precede him past the two lemon pots that marked the beginning of the path.

Lavinia walked in her Indian sandals looking straight ahead. What an idiot, what an idiot. She was an idiot, but he was a scoundrel. Clearly his gesture had been deliberate, a dirty trick to embarrass her. He had left her there, leaning toward him, looking stupid and pathetic.

As she pulled off her dress in the little bamboo cabin by the edge of the pool—and immediately put it back on because she had lost all desire to display her cadaverous length and pallor in a bathing suit—she convinced herself that, in fact, Marco had not meant to offend her. He had acted on an impulse and, midway, the thought of the steaks had distracted him. In other words, he was a bastard, a two-bit egoist, whose indifference to everybody else verged on cruelty.

At the thought, she felt something new and exciting stirring inside—though maybe it had already started the previous evening but was now assuming a dimension that could be registered by her consciousness—something deplorable and viscous which, for lack of any other word, she had to call love. It was a newly born feeling, barely hatched: the yacht rocking on the quiet Aegean waters still occupied the center of her thoughts, but in the distance she could already glimpse other waters, other surfs: Marco and Cynthia—she white and soft, he slim and silvery—were playing in the pool. They really were, in flesh and blood, not as the creatures of her imagination. On second thought, Lavinia decided to undress and join them.

Fatima arrived carrying the lasagna just as Lavinia was diving in. Marco and Cynthia climbed out of the pool on the opposite side and started drying themselves with their white terry cloth towels. With a confident, American gesture, Cynthia pulled off her rose-petaled swimming cap and tossed her blond hair in the sun.

Fatima had left the tray on the table and was starting to place the steaks onto the grill; everybody was already sitting down—dry and combed in their multicolored bathrobes ("Come on, Lavinia, you're the last one as usual")—everybody except for Aldo, who waited for her and pulled out a chair so that she, hair dripping all over her lasagna, could sit down too.

17

ONE SINGLE NOTE, relentlessly whirred by the cicadas, fills the valley; the scents of the country have all surrendered to the overwhelming fragrance of cut grass; and its colors, radiating as far as the eye can see in that large circle of which the Arnolfina is the center, have all been blurred and unified by the opaque yellow characteristic of the summer sun around three in the afternoon.

I am posted at my tower window, watching the Santini park, waiting for something to happen, for the show to begin.

Of course, I am way ahead of time—what could possibly happen at this blazing hour? But I am in no hurry. The sun and the white wine drunk by the swimming pool have dilated my mental processes, which now unfold in slow motion, as if underwater, lazily spiraling along a constantly changing plane.

From up here—shuttling back and forth from one window to the next—I command an optimal view of the three houses, each of which offers me a privileged insight into its most vital center: the drawing room and, immediately below it at the base of the steps, the flower beds and borders of Villa Grande; the second-floor gallery with the three French windows—corresponding to the three main bedrooms, Cynthia's, the unborn child's, and Leopoldo's—of Villa Piccola. It is obvious that if anything significant is, or is not, to happen in those two houses, it will happen in those settings and nowhere else: anything concerning Violante, the queen, will take place in the throne room, whereas anything affecting a marriage on the rocks—whatever the reasons for its demise—will inevitably occur in the no-man's-land between the two beds.

As for the Limonaia, my princess's home, with its three huge arched windows, it offers itself to my eyes like a glass cage through whose walls I can follow not only all the gestures that Lavinia will enact as a character in my play, but also those that have nothing to do with the supreme performance, but are nonetheless meaningful to me, who loved her when she was still a gangly child in knee socks and pleated skirt, and still love her now that I am old and she is no longer young—as each new meeting fills me with adolescent languor and the yearning to offer her flowers, send her love notes with pierced hearts, and cover the walls of the city with the same peremptory words: Aldo loves Lavinia.

This morning, I watched her walk toward the swimming pool with those dragging, lazy movements of hers, as if, at every step, her hands and feet were loath to change their position, regretful of what they were leaving behind and fearful of what they were going toward, wavering between doing and not doing, deciding and postponing. The country sun had already faintly colored her cheeks; the soft halo of her hair and the rosy pattern of her light cotton dress swelled and swung in rhythm with her supple step. She seemed to be wearing an anadem of flowers, and to have been prepared by priestly hands for a cruel ceremony: Iphigenia led to her sacrifice before the departure of the Greek ships.

She was a conscious victim, indeed, quite enthusiastic, as her face bore the marks of a joyous anticipation, whose motive I immediately guessed while cursing my stupidity for having spent last night dallying in vague fears rather than getting straight to the heart of the matter.

It was the boy, of course. I had been quite lacking in the most basic mental acumen not to realize that he was exactly the right type.

Like a Leporello who has changed his master, for years I have been updating my poor Donna Elvira's love records: not out of pleasure, but because she insists on ruthlessly baring her heart to me. As a result, I know all the most essential characteristics of all the scoundrels who have mistreated her for twenty years, from the very first to the very last, starting with Filippo and ending with Sandro, the sociologist.

Of course, superficially they would seem quite different from Marco. First of all they are all grown men, and—as if stamped out by the same cookie cutter—all cultivated, elegant, somewhat snobbish, seductive, and influential. Interesting men, full of charm, as Lavinia describes them in the course of her outpourings.

She also adds, however, that with such men—top-quality, the cream of the human race—there is always a catch: they are unfaithful, sadistic, mendacious. The way she says this, one could think it tickles her pink. She manages to turn her own humiliation into some source of pride—at least when she talks to me. I sincerely, if not nobly, hope that when she is alone she doesn't find it quite as exalting. In any case, the version I hear would seem to suggest that her predilection for those wretches is a feather in her cap. She wants her men to be special; she is selective, aristocratic. She likes to aim high, and every time, she faces the consequences with a small, courageous smile.

I could strangle her when she starts singing this tune. It is as if, with utter cruelty, she wanted to build herself up at my expense. Since, needless to say, the immediate corollary to her theory is that a good man—which I have been almost by definition for over twenty years, and for which I have often been praised like an old dog, with a pat on the head and a light rub behind the ears—is inevitably devoid of charm.

And I cannot defend myself. How could I—poor, dear, loyal Aldo, always at one's disposal—say that I am also a handsome man? Cultivated, intelligent, known the world over as an art expert? A friend to artists and men of letters? The owner of a house full of treasures? Long-limbed, broad-shouldered, straight-backed, and with healthy teeth? How could I say all this without appearing ridiculous, even though it is all true?

What I can do—and never fail to—is to suggest to her that she does not love certain men in spite of the fact that they are scoundrels, but precisely because they are. Not only is this so obvious that her shrink should have told her about it long ago, but it also provides my wounded ego with an acceptable explanation for the fact that this woman doesn't seem to want to love me, as she reasonably should.

This morning, as I watched her gaze longingly at Marco, who ignored her, my theory about her vocation was quite confirmed.

That punk in tennis shoes, that pipsqueak out of nowhere, has exactly what it takes to inflame Lavinia's heart: shallow, unperturbed eyes, the inscrutable face of a second-rate idol, hair so soft and bright as to reflect the blue of the sky, sensuous lips, an air of danger—the perfect alien. Besides, he is twenty-two, wanders through the world with a knapsack on his back, and is the first to acknowledge he bears no kinship with any of us. And I am sure there are other reasons that I can't even begin to guess because of the abyss that my fifty-five years and my handmade shoes have put between us.

He has crept into our world like a virus, wagging its tail, tickling this and that organ. Now something has to happen in the organism that has so regardlessly hosted him. I'll stay posted at my window ready to detect the first symptoms of illness.

Indeed, something is happening, but not where I expected.

Leopoldo has opened his bedroom window and has stepped onto the gallery. He looks around. A few tentacles of the vines climbing around the columns have spread out toward the windows and are now creeping through the shutters of the middle room. I feel I can hear Leopoldo's thoughts as clearly as I can see his gestures. A bedroom that's been locked up for years. No children, no guests. No reason, however, to let its casements go to seed. He tears off a few stems with his hands and then goes down to the ground floor to fetch the tools necessary to finish the job.

The shutters are closed from the inside. As soon as Leopoldo has freed them from the creeper, he walks into his bedroom and, via the landing, into the middle room to thrust them wide open. From where I stand, I can see the light pour in and fill every corner. I imagine I can smell the scent—a light aroma of dried flowers—that the afternoon warmth stirs and reawakens. Leopoldo steps out onto the gallery and sits down in one of the wicker chairs.

But he is restless. After a short while he gets up, walks downstairs, comes outside. He is wearing only a pair of white trousers. Bare-chested, he directs his steps toward the Limonaia.

I may well be biased, since I am waiting for something meaningful to happen, but the way he leaves his house at this hour, in this heat, looks somewhat furtive: as if he were seeking secrecy and solitude—more than if he had snuck out in the middle of the night.

For a while, he proceeds at a fast clip, until the gravel path ends and the stone patio of the Limonaia begins.

At this point, his pace changes, and his entire mien becomes awkward and clumsy, as often happens when someone wants his actions to suggest an intention other than the one that prompted them. With phony nonchalance, he plucks a dry flower from a pot of geraniums; stops and shifts his weight from one foot to the other; takes a few steps on the patio as if he were just out for a stroll; then he turns his back to the Limonaia, picks up a rock from the ground, and throws it into the cherry laurel bushes.

Sigmund immediately shoots out of one of the windows and dives into the shrubs; after some rustling about, he reemerges, panting, with the rock in his mouth. He deposits it delicately at Leopoldo's feet, then, with a smile so wide I can see it from up here, sits still and waits.

Leopoldo tells him something in a low voice—I can barely hear a murmur—and takes a few steps toward the Limonaia. The dog picks up the rock with his teeth, places it a few inches away from the blue espadrilles, and lets out a low, discreet, but nonetheless audible yelp—sort of like a civilized little honk to remind the driver of the car ahead that the light has just turned green. Leopoldo pays him no attention and takes two more steps toward the house.

Sigmund picks up the rock again and follows him when suddenly Marco, barefoot and naked, with tousled hair and a shocking-pink towel wrapped around his loins, steps out of his room.

Crazed with joy, the dog starts running back and forth between Leopoldo's and Marco's feet, wagging not just his tail but his entire rear, arching it like a shrimp. As I watch the scene, I realize that I can only observe it, without trying to understand it; at the moment, the dog's thoughts are the only ones I can interpret. Leopoldo feels like playing, Sigmund thinks, and this is a rare opportunity. He threw the rock even though, as usual, he now refuses to pick it up and throw it again. Generally, he behaves like everybody else with the exception of Nicky. He doesn't want to hear about playing with me: "Stop it," he says. "Sigmund, enough"—everybody's favorite expression. But today it's different; even Marco has come out to have fun with us. We will all play together, a real party.

He picks up the rock and, at a gallop, brings it to the boy's feet.

I am too far away to understand Marco's words, but I am sure they are addressed to the dog and not to the man who is only standing a few feet away. He bends to pick up the rock and throws it along the path, past Leopoldo; while Sigmund takes off in pursuit, he starts walking in the same direction.

When the two men are side by side, they pause for a while and then proceed together toward the swimming pool; the older of the two confidently trampling the gravel of the path with his espadrilles, the younger one walking barefoot on the grassy edge, his hips gently swaying. Sigmund keeps running back and forth to fetch the rock they take turns throwing. Leopoldo and Marco don't seem to be exchanging a single word; now and then one of them says something to the dog.

At the pool, Leopoldo sits on the edge; Marco discards his towel, stands stark naked on the edge to test the water with his foot, and then dives in. After a few strokes, he hoists himself up on the silvery air mattress that's gently rocking with the rippled surface.

"You know, I thought Nicola was a real orphan. I mean on both parents' side," he says. Marco's voice reaches me crystal clear, carried by the sheet of water. I can't make out Leopoldo's answer but I can easily imagine it: Filippo's horrid behavior, his fall from the viaduct (Leopoldo stands up and starts walking up and down along the edge of the pool), the birth of the child, Lavinia—herself very young—who had ample reason to forget and start anew, and Violante, who had been Nicola's real mother. At the end of the speech, Leopoldo turns to gesture in the direction of the villa, and a few words manage to reach my ears. "On the other hand, Nicola has always been mature for his age. Even when he was a child, with his father dead and his mother gone most of the time, he did not seem to miss his parents. At least, on the surface. Who knows how he really felt inside, the poor child."

"I am a child too, delicate and with a fair complexion. I don't want to get burnt," Marco declares. Even from this distance, I can detect the coquetry in the tone of his voice. I can imagine

114

his lips, halfway between a childish pout and an ironic smile. With the palms of his hands, he paddles to the edge of the pool. Leopoldo picks a jar from the small table with all the suntan lotions, kneels on the ground and starts spreading the cream on the boy's body. Now they are close to each other. They speak in a low voice and I can no longer hear them.

Sigmund has crawled into the shade of an easy chair and is now asleep.

18

"WE COULD TRY to lift it up a bit around the temples,"
Lavinia said. Margherita, standing behind her chair, turned off
the hair dryer and unrolled the blond strand from the cylindrical brush.

"It would only last ten minutes," she answered. She placed
hair dryer and brush on the dressing table; with expert fingers,
she tousled Lavinia's hair. She pulled it up, as if to let it fill with
air, then, opening her hand, let it fall back in place. "See. We
have worked on it for half an hour, and it's already going every
which way. The only thing to do is to respect its natural inclination. The color is fine, distinctive," she said, sweetening the pill.
"And it is as soft as a child's."

Lavinia looked at herself in the mirror with dislike. Something soft and transparent (but what color was it? It had no
color!) framed her face, hanging limply, like torn spiderwebs in
chilly old attics. Respect the natural inclination—her hair's and
everything else's. Keep in mind the way things and people are:
take them or leave them. And when you take them, do not
expect the impossible—Filippo's love, Sandro's fidelity, a nice
curl in your hair—but only the best possible result. She picked

up the brush from the top of the dressing table and rearranged a strand on her forehead. Knowing what was right was no help at all.

"Thank you, Margherita," she said. "You couldn't have done a better job."

The best possible result meant that her hair was clean and fluffy; that, twenty-three years earlier, Filippo had married her and rescued her from poverty; that, today, Sandro loved her his way, that is, not at all, or almost. And what about Marco? What could she reasonably expect from him?

"If you don't need anything else, I'll go downtown with Nives," Margherita said.

Why should she expect anything from Marco? He was as innocent as an animal—a white, slightly bloodthirsty ermine, with much grace, immaculate paws, and not a doubt clouding its mind.

"Of course," she said. "You may go."

She was going to be left alone with him, provided Aldo did not drop in on them.

A touch of rouge on her cheekbones? She smoothed it on with her fingertips. Once, in London, she had walked into a beauty salon and had given the manager carte blanche. "Do what you want. See what's wrong and fix it." She had told her how much she could spend, a considerable sum. She had come to buy clothes in Carnaby Street, and midway through her purchases had reached the conclusion that the boutique was a stupid mistake. It brought her very little profit, and no longer amused her. "You must love yourself," her therapist kept telling her; it was the perfect opportunity. Her eyes had fallen onto that convincing pink-and-gold sign. She had the money. She was alone in a foreign country. All she wanted was not to have to decide anything. They had to make her over as they saw fit, without consulting her, otherwise it would all be for nothing. Someone had to give birth to her again, so that she could really emerge a different woman.

The result was disastrous. Her plucked eyebrows made her look like a rabbit, her hair color, "revamped" according to the aesthetic standards of the hairdresser, had turned into a metallic beige that made one think of car paint, while her eyes, greatly enlarged by the makeup, looked meekly bovine.

She got up from her chair, undid her belt, pulled off her bathrobe, and threw it onto the bed. Margherita was leaving through the living-room door; Lavinia saw her cross the patio, pass between two geranium pots and proceed on to the path, her straw bag strapped across her shoulder.

Lavinia slipped into a jade-colored, light cotton kimono, and opened the door that led to the hallway.

"Marco," she called.

He answered after a few seconds. "I'm here." The voice came from the living room. He was lying on the couch, a glass of orangeade nearby on the rug. He was all dressed in white: pants, espadrilles, T-shirt.

"You really look like an ermine," Lavinia said, as she sat on the low table in front of him.

"Your mother-in-law can't stomach me," Marco suddenly exclaimed. "And neither can Aldo. Those two really hate me."

"That's not true. It's all in your mind. You're wrong."

"No, I'm not wrong. I'd like to know what I have done to them." His eyes filled with tears. He turned onto his belly and sunk his face in the cushions: "I hate to be hated. I'm leaving."

"You don't know what you are saying. . . . Make some room for me." Lavinia sat on the edge of the sofa and started caressing the boy's hair. Marco remained motionless for a while, then he moved an arm slightly, and suddenly his hand was under the jade-colored kimono and between Lavinia's thighs.

Once again, as in the morning by the window, she found herself thrown off balance by the wrong gesture, which, however, having been made, could no longer be taken back and had to be brought to a conclusion as quickly and as painlessly as possible. The duet was so ridiculous as to appear obscene, Lavinia thought: her hand, tenderly and maternally caressing Marco's hair, his brisk fingers finding their way without wasting any time on foreplay. The dissonance was horrible and, once again, humiliating for her. Now she had to come to terms with the situation—as usual, clumsily and a touch too late—and get in tune with the music.

She stopped caressing Marco's hair and lay down on the couch next to him, letting the kimono slide open to reveal the pale length of her body. Just as she saw her legs stretch out and the jade-colored corner of her kimono dip into his glass of orangeade, she had the mathematical certainty that he might once more leave her in the lurch, and suddenly sit up and start chatting about this and that while she lay there, indecently spread out. As if, with Marco, she had already shared a past fraught with the disappointments and deceptions of promises made and seldom kept—just another absentminded trapeze artist who forgets to extend his arms at the right moment and lets his trusting partner fall and crash right in the middle of the ring.

Instead, this time he surprised her precisely by not surprising her: what had been begun was concluded, and his elfin body mounted Lavinia's and abandoned itself to her embrace. And she felt as if she had suddenly dilated and deepened, as if she had turned into a nest to welcome and protect something infinitely small and precious.

But later, when the little ermine snuck out of its nest and curled up in the corner of the sofa, Lavinia closed the front of her jade-colored robe and realized that there were still two hours to dinner and that she had nothing to tell that stranger, and not a clue as to how else to entertain him and fill the abyss between them.

With Sandro—whether in her apartment under the eiderdown, or at his place on the posturepedic mattress with its stainless-steel frame and black linen sheets, leaning against the pillows with their knees up and a glass of tomato juice in their hands—she fully enjoyed that magic moment of truce. For half an hour, and from both of them, words would spontaneously pour out without her having to wrest them from him or him having to yield them to her. It was a pleasant, friendly sort of chat, touching on common interests and tinged with irony, the fond intimacy of exchanging advice—don't miss that movie, read that book, the homeopathic doctor, the upholsterer, the plumber—punctuated by a "you" that suddenly echoed with an unusual brotherly timbre, the pleasure of being the same age and having a large base of common allusions on which to anchor the stories of one's personal experience.

Marco was no help to her. Silence did not bother him. Quite the contrary, one might wonder whether that nacreous look did not hide the deliberate intention of increasing his interlocutors' discomfort so as to get the better of them—he could walk without fear through the poisonous vapors that threatened her, as if he were protected by some secret antidote. She tightened the belt around her waist and, like a turtle, coiled back upon the center of her body, where the usual pain had again started to flare up. My God, she silently groaned. My God, my God. She needed someone to take care of her, comb her, pet her, cherish her, and if necessary even chide and punish her. Provided she was not abandoned in a corner, forsaken, forgotten, and forced to fend for herself. Why in the world hadn't she gone to Villa Grande as usual? It was so comforting to be in a house where everything ran like clockwork and nothing depended on her.

As comforting as men with initiative, men who came to take her out with theater tickets already in their pocket, reservations at the restaurant, and everything already clearly mapped out for the rest of the evening—political opinions, topics of conversation—including, at the end, the words and gestures necessary to bring the encounter to the right level of intimacy. Men who allowed her to listen to them with that famous enigmatic smile of hers, and just nod and drop a word here and there to show them what an attentive and intelligent listener she was, and how independent she was in her judgment since, though she always eschewed polemics, that little smile of hers made it impossible for anyone to figure out whether she agreed with what they had said or not.

She cast a powerless, forlorn glance around the room: the furniture, the rugs, the hallway beyond the door. Violante's reach stretched far, even as far as the Limonaia, where a benevolent presence could be felt in just about everything, from the soap in the bathroom and the flowers on the console table to the soft drinks in the fridge; but why, why hadn't she sought shelter, as usual, at the heart of that protective sphere?

And, above all, why had she let such a puny creature climb on top of her, that tiny little thing that now looked to her like one of those diminutive males nature occasionally enjoys producing—an impudent little toad clinging with anthropomorphous hands to the huge body of its gigantic female?

He had withdrawn into a corner of the sofa; crouched on his heels, like a fakir, he looked as if he were waiting for something to happen.

Lavinia picked up the phone and dialed 161. Six-forty. "Good Lord, I didn't know it was so late," she lied. "I must get ready for dinner."

She ran away to take refuge—alone, thank heavens—in her bedroom. Rid of Marco's presence, she could wallow in the memory of his beauty, relive, as she lay on the bed, the grace of his movements, the divine lightness of his body, the scent of his hair. She saw him abandoned in her arms, his eyes closed, while she whispered sweet nothings in his ear. Everything cohered: dream bodies have no elbows, and imaginary lovers are not always about to say the wrong thing.

Sandro and Rosylips floated on the Aegean sea, smeared with antiwrinkle lotions—heavy, awkward, and, for the time being, harmless. They spoke of expensive things, intellectual fads, exclusive places. Their drawling voices nonchalantly skimmed through the Great Issues, and fiercely churned up inanities according to the ancient model of chic humor. They got along fine.

Knew the same people. Despised the same columnist. Detested the same psychologist. Adored the same comic-strip writer. In Paris, they checked in at the same hotel. At the bottom of their respective hearts, they were absolutely convinced that there were no more than three hundred people in the world, since the tracks of their six hundred feet formed a web into which one couldn't help bumping at every step.

Lavinia smiled at the ceiling. She felt oddly indulgent toward Sandro, Rosylips, and even toward herself. Because, after all, she had also been like them, indeed, still was. She was one of the three hundred people, with their silly social games complacently delighting in all sort of trifles. And if someone made her feel like an outsider, she felt stupidly hurt for having no longer been allowed to feel stupidly complacent. She was an idiot, through and through, but it was not her fault. It was never anybody's fault, and hers least of all. She had never looked for trouble; it just happened that she had often found it, ready-made and handy. She was born in the middle of it, whether she liked it or not.

However, she now had her little ermine. Finally she had something so small she could hold it in her hand, something precious and delicate that she could never confuse with anything else she knew: it was a sliver from another world, compared to which any object belonging to this one looked coarse, opaque, heavy.

Of course, the only place where she and Marco could meet was in a dream: to be friends with him would be ridiculous, to confide in him obscene, to be tender with him preposterous; even making love with him, at least when it came to its more concrete expression, was out of balance, at least judging from the sort of disturbance that the mere thought of it stirred up in her.

She had caught an ermine: a perfect creature, wrapped, by birthright, in a royal cloak. Or was it in fact the ermine that had caught her and was leisurely preparing to tear her apart with its sharp little teeth? It was one or the other, or both at the same time. What difference could it make? She curled up around her nervous gastritis like a hen warming up its favorite chick, and fell blissfully asleep.

19

VIOLANTE STARED AT HER DIAGRAM for a long time. The lines pointed in a strange direction, and seemed to suggest an answer that she could not understand, and for which she had not formulated any question. This was the trouble with pulling things out of one's head to put them down in black and white. Out there, out of reach of whoever had thought them up, they were what they were, and had their own laws and their own destiny. No one could stop them.

The diagram had grown beyond her expectations—she had added one sheet of paper, then another—and the desk in her study was no longer large enough for it.

She had moved everything to the basement, on the old Ping-Pong table that had once been Filippo's, then Leopoldo's, then Nicola's, and was now kept down there, waiting for other grandchildren to decide to be born.

The room was enormous and silent. Nobody knew she was there. What if she suddenly became ill? She was old, very old. The certainty of death fell within an increasingly smaller span of time. By now, she could no longer die in her infancy, or in her childhood, adolescence, adulthood, or advanced maturity. She had hardly any choice left as to the time of her death; but she could still choose the place. She would have liked to die in her bed, or in the garden. Not in that cold, enormous room.

Here or there, in any case she did not have much time left. She had already buried a son—the most unnatural thing, and he her beloved son, and she not there when it happened . . . and yet she had survived. A real miracle.

The diagram had not grown by itself, of course. The fact is that when she started working on one end, she forgot the other, remote extremity, so that when she turned around the table she could no longer recognize the lines she had herself drawn.

She pulled out one more sheet of paper and tacked it onto the table.

On the top left corner she wrote: Aldo.

I saw her leave her house but until the last minute did not realize that she was coming to see me. I lost sight of her the moment she crossed the gate and was swallowed by the trees; she reappeared along the path leading to the Arnolfina, and judging from the way she tackled the slope I assumed this was not going to be just another visit.

I rushed downstairs and opened the door at the very second Violante was reaching for the small bronze bell.

Sigmund must have met her on the way. He has accompanied her here and is now confidently making himself at home. We follow him into the blue-green coolness of the living room.

It is a large, square room built on two levels. The outer level is a sort of landing which entirely surrounds the central part of the room, some thirty inches below it. This is how I found it when I bought it, maybe for reasons connected to its original function as an olive press, and I have not changed it. In fact, I have emphasized its Roman swimming pool aspect by decorating it entirely in aquatic colors. The few pieces of furniture in it—few but, I must add, of great value—seem to float; all along the walls, the paintings—my small private collection—glow and vibrate with liquid reflections.

Violante sits down in a turquoise armchair. "Did you know that last week Filippo's famous friend died?" she asks.

I knew, I read her obituary in the papers. I tell her as much.

"Well, it has had the strangest effect on me. I haven't been able to get it out of my mind. Not her, of course. I didn't even know her. Not even Filippo: not more than usually, I mean. I always think of him, night and day. What I mean is that I have been thinking of her death. I've been struck by the fact that the woman who was my son's mistress has now died—and not in an accident, but worn out by the years. Do you understand? It is as if the generation after mine had already started to die out. How can I be still around?"

"But you know why: Mafalda was much older than Filippo. Maybe she was even older than you . . . and probably sick. . . . What preposterous ideas!"

"Come, come. Don't pretend you don't understand. All I mean is that now and then things happen that remind us of the inexorable flow of time. When I heard about Mafalda's death, I felt old, that's all."

"Hard to believe, seeing you dig in your garden."

She starts laughing like a bird flapping its wings. "I know, I know. I'm doing fine. Nevertheless, I feel the need to put my affairs in order, just as if a doctor had pronounced a fatal sentence on me. I've got to do it: I have ruled like a czarina, and now they are all good-for-nothing."

"Are you thinking of the paper mill?" I venture.

"Good heavens, no! For three centuries the men of the family have taken care of it without my help . . . I have never had anything to do with it. Leopoldo is excellent, and in a few years Nicola will join him. No, I am not worried about the paper mill. I worry about what's up here." She gestures toward the window, beyond which lies the garden with the three houses and the farmland. "Walls, furniture, plants, sons, daughters-in-law, grandchildren, servants, farmhands, peasants . . . what keeps it all together. Our life."

"A kingdom," I say, with a voice full of admiration.

She looks at me askance, as if to make sure I am not teasing her. "A small one," she admits. "But it won't hold together if someone doesn't look after it once I am gone. There are things which, taken one by one, may seem mere trifles, but there are so many, so many . . . someone must go to the trouble of holding them all together. Not just keeping up with what has to be done. That too, of course, but mostly . . . I don't know how to put it. A general commitment."

"The crown," I say. "I would think a head must satisfy some requirements to be able to support a crown."

"Yes," she admits. "And the first one is to not move too abruptly. One must be unperturbable, in control. Authority is a way of walking, of speaking to the dog, of opening a door. And one can never say, 'Now I'm tired. Someone else will take care of it.' Never. To let go, even if only for a moment, is like punching a hole in a sack of corn: pretty soon there is nothing left."

"I would like to be able to tell you that I will take care of Lavinia. I'd like to, with all my heart, you know."

"I know. Loyal to the end." She smiles and strokes my hand. The armchair cushion slightly rustles under her weight. I picture her with hollow bones, covered with feathers, ready to take flight and land a little further away.

"One day," I tell her, "she'll tire of being knocked about by one scoundrel after another. Then, I'll be there, waiting for her." As I say this, my sentence appears to be utterly comic, and I blush. I assume a worldly tone and conclude, "Therefore, my queen, one of your subjects is already taken care of."

She does not want to humor me. "Did you see how they were all excited by that boy's arrival? And yet he is totally insipid. He's young, that's all. He is one of those characters who can be defined by just one adjective: young. By profession, by destiny. He won't survive his youth, he will dwindle down to two little heaps of ashes at the bottom of his tennis shoes. . . . Can you tell me what's so exciting about him?"

"I'm afraid Lavinia likes him."

"Nonsense!" Just as she's saying this, she is seized by a sudden doubt. "You think so?" But she does not wait for an answer. "You see, I've drawn a sort of diagram—I've been working on it for a week."

"Is this what you wanted to tell me about last night?"

"Yes. You are the only person who can understand me. You don't seem to lead your life carelessly. You won't be too surprised when I tell you that I like to see things clearly to be able to organize a good strategy. So, I put everything on paper."

"In a diagram?"

"Precisely." She sounds slightly petulant, as if she isn't entirely sure I am taking her seriously. "I've put everything in it, including what I don't know, like, for instance, the reason why Cynthia and Leopoldo don't get along. Lavinia says they have problems in bed. Is that possible? Personally, I don't think that what goes on in a bed is all that important." She glances at me, leaning her head on her shoulder. "This shouldn't make you think I am old-fashioned." She bats her eyelashes like an owl in the sun. "If anything I am postmodern, as Nicola says."

"It's not all that important?" I repeat.

"It depends. It may even not matter at all, believe me. One day people will realize they have given it much too much importance."

"Your diagram also includes Cynthia and Leopoldo's intimate life?"

"That is one of the unknowns. What is obvious—maybe the only obvious thing I noticed as soon as I drew the first lines—is that they need a son. In fact, all three of them do, Lavinia included. The way they have reacted to Marco's arrival has quite confirmed it. That boy's appearance has awakened something in them, some natural instinct."

"I'm afraid the instinct he has awakened in Lavinia may be natural enough but not all that maternal," I note.

Violante grabs a couple of peanuts from a Chinese bowl, pops them into her mouth, and starts pecking away at them with her front teeth while staring at me with her round eyes. "I would really like to know who has invented all these different kinds of love. Luckily, I am old enough to be allowed to speak the truth, at least among friends." She cranes her neck forward, and leans her head toward mine as if to confide a secret. "All those distinctions are phony. Love is a huge melting pot, my dear man."

She doesn't give me time to answer and goes on. "The fact that Lavinia asked to go stay at the Limonaia is in itself a sign."

"A sign? A sign of what? Besides," I continue, "Lavinia has a son, don't forget."

"She gave birth to one and I took him away from her. This is the sacred truth. It seemed the right thing to do . . . unless it was because I missed Filippo so much. I myself have never fully believed that mine was a totally altruistic gesture intended to give Lavinia a second chance. Anyway, it no longer matters. That's what happened. The fact is, now I have to give him back to his mother. I have put everything down in my diagram. Everything seemed quite simple, until yesterday: Lavinia takes her son back and, as a direct result, rises one notch on the scale of maturity, so that, when I die, she is ready to take care of everybody. Two birds with one stone, if not three or four. Order reigns, Lavinia experiences the joys of maternity, Nicola finds a young mother who will be close to him for several more years, and as for you, my dear friend, what a great opportunity. . . . Because I am sure that Lavinia would lose her perverse need to be abused. A son—even a good son like Nicola—provides a mother with all the suffering the staunchest masochist might want, believe me. She could at last appreciate the simpler joys of a happy, requited love."

"And you have drawn a diagram of all these future events?"

"Yes, my dear. And don't look at me as if I were crazy. Everybody thinks of tomorrow, of all the things they must do to carry out certain plans, and they rely on whatever data they have at their disposal. I do the same thing in a more methodical way. What's wrong with using a pencil and a sheet of paper? Do you think people who go to a palm reader are saner?"

I am so glad I figure in her projection of Lavinia's life that I wouldn't dream of criticizing her method. Instead, I ask her, "Why did everything seem so simple until yesterday?"

"I don't know. Some new things have cropped up that I can't understand. The central knot seems to have moved. . . ."

"The central knot being, if I have understood you correctly, the necessity to provoke the maturation—albeit a belated one—of Lavinia's personality. Right?"

"Yes, yes. Or rather, that's just one of the knots, the one that concerns me most. That woman must stop thinking exclusively of herself, and of the effect she has on others. Also because," she adds with a more confidential tone of voice, "one does get older, and I can assure you that after seventy to think only of oneself is not that pleasant."

I tell her that I believe her, but I stifle my deepest hope: that Lavinia will mature, like a late-bloomer, the day she notices me. That day, she will be mine: intact, the way I saw her for the first time, the sullen lip, the naked knee above the blue knee sock. In one eternal present, I will possess all the overlapping images of her I have accumulated during the thirty years I have loved her: the slender stalk gradually blooming and gradually mutating into an Oriental slave weighed down by chains; the haughty, melancholy frailty; the bright buoyancy of the hair, and the pensive eyes beneath the white veil (as she knelt by another man in the Romanesque nave); the furtive flash of a pale thigh in an eight-millimeter movie—filmed by me—of

Nicola, aged two, wrestling with his mother on the lawn in front of Villa Grande; in furs and carrying her beauty case as she boards a plane for London; in a wisteria-colored robe, with large pleated sleeves, basking in the opalescent light of her Milan apartment; in a business suit during her brief career at Olivetti.

She has never cared about anyone but herself, Violante says. In other words, she has never loved anybody: does this mean that she will only love me? That they will only love me? That entire harem of images piled up over the years to form my divine woman-in-her-forties will belong to me, exclusively?

"It seems she is always crazy about something, always pursuing some new idea. In fact, she doesn't give a damn," Violante continues. "Every time she radically redecorates her apartment . . . Remember when she developed a sudden passion for the Orient, a couple of years ago? She changed everything according to her new passion, and spent loads of money on it, but do you really think that—when the painters were gone and she squatted on her tatami mats, in the middle of all that bamboo and rice paper—do you really think she tasted even a single second of sincere aesthetic pleasure, an instant of true joy—as we could have, you with your paintings and I with my flowers? Do you really think she did?" She emits a scornful giggle and shakes her feathers. "The only thing she cared about was that crazy idea that all that stuff would somehow transform her into an ivory doll adored by the rascal on duty. That's all: she didn't care about anything else." She looks at me askance, with just one eye. "Did you go to Milan during that period?"

"Yes," I answer.

"Fortunately it didn't last. It didn't take her long to realize that she was only a barefoot beanpole sitting on the floor in a very uncomfortable apartment."

I remember. She had walked toward me with little steps, had bent her neck in a little bow, and had looked at me with a small, impenetrable smile. . . . Oh, Lavinia, Lavinia!

This afternoon never ends. The sun sits still, three quarters of the way through his journey, waiting for Violante to organize her own death. What can she offer to each of her three old children so that they will grow according to nature and, one day, die, as decently as she means to? And her offer, how can she let it lie around as if it were nothing, hoping that they will find it and pick it up on their own? But, above all, *what* can she offer them?

If it is true that they need a child to become adults, what could serve as a magical love and fertility potion for Leopoldo and Cynthia? And how to provoke that spark of recognition between Lavinia and Nicola that would allow them to readopt each other as mother and son?

She speaks of possible interventions in the warp of personal histories whose intersection she seems to occupy, and I imagine her crouching among her dahlias, busy pulling up weeds. She is so much at the center of the picture that her control over it seems unquestionable and destined to last far beyond the limits of her mortal existence.

I would really like to know how it feels to occupy such a perfectly central place in one's own world; I wonder about it with a pang of nostalgia for the man I could have been if, forty years ago, I had not torn my heart out of my body to hurl it away, as far as possible, while, from my hiding place, I watched it bounce on the floors of the stage, among the characters I had chosen as the protagonists of my life.

To be there or not to be there: it would have made a great deal of difference. What would have become of me—given my mother's ambition, my tenacity, and all the rest—had I not conceived that fatal passion, that night, behind the shutter?

I can imagine a wealthy pharmacist, with his own little villa on what once was millionaires' row—wife, two children, a false antique bed covered with a handwoven, spun-silk bedspread, a VCR, a Rotary Club card, a passion for organized tours (China, Seychelles, Las Vegas, the Arctic Circle) and slides, a vicuna overcoat: the point of intersection between what could have been and what has come true. That mythical piece of clothing serves me as a metaphorical bridge between the two existences. Without regrets, I leave the pharmacist in his little world and turn toward the image of myself as I really am, as I have chosen to be, solitary and eccentric on top of a tower, behind binoculars.

20

IF I ONLY KNEW WHAT'S on his mind, Lavinia thought. There was no exception: all men shared the same inhuman habit of leaving things hanging. Was it so unreasonable to expect that a carnal encounter be granted if only the slightest meaning by a few words? She felt herself blush: the warm wave that was invading her flowed down her arms all the way to her hands, changing their color. Obviously, she couldn't ask for anything. She would rather cut out her tongue.

This was the problem: what one needed the most was, generally, precisely what one should never ask for. Never ask for an explanation, never give one, never write letters, never demand anything, never complain. Nobody knew those rules better than she; just as nobody transgressed them with as much stupid obstinacy. To know certain things did not help. One also had to discover the right formula to act according to common sense: it would be a new Columbus's egg, and it would radically change her life.

She got up and, daydreaming, started preparing for dinner. It was sure to be the simplest trick, a brilliant little gadget, like a zipper. She could get rich selling the patent: she would rid the world of all its heartaches. Because it was just a habit, an addiction, like smoking: dangerous for the person addicted, and annoying to others. She would be able to love Aldo; but then again—and suddenly she felt as if she were hanging in midair, as if the ground had caved in right under her feet—he would be able to stop loving her. Could such an unnatural thing happen? Could he stop loving her or, even worse, fall in love with someone else? She pictured him sitting at the head of the table in the Arnolfina dining room, surrounded by friends, and, sitting directly opposite him at the other end of the table, an attractive woman, his wife. She might even be young, younger than herself. After all, he was a handsome man, and famous at that, a real authority in his field. . . . The attractive young woman kept her eyes fixed on the other end of the table, gleaming with the certainty of a secret understanding. Hey you, down there, beyond all those people, do you remember? Do you know what's on my mind? And he would answer with a similar look. It was an intolerable thought. She shooed it away and concentrated on her appearance.

She opened her wardrobe and pulled out one dress after another. Her mind turned back to Marco. The question was: what to do with that twenty-year gap? When a boy is attracted by an older woman, what seduces him most, the fact that she is older or the fact that she looks younger? What would be the point of showing up in a ponytail, jeans, a pink T-shirt, and espadrilles if in fact he liked the idea of being involved with a lady?

Marco knocked on the door. He was squeaky clean and had a sweater tied around his neck. He looked like a young boy on his first date.

"I'm going ahead, I have to stop at Cynthia's," he said.

"Fine, go ahead."

Through the window, Lavinia watched him walk away. She couldn't dress like a young girl, it would be grotesque.

Until a minute ago she had been trying to decide what was the best thing to wear; now, having piled up all her dresses on the bed, she was looking around disconsolately trying to figure out which one was the least bad. Maybe a St. Laurent and high heels. But in high heels she was over six feet tall, a real camel.

21

I HAVE COME BY to pick her up at eight-thirty. I wait for her to be ready and escort her to Villa Grande. The jets of the automatic sprinklers fill the air with a slight buzz, the nightingales sing, the flowers exude their fragrances, the first star twinkles in the still-light sky: everything in Violante's garden is behaving as well as could be wished. As we cross the jasmine bower, I slow down, and take Lavinia's hand between mine.

"Wait a second," I sigh. "Let me look at you. You are so beautiful I can't find the right words to tell you."

"Really? You think so?" she answers nervously, patting the hair on her forehead. "If I could only tame this hair." Then she adds, "I wish I were dead." She holds her words back for a minute, and then lets them all pour out on top of me: Marco's hand on her breast as they were walking toward the swimming pool, their lovemaking on the couch, their silence—unbearable to her, while to him . . . "Have you noticed it? He looks so indifferent, so irresponsible: the entire burden falls on us. To speak or not to speak, to take an initiative or not to take it. As if we had conjured him up from nothing, as if he were a dream of ours, a child of our fancy, and it were up to us to set him in motion. . . . Are they all like that at his age? Do you think Nicola is like him?"

"Nicola . . . ," I begin. I would like to keep the conversation on the subject of her son, to keep it away from what I suspected and now know, and will have to hear from her lips down to the last word. But she does not allow it. She interrupts me and goes on. "He doesn't even try to understand or to be understood, he moves among us in a condition of total incommunicability, and doesn't seem to be a bit bothered by it."

"To tell you the truth, it doesn't bother me either. He has come, he will go, we'll never see him again: who cares whether we have had a human relationship? I don't, and neither does he."

A few minutes have been enough to demolish the entire scene. I hate the nightingales, the sprinklers, the flowers, the stars. I only wish I could go back to my tower and didn't have to see anyone except through my binoculars.

Fortunately Violante seems to want to get through the evening as quickly as possible.

"We are all tired," she says when she sees us approach the loggia of Villa Grande. "We'll all go to bed early."

She is lying on an easy chair, smoking a cigarette. Cynthia and Leopoldo are sitting next to each other on the bamboo couch, with Marco curled up on an emerald cushion at their feet. The boy's head is leaning against Cynthia's knees and her fingers play with his hair. Her diamond ring and polished nails sparkle at every movement. Leopoldo is saying, " . . . quite possible that tonight you will have a fever and that tomorrow you'll be peeling all over."

"Right now I am just very hot," Marco answers.

Lavinia pauses briefly under the arcade, then takes a few faltering steps toward the group of chairs. She looks around anxiously, as if to choose to sit in one place rather than another were a vital question that left absolutely no margin for error. I realize how much she wishes she were the sort of woman she

is not: casual, self-confident, capable of making the right movements to achieve the desired ends, which in this case could be
to take three long strides toward the bunch of cushions on the
corner sofa, grab one, toss it on the floor next to Marco, and
then let herself gracefully drop onto it, at the center of that odd
little family, throwing it off balance and reclaiming what was
hers.

Instead, she comes back to me, grabs my arm, and, peremp-
torily rubbing her breast against my elbow, tows me along
toward a small sofa with two seats. For the entire evening—
which fortunately lasts only a short while—while Marco lets
Cynthia and Leopoldo baby him, she flirts with me with a dark
vengeance.

She is still clinging to me as we leave to go back home.
Cynthia and Leopoldo are walking ahead of us with Marco in
the middle, all three clasping each other, partly because of the
wine they have drunk, partly because of the narrowness of the
path, and partly to support the boy, who seems to be getting
a bit feverish because of all the sun he was exposed to in the
afternoon.

At the fork with the path leading to Villa Piccola, they whisk
him away with a perfect sleight of hand. "I have an American
lotion for your shoulders," Cynthia says. "Come have a glass
of orange juice with us," Leopoldo echoes her. Then, almost in
unison, turning back toward Lavinia: "We're going to put him
to bed in the children's room," they say with laughing voices,
as if playing a very exciting game.

All three disappear in the darkness, pushing and pulling one
another, shouting and answering the nightingale's song
through the warm summer night. Then, as we walk on past the
fork leading to the swimming pool, they reappear through the
arches of the gallery—the windows all wide open, the lights all
on—unfolding sheets, billowing them out in midair, as in a
scene out of a play.

22

I SUSPECTED IT from the start and am every day surer of it: this is a special summer. Time hiccups on: now it flies, now it drags on as if to sum itself up. This afternoon Violante's strong little hand has pulled in the reins a bit so as to allow both her and me to catch up with what has been going on and look around ourselves, impartially, as if people and things were sitting around us like the knights of the Round Table: without hierarchy, without before and after, just one next to the other, offering themselves to a benign general view. Thus both of us have contemplated our respective landscapes, and pinpointed where our two horizons overlap and our programs—my dreams and Violante's strategies—could usefully join forces.

But now everything seems to move faster than usual—first the quick dinner, then the telephone ringing the very minute we stepped into the living room of the Limonaia, and Lavinia letting herself collapse on the sofa with a long moan: her son, from New York.

Lavinia has picked up the phone, and is now holding the receiver glued to her ear; and yet, Nicola's distant voice resounds through the room as if it had passed through her body and, amplified by it, had reached my ears loud and clear. He should have spent one more week in New York, he says, but he has changed his mind. He is taking advantage of a special nonstop flight to Pisa. He is calling from the airport just before boarding. In a few hours he will land at San Giusto.

Even this phone call seems a trick of time: at once absurd and yet exceedingly significant: first of all the conversation between today and tomorrow—ten past six in the evening in New York, and ten past midnight here—and secondly because Lavinia will barely have the time to take a nap before jumping in her car to go fetch her son at the Pisa airport at seven tomorrow morning.

It is as if the three of us had found ourselves at the point of intersection between past and future. As I am making a mental note of this, I suddenly realize that this is precisely the peculiarity of the hours I have lived since receiving Violante's note inviting me to dinner: we are all teetering on the edge of time, in a continuous present which my old friend could easily represent in her diagram as the very point where the two circles of the infinity symbol touch.

When Lavinia hangs up, Sigmund bursts into the living room like a shot and cheerfully leaps onto his mistress's lap. Hugging him to her breast, she stammers, "N . . . Nicky's coming home," and bursts into tears.

I hope that those tears, in unconscious submission to Violante's projects, represent a sort of liquid bridge between the anguish of the lady brutally neglected by both her old and new lovers and the feelings of the mother moved by her son's sudden return; and maybe also—in a few minor drops at the corner of the eyes—a token of gratitude, however absentminded, for the presence of two faithful creatures, one fuzzy and wriggling in her arms, and the other dressed in white linen, standing stiffly by an armchair.

23

LEOPOLDO HELPED HER make the bed, his fine dark hand smoothing down the sheet with long strokes that ran parallel to those made by her white chubby one. "You sit still," they had told Marco. "You have a temperature, and besides, three people cannot do this." They had lent him pajamas—the right size. The two men, Cynthia thought fondly, had very similar bodies, the same form filled with different substances: muscles and bones in Leopoldo's case, and some mysterious substance, as delicate as the flesh of a fruit, in Marco's. It moved her perhaps, she reflected, because she was a little tipsy. All three of them were.

She went to the bathroom to fetch her American sunburn lotion; she glanced at herself in the mirror and saw herself as very blond, very rosy, with no hard lines or edges: curves, planes, and colors gently shaded into one another culminating in the harmonious brightness of her hair. She smiled at her reflection and her eyes filled with tears. She felt that familiar delight—like an infinite sweetness painfully pressing to be released. Nothing new to her. Other things had provoked it in the past: her mother approaching her bed, centuries ago, to give her something, something that could have been either medicine, or a scolding, or a present; the pages of certain books which she mentally recited to reproduce the same agonizing fullness of the heart: "The candle, by the light of which she had been reading that book filled with anxieties, deceptions, grief, and evil" (Anna Karenina's death was her favorite passage), "flared up with a brighter light than before, lit up for her all that had before been dark, flickered, began to grow dim, and went out for ever." No, it was not a new emotion, she recognized its quality; but she had never, ever felt it to such an extent. This time it was infinitely larger, it filled her up and kept on growing, giving no sign it might be about to stop.

Marco—hair tousled, eyes shining, and face flushed above Leopoldo's blue pajamas—was already in bed.

"Are you thirsty? Leopoldo could go downstairs and get you some fresh grapefruit juice. Would you like some?"

"Yes, please."

Leopoldo tiptoed out of the room. "Poor baby, so sick," Cynthia murmured. She was panting slightly, as if she had run upstairs. She sat down on the bed, placed her hand on Marco's forehead. "Poor baby, poor baby." She moved toward the bedstead and leaned against the pillows. "Show me your back." She helped him remove the pajama top and made him lean over across her lap. He was as light as a child and much more docile. She gently rubbed his back with her American lotion, while through the fuchsia-colored silk of her dress she felt his breath damp and warm between her thighs.

That was the last sensation of the night Cynthia could remember with any precision: time—twelve-thirty; place—the children's room; cause—the breath of a feverish boy through a silk fabric; characters—she and Marco.

Up to that moment she could still clearly distinguish the boundaries between all the things that had really happened and those, however happily similar, she had wished would happen. But later everything got all tangled up: other things happened, unless she had dreamed them or dreamed of dreaming them. Had she really drawn that child to her bosom, and had he really placed his trusting hand on her white breast as he suckled it with closed eyes? And when had Leopoldo come back, how had he come into the game, what role had he played, and ultimately, when had he picked her up in his arms, carried her down the gallery, laid her down among the virginal ruffles of her bed, and loved her, quietly, not to wake up the boy sleeping in the next room?

The next morning her husband was still by her side. The shutters had been left open, and the daylight pouring in through the jasmine-trimmed arches lapped the lace of the rumpled bed with its green ripples. Leopoldo felt Cynthia move and, without opening his eyes, stretched his arms toward her and clasped her against his body—a gesture he had never had the opportunity to make, but must have dreamed of over and over again for years, Cynthia thought with a shudder of happiness, because it felt so familiar, as if it had happened every morning since the day they got married.

"Hi there, blondie," he said to her. "We'd better get a larger bed, soon." He changed his position and let out a groan. "I'm aching all over."

"We'll ask your mother," Cynthia answered. No use buying a new bed with all the things they had at Villa Grande, she thought. Mentally, she moved a few pieces of furniture from one house to the other until she had reached a satisfactory balance from an aesthetic, economic, and emotional point of view.

As she was refurnishing the children's room, her imagination stumbled against an obstacle, an object out of place, Marco's sleeping body. They had to transfer him back to Lavinia's as soon as possible.

She tried to remember. Or was it better to try to forget? In fact, she decided, it did not matter: the things that had happened that night in the room next door—granting that they had happened—fell so far beyond the bounds of any law that they would automatically slip away from a reality with which they had no connection. In any case, Nicola was about to arrive; his presence would put everything back into place. Cynthia loved and trusted her nephew. There was something strong and authentic in him. Paradoxically, he reminded her of her grandfather, from Jacksonville, Texas, who read her the Bible every night—odd that it should be Nicola, the baby of the family.

Only for the time being, she thought, and cuddled up in Leopoldo's arms, pressing against him. They would have a boy right away—at thirty-five, she had no time to waste—then a girl.

"A boy for you and a girl for me," she sang mentally. "Can't you see how happy we will be?"

24

LAVINIA TURNED ON the headlights and, murmuring a prayer, drove into the darkness of the San Giuliano tunnel. She was a good driver, but had to overcome a great many fears: vertigoes on viaducts, panic at the mere approach of a truck, claustrophobia in tunnels. The prayer poured out of her mechanically, in spite of herself—a relic of the past. She had been brought up by parents so old they could have been her grandparents; as a result, the education she had received was far more old-fashioned than that of her schoolmates. The same fate had befallen Nicola, brought up by Violante, his actual grandmother. He had also gone through a religious discipline—like any other discipline, it did not require or propose any conviction; it had only been a formal obligation, like a polio shot. It was part of the system of norms—such as good manners, personal hygiene—that governed his life: to stand up when a lady entered a room, to brush one's teeth after each meal, to tidy up after playing, to speak only if addressed when sitting at table, to say one's prayers before going to sleep.

He took everything so seriously. Like that evening . . . how old was he? Four, maybe. It was during the tenure of Mademoiselle Claudine, the French governess. Kneeling by the bed, in his yellow pajamas, dead tired after a day of romping in the fields with his dog, he was drooping with sleep, unable to keep his eyes open.

"Allons-y, Nicky, dis vite tes prières," Mademoiselle was telling him. Lavinia was already dressed, ready to go out. She had stopped by the door so as not to interfere with the ritual established by the governess.

"Commence: Père Eternel . . . ," Mademoiselle urged him.

"Père Eternel," Nicola said.

"Et après? Vas-y, Nicky."

"Père Eternel . . . Père Eternel, sur un arbre perché, tenait dans son bec un fromage."

Mademoiselle, who had little or no sense of humor, was honestly shocked. "Mais voyons, Nicholas! Fais donc attention!" How could he confuse the Paternoster with one of La Fontaine's fables?

Nicola, now quite awake, his little face dismayed and his chin all puckered up, really looked as if he considered himself guilty of some impiety. So, Lavinia had entered the room and had picked him up—a warm, moist little bundle. She had held him tight and had whispered, in his ear so that Mademoiselle would not hear her, "Don't worry, my love, I'm sure the Good Lord had a laugh!"

Oh, if she could always find the right words! If she could only feel as close to someone as she had to her child that evening!

She went on rehearsing the same scene in her mind—his yellow pajamas, his naked feet crossed at the toes, pink soles turned upward, his serious face. . . . "Père Eternel, sur un arbre perché . . ." She lingered over the details, delighting in the feelings they stirred up in her, while she drove down the winding road, under the plane trees of the boulevard, across the Arno, and looked for a spot in the parking lot. "Don't worry, my love, my baby." If she could only have him back at that age, and even earlier, when he was born, and start everything anew, from the beginning. . . . Suddenly, through the buzz of the crowd waiting at the airport, she heard a voice right behind her say, "Mother."

He drove the way back. She curled up in the passenger's seat so that she could see him more comfortably. He looked much more like her than like Filippo; she had never noticed it before.

"You have grown," she told him. Too late, too late. How could she pick up a six-foot-four man in her arms, wipe his tears, tuck him in bed? She told him how she had decided to reopen the Limonaia, but forgot to tell him about Marco. He was the one who asked. "Has a friend of mine come by?"

So it was true, after all, he had invited him. A good fellow, a land surveyor at Sesto San Giovanni. "Awfully shy. I wonder how he managed to face all of you without my protection." Every year, on the occasion of his village's patron saint's day, he went back south to visit his family. "He wrote to me in April to ask me if he could stop by on his way down, and I told him to come. I didn't know I would come back later."

A good fellow, a land surveyor at Sesto San Giovanni. And she had mistaken him for a bloodthirsty little beast, an ermine!

Once in the driveway, Nicola honked according to a special code that told his grandmother and everybody else that he had arrived. "Let's head straight for the Limonaia," Lavinia said. "Home."

25

GET HOLD OF TIME, and gather all its moments together so that they won't disperse like a flock without a shepherd. Each instant should mark at once the accomplishment of an old commitment and the promise of a new one. Never live "at random," never say "I can't." Above all, and most crucially, never look for an excuse: to reign simply means there is no one to call in sick to.

Violante put her pencil down and drew a small circle around the main point of intersection. That was undoubtedly the navel of the entire plan. All the lines had almost spontaneously converged there, aligning themselves with utter clarity.

And yet, somewhere there must have been a mistake because every time she tried to insert the last and most important datum into the diagram, everything fell into disarray and the drawing became a shabby, casual tangle meaning nothing.

Everything had worked according to plan until the very last. When Nicola had called her from the New York airport at midnight, she had given him the phone number at the Limonaia: "Call your mother and arrange everything with her." As she had expected—and much to her dismay, but it couldn't be helped—there was an immediate change in the tone of the distant voice. An imperceptible variation had crossed the ocean and reached her ears: a controlled tremor, happy incredulity, impatience. "Why, are we staying there this year?" "Yes, the two of you, you and your mother."

She heard steps coming down the stairs that led to the basement.

"Nives? I am here."

The steps stopped a moment, and then resumed, more rapidly. Nives appeared through the doorway.

"I've been looking for you everywhere," she said.

"What's the matter?"

"Nothing. But you are always disappearing."

She's also beginning to realize that I am old, Violante thought. She's afraid I might fall sick and die alone in one of these deserted dens. She looked around the enormous room, quite empty but for the Ping-Pong table. "It's freezing down here."

"It's because we are underground," Nives said. "Besides, this room is so huge."

"I know. The entire apartment where I was born, in Parma, could fit in it. Twice. For a whole year, after I got married, I kept getting lost in this house."

"Me too, at first. I cried for days on end, remember?"

"I certainly do. But then we both managed fairly well, don't you think?"

"I'd say so."

Violante dropped her pencil into the silver cup, among the others. "What will my daughter-in-law do when I am dead? And please, don't tell me, as you usually do, 'Madam, don't even think of it.' You think of it, too. That's why you're always watching me so closely. You don't want me to die in the wrong place."

Nives hesitated. There were so many little things Violante had been forgetting in the last few months: instructions to give, bills to pay. And Cynthia had punctually, and quietly, done it for her, without her noticing it. Should Nives tell her? Would she feel reassured or humiliated by the certainty that everything could go on even without her? Ironically enough, when Violante said "my daughter-in-law," she generally referred to Lavinia. Just imagine . . .

"Your daughter-in-law will do very well," Nives said.

"You think so?"

"Don't you worry. She has already learned a great deal. You needn't worry about a thing, I assure you."

They heard a brief honk in the distance, then another, and then a third: Nicola's signal.

"He's here!" the two women said in unison.

26

I DON'T KNOW whether it has all happened because of Violante's diagram, but I'm tempted to believe so. I have often
been convinced that thoughts, once down in writing, tend to
evolve rapidly toward reality. This is how it was with the Master of the *Virgin in Red,* who started existing after I wrote about
him; I hope the same thing will happen to my kingfisher.

But, to get back to the diagram, even in this case one could
say that things—which had long been ready to happen—were
waiting to be methodically drawn on paper to become true. As
the events of this Sunday keep unfolding, I seem to hear each
of them produce the sort of click that occurs when a gear locks
into place, setting the whole machinery in motion.

First of all there is the omelette that Lavinia prepared for
Nicola in the kitchen at the Limonaia: there is nothing sensational about this scene, indeed it may not even be the first meal
Lavinia has prepared for her son. And yet, it is as if, in every
gesture she makes as she bustles about the kitchen, and in the
way he sits waiting at the table, there is a new intensity of
meaning reminiscent of the last scene in so many nineteenth-
century novels—"Yes, my lord, I can no longer conceal the

truth: I am your mother!" "You . . . madam . . . my mother!"

Drawn by the sound of the horn, we all gathered in front of the Limonaia: first Violante and Nives, followed by me, and then Leopoldo and Cynthia, hugging and visibly happy. A definite click. In the course of the night, I saw enough of what was happening beyond the windows of Villa Piccola to be quite confident that even there they have found the right gear. The last to arrive was Marco, with a red nose and the circumspect movements of someone with sunburnt shoulders.

"I'm sorry I wasn't here when you arrived," Nicola apologized kindly. "Can you stay a little longer?"

"I'm afraid I can't. My folks are expecting me tomorrow."

"I'm sorry," Nicola repeated. He glances at his watch. "For me it is four in the morning," he explains. "I really need to take a nap."

We all gather around him while he eats his omelette; Lavinia hovers attentively. Then we let him go to sleep and withdraw to the pool for a quick dip.

The day is very hot, but we can hear thunder in the distance.

As we are walking down the path I hear another click: I have found a solution to the main problem in Violante's diagram, a perfect solution, just as I have located the exact place where Violante's plans seemed to go wrong and where the mechanism she had set in motion has clicked by itself, automatically correcting, as the most sophisticated machines often do, the human error.

Cynthia grabs my arm and pulls me aside.

"Just a second," she tells me. She asks me for my pen and writes a telephone number on a matchbook. "I'm counting on you," she whispers. Leopoldo, Lavinia, and Marco are walking a few steps ahead of us; Violante and Nives have already turned toward Villa Grande. "It's about the Ferragosto procession," Cynthia goes on.

"The procession?"

"Yes, the procession that goes through the park."

"I know. What about it?"

"We are leaving, my husband and I. We want to take a trip somewhere, the two of us, alone. We are leaving tomorrow."

"I'm delighted to hear it."

"I won't be here for the procession. This is what I wanted to tell you. It's about the flower carpet. I suppose you know that once the tenant farmers used to go to the olive groves to gather the wild thyme they then offered to their masters to make the green background for the flower carpet."

"I know. They still do it. That's what I like best: that fragrance, midway between incense and myrtle, Christianity and paganism. Last year I invited some Japanese friends. They were so excited, they must have taken a thousand pictures!"

"But things have changed a bit. The tenant farmers haven't gone to gather wild thyme in the olive groves for the last four years. Time, my dear, has acquired a value it did not have in the past. Why, it's already hard enough to convince them to go gather the olives!"

"But I remember the fragrance was there last year, as it has always been."

"I've been taking care of it myself. I secretly order the wild thyme from Bruschini, the man who sells funeral garlands." She hands me the matchbook. "This is his number. Remember, you must call him four or five days ahead of time. And make sure that Violante doesn't know. No one does, except for Nives. She knows. We have been doing lots of things in secret, she and I. Violante is no longer a girl, poor dear."

Click. The new queen is ready to take Violante's place when the moment comes. But it is not Lavinia: and this is where Violante's plans have gone wrong, where the curves she has drawn have taken a different direction, refusing to follow the one traced by her pencil.

How could she possibly think her place would be filled by Lavinia! Not only is she not the right woman, but the days of natural succession are long gone. Today, it takes a good-willed barbarian, a parvenu in love, to devotedly pick up the spoils—someone like Cynthia, coming from far away, like an explorer full of enthusiasm and respect for the exotic places she is going to discover, strong and disciplined. Like me, in a way: I too come from afar and don't give up easily. Or like Violante herself, the daughter of a poor musician from Parma. But not Lavinia. Nives has certainly known this for sometime, and without the help of diagrams. As Cynthia just said, "We have been doing lots of things in secret, she and I."

27

MARCO HAS REGAINED THE POWER of speech and lost all his glamor. He is no worse than many others. A bit pretentious—like someone who tries to impress by using supposedly elegant words. The poor thing is trying to dazzle us with his rather boring knowledge of all the brand names of sports-clothes, shoes, cars, whisky, boats. "Even at the level of pure economic calculation," he says, "the optimal selection is always the one involving the authentic product."

It is more than obvious that nobody—not Lavinia, nor Leopoldo or Cynthia—cares to listen to him. They had thought he was a special creature from a different world: beautiful, mysterious, and slightly pernicious. How can they possibly forgive him for being just another young man begging to be liked who says, "By now even the general public has been sensitized to Timberland"?

There is absolutely no doubt, judging from the polite way the conversation is proceeding, that they are all counting the minutes to Marco's departure. I couldn't even say whether he is aware of how vain his efforts are to appear cool and worldly:

I truly hope he isn't, because all my jealousy of him has vanished to be replaced by incommensurable pity.

They are speaking among themselves—Lavinia, Leopoldo, and Cynthia—occasionally glancing at Marco with vacant eyes that do not seem to recognize him. Now and then, they slide into the water, lean with an elbow on the edge of the pool, and let their legs float behind them.

Lavinia looks longer and whiter than usual. Her drawling, slightly querulous voice grates on my nerves unbearably.

For the first time in my life I try to imagine—not without some regret—what my life would have been like if, on that memorable night when everything started, instead of being seduced by the vision of the table setting, the ancient domestic, and the old woman in her fur stole, I had been inspired with a simple but natural feeling of rebellion. Indeed, this is a very plausible third hypothesis, besides becoming the man I am or the pharmacist with a passion for organized tours—which, however, I have never seriously considered. And yet, it could have happened. I could have devoted my life to fighting that world instead of struggling to be part of it. I could have fought to make sure that no one would ever have to endure a crooked kitchen or a cracked cup with a greenish rim. It would have been enough to replace one detail with another, equally plausible, one. At this very moment, I find Lavinia so detestable that I enjoy imagining a slightly different starting point. Let's assume, for instance, that thirteen-year-old Aldo Rugani had a poorly developed aesthetic sense and a strong bent for moral outrage. It would have been enough to change everything. He would have been appalled by the meaningless waste of all that luxury, by the inanity of the conversation, and the imbecility of all that formality. I turn my eyes to Lavinia, squatting on a cushion, wholly absorbed in a profound study of her left knee, and shudder at the mere thought of her affected pronunciation, at her utter uselessness.

157

Not to mention myself: the deft forger who has always thought of himself as his most successful forgery. What am I, in this case? The fake of a fake?

"You said you're leaving this evening?" I ask Marco.

"I have to, yes."

"If you come with me, I'll take you to Poveromo to have lunch at a friend's, and then I'll drop you off at the train station in Viareggio. You'll meet two very interesting people, you'll see. He—he's more than a friend, he's my mentor—is not only the greatest living art critic, but also one of the nicest, least pretentious people I know."

"But then I won't see Nicola."

"Who knows how long he's going to be sleeping," Lavinia immediately interposes. "You'd better take advantage of Aldo's offer."

I stand up. "Come on, let's go. What are we waiting for?"

As I am drying myself, Lavinia comes out of the pool and approaches me. "When are you coming back?" she asks.

"No idea. It depends."

"Will you be back for dinner?"

"I don't know."

She pulls a long face, and looks at me with eyes that are at once pleading and resentful. I know, at the bottom of my heart, that soon my usual feelings for her will again take over, but for the time being I identify with Sandro, the sociologist, or one of his predecessors. For a moment, I enjoy being the very character I have hated and envied for years: the sort of man on whom Lavinia has lavished her demanding and sticky attentions.

I tell myself I am crazy and that I am going to be sorry, but I am acting to get out of there without answering her plaintive questions with a promise.

"What do you mean you don't know!"

I find an excuse—as I increasingly feel like Sandro, the sociologist—a half excuse since there really are some photos I want to show to Levi, but that wouldn't take more than an hour and

I could easily be back for dinner. "I must talk to Levi about the painter I am working on. I don't know how long it will take. I may even spend the night."

After all, I think, I could really spend the night at Poveromo. I have lots of things I want to tell Levi. I want to talk to him about my lansquenet painter before I send the book to a publisher. The mere thought of the work I have ahead of me suddenly fills me with excitement. I run away dragging Marco along, and on the way I keep thinking of the little kingfisher perched on a tuft of bullrushes.

28

I SPENT THE ENTIRE DAY at Poveromo. We sent Marco off swimming with my old friends' grandchildren, and I stayed home with them to talk about Martin Lansquenet. Their home is quite far from the beach, has two trees full of apricots, a small pergola, and a vegetable garden in back. Elvira, Levi's wife, having worked in a bank for forty years, retired six months ago. Now that she has the time she has started raising chickens. While David was examining the photos I had brought him on the cast-iron table under the pergola, Elvira showed me the chicken coop the two of them had built together with some wire fencing and varnished wood. Chicken and guinea hens were roaming freely all over the place.

"I lock them up at night because of the foxes," Elvira said. "They're much better when they are allowed to scratch about. They eat earthworms, grass. They've even eaten all my flowers." With a lash of her apron, she shooed a fat white hen away from a geranium stump. "When is your kingfisher going to be ready?"

"The book should come out in the fall. I'm just about done."

"It must be nice to have a book published. You're lucky, the two of you," she said waving her apron in her husband's direction.

"Why, you're not?"

"Yes, I'm lucky too. We have left our house in Florence. Now we live here year-round. I have my chickens, my garden. And I have him. And in the summer we have our grandchildren. What more can I want? When some of his stuff gets published I am as excited as he is."

I am sure she has listed the reasons for her happiness in the exact same order they occupy in her heart; I find it very wise.

We waited for the kids to come back from the beach to have lunch. The afternoon flowed leisurely on. We took a nap under the pergola, looked at the photos, talked about my painter; at dusk, we took a short walk toward the hills. Marco fixed Elvira's washer. When the kids drove him to the train station, she hugged him as if he were her own, and gave him a bag full of freshly picked apricots for the trip.

We ate alone, the three of us—Pecorino cheese, a zucchini omelette, and red wine—under the pergola; the grandchildren had gone out for a pizza with their friends.

I left them at eleven, and drove slowly home taking the Quiesa mountain road, the finest and longest. When I reached the pass, I made it longer yet by turning toward Stabbiano. I drove up the woody hill and stopped at the topmost curve. I got out of the car and stood there a while, staring at the moonlit sea; I could hear the thunder in the distance.

The wood behind me resounded with the rustlings of the night: the velvety flight of the predators, the wailing of their prey. The dry barking of a fox reached me from the vines below, like a sudden coughing fit.

Only a small part of my soul was inside my body; the rest, large, soft, and flexible, stretched over the silvery surface of the sea, skimmed over the rounded tops of the chestnut trees, dipped, with roots and worms, under last year's dry leaves and into the damp darkness of the earth, wandered along the strip of country between the beach and the hills, looking for Elvira's and David's house.

I knew ours had been a farewell evening, my farewell to the unlimited breadth of everything, to the possibility of choosing, of changing. In my fifties, I was like Peter Pan, about to fly back through his window to slip into bed.

I am now climbing the steps to my tower: it is one o'clock. The telephone starts ringing even before I can open the door to my bedroom.

"I've been looking for you all day . . . where on earth . . . Oh, Aldo, you're back at last!"

"Lavinia, what is it? What's going on?"

"Nothing, I've missed you. . . . Come down and have a drink with me."

"R . . . right now?" I was about to say "right over." Out of habit—not the habit of answering to such a call, but of dreaming of it: waking up with a pounding heart and lying in bed motionless, trying to prolong that instant of delight and slide back into sleep, into a dream which, instead, keeps receding, farther and farther away from the darkness, into the light of day. Because this time I have no doubts as to the meaning of Lavinia's call: it is the one I've been expecting all my life. But then, how can I explain the fact that I'm not rushing to her side? That I'm not swooping down from my tower window, a solitary crow no longer, but a romantic hawk answering the call of a sweet turtledove? That I carefully turn off all the lights and even find the time to spray my bedroom so that I won't find it full of mosquitoes when I come back?

And, why is it that, as I grab a bottle of champagne from the fridge and walk down to the Limonaia at a fairly swift pace, I feel empty inside, oddly nostalgic, as if I were about to leave a beloved place forever?

I find her on the patio. We open the champagne and symbolically taste it; then we leave the glasses on the stone table and walk away so as not to wake up Nicola.

Our steps lead us toward Villa Grande along the same path we followed the night before. The twenty-four hours that have gone by now seem like an insurmountable caesura. Even the weather has changed: summer, which officially began only yesterday, is already showing the first signs of its end. The thunder rumbles on in the distance, from the gorges of the Alpi Apuane. Over her jeans, Lavinia is wearing a sweater that exudes a faint smell of camphor.

This time she is the one who stops under the jasmine bower. Aside from the thunder and the cooler air, everything is like last night—stars, nightingales, the scent of flowers. But then why does everything seem so different?

"This is the spot where, last night, you took my hand," Lavinia says. Her voice is still quite childish: in the semidarkness, the slender figure by my side could be that of the young girl I met so many years ago. If it is true that a head must have certain requisites to wear a crown, then I am sure hers does not possess them. Just as I am sure that she is not even aware that there is a kingdom to inherit, a kingdom that won't be hers. If she knew it, she would only feel relief.

I wonder whether I should tell Violante that she has made a mistake in her choice of an heir.

"Cynthia and Leopoldo are leaving tomorrow," I say.

"I know. She came to bring Nicola the chemicals to test the water of the swimming pool. Why were you gone so long? Were you angry at me?"

I hold her hands in mine. "No, I was not angry." It will be interesting to see the style of Cynthia's reign. It will certainly be quite different from Violante's. "You know I forgive you everything."

The jasmine gives off a very sweet perfume. I kiss the tips of her fingers and hug her. "Lavinia," I say.

"Yes."

I know I will have to give up something for good. It is like when I see a plane fly very high into the sun: seen from the earth, in the rarefied limpidity of the air, that spot could be paradise. And yet that is not at all the sensation I have when I am on a plane.

I hug her tight. "You have no idea how unhappy I was all day," she murmurs. "I thought I had lost you." She puts her arms around my neck. "You are so tall. The right height for me."

Logically, we would live at the Arnolfina so that Nicola could settle at the Limonaia as soon as he comes back from America for good. And we might want to keep the apartment in Milan. . . .

"I love you, you know," I tell her.

"The funniest thing is that I love you too."

In any case, we are in no hurry. Nicola must spend three more years in America: if we decide to stay at the Limonaia we will just have to make some room for him for two months, during the holidays. . . . Suddenly I feel I couldn't go on living at the Arnolfina. It wouldn't make any sense.

Something is slowing me down, almost paralyzing me. I am suddenly asked to abandon my observatory and step onto the stage. My hands, heavy and awkward as in a dream, move with difficulty as they stroke her supple back. "I can't believe it," I say. Of course, we are in no hurry. A few large drops of luke-warm water are starting to fall from the sky. First we have to wait for the book on Martin Lansquenet to come out. A wave of happiness invades me at the mere thought of the bluish green bird I discovered, of the work ahead, of the book that will be published, of the excitement while waiting for the reviews . . . "I've loved you for such a long time."

Here I am, right at center stage, with the garden and the three houses as a backdrop. Nicola is sleeping in his bed. Violante is organizing her death without knowing that she needn't worry about a thing since everything has already been happily decided. Nives is ready to offer her loyalty to the new queen. Cynthia is about to leave on her second honeymoon, but when the day comes she will be ready to dust all the cobwebs off this old kingdom, spray it with a disinfectant, and give it a few fake *settecento* touches; in other words, to do her best, as is her nature. She will have her own personal style, but like Violante, she will behave as if, any moment, she might have to stow all her precious things on an ark, to keep them safe till after the deluge. Marco is traveling south carrying—along with the memory of a strange family—the bag of apricots Elvira Levi gave him—the only thing he has brought back from this trip, his only reward for having set everything straight.

And Lavinia is in my arms. My hands wander up to her hair, so soft. It is starting to rain. Summer seems to have ended; soon we'll move into a very mellow winter, during which we'll decide on lots of things.

Then, we'll see.

SUSAN HILL

Air & Angels

Celibate, irreproachable and distinguished, Thomas Cavendish is in his mid-fifties and the obvious man to become Master of his college. But, walking by the river, Thomas sees a young girl standing on the bridge. It is an apocalyptic vision, one that alters Thomas's life irrevocably and tragically, but with the beauty and joy of a love never previously imagined.

'It is a novel that Colette might have been proud to have written. It contains some of the most beautiful and evocative writing you could wish for . . . It is a novel to treasure. It has been worth waiting for'
Allan Massie, *Scotsman*

'Subtle and profoundly moving, this novel is rich in the qualities for which Hill has won such high praise in the past. She returns to the eerie landscape of the East Anglican marshes, which was used to such magnificent effect in her classic ghost story *The Woman in Black* . . . One of our finest novelists'
Miranda Seymour, *Sunday Times*

'An extraordinary and haunting psychological tour de force, a novel you can't put down while the desire remains to make it last'
Birmingham Post

NICHOLAS MOSLEY

Hopeful Monsters

WHITBREAD BOOK OF THE YEAR 1990

'Quite simply, the best English novel to have been
written since the Second World War'
A.N. Wilson, *Evening Standard*

'This is a major novel by any standard of
measurement. Its ambition is lofty, its intelligence
startling, and its sympathy profound. It is
frequently funny, sometimes painful, sometimes
moving. It asks fundamental questions about the
nature of experience . . . It is a novel which makes
the greater part of contemporary fiction seem
pygmy in comparison'
Allan Massie, *The Scotsman*

'A gigantic achievement that glows and grows
long after it is put aside'
Jennifer Potter, *Independent on Sunday*

'Enormously ambitious and continuously fascinating . . . There is an intellectual engagement
here, a devouring determination to investigate, to
refrain from judgement while never abandoning
moral conventions, that is rare among British
novelists – for that matter, among novelists of any
nationality'
Paul Binding, *New Statesman and Society*

'Nicholas Mosley, in a country never generous to
experimental writing, is one of the more significant instances we have that it can still, brilliantly,
be done'
Malcolm Bradbury

MICHELLE CLIFF

Bodies of Water

'*Bodies of Water* pulls off the remarkable feat of being tender, often moving, and statuesque at the same time. From the first story, set in Jamaica and reminiscent of the best of Paul Bowles, sensual and rich and sad, the style and geography slowly changes. By the final story we are in the God-fearing deserts of Nevada and Omaha, with a garage owner who builds an altar out of tin-foil . . . Breathtakingly good'
Roger Clarke, *New Statesman and Society*

'Michelle Cliff's stories move with great authority from her native Jamaica to her adopted United States. She never wallows in sentiment, yet she has the rare gift of moving the reader. Her insights into the iniquities of both historical and contemporary America are pellucid, her tone one of controlled urgency'
Caryl Phillips

'Cliff's stories have the lyrical, slow-motion quality of a gorgeous dream that slides into strangling nightmare. Her writing is clear as a bell and sharp as a scream'
Clare Boylan, *Sunday Times*

'Cliff's slight, delicate fictions tackle their themes like a Tai Chi master, sinuously evasive, as though the violence and pain they record would be unbearable if confronted directly . . . These pieces have an effect out of all proportion to their length'
Michael Dibdin, *Independent on Sunday*

ROBERT EDRIC

A Lunar Eclipse

'In *A Lunar Eclipse* Robert Edric traces the emotional disintegration and collapse of a woman, following the death of her husband.

'Rachel's husband, Colin, died in a car accident in the fourth year of their marriage. Rachel is a writer. She has friends, and a proven gift as a writer. But freelance existence is hazardous. More importantly, it does not offer the social framework of a regular job, valuable prop in bereavement.

'The uncertainties of her future throw Rachel into the past – her life with Colin, which she attempts to re-live through a collection of mementos.

'To write a novel about bereavement and its after effects is no easy task. Few novelists have done it successfully. Edric writes eloquently. His insights are acute; his sensitivity unfailing'
Yorkshire Post

'Original and diverting'
Literary Review

'The whole sad process is brilliantly chronicled in detail by Robert Edric, who writes with the authority and perception that has already won him much acclaim (his previous two novels carried off the James Tait Black Memorial Prize and second place in the *Guardian* Fiction Prize)'
Metropolitan

A Selected List of Titles Available from Minerva

While every effort is made to keep prices low, it is sometimes necessary to increase prices at short notice. Mandarin Paperbacks reserves the right to show new retail prices on covers which may differ from those previously advertised in the text or elsewhere.

The prices shown below were correct at the time of going to press.

☐	7493 9137 5	**On the Eve of Uncertain Tomorrows**	Neil Bissoondath	£5.99
☐	7493 9050 6	**Women In A River Landscape**	Heinrich Boll	£4.99
☐	7493 9921 X	**An Instant in the Wind**	Andre Brink	£5.99
☐	7493 9147 2	**Explosion in a Cathedral**	Alejo Carpentier	£5.99
☐	7493 9109 X	**Bodies of Water**	Michelle Cliff	£4.99
☐	7493 9060 3	**Century of the Wind**	Eduardo Galeano	£4.99
☐	7493 9080 8	**Balzacs Horse**	Gert Hofmann	£4.99
☐	7493 9093 X	**The Notebook**	Agota Kristof	£4.99
☐	7493 9174 X	**The Mirror Maker**	Primo Levi	£4.99
☐	7493 9143 X	**Parents Worry**	Gerard Reve	£4.99
☐	7493 9172 3	**Lives of the Saints**	Nino Ricci	£4.99
☐	7493 9003 4	**The Fall of the Imam**	Nawal El Saadawi	£4.99
☐	7493 9924 4	**Ake**	Wole Soyinka	£5.99
☐	7493 9139 1	**The Four Wise Men**	Michel Tournier	£5.99
☐	7493 9092 1	**Woman's Decameron**	Julia Voznesenskaya	£5.99

All these books are available at your bookshop or newsagent, or can be ordered direct from the publisher. Just tick the titles you want and fill in the form below.

Mandarin Paperbacks, Cash Sales Department, PO Box 11, Falmouth, Cornwall TR10 9EN.

Please send cheque or postal order, no currency, for purchase price quoted and allow the following for postage and packing:

UK including BFPO

£1.00 for the first book, 50p for the second and 30p for each additional book ordered to a maximum charge of £3.00.

Overseas including Eire

£2 for the first book, £1.00 for the second and 50p for each additional book thereafter.

NAME (Block letters) ....

ADDRESS ....

....

☐ I enclose my remittance for ....

☐ I wish to pay by Access/Visa Card Number

Expiry Date